Rethinking Religion and World Affairs

Rethinking Religion and World Affairs

Edited by Timothy Samuel Shah,
Alfred Stepan, and Monica Duffy Toft

OXFORD
UNIVERSITY PRESS

Oxford University Press, Inc., publishes works that further
Oxford University's objective of excellence
in research, scholarship, and education.

Oxford   New York
Auckland   Cape Town   Dar es Salaam   Hong Kong   Karachi
Kuala Lumpur   Madrid   Melbourne   Mexico City   Nairobi
New Delhi   Shanghai   Taipei   Toronto

With offices in
Argentina   Austria   Brazil   Chile   Czech Republic   France   Greece
Guatemala   Hungary   Italy   Japan   Poland   Portugal   Singapore
South Korea   Switzerland   Thailand   Turkey   Ukraine   Vietnam

Stepan, Alfred. "Religion, Democracy and the 'Twin Tolerations'". Journal of Democracy 11:4 (2000), 37–57. © 2000 The National Endowment for Democracy and The Johns Hopkins University Press. Reprinted with permission of The Johns Hopkins University Press.

Mead, Walter Russell. "God's Country." Reprinted by permission of FOREIGN AFFAIRS (85, September/October 2006). Copyright (2006) by the Council on Foreign Relations, Inc. www.ForeignAffairs.com.

Philpott, Daniel, "What Religion Offers for the Politics of Transitional Justice" is adapted from an earlier article, "What Religion Brings to the Politics of Transitional Justice," originally published in the *Journal of International Affairs* 61:1 (Winter 2007), 93–110.

Published by Oxford University Press, Inc.
198 Madison Avenue, New York, New York 10016
www.oup.com

Oxford is a registered trademark of Oxford University Press

Library of Congress Cataloging-in-Publication Data
Rethinking religion and world affairs / edited by Timothy Samuel Shah, Alfred Stepan, and Monica Duffy Toft.
    p. cm.
    Includes bibliographical references and index.
    ISBN 978–0–19–982797–8 (hardcover : alk. paper) — ISBN 978–0–19–982799–2
(pbk. : alk. paper) 1. Religion and international relations. I. Shah, Timothy Samuel.
II. Stepan, Alfred C.   III. Toft, Monica Duffy, 1965-
    BL65.I55R48 2012
    201'.727—dc23   2011027612

9 8 7 6 5 4 3 2 1
Printed in the United States of America
acid-free paper

CONTENTS

CONTRIBUTORS

Nichole J. Allem received an M.A. in International Relations and an M.S. in Public Relations from Syracuse University in 2010.

Thomas Banchoff is Associate Professor of Government and Director of the Berkley Center for Religion, Peace, and World Affairs, Georgetown University.

Michael Barnett is University Professor of International Relations and Political Science at the George Washington University.

Frederick D. Barton is a former Codirector of the Post-Conflict Reconstruction Project at the Center for Strategic and International Studies.

Rajeev Bhargava is Director of the Centre for the study of Developing Societies, Delhi. He is the editor of *Secularism and its Critics* (OUP,1998).

Mehrzad Boroujerdi is Associate Professor of Political Science, Founding Director of the Middle Eastern Studies Program, and Founding Codirector of the Religion, Media and International Relations Program at the Maxwell School of Citizenship, Syracuse University.

José Casanova is Professor of Sociology at Georgetown University and a Senior Fellow of the Berkley Center for Religion, Peace, and World Affairs.

Thomas F. Farr is a former U.S. diplomat, Director of the Religious Freedom Project at the Berkley Center for Religion, Peace, and World Affairs at Georgetown University, and Visiting Associate Professor at the Edmund A. Walsh School of Foreign Service, also at Georgetown University.

M. Christian Green is a Senior Fellow of the Center for the Study of Law and Religion, Emory University.

Nicole Greenfield is a Research Associate for the Social Science Research Council.

Shannon Hayden is a former Project Coordinator for the Post-Conflict Reconstruction Project at the Center for Strategic and International Studies.

Robert W. Hefner is Professor of Anthropology and Director of the Institute on Culture, Religion, and World Affairs, Boston University.

J. Bryan Hehir is the Parker Gilbert Montgomery Professor of the Practice of Religion and Public Life at the John F. Kennedy School of Government, Harvard University and secretary for Health and Social Services for the Archdiocese of Boston.

Karin von Hippel is a former Codirector of the Post-Conflict Reconstruction Project at the Center for Strategic and International Studies.

Elizabeth Shakman Hurd is Associate Professor of Political Science at Northwestern University.

Katherine Marshall is Visiting Professor of Government at Georgetown University and a Senior Fellow of the Berkley Center for Religion, Peace, and World Affairs.

Walter Russell Mead is the James Clarke Chace Professor of Foreign Affairs and Humanities at Bard College.

Daniel Philpott is Associate Professor of Political Science and Peace Studies at the Joan B. Kroc Institute for International Peace Studies, University of Notre Dame.

Timothy Samuel Shah is Visiting Assistant Professor of Government at Georgetown University and Associate Director of the Religious Freedom Project and Scholar in Residence at the Berkley Center for Religion, Peace, and World Affairs, also at Georgetown University.

Alfred Stepan is the Wallace S. Sayre Professor of Government and Director of the Center for the Study of Democracy, Toleration, and Religion at the School of International and Public Affairs, Columbia University.

Monica Duffy Toft is Associate Professor of Public Policy at the John F. Kennedy School of Government, Harvard University.

Diane Winston is the Knight Chair in Media and Religion at the Annenberg School for Communication and Journalism, University of Southern California.

John Witte Jr. is the Jonas Robitscher Professor of Law, Alonzo L. McDonald Family Foundation Distinguished Professor, and Director of the Center for the Study of Law and Religion, Emory University.

Rethinking Religion and World Affairs

Introduction

RELIGION AND WORLD AFFAIRS: X
BLURRING THE BOUNDARIES

Timothy Samuel Shah

I.

Four guided missiles packed with explosive material hurtled into the morning sky. Though the day was brilliant blue and cloudless, no one saw them coming. They were aimed at a nation that did not see itself at war. Moreover, it was a nation convinced that missiles fired in anger no longer posed a serious threat to its security. The weapons were conventional in the strict sense: they did not carry nuclear warheads.

But the weapons and the attackers who launched them were anything but conventional. The 19 hijackers who commandeered four civilian jetliners on the morning of September 11, 2001, were not sent by a state or nation. They were not motivated by any purely secular or political cause. Born of religious zeal, they sought to strike a blow against a power they believed was in thralldom and service to Satan. Motivated by faith, they wanted to strike a blow for Allah.

Religion, which was supposed to have been permanently sidelined by secularization, suddenly appeared to be at the center of world affairs. Seemingly without   X
warning, faith had transgressed the neat boundaries that organized the thinking and planning of our best and brightest policy makers, policy analysts, and scholars. Religious believers were supposed to stay confined to one side of the boundary that sealed private faith off from global public affairs—a boundary that separated the irrational from the rational, the mystical from the purposeful. However, guided by an astonishing combination of zealous faith and coolly calculating rationality, September 11 showed that organized religious believers could act with purpose, power, and public consequence.

And we—not only America, but the whole world of professional policy making and analysis—were unprepared. As Robert Keohane, a leading international relations scholar, had the humility to admit shortly afterward:

> The attacks of September 11 reveal that *all mainstream theories of world politics are relentlessly secular with respect to motivation.* They ignore the impact of religion, despite the fact that world-shaking political movements have so often been fueled by religious fervor. None of them takes very seriously the human

1

desire to dominate or to hate—both so strong in history and in classical realist thought. [emphasis added]

In his own post-9/11 analysis, however, Keohane also had the honesty to say: "Since I have few insights into religious motivations in world politics, I will leave this subject to those who are more qualified to address it."

This edited volume picks up where Keohane left off. In the light of religion's global resurgence, most dramatized by 9/11, it attempts a radical rethinking of the relationship between religion and world affairs, hence the title. It brings together scholars who are eminently qualified to analyze how and why religious motivations, actors, ideas, and organizations matter for contemporary world affairs. It addresses some of the reasons that theories of world politics and world affairs have been slow to address religious factors, how and why religious factors are influencing important global dynamics, and how we need to adapt our theories of world affairs to the realities and implications of this resurgence.

II.

There was once a virtually unbroken consensus in the foundational works of social science about modernization and religion. One part of this consensus was empirical or factual. The other was normative or ethical. The empirical assumption was that with economic modernization or "development," religion *would* decline. The ethical assumption was that with political modernization and its attendant "democratization," religion *should* be confined to the private sphere. Description and prescription went happily together.

Both parts of this consensus are now in question. The September 11 attacks clearly demonstrated that the consensus was wrong. Well before and apart from September 11, however, the consensus was increasingly difficult to sustain. A multitude of simultaneously developed and vibrantly religious societies—starting with the United States—explodes the empirical assumption. A multitude of simultaneously democratic and luxuriantly faith-saturated societies—including India, Turkey, and Indonesia—explodes the ethical assumption. And ten years after September 11, 2001, religious militancy remains a powerful force—in Iraq, Afghanistan, Pakistan, Nigeria, and numerous other locales—that individual governments and the international community have proven unable to defeat or even contain.

This old consensus is nevertheless stubborn. It still structures much of our study and understanding of the role of religion in world affairs. It does so because many of the concepts and conceptual distinctions on which it was founded remain firmly lodged in the minds of international relations scholars, as Bryan Hehir describes in chapter 1 of this book. The meaning of concepts such as "secularism," "modernity," "power," and "public life" is assumed without hesitation or complication. With equal confidence, a sharp boundary is drawn between these concepts and phenomena assumed to be their polar opposites: "religion," "tradition," "theology," "faith," and "private worship."

Much classical thinking and practice in world affairs is thus a form of border patrol. It is concerned with policing and strengthening the fence between two worlds. The first world is the "secular" and "public" world in which international actors—nation-states and the multilateral organizations that bind them together—are presumed to make rational choices in the pursuit of political and economic power. The second world is the "spiritual" and "private" world in which religious actors—everything from church hierarchies to clerical councils to violent organizations such as Al Qaeda and Hizbollah—are presumed to make faith-based choices in the pursuit of nonrational or irrational goals. As with the empirical assumption about religion and economic development, the factual assumption about these two worlds is that they are two separate universes, with little to no mutual contact or interaction. As with the ethical or normative assumption about religion and political democratization, the ethical or moral assumption about these two worlds is that they should be kept as far apart as possible.

However, it is true that what could be called classical secularization theory recognized the reality and legitimacy of some traffic between these two universes. Classical secularization theory assumed the descriptive and prescriptive forms noted at the beginning: it expected the automatic decline of religion in the face of development and required the hermetic isolation of religion in the face of democracy. On one hand, the forces of development and progress would so impinge on the world of religion that religion would have little to do and less space in which to do it. Modern progress would make the security and comfort offered by religion increasingly unnecessary. Modernization, in other words, would infiltrate, occupy, and diminish the world of the spirit, fostering the "disenchantment" that Max Weber made central to his understanding of modernity. On the other hand, secularization theory held that the forces of democracy should reform and regulate religion to make it compatible with freedom—to inculcate habits of autonomy and rational reflection and encourage individuals to forge new identities as democratic citizens. On closer inspection, in other words, classical secularization theory imagined that the religious and political worlds would and should interrelate to a significant extent.

The crucial point, however, is that the secularization theorists who assigned themselves the task of managing the points of contact between the public "secular" world and the private "spiritual" world *allowed—and expected—traffic to flow in only one direction.*

The result of this stringent and one-way boundary maintenance has been the long-standing exclusion of religion and religious actors from the systematic study of world politics in general and international relations in particular. This has created a paradoxical situation: religion has become one of the most influential factors in world affairs in the last generation but remains one of the least examined factors in the professional study and practice of world affairs.

For example, the lead journal for political science in the United States is the *American Political Science Review* (APSR). In its 100th anniversary issue, an article concluded that "prior to 1960 only a single APSR article sought to use religion as a variable to explain empirical phenomena" and that in APSR "from 1980 on, just one article in American Government put religious factors at the center of analysis; and just two in Comparative Politics."[1] A similar neglect marked the international relations literature. Daniel Philpott, a contributor to this book, judged that in his survey of leading journals of international relations from 1980 to 1999, "only six or so out of a total of about sixteen hundred featured religion as an important influence."[2] This neglect of religion in research is echoed in teaching. One of the coeditors of this volume, Alfred Stepan, teaches at one of America's largest and oldest schools dedicated to training graduate students for international careers in government, political analysis, international organizations, the media, human rights, the private sector, and academia: the School of International and Public Affairs at Columbia University. He is currently teaching the first general course on the role of religion in world affairs in the school's fifty-year history.

III.

Rethinking Religion and World Affairs represents a collective effort to rethink religion and world affairs by questioning the sharp empirical and ethical boundaries that have separated the two. A working group of leading scholars and policy practitioners concerned with religion in the contemporary world was convened by the Social Science Research Council (SSRC) in New York, with the generous support of the Henry Luce Foundation, to devise strategies to transcend this state of affairs. It soon became apparent that thousands of professors never trained in religion and world affairs would be asked to design and teach new courses, media newsrooms to report on religion in greater depth, and legislators, foreign policy makers, humanitarian organizations, development agencies, and feminist and human rights groups to devise new and more appropriate approaches to religion.

This book has chapters on all these areas and more. Each chapter has a guide to additional literature and resources. Furthermore, perhaps one of the book's more innovative and valuable features is an "Internet Resource Guide," included as an Appendix. Led by M. Christian Green and Nicole Greenfield, this guide was compiled in consultation with the SSRC Advisory Committee on Religion and International Affairs, many of whose members have contributed articles to this book. In addition, Green and Greenfield consulted with other scholars and practitioners active in this nascent field. Because much information in this field is being conveyed, interpreted, and driven by the Internet, we present a selection of the significant Web sites that have been compiled and present them in the appendix. This appendix serves as a guide that will help readers navigate this new and complex terrain by means of a regularly updated directory of Internet materials on religion.

This book contains six parts. Part I, "Religion, Secularism, and Secularization," addresses one of the major debates of our time: do the classical empirical and ethical assumptions about the relationship between religion and modernization noted earlier have any meaning and validity today? Empirically, *do* the dynamics of the modern world force religion into a private sphere with little to no public voice? In other words, is some process of *secularization* occurring in modern societies? Ethically, *should* religion be restricted to a private sphere to help make democracy more durable and robust? Is some doctrine of *secularism* that limits the role of religion in public life necessary to build free and healthy societies? To launch this volume's rethinking of the relationship between religion and world affairs, we could not be more fortunate than to have a contribution from J. Bryan Hehir. As Professor of the Practice of Religion and Public Life at Harvard's Kennedy School of Government and Secretary for Health and Social Services for the Catholic Archdiocese of Boston, Hehir embodies the robust and creative interplay between faith and public life. As a scholar, Hehir began to reflect deeply on the necessary nexus of religion and international affairs long before it was fashionable to do so; as a practitioner, he helped to shape the thinking of the U.S. Conference of Catholic Bishops on issues of war and peace. Here he offers a magisterial (a word even more appropriate here than in most cases) account of the reasons for the stubborn hold of secularism on both the theory and practice of international affairs. Yet he also provides an exploration—as comprehensive as it is concise—of the ongoing shift in favor of greater scholarly and policy attention to religious factors in world politics. According to Hehir, this shift has been prompted more by events than ideas; it began in earnest in the 1970s; and it has accelerated since that time, particularly in the 1990s and after September 11, 2001. Though events led the way, he concludes, new and creative ways of integrating religion into the study of world affairs are rapidly catching up to reality.

The second contributor to our book, Georgetown University sociologist José Casanova, formulated singularly illuminating and influential answers to basic questions about secularism and secularization in his modern classic, *Public Religions in the Modern World* (1994). On the empirical question, Casanova displayed nuance on the fierce debate about secularization. On one hand, he argued that modernization has entailed secularization in one sense: it has fostered functional and institutional differentiation in societies, in which distinct social institutions such as governments and churches increasingly assume independent roles and functions, as well as assume discrete institutional forms. Religious institutions no longer help prop up overarching "sacred canopies" that envelop entire societies in systems of religious meaning but instead come to serve specialized religious functions and conduct specifically religious activities. On the other hand, however, Casanova argues that this differentiation of spheres has not entailed the privatization of religion. Functionally differentiated religious actors still shape civil society and political society—by delivering social services or organizing grassroots campaigns to influence legislation—even when they are no longer fused with the state or with other societal institutions.

In Casanova's contribution to this book, he refines and expands this pathbreaking argument, here outlining even more forcefully that the only aspect of the secular model that remains valid is that there must be an element of institutional differentiation between elected democratic authorities and religious authorities. In terms of privatization, he now argues that his initial argument was not strong enough. Fifteen years ago, he argued that religion, religious arguments, and participants played a legitimate role in civil society but not political society. As an ethical or normative matter, he now argues how and why religious actors have the right to shape political society. In particular, he makes three provocative self-criticisms about his concept of "public religions." First, he now argues that his attempt to restrict—at least normatively—modern public religions to the public sphere of civil society was a mistake. Second, he believes his original argument suffered from an "empirical framing of the study as church-state-nation-civil society from a comparative national perspective, neglecting the transnational dimensions" of religion so apparent today. Third, he moves away from his original focus on secularism as a Western Christian concept to look at its quite diverse manifestations in an increasingly "deterritorialized" world.

Our third article, "The Politics of Secularism," is by a rising scholar of international relations theory, Elizabeth Shakman Hurd. As Bryan Hehir demonstrated, both the international relations literature and diplomatic history neglect religion in international affairs. Author of a recent groundbreaking monograph, *The Politics of Secularism in International Relations,* Hurd takes on the task of unearthing the deep conceptual roots of this neglect, calling for a thorough reappraisal of the category of the "secular" as it has been used, understood, and applied in the study of international relations.[3] Secularisms (in the plural) are not fixed and final achievements of European-inspired modernity, she argues, but a series of social constructs and patterns of political rule that are contested and contestable. Failure to see this has led to a selective blindness in the study of world politics, as the blanket usage of the categories of the secular and the religious masks the diversity, history, and politics surrounding claims to secularism, secular democracy, and related concepts. In a powerful analysis of core assumptions held by the three major schools of international relations—realist, liberal, and constructivist—Hurd explores the different ways in which religion is understood and managed in secularist international relations theory and practice.

Part II, "Religion, Democracy, and Human Rights," turns to questions of democracy, human rights, and international law. Virtually all the religions of the world are considered. In chapter 4, Alfred Stepan advances his theory of the "twin tolerations." He argues that "secularism" is neither a necessary nor a sufficient condition for democracy. What is a necessary condition is that democratic political authorities have a sufficient degree of autonomy from religious authorities to be able to execute their legitimate democratic functions and that religions in the polity be given sufficient toleration, not only to privately exercise religious freedom of worship and to participate in public debates in civil society but also to organize in political society. Such religious freedoms may violate doctrinaire

French secularism but they do not violate democracy. In this and other works, Stepan develops the theory and practice of what he calls the "multiple secularisms of modern democratic and non-democratic regimes." He shows that many completely different state-religion-society models, and all major world religions, can conceivably be democratically contained within the twin tolerations.

One of the most novel and effective of these nonclassic but democratic secularisms is found in India. Rajeev Bhargava is the major theorist of this model. In his article "How Should States Deal with Deep Religious Diversity? Can Anything Be Learned from the Indian Model of Secularism?" he shows that the answer is clearly yes. Unlike the "wall of separation between church and state" found in the U.S. and enshrined in the U.S. Constitution, the Indian democratic state financially supports *all* religions. Also, unlike the U.S. idea of the state maintaining "equidistance" from all religions, the Indian model calls for "principled distance" from all religions. Principled distance allows the democratic state to act against a religion if it is violating other citizens' rights.

Robert Hefner explores the relationship between Islam and democracy. Using standard rankings of world polities concerning democracy and drawing on his expertise on non-Arab Indonesia, the world's most populous Muslim country, his article "Rethinking Islam and Democracy" shows that there are important differences in political culture and performance across Muslim countries. Taken as a whole, non-Arab Muslim-majority countries are, given their socioeconomic conditions, "democratically overachieving," while Arab-majority countries are "democratically underachieving." In one sense, this bodes well for the Muslim world's democratic prospects, since only about 22 percent of the world's Muslims live in Arab states. This is so despite the fact that support for democracy is roughly as high in Arab as in non-Arab-majority countries. However, just as there are some differences in Europe between Social Democratic and Christian Democratic polities, Hefner argues that emerging democracies in Muslim-majority countries may well be characterized by distinctive qualities and public-cultural concerns, owing to their ethico-legal and organizational legacies. In particular, even as democracy takes hold, religion is not likely to be privatized, and questions surrounding the status of women, non-Muslims, and Muslim nonconformists—and thus questions of religious freedom—may well continue to figure in public arguments over politics and the common good. Notwithstanding these dynamics, democracy is alive and well in parts of the Muslim world, and it will probably continue to expand and improve in quality.

The final article in this section is by John Witte Jr. and M. Christian Green of the Center for the Study of Law and Religion at Emory University. Their chapter outlines the importance of religious freedom for questions of human rights and democracy. They review the major international covenants concerning religious freedom and describe and analyze their evolution. They also analyze a "new alphabet" of religious freedom violation that has made the international headlines in recent years, concerning charges of apostasy, blasphemy, conversion, and defamation. Their argument, overall, is that human rights needs religion and religion needs human rights, and that conscience and freedom are essential to religion, human rights, and democracy.

The ambivalence of religion is reflected in the two essays that make up Part III, "Religion, Conflict, and Peacemaking." Although the essayists, Monica Duffy Toft of Harvard's John F. Kennedy School of Government and Daniel Philpott of the University of Notre Dame, are careful not to cast religion as intrinsically violence-prone or intrinsically peaceful, they nevertheless agree that religion is a force with serious political implications. Toft, for instance, provides a critical examination of the motivations religious actors have used to justify their use of violence. When violence takes a religious turn, it is often more deadly and intractable than other sorts of violence. Nevertheless, religious actors are not irrational. In fact, Toft shows that the ways in which religious actors reason and calculate can be understood, even when their calculations lead them to adopt violent courses of action. She also shows that it is vital for scholars and practitioners to consider the different forms and foundations of rationality that religious actors employ in the political arena, with or without accompanying violence.

While Toft's essay examines religion and violence, Philpott turns our attention to reconciliation efforts by religious actors following civil wars, genocide, and dictatorship. He first explains the paradigm of reconciliation that religious theologians and leaders have developed, one that poses an alternative to the liberal peace, now the globally dominant paradigm among the world's most powerful institutions. In the second half of the piece, he offers a comparative analysis that shows where and under what conditions religious actors have drawn on reconciliation to shape institutions of transitional justice.

In Part IV, "Religion, Humanitarianism, and Civil Society," the contributors address major global dynamics that often proceed under the radar of international politics and diplomacy—namely, the role of religion in humanitarianism, development, gender relations, and interreligious dialogue. These dynamics do not normally grab headlines quite the way suicide bombings do. But they are an increasingly salient issue in bilateral and multilateral diplomacy, numerous international organizations devote enormous time and resources to addressing them, and they have an enormous and direct impact on the quality of life of most of the world's people. What is more, they are all issues in which religious discourse and religious institutions play a large and increasing role.

Opening this section is a rich contribution by political scientist Michael Barnett, a senior scholar of international relations and of the history and role of humanitarianism in shaping global affairs. He explores the profound complexities and developments that characterize the relationship between religion and humanitarianism, both today and in history. Though much academic and policy discussion takes for granted an unproblematic distinction between secular and faith-based social service organizations operating in the humanitarian field at home and abroad, Barnett shows that the history and contemporary reality of humanitarian practice forces us to blur this presumed conceptual boundary. For one thing, many formally secular humanitarian workers and aid agencies are demonstrably motivated by a great deal of faith and drive to connect with the transcendent. In addition, evangelical Protestants pioneered the formation of voluntary societies that specialized in meeting humanitarian goals, such as abolishing slavery. At the same time, many officially faith-based organizations operate programs and follow procedures that are virtually indistinguishable from those of secular aid organizations. His essay demonstrates that the neat distinctions we take for granted in scholarship and policy debates should be interrogated, not assumed.

Development expert Katherine Marshall of Georgetown University treats a contentious relationship in the next chapter, "Faith, Gender, and International Affairs." Marshall focuses on the respects in which religion is both a major vehicle of women's empowerment in the developing world and a frequent barrier to women's emancipation. To advance cooperation and partnership between women and mostly male religious hierarchies, Marshall urges greater dialogue and efforts at mutual understanding. But she also urges that the two sides focus on shared concerns on which they can undertake practical partnership—in areas such as sanitation, for example.

To open up the many-sided relationship between religion and development, Marshall, in a separate contribution, also explores numerous cases in which religious actors cooperated and clashed with the activities of multilateral development organizations including the World Bank. Marshall knows this fraught relationship well: for four decades, she served at the World Bank and helped launch an effort to establish a formal initiative there to strengthen dialogue and partnership between it and religious leaders and institutions. Her chapter documents the skepticism about religion's role in development she encountered firsthand during her tenure at the bank. But it also documents how the goals of both religious organizations and development institutions like the World Bank can be advanced through improved mutual understanding and practical partnerships.

If dialogue is a persistent subtheme in this section's chapters, it moves to center stage in the contribution by Thomas Banchoff, the director of the Berkley Center on Religion, Peace, and World Affairs at Georgetown University. Banchoff examines the evolution of interreligious dialogue over the last century, its intensification after the attacks of September 11, 2001, and its interaction with politics across societies and in interstate relations.

Part V, "Religion and the Media," turns to the role of the media and how religion is covered. Both chapters in this section reveal that new media and technologies have challenged fundamental understandings about what exactly religion is and its impact in global politics. The first chapter, by Mehrzad Boroujerdi and Nichole J. Allem, takes the reader through media in the Muslim world. What we discover is how the Muslim and Arab worlds have taken hold of media to challenge Western conceptions of how the world works, as well as to challenge domestic regimes.

Diane Winston's essay is complementary, showing the interplay between journalists, religion, and foreign policy and how the relationship has changed. Although religion has played a role in the coverage of some events, the quality of that coverage has shifted over time as new technologies and journalistic methods such as the Internet and blogging, for instance, have allowed a multitude of different perspectives to be heard in corners of the world that receive little to no coverage. Using the case of the Saffron Revolution, a series of demonstrations that involved monks in Burma protesting the policies of the country's oppressive junta, she argues that mainstream media outlets would not only have failed to cover the demonstrations but also have probably misinterpreted them. The ability of citizen journalists to post online their videos, photographs, and reporting about what is happening has transformed reporting in general and, in Winston's view, the reporting of religion. Moreover, by subjecting the political system to more scrutiny, it has helped to transform Burma's/Myanmar's politics in a positive direction through elections, freeing of dissidents and civilian rule.

Part VI, "Religion and American Foreign Policy," explores the relationship between religion and American foreign policy from diverse perspectives. Numerous difficult questions underpin this relationship. Do some religious groups have a dangerous influence on American foreign policy? Have efforts by the U.S. foreign policy apparatus to engage religious dynamics borne any policy fruit? Can U.S. foreign policy makers learn to engage religious dynamics more nimbly and effectively to advance not only the interests of the United States but also the global common good? Does it make sense for a country with a constitutional separation of church and state to do so?

The essay by Walter Russell Mead, reprinted from the September 2006 issue of *Foreign Affairs*, tackles the first of these nettlesome issues head-on: do some religious groups have a dangerous influence on American foreign policy? As a leading analyst of the history of American foreign policy and strategic thinker at the Council on Foreign Relations, Mead has had a sustained interest in the interplay of religious ideas and America's conception of its global role and interests. He brings the weight of his historical expertise and strategic acumen to the issue of how American evangelical Protestants are shaping American foreign policy. Though the influence of conservative Protestants on American foreign policy worries some and terrifies others, Mead observes that missionary Protestantism has been an almost constant shaper of American self-understanding and contributor to American perceptions of the world. This is sometimes for ill, Mead finds, but often for good. Mead concludes that evangelical Protestants are already showing signs of maturing in their thinking about foreign policy, though they still have a way to go. The more evangelicals can become conversant with the concepts and debates that shape American foreign policy, the better off both evangelicals and the United States will be. This is true, Mead argues, not least because evangelicals have the potential to play a positive and strategic role in helping American foreign policy elites to grasp the importance of global religious dynamics.

One area where the activism of American religious communities made a concrete difference in the crafting of American foreign policy is international religious freedom. Not only evangelical Protestants but also a broad coalition of Catholics, Protestants, Jews, and others mobilized between 1996 and 1998 to push for the passage of congressional legislation on international religious freedom. When the International Religious Freedom Act passed Congress by unanimous votes in the House and Senate and was signed into law by President Bill Clinton in October 1998, it mandated the systematic integration of religious freedom into the priorities and structures of American foreign policy.

But more than ten years later, Thomas Farr asks in this book, how well has America's new religious freedom policy really worked? Farr's long experience as a diplomat and, in particular, as the first director of the International Religious Freedom office at the State Department gives him a unique ability to deliver an authoritative assessment. As implemented, Farr argues, the policy has fallen far short of its promise. It has focused too much on the narrow and short-term goal of rescuing particular victims of religious persecution in a relatively small number of countries. Instead, Farr argues, America's religious freedom policy could and should be tasked with advancing the "twin tolerations" Alfred Stepan articulates in his contribution to this book: liberty for religious organizations to express themselves fully and freely in public life, along with freedom for states to formulate laws democratically without being trumped by religious authorities. This kind of robust freedom for religious communities would not only secure their basic civil and political rights, Farr explains, but also advance U.S. strategic interests, such as countering extremism and stabilizing religiously divided societies.

In many ways, any book on rethinking religion would not be complete without the final chapter in this section, contributed by three senior fellows at one of Washington's most respected and influential think tanks. Karin von Hippel, Frederick Barton, and Shannon Hayden, the former codirectors and project coordinator, respectively, of the Post-Conflict Reconstruction Project at the Center for Strategic and International Studies, provide a practical, how-to user's manual for advancing the integration of religion into American foreign policy They note the parts of the U.S. government that have been most open to integrating religion—mostly in the Pentagon, it turns out—and why most other parts of America's foreign policy apparatus have proven relatively resistant. More than this, they specify a series of doable steps forward that American government officials can take to make progress in this neglected area. With these steps, U.S. policy makers will not only be smarter about religion but also better equipped to negotiate the challenges and opportunities the blurring of the boundaries between religion and world affairs poses for American interests.

A final word is in order about "religion," perhaps the most important concept explored in this book. Since it is of such obvious importance in a book about "religion and world affairs," it is reasonable to ask: What is it exactly? How do we define it? The answer is: We don't. Or, more accurately, we do not impose a single definition on the diverse authors and perspectives represented in this volume. The reason is not that we consider "religion" a meaningless category, as some suggest. Nor is the reason that we must simply throw our hands up in despair because there are just too many ways to define it. William Cavanugh's profound and perceptive recent book, *The Myth of Religious Violence*, cites a 1912 psychology of religion textbook that lists more than fifty different definitions of religion.[4] The increasing self-criticism and self-consciousness of religion scholars in the hundred years since that textbook was published has no doubt doubled or tripled the available definitions.

Aware of the proper complexity, capaciousness, and multivalence of "religion" as a concept, we invited the scholars and practitioners selected to contribute to this book to adopt and apply their own definitions and methods to the task of rethinking the place and influence of religion in world affairs. We encouraged each contributor to approach religion from within his or her own disciplinary framework in order to enrich our understanding of the variety of ways in which religion interacts with global affairs.

As this book makes clear, religion cannot and should not be confined to a narrow category of scholarship or thought. Rethinking religion properly, therefore, requires that we encourage multiple strands of scholarship and practical insight. In any case, if history and prior scholarship are any guide, no matter what we do, religious phenomena will sooner or later "trespass" almost any boundary, conceptual or practical, we seek to impose.

Notes

1. Kenneth D. Wald and Clyde Wilcox, "Getting Religion: Has Political Science Rediscovered the Faith Factor?" *American Political Science Review* 100:4 (November 2006), 525.

2. Daniel Philpott, "The Challenge of September 11 to Secularism in International Relations," *World Politics* 55:1 (October 2002), 69.

3. See Elizabeth Shakman Hurd, *The Politics of Secularism in International Relations* (Princeton: Princeton University Press, 2007).

4. William Cavanaugh, *The Myth of Religious Violence* (New York: Oxford University Press, 2009), 119.

PART I

Religion, Secularism, and Secularization

1 }

Why Religion? Why Now?

J. Bryan Hehir

The theme of this book of essays, religion and world politics, embodies a paradox. The authors, explicitly or implicitly, will refer to the emergence or resurgence of religion in international affairs. But religion has never been absent from the international arena or the reality of world politics. Rooted as it is in the deepest dimension of human personality and societal life, religion has been entwined with the basic dynamics of men and women, states and nations for millennia. Religious beliefs and convictions have moved societies to cooperate and to collide, to seek understanding of each other and to plan domination of others. The role of religion has never been one-dimensional: it has fostered the search for peace, and it has intensified the motives for war; it has united some at the price of dividing others. The narrative of religion in world politics cannot be conceived or written parsimoniously; the story, like the reality, covers a broad canvas.

Yet, the paradox is that the scholars in this book and in other sources who speak of a return or a resurgence of religion have a valid point.[1] In reality, religion has never been absent from international affairs. But the study of world politics, particularly the formal discipline of international relations, and the practice of world politics, particularly formal interstate diplomacy, have both treated religion as inconsequential, a reality that could be ignored by scholars or diplomats without any diminishment of their understanding of the world.[2] The claim here is not that there has been, in the academy or diplomacy, a widespread animus against religion, much less systematic efforts to persecute it. Part of the narrative does include persecution: sometimes states persecuting believers, sometimes one faith against another. But at the level that concerns this book—the level of scholarship and the quest for understanding, the level of how states and global institutions actually practice diplomacy, make war, or make peace—at those levels, the dominant reality has not been active opposition to religion but benign disregard of it. Religion has effectively been treated as a black box. In other words, the operative assumption has been that the influence of religious beliefs and communities on "high politics" is so marginal—and so opaque—that one can safely ignore religion altogether and still successfully interpret the international system and the policies of states.

Sorting out the paradox of this book, therefore, requires a determination of why religion has been marginalized in the past, what factors have brought about its "resurgence" in fact and in theory, and how the relationship of religion and international affairs should be pursued in theory and practice.

The Past: Why the Absence?

The absence of serious attention to the role of religion in world politics has a remote cause and an immediate cause. Locating the remote cause requires retelling the modern history of the state system, a story that runs from the mid-seventeenth to the mid-twentieth century. In his widely respected work, *Diplomacy*, Henry Kissinger charts the emergence of the modern era of international relations in terms of the collapse of universalist values and the rise of state-centric conceptions of national interest.[3] Universalism had a clear religious component and realization in the role and teaching of the Catholic Church. This universalism had a secular counterpart in the aspirations of the Holy Roman Empire. The secular decline of both parties involved a process of evolution; it was not the product of a single event. Kissinger, along with many other analysts, identifies the principal historical divide as the rise of the Westphalian order of politics in the seventeenth century.

The transition across the divide from medieval universalism to modern states involved three major changes stretching from the fourteenth to the seventeenth century. The first was the gradual emergence and spread of state sovereignty, the consolidation of state power within a defined territory in a style distinctly different from the medieval pluralist structure of overlapping powers and conflicting loyalties. The second was the decisive event of the Protestant Reformation. While sovereignty challenged political universalism, the Reformation challenged religious universalism, thus weakening the Catholic Church as a transnational political actor and strengthening emerging nation-states. Due to the Reformation, a unified church under a single papal authority gave way in many parts of northern Europe to divided, territorialized churches under a multitude of princely authorities. The third factor was the substantial erosion of a unified conception of moral norms to direct and restrain politics and war.[4] Each of these transitions was a complex process, better recognized in retrospect than in the midst of their evolution.

The Westphalian order, symbolically tied to the Treaty of Westphalia (but not exhausted by it) had a double meaning. The treaty itself ended the Thirty Years' War, in which confessional divisions played a crucial role, and in a wider sense attempted to contain the political-military consequences of the religious divide in Europe. Beyond these immediate purposes, however, the Westphalian order had a broader and more lasting impact on the modern era of statecraft. It produced a conception of international order that was sovereign and secular in character, committed to a conception of state interests as the best guide to understanding international relations. This whole narrative of the transition from medieval universalism to modern sovereignty has a distinctively Western character that should be explicitly acknowledged. But its Western roots did not prevent the Westphalian order from extending its ideas and influence across the expanding area of international relations over the next three centuries. The expansion of Westphalia—to some degree, a universalism of a different kind—has been embodied in the United Nations, an institution that exemplifies the sovereign and secular elements of the new order.

One of these elements of the new international order—the emphasis on states as autonomous and sovereign political entities—has attracted the lion's share of attention. The sovereignty theme of the Westphalian-UN order has been the subject of endless analysis and commentary. This critical attention has been merited insofar as a state-centric view of world politics provided a powerful (if not fully comprehensive) understanding of the world through the first half of the twentieth century.

While sovereignty was the subject of extensive attention and analysis, the secular character of the modern era was taken for granted in the study and practice of world politics. Certainly, in much of the twentieth century, there were no more than a few glancing references to the transition to a secular conception of politics. That world politics is and ought to be secular was presumably a truth so clear it needed neither explanation nor commentary. Secularity, the assertion of a political order (within states and among them) that stood beyond the range of religious authority, control, or even influence, was a purposeful result of Westphalia, but its status seemed so certain that it has not been an object of inquiry or analysis. In a sense, Dr. Kissinger is an exemplary representative of this view. He acknowledges a past when religion was an essential element of politics, but the recognition is retrospective, a historical note about a world that has been surmounted by secularity. In this view, discussion of a return of religion to a significant role in world politics is likely to be seen as a regression, more of a threat to order than a contribution to it—which may be why *religion* doesn't even make it into the index of Kissinger's 900-page *Diplomacy*.[5] The threat arises from the potential impact religious conviction can have on politics. The word *potential* is critical in the previous sentence; there are examples—past and present—of religion enhancing political relationships and contributing to justice and peace. But the more powerful lasting memory for most analysts of world politics, as well as statesmen, seems to be the way religion can deepen and intensify political competition and military conflict. Holy war always sounds more ominous than simply war. Echoing this prevailing sentiment, President Barack Obama pithily observed in his speech accepting the Nobel Peace Prize on December 10, 2009, that "no holy war can ever be a just war."

In brief, at the level of schools and theories of international relations, the proposal to create greater space for religious ideas, convictions, and institutions has been considered more a threat than a promise. The unfortunate legacy of this diffidence about religion is impoverished theorizing about world politics. As Professor Robert Keohane, one of America's preeminent scholars of international relations, observed: "The attacks of September 11 reveal that all mainstream theories of world politics are relentlessly secular with respect to motivation. They ignore the impact of religion, despite the fact that world-shaking political movements have so often been fuelled by religious fervor."[6]

If anything, the diplomats and statesmen who practice world politics are even more nervous about religion than the international relations scholars who study it. The past—including the very recent past—manifests a spectrum from skepticism to opposition when the theme of religion arises in foreign ministries, among professional diplomats, and in the halls of international institutions. This is the immediate cause of the absence of religion. Thomas Farr, a career U.S. Foreign Service officer and contributor to this book, recounts his experience within the State Department bureaucracy.[7] At one level, he observed a presumptive doubt that knowledge of religious dynamics could contribute useful insight to foreign policy analysis. Beyond intellectual doubt, there looms the assumption that including religious ideas or religious actors in U.S. foreign policy may lead to constitutional issues concerning the First Amendment. Finally, the religious pluralism of the world in which the United States must function shapes the cost-benefit calculus among professionals that far more cost—and controversy—is likely if one engages with religion. As former Secretary of State Madeleine Albright has said, "Diplomats trained in my era were taught not to invite trouble. And no subject seemed more inherently treacherous than religion."[8]

The combination of doubts in the academy and skittishness among diplomats about the dangers of addressing religion in world politics has been reinforced—at least in the West—by one other assumption. The assumption is rooted in the democratic revolutions of the eighteenth century. Their influence in the West has been virtually equal to the power of the Westphalian conception of politics, precisely in terms of the conviction that freedom of religion is a basic human right. The correlative idea has been that a democratic polity that guarantees religious freedom for all citizens should regard religion as a private reality, not a public influence on society. The correlative concept is not universally shared in democratic societies, and its meaning is often assumed but not articulated. Its influence on diplomacy and international relations, however, has been pervasive. It undergirds the idea that religion need not be addressed in understanding the public nature of world politics. This reinforces the notion, identified earlier, that religion can safely be treated as a black box—inscrutable and irrelevant—without detriment to policy analysis. The legacy of Westphalia and the democratic era go some distance in explaining the absence of religion in international relations for much of the last four centuries. But the picture is now changing. That changing picture is our next topic.

The Present: Describing the Return

If change is occurring, what accounts for it? The change is clearer in the study of world politics than in the policy arena. But both show signs of a necessity and/or a willingness to rethink the relationship of religion and international relations.

The primary catalyst for change was concrete events; events preceded ideas. In the study of international relations, scholars and analysts were confronted with facts that cried out for explanation. The events began in the 1970s and continued throughout the last century. In Latin America, beginning in Brazil, then Chile, and on to Central America in the 1980s, religious leaders and communities confronted the power of authoritarian regimes (usually military) in the name of protecting human rights and in support of the struggle of peasants and workers for social justice. In these cases, it was not surprising that the dominant religious voice was the Catholic Church. In the 1980s in South Africa, it was the South African Council of Churches, led by Anglican Archbishop Desmond Tutu, that was in the forefront of the antiapartheid movement. In the Philippines and South Korea, local religious leaders and their communities clashed with authoritarian regimes allied with the United States. In all of these cases, the religious community in the United States provided a complementary voice within the U.S. political process through public campaigns, congressional testimony, and other forms of support to coreligionists abroad. In the late eighties, the focus of attention shifted to the very center of the Cold War competition, as Lutherans in Berlin and a Polish pope allied with Solidarity helped erode the power of the communist states in Central and Eastern Europe. In none of these instances was the role of religion the sole cause of change; each case was unique, and in all cases religious communities worked with other groups and nongovernmental organizations to oppose state power and/or work for basic changes in society.

The relevant point for this book is that religious convictions, institutions, and ideas demonstrated a growing ability to play a significant role in highly complex and often dangerous political situations. That ability in turn attracted the attention of governments, scholars, and other key players in international relations seeking to determine the kind and degree of influence religion actually was exercising in these conflicted cases.

The broad theme of religion and world politics attracted new visibility with the publication of Samuel Huntington's article "The Clash of Civilizations?" in *Foreign Affairs*;[9] Huntington's reputation for making numerous and decisive contributions to the field of international relations and American foreign policy immediately drew attention to his argument "that the fundamental source of conflict in this new world will not be primarily ideological or primarily economic. The great divisions among humankind and the dominating source of conflict will be cultural."[10] Huntington then went on to specify his view of civilization: "Civilizations are differentiated from each other by history, language, culture, tradition and, most important, religion."[11] The argument he made was characteristically about large ideas and a capacious theme; it left much room for commendation and critique, and plenty of both followed. In terms of this book, the most important fact about the article was its existence. For forty years, Sam Huntington had been a major voice in the academy and the policy world; to have him address religion and world politics signified to many a legitimization of the theme.

It is to stress the obvious to say that the events of 9/11, with their transnational destructive consequences, their explicit religious references, and their threat to combine religion and war in new ways did nothing but intensify the drive to understand factors that, as Keohane asserted, had been ignored or undervalued in mainline political analysis. The research and debate about 9/11 moved in different directions: some sought to establish a barrier between religion and politics; others sought deeper analysis of how religious traditions interpret the world, who speaks for the authentic tradition, and how traditions can be manipulated or distorted from within and without.

In retrospect, looking back on world politics as it took shape in the last half of the twentieth century, it is possible to identify substantial forces that emerged and created open space for the religious voice to be heard in new ways. The rise and recognition of transnationality, a reality that found expression in the work of Bob Keohane and Joe Nye in the 1970s and was carried forward on multiple fronts drew from scholars analogies between religious communities and other transnational actors as they interacted with states and international institutions. Transnationality as a theme pointed to transnational actors and transnational problems (food, population, environment, economics), both of which were reshaping the international agenda. A broader theme than transnationality was the growing fabric of interdependence, not a new reality in world politics, but one that moved rapidly toward ever greater integration of nations and states. The conceptual and factual journey from interdependence to globalization offered topics that drew religious voices and analysis closer to mainline analysis of international relations. This linkage was expanded and intensified as normative themes captured the attention of governments and scholars: the ethics of war was revisited in light of nuclear weapons and then terrorism; the role of human rights in an interdependent globe engaged both religious ethics and religious institutions; questions of international economic justice, including the visible campaign about Third World debt, drew on religious resources for intellectual and organizational support.

These secular changes in world politics, grounded independently from religion, converged with aspects of religious analysis and activity. This book, in terms of its authors and its themes, testifies to the change that has occurred on the religion–world politics frontier. There is a body of solid scholarship arising from students of international relations and comparative government on one hand and theologians and social scientists interested in religion on the other. Professor Eva Bellin has provided an illuminating review of this literature in *World Politics*. She assesses the past in terms similar to this chapter and then pushes on to a literature review probing distinct areas in political science, where she charts an impressive array of basic works on which broader theoretical contributions to religion and politics, particularly world politics, can be made. Bellin acknowledges that her review article builds on other solid surveys in the field of religion and politics, and she usefully reminds all that this is a journey with many miles to go.

She focuses on international relations theory and comparative politics. Although this introduction has a much more limited scope than Bellin's essay, its purpose is similar. It is to point toward the connections being made in this text with mainstream conceptions of world politics. Making these connections is still a major challenge, but two recent examples of a similar nature do exist and provide resources for reflection.

The first is the post–World War II narrative concerning ethics and international relations (IR). All too often, the study of religion and the study of ethics are conflated. While it is clear that religious traditions are a source for ethics, practically and theoretically, they are distinct sources of normative wisdom. Hence the relationship of ethics and international relations has its own story. The modern version begins with the triumph of realist theory in IR in the 1940s and 1950s; the perspective coincided with the main lines of the Westphalian order: realism had a well-known skepticism about ethical reflection. Although prominent realists, like Morgenthau, Kennan, and Niebuhr, did grapple with the questions, realist skepticism was rooted in three concerns: complexity, consequences, and crusades. Realism is famous for parsimonious explanations of the world; in line with this preference, realists typically concluded that foreign policy problems were sufficiently complex in themselves (i.e., in their secular, empirical characteristics) that expanding these questions to include their ethical dimensions would only increase the likelihood of mistaken analysis and faulty decisions. The early Morgenthau famously argued that a precise, enlightened view of national interest would simultaneously coincide with the best ethical answers to a policy problem. Beyond complexity, realists feared the multiplication of unintended consequences if ethical reflection played a major role in policy; students of history as they were, realists could cite multiple cases where good moral intentions had produced bad moral consequences. The argument, of course, is joined with the concerns about complexity. Finding one's way through both the fact of complexity and the possibility of unintended consequences diminished the realist's interest in addressing the ethics of policy. More precisely, those realists who were interested in this move always stressed how difficult the task would be. The final realist hesitation was crusades; here the argument was that a concern for the morally right course of action can easily decline into a simplistic conception of good and bad and right and wrong in the world, which in turn can produce a sense that pursuing the good and the right is so clearly one's obligation that restraint on means is overridden and ends are pursued without a sense of limits and prudence.

There were responses to all these questions and concerns, but the immediate postwar triumph of realism overwhelmed arguments that ethics could be systematically addressed in policy analysis while taking into account the realist's cautions. The three most visible postwar realists—Morgenthau, Kennan, and Niebuhr—later gave increasing scope to moral arguments in the policy process. Their evolution reflected the broader movement over the next forty years to incorporate systematic, sophisticated moral arguments in the field of international relations. It is possible to trace the evolution in terms of specific issues and broader thematic developments.

Here again, issues led the way, beginning with the postwar debates about the ethics of war. A leading voice in this area, John Courtney Murray, S.J., lamented in 1960 the absence of serious moral debate during World War II, when obliteration bombing directly contradicted core principles of the traditional ethics of war. But the next thirty years saw a revival of the ancient ethic and its development—in method and content—to address nuclear weapons, counterinsurgency warfare, and humanitarian intervention. The theologians led the way—Murray, joined by Paul Ramsey and Niebuhr—but the broader development involved historians and philosophers (Michael Walzer and James Johnson) and, particularly important for our purposes, international relations scholars like Stanley Hoffmann, Joseph Nye, and Bruce Russett.[12]

By the 1970s, these developments in the area of human rights required explicit and systematic ethical reflection on the nature of rights, their role in the UN system, their inclusion in foreign policy making, and their standing in debates about sovereignty and intervention. From the 1970s onward, a virtual cottage industry developed that simply assumed that normative considerations about human rights must be part of the policy equation and part of international regimes. The assumption itself constituted a major shift from the realist arguments of the 1950s and drew strong critique from George Kennan, whether the human rights debate was about the Soviet Union or South Africa. But the pattern set by policy debates about war was repeated on human rights. Not only the moralists and the theologians but also IR scholars, foreign policy analysts, and diplomatic debates were filled with human rights arguments.

Finally, a third stage in the ethics and international relations narrative has been the normative questions raised as the international system moved from early analysis about interdependence through the increasingly dense arguments about globalization. Classical questions about distributive justice, the role of markets, and the responsibilities of states for basic human rights and the satisfaction of human needs have been played out at the macrolevel of systemic relations. The issues of trade, debt, and foreign aid are regularly cast in normative terms.

Each of these cases—war, human rights, social justice—could be developed in detail, but the broader point relevant to this book is that the subfield of ethics and international relations today has substantial standing in terms of how world politics is studied in the academy, debated in international forums, and decided in policy bureaucracies. Examples abound: the recent *Oxford Handbook of International Relations* pairs each chapter describing schools of international theory with a chapter on the ethical vision embedded in each theory;[13] the UN Millennium Summit had pervasive normative themes in its debates and its declarations; U.S. policy engaging the use of force from Kosovo to Iraq to Afghanistan is simultaneously debated in strategic and normative terms. It may be an overstatement to describe the journey of ethics and IR over the last fifty years as one of movement from isolation to integration, but an approximation of this description is sustainable.

The second case of integration of new themes in the standard discourse of IR is better known in the discipline. Often described as the recasting of the distinction between "high-politics" (politics and war) and "low-politics" (politics and economics) so that both dimensions are accorded equal status, it has been a narrative of changing facts and changing theoretical perspectives. The basic fact—with multidimensional sources and consequences—has been increasing economic interdependence. That phenomenon, in turn, provided increasing salience for political economy, not only as a sphere of private, market-driven significance but also as an issue for the policies of governments. The increasing significance of political economy as a policy issue and the growing density of transnational relationships and actors in world politics attracted widespread scholarly attention in the 1970s and 1980s. Keohane and Nye's *Power and Interdependence*,[14] a uniquely influential work, argued for the recognition of the changing landscape of world politics and the need to move beyond the "high versus low" conception of international relations. Their work had the distinct benefit of acknowledging the continuing role of political-strategic issues but also defining the limits of a strategic, state-centric perspective in a world of multiple hierarchies, many actors, and a growing agenda of related transnational problems. Over time in the scholarly and diplomatic worlds, this broader conception of world politics gained currency. The result was a redefined conception of the core issues of world politics.

All analogies are limited, but these two examples illustrate the challenge and potential of systematically integrating the role of religion in the study of world politics and international diplomacy. The work that has been accomplished academically thus far has established a solid foundation for integration. But deeper and broader analysis is needed.

The essays in this book—by leading scholars and practitioners of international politics and diplomacy—articulate why religion has a rightful place in the study of world politics. Not only that, they offer creative analytical tools and approaches that significantly advance religion's integration into the systematic study of international relations and world affairs. One hopes that when future Henry Kissingers and Madeleine Albrights write the story of world politics and international diplomacy in the twenty-first century, these essays will make it a little more likely that religion will be a central subject of their analysis—or at least make it into the index.

Notes

1. Several works now trace this theme of resurgence: cf. Scott Thomas, *The Global Resurgence of Religion and the Transformation of International Relations* (New York: Palgrave Macmillan, 2005), 45; Peter Katzenstein and Timothy Byrnes, "Transnational Religion in an Expanding Europe," *Perspectives on Politics* (December 2006), 679–694; Eva Bellin, "Faith in Politics: New Trends in the Study of Religion and Politics," *World Politics* 60 (January 2008), 315–347.

2. Bellin, in her review article, identifies the perspective: "Perceived as limited in theoretical reach and methodological sophistication, studies of religion in politics have typically been shunted to the margin of the profession." "Faith in Politics," 315.

3. Kissinger contrasts the two images of the world. The medieval universalist perspective: "The world was conceived as mirroring the Heavens. Just as one God ruled in Heaven, so one emperor would rule over the secular world and one pope over the Universal Church." In the modern world: "With the concept of unity collapsing, the emerging states of Europe needed some principle to justify their heresy and to regulate their relations. They found it in the concepts of *raison d'état* and the balance of power." Henry Kissinger, *Diplomacy* (New York: Simon and Schuster, 1994), 56, 58.

4. The normative vision that held the medieval order together was a mix of faith and reason, the latter embodied in the philosophy of Natural Law. When the religious unity of the West collapsed, three key figures—Vitoria, Suarez, and Grotius—sought to salvage the Natural Law philosophy of statecraft as a source of restraint. Eventually, the field of positive international law emerged from their efforts.

5. Describing the transition away from medieval ideas achieved by Richelieu, Kissinger comments: "In an age still dominated by religious zeal and ideological fanaticism, a dispassionate foreign policy free of moral imperatives stood out like a snow-covered Alp in the desert." *Diplomacy*, 62.

6. Robert O. Keohane, "The Globalization of Informal Violence, Theories of World Politics and the Liberalism of Fear," *International Organization*, IO-Dialog (Spring 2002), 29–43; quoted in Thomas, *The Global Resurgence*, 11.

7. Thomas F. Farr, "Diplomacy in an Age of Faith," *Foreign Affairs* 87:2 (March–April 2008), 114. Farr's summary statement is: "The problem is rooted in the secularist habits of thought pervasive within the U.S. foreign policy community. Most analysts lack the vocabulary and the imagination to fashion remedies that draw on religion, a shortcoming common to all major schools of foreign policy."

8. Interview of Madeleine Albright with Bob Abernethy for PBS, "Madeleine Albright: The Intersection of Religion and Foreign Policy," May 19, 2006. Also see "Madeleine Albright, the Cardinal?" by Peter Steinfels, *New York Times* (May 6, 2006). Available at www.nytimes.com/2006/05/06/us/06beliefs.html.

9. Samuel P. Huntington, "The Clash of Civilizations?" *Foreign Affairs*, 72:3 (Summer 1993), 22.

10. Ibid., 25.

11. Ibid.

12. Stanley Hoffmann, *Duties beyond Borders* (Syracuse, NY: Syracuse University Press, 1981); Joseph S. Nye Jr., *Nuclear Ethics* (New York: Free Press, 1986); Bruce M. Russett, "Ethical Dilemmas of Nuclear Deterrence," *International Security* 8:4 (Spring 1984), 36–54.

13. Christian Reus-Smit and Duncan Snidal, *The Oxford Handbook of International Relations* (New York: Oxford University Press, 2008), 109–408.

14. Robert O. Keohane and Joseph S. Nye Jr., *Power and Interdependence: World Politics in Transition* (Boston: Little Brown, 1977).

2 }

Rethinking Public Religions

José Casanova

The aim of this chapter is to revisit the argument first presented in *Public Religions in the Modern World* in order to ascertain the extent to which the theoretical-analytical framework developed there needs to be critically revised and expanded to make it more applicable beyond Western Christian contexts.[1] The central thesis of the book was that we were witnessing a process of deprivatization of religion as a relatively global trend. As an empirical claim, the thesis has been amply confirmed by subsequent developments practically everywhere. In a sense, the best confirmation of the thesis can actually be found in the heartland of secularization, that is, in Western European societies. Even though there is very little evidence of any kind of religious revival among the European population, if one excludes the significant influx of new immigrant religions, religion has certainly returned as a contentious issue to the public sphere of most European societies.[2]

In this respect, more important than the empirical confirmation of the global trend of deprivatization of religion has been the widespread acceptance of the basic analytical-theoretical and normative claims of the thesis, namely, that the deprivatization of religion did not have to be interpreted necessarily as an antimodern, antisecular, or antidemocratic reaction. In my view, the most important contribution of the book was the critique it offered to prescriptive theories of privatization of religion and to the secularist assumptions built into social theories of Western modernity and into most liberal theories of modern democratic politics. The critique was made possible by two new analytical contributions.

The first contribution was the analytical disaggregation of the theory of secularization into three disparate components or subtheses: (1) the theory of the institutional differentiation of the secular spheres, such as state, economy, and science, from religious institutions and norms; (2) the theory of the decline of religious beliefs and practices as a concomitant of levels of modernization; and (3) the theory of privatization of religion as a precondition of modern democratic politics. Such an analytical distinction enables testing each of the three subtheses separately as different empirically falsifiable propositions. Because in Europe the three processes of secular differentiation, religious decline, and privatization have been historically interconnected, the tendency has been to view all three processes as intrinsically interrelated components of a general teleological process of secularization and modernization, rather than as particular contingent developments. In the United States, by contrast, one finds a paradigmatic process of secular differentiation that is not accompanied either by a process of religious decline or by the confinement of religion to the private sphere. Processes of modernization and democratization in American society have often been accompanied by religious revivals, and the wall of separation between church and state, though much stricter than the one erected in most European societies, does not imply the rigid separation of religion and politics.

The second main analytical contribution was the distinction of three different types of public religion, corresponding to the analytical distinction between three different areas of a modern democratic polity: state, political society, and civil society. Established state churches would be the paradigmatic example of public religion at the state level. Religions that mobilize their institutional resources for political competition through political parties, social movements, or lobbying agencies would be examples of public religion at the level of political society. Finally, public religions at the civil society level would be exemplified by religions that enter the public square—that is, the undifferentiated public sphere of civil society—to participate in open public debates about the res publica, that is, about public issues, public affairs, public policy, and the common good or commonwealth.

Obviously, this is an analytical, "ideal-typical" distinction. In actual empirical reality, the boundaries between the three areas of the polity are by no means so clear-cut, and therefore the delineation of the different types of public religion can also not always be clear and distinct. Nevertheless, the purpose of the analytical distinction was to put into question any rigid theory of privatization that would like to restrict religion to the private sphere on the grounds that any form of public religion represents a threat to the public sphere or to democratic politics.

Although I think that the analytical-theoretical framework developed in *Public Religions* is generally useful and still defensible today, I can see three main shortcomings or limitations of the argument: (1) its Western-Christian centrism; (2) the attempt to restrict, at least normatively, modern public religions to the public sphere of civil society; and (3) the empirical framing of the study as church-state-nation-civil society relations from a comparative national perspective, neglecting the transnational global dimensions.

Since my study was focused on the two main branches of Western Christianity, Catholicism and Protestantism, it could function with a relatively unreflexive category of "religion." The moment one adopts a global comparative perspective, however, this is no longer possible. In fact, within the academic discipline of religious studies, the very category of religion has undergone numerous challenges, as well as all kinds of critical genealogical deconstructions.

Thus, any discussion of religion in the contemporary global age should begin with the recognition of a paradox, namely, that scholars of religion are questioning the validity of the category of religion at the very same moment when the discursive reality of religion is more widespread than ever before and has become, for the first time, global. I am not claiming that people today everywhere are either more or less religious than they may have been in the past. Here I am bracketing out altogether the question that has dominated most theories of secularization, namely, whether religious beliefs and practices are declining or growing as a general modern trend. I am claiming only that religion as a discursive reality—indeed, as an abstract category and as a system of classification of reality, used by modern individuals as well as by modern societies across the world—has become an undisputable global social fact.

It is obvious that when people around the world use the same category of religion, they actually mean very different things. The actual concrete meaning of whatever people denominate as religion can be elucidated only in the context of their particular discursive practices. But the very fact that the same category of religion is being used globally across cultures and civilizations testifies to the global expansion of the modern secular-religious system of classification of reality that first emerged in the modern Christian West. This implies the need to reflect more critically on this particular modern system of classification.

Rethinking Secularization beyond the West: Toward a Global Comparative Perspective

While the two minor subtheses of the theory of secularization, namely, the decline of religion and the privatization of religion, have undergone numerous critiques and revisions in the last fifteen years, the core of the thesis, the understanding of secularization as a single process of functional differentiation of the various institutional spheres or subsystems of modern societies, remains relatively uncontested in the social sciences, particularly within European sociology. Yet, I do not think it is appropriate to subsume the multiple and very diverse historical patterns of differentiation and fusion of the various institutional spheres (that is, church and state, state and economy, economy and science) that one finds throughout the history of modern Western societies into a single teleological process of modern functional differentiation.

Moreover, rather than viewing secularization as a general universal process of human and societal development culminating in secular modernity, one should begin with the recognition that the very term *secularization* derives from a unique Western Christian theological category, that of the *saeculum*, which has no equivalent term in other world religions, not even in Eastern Christianity. The modern Western process of secularization, therefore, is a particular historical dynamic that can best be interpreted as a response and reaction to the particular medieval Latin Christian system of classification of all reality into spiritual and temporal, religious and secular.

As Charles Taylor has clearly shown, the historical process of modern secularization begins as a process of internal secular reform within Latin Christendom as an attempt to spiritualize the temporal and to bring the religious life of perfection out of the monasteries into the *saeculum*, thus literally as an attempt to secularize the religious. These medieval movements of Christian reform already established the basic patterns of secularization that would be later radicalized by the Protestant Reformation and by the French Revolution.[3]

The Protestant path of secularization, which attained its paradigmatic manifestation in the Anglo-Saxon Calvinist cultural area, particularly in the United States, is characterized by a blurring of the boundaries and by a mutual reciprocal infusion of the religious and the secular, in a sense making the religious secular and the secular religious. Even the separation of church and state that was constitutionally codified in the dual clause of the First Amendment was promoted by the religious sects and was as much about protecting the free exercise of religion from state interference and from ecclesiastical establishments as it was about protecting the federal secular state from any religious entanglement. This pattern of secularization does not necessarily entail the decline of religion. On the contrary, from the American Revolution till the present, processes of radical social change and secular modernization have often been accompanied by great awakenings and by religious growth.

The French-Latin-Catholic path, by contrast, takes the form of laicization and is basically marked by a civil-ecclesiastical and laical-clerical antagonistic dynamic. Here the boundaries between the religious and the secular are rigidly maintained, but those boundaries are pushed into the margins, aiming to contain, privatize, and marginalize everything religious, while excluding it from any visible presence in the secular public sphere. When the secularization of monasteries took place first during the French Revolution and later in subsequent liberal revolutions, the explicit purpose of breaking down the monastery walls was not to bring the religious life into the secular world but rather to laicize those religious places, dissolving and emptying their religious content and making the religious persons, monks and nuns, civil and laical before forcing them into the world, now conceived as merely a secular place emptied of religious symbols and religious meanings. This could well serve as the basic metaphor of all subtraction narratives of secular modernity, which tend to understand the secular as merely the space left behind when this-worldly reality is emptied of religion.

A recognition of the multiple and diverse historical patterns of secularization and differentiation within European and Western societies should allow a less Eurocentric comparative analysis of patterns of differentiation and secularization in other civilizations and world religions and, more important, the further recognition that with the world-historical process of globalization initiated by the European colonial expansion, all these processes everywhere are dynamically interrelated and mutually constituted.

If the European concept of secularization is not a particularly relevant category for the "Christian" United States, much less may it be directly applicable to other world religions and other civilizational areas with very different dynamics of structuration of the relations and tensions between religion and world or between cosmological transcendence and worldly immanence. Moreover, in the same way as Western secular modernity is fundamentally and inevitably post-Christian, the emerging multiple modernities in the different postaxial civilizational areas are likely to be post-Hindu, post-Confucian, or post-Muslim; that is, they will also be a modern refashioning and transformation of already existing civilizational patterns and social imaginaries.

Public Religions beyond Ecclesiastical Disestablishment and Civil Society

THE DUAL CLAUSE AND THE "TWIN TOLERATIONS"

My own analysis of the deprivatization of religion tried to contain, at least normatively, public religions within the public sphere of civil society, without allowing them to spill over into political society or the democratic state. Today I must recognize my own modern Western secular prejudices and the particular hermeneutic Catholic and ecclesiastical perspective on religion that I adopted in my comparative analysis of the relations between church, state, nation, and civil society in Western Catholic and Protestant societies. The moment one adopts a global comparative perspective, one must admit that the deprivatization of religion is unlikely to be contained within the public sphere of civil society, within the territorial boundaries of the nation-state, and within the constitutional premises of ecclesiastical disestablishment and juridical separation of church and state. We need to go beyond the secularist discourse of separation and beyond the public sphere of civil society to address the real issues of democratic politics across the world.

My theory of modern public religion was largely informed by the experience of the Catholic aggiornamento of the 1960s. The official recognition of the inalienable right of every individual to religious freedom, based on the sacred dignity of the human person, meant that the church abandoned its traditional compulsory character and accepted the modern principle of disestablishment and the separation of church and state. The most important document of the Second Vatican Council, *Gaudium et Spes*, represented the church's acceptance of the religious legitimacy of the modern secular age and of the modern secular world, putting an end to the negative philosophy of history that had characterized the official Catholic position since the Counter-Reformation.

The aggiornamento led to a fundamental relocation of the Catholic Church from a state-oriented to a civil society–oriented institution. Moreover, the official adoption of the modern discourse of human rights allowed the Catholic Church to play a crucial role in opposition to authoritarian regimes and in processes of democratization throughout the Catholic world. But the Catholic Church's embrace of voluntary disestablishment did not mean the privatization of Catholicism but rather its relocation from the state to the public sphere of civil society. This is the hermeneutic context within which I developed the analytical framework of modern public religions and the theory of deprivatization. But obviously, there are many other forms of modern public religions and other forms of deprivatization.

I cannot find a compelling reason, on either democratic or liberal grounds, to in principle banish religion from the public democratic sphere. One could at most, on pragmatic historical grounds, defend the need for separation of church and state, although I am no longer convinced that complete separation is either a necessary or a sufficient condition for democracy. In any case, the attempt to establish a wall of separation between religion and politics is both unjustified and probably counterproductive for democracy itself. Curtailing the free exercise of religion per se must lead to curtailing the free exercise of the civil and political rights of religious citizens. Particular religious discourses or particular religious practices may be objectionable and susceptible to legal prohibition on some democratic or liberal ground, but not because they are religious per se.

Tocqueville was arguably the only modern social theorist who anticipated, rather presciently, that the democratization of politics and the entrance of ordinary people into the political arena would augment, rather than diminish, the public relevance of religion. The history of democratic politics throughout the world has confirmed Tocqueville's assumptions. Religious issues, religious resources, interdenominational conflicts, and secular-religious cleavages have all been relatively central to electoral democratic politics and to the politics of civil society throughout the history of democracy.

As the example of many modern secular authoritarian and totalitarian states have shown, from the Soviet Union to Kemalist Turkey, strict no establishment is by no means a sufficient condition for democracy. On the other hand, several countries with at least nominal establishment, such as England or Lutheran Scandinavian countries, have a relatively commendable record of democratic freedoms and of protection of the rights of minorities, including religious ones. It would seem, therefore, that strict separation is not a necessary condition for democracy. Indeed, one could advance the proposition that of the two clauses of the First Amendment, "free exercise" is the one that stands out as a normative democratic principle in itself, while the no establishment principle is defensible insofar as it might be a necessary means to free exercise and to equal rights. In other words, secularist principles per se may be defensible on some other ground, but not as intrinsically liberal democratic ones.

Alfred Stepan has pointed out how the most important empirical analytical theories of democracy, from Robert Dahl to Juan Linz, do not include secularism or strict separation as an institutional requirement for democracy, as prominent normative liberal theories, such as those of John Rawls or Bruce Ackerman, tend to do. As an alternative to secularist principles or norms, Stepan has proposed the model of "twin tolerations" between religious and political institutions and authorities. Within this framework of mutual autonomy and toleration, Stepan concludes that "there can be an extraordinarily broad range of concrete patterns of religion-state relations in political systems that would meet our minimal definition of democracy."[4]

Notwithstanding the official discourse of European secular democracy, the complex diversity of institutional patterns of church-state relations in Europe's "really existing democracies" offers a perfect illustration of Stepan's argument. Indeed, only a handful of European states may be said to be strictly secular, and none of them lives up to the myth of secular neutrality. Even the French state, the only self-defined secularist state in Western Europe, is far from being neutral or distant from religious institutions. It frequently regulates religious affairs, has established institutional relations with the Catholic Church through concordats, and has tried at different times to organize the other religious communities, Protestant, Jewish, and Muslim alike, into churchlike ecclesiastical institutions, which the state can use as interlocutor and institutional partner.

At the other extreme, several European countries with long-standing democracies have maintained officially established or national churches, including the Church of England, the Church of Scotland, the Lutheran churches in most Nordic countries, and the Orthodox Church in Greece. Ironically, this means that with the exception of the Catholic Church, which has eschewed establishment in every recent transition to democracy in Southern and Eastern Europe, every other major branch of Christianity (Anglican, Presbyterian, Lutheran, Orthodox) is officially established somewhere in Europe, without apparently jeopardizing democracy in those countries.

One could, of course, retort that European societies are de facto so secularized, and, as a consequence, what remains of religion has become so temperate that both constitutional establishment and the various institutional church-state entanglements are, as a matter of fact, innocuous, if not completely irrelevant. This may well be the case for the national majorities, whether they maintain implicit (i.e., vicarious) or explicit religious affiliation with their national churches. But it can hardly be said to be the case for most religious minorities, least of all for new immigrant religious minorities.

One should remember also that the drastic secularization of most Western European societies came after the consolidation of democracy, not before, and therefore it would be incongruent to present not only the secularization of the state and of politics but also the secularization of society as a condition for democracy. Moreover, at one time or another, most continental European societies developed confessional religious parties, which played a crucial role in the democratization of those societies. Even those confessional parties that initially emerged as antiliberal and at least ideologically as antidemocratic, as was the case with most Catholic parties in the nineteenth century, ended up playing a very important role in the democratization of their societies. This is the paradox of Christian Democracy so well analyzed by Stathis Kalyvas.[5] The story of the transformation from Political Catholicism to Christian Democracy is particularly relevant at a time when the alleged incompatibility of Islam and democracy and the supposedly antidemocratic nature of Muslim and other religious parties is so frequently and publicly debated.[6]

Transnational Religions, Transnational Imagined Communities, and Globalization

The empirical case studies in *Public Religions* were still framed as national case studies under the premises of the kind of methodological nationalism that has framed so much of the comparative work in the social sciences, whether comparative historical sociology, comparative politics, or comparative economic development. While one may take for granted the transnational dimensions of Catholicism, what is truly revealing is the extent to which, from the sixteenth to the early twentieth century, all the transnational dimensions of Catholicism that had been characteristic of medieval Christendom, from the transnational papacy to transnational religious orders, ecumenical councils, transnational universities and centers of Catholic learning, and transnational pilgrimages, had all been substantially diminished, if they had not altogether disappeared. Since the end of the nineteenth century, however, one can witness the reemergence and reconstruction of all the transnational dimensions of Catholicism on a new global basis.

Catholicism has been reconstituted as a new transnational and deterritorialized global religious regime.[7] Other world religions are undergoing their own peculiar transformations as a response to the same global processes. The contemporary worldwide expansion of Pentecostalism may serve to illustrate the equally favorable opportunities globalization offers to a highly decentralized religion, with no historical links to tradition and no territorial roots or identity, which therefore can make itself at home anywhere in the globe where the Spirit moves.[8]

Similar illustrations could be offered from other branches of Christianity and from other world religions. The dynamic core of Anglicanism no longer resides in post-Christian England. But today, immigrants from all over the British post-colonial world are reviving Anglicanism in secular England. For the world religions, globalization offers to all the opportunity to become for the first time truly world religions, that is, global, but also offers the threat of deterritorialization. The opportunities are greatest for those world religions like Islam and Buddhism that always had a transnational structure. The threat is greatest for those embedded in civilizational territories like Islam and Hinduism. But through worldwide migrations, they are also becoming global and deterritorialized. Indeed, their diasporas are becoming dynamic centers for their global transformation, affecting their civilizational homes.

Until very recently, the civilizational *oikoumenē* of all world religions had very clear territorial limits, set by the very world regimes in which those religions were civilizationally and thus territorially embedded and by the geographically circumscribed limitations of the existing means of communication. The Bishop of Rome may have always claimed to speak *urbi et orbi*, to the city and to the world. But in fact this became a reality first in the twentieth century. What constitutes the truly novel aspect of the present global condition is precisely the fact that all world religions can be reconstituted for the first time truly as deterritorialized global imagined communities, detached from the civilizational settings in which they have been traditionally embedded. Paraphrasing Arjun Appadurai's image of "modernity at large," one could say that the world religions, through the linking of electronic mass media and mass migration, are being reconstituted as deterritorialized global religions at large or as global *ummas*.[9]

For that very reason, Samuel Huntington's thesis of the impending clash of civilizations is simultaneously illuminating of the present global condition and profoundly misleading.[10] It is illuminating insofar as it calls attention to the increasing relevance of civilizations and civilizational identities in the emerging global order and in global conflicts. But it is also profoundly misleading insofar as it still conceives of civilizations as territorial geopolitical units, akin to superpowers, having some world religion as its cultural core.

When it comes to Islam, there is today, perhaps unavoidably, an obsession with state Islamism and *khilafist jihādism* as the two contemporary dominant forms of globalized Islam. But one could argue that the majoritarian currents of transnational Islam today and the ones likely to have the greatest impact on the future transformation of Islam are transnational networks and movements of Muslim renewal, equally disaffected from state Islamism and transnational *jihādism*. They constitute the networks of a loosely organized and pluralist transnational *ummah*, or global Muslim civil society: from the "evangelical" *Tablighi Jama'at* and other transnational *dawa* networks, to the neo-Sufist Fethullah Gülen's educational network, to other Sufi brotherhoods, such as the Mourids of West Africa, all of which have expanded their transnational networks into the Muslim diasporas of Europe and North America.

One could make a similar analysis of the formation of a global Hindu *ummah* linking the civilizational home, "Mother India," with old diasporic colonial Hindu communities across the former British Empire from Southeast Asia, to South Africa, to the Caribbean and with new immigrant Hindu communities throughout the West. It is this proliferation of deterritorialized transnational global imagined communities, encompassing the so-called old world religions, as well as many new forms of hybrid globalized religions, such as the Baha'is, Moonies, Hare Krishnas, Afro-American religions, and Falun Gong, that I call the emerging global denominationalism. Of course, they compete with modern nationalisms and with many other forms of secular imagined communities. But all those transnational imagined religious communities present fundamental challenges to international relations theories that are still functioning within the premises of a Westphalian international system and to secular cosmopolitan theories of globalization.

Notes

1. José Casanova, *Public Religions in the Modern World* (Chicago: University of Chicago Press, 1994).

2. José Casanova, "Religion, European Secular Identities, and European Integration," in *Religion in an Expanding Europe*, ed. Timothy A. Byrnes and Peter J. Katzenstein (Cambridge: Cambridge University Press, 2006), 65–92.

3. Charles Taylor, *A Secular Age* (Cambridge, MA: Harvard University Press, 2007).

4. Alfred Stepan, "The World's Religious Systems and Democracy: Crafting the 'Twin Tolerations,'" in *Arguing Comparative Politics* (Oxford: Oxford University Press, 2001), 217.

5. Stathis N. Kalyvas, *The Rise of Christian Democracy in Europe* (Ithaca, NY: Cornell University Press, 1996).

6. José Casanova, "Catholic and Muslim Politics in Comparative Perspective," *Taiwan Journal of Democracy*, 1:2 (December 2005), 89–108.

7. José Casanova, "Globalizing Catholicism and the Return to a 'Universal Church,'" in *Transnational Religion and Fading States*, ed. Susanne Rudolph and James Piscatori (Boulder, CO: Westview, 1997), 121–143.

8. José Casanova, "Religion, the New Millennium and Globalization," *Sociology of Religion* 62:4 (2001), 415–441.

9. Arjun Appadurai, *Modernity at Large* (Minneapolis: University of Minnesota Press, 1996).

10. Samuel P. Huntington, *The Clash of Civilizations and the Remaking of World Order* (New York: Simon & Schuster, 1994).

Annotated Bibliography

Almond, Gabriel A., R. Scott Appleby, and Emmanuel Sivan, *Strong Religion. The Rise of Fundamentalisms around the World*. Chicago: University of Chicago Press, 2003.
An invaluable source on "illiberal" religious political movements around the world, which summarizes the findings of The Fundamentalism Project: highly recommended, despite the problematic assumption that they are all manifestations of a singular global religious fundamentalism, resisting modern secularization.

Asad, Talal, *Formations of the Secular*. Stanford, CA: Stanford University Press, 2003.
A pathbreaking "genealogical" account of the secular, which builds upon Asad's pioneering *Genealogies of Religion*. It has been the single most influential source in reorienting the focus of much of social science from the study of "religion" to the comparative study of "the secular" and "secularisms."

Bader, Veit, *Secularism or Democracy? Associational Governance of Religious Diversity*. Amsterdam: Amsterdam University Press, 2007.
A sociologically grounded theoretical political critique of secularism as a model of governance of religious diversity and a compelling normative defense of democratic pluralism that incorporates religious groups into its institutional arrangements.

Beyer, Peter, *Religion in Global Society*. London: Routledge, 2006.
An invaluable reconstruction of the emerging world system of religions as a function of processes of globalization that illuminates both the role of globalization in the contemporary

transformation of all religions and the central role of religion in ongoing processes of globalization.

Hurd, Elizabeth Shakman, *The Politics of Secularism in International Relations.* Princeton, NJ: Princeton University Press, 2008.

A pioneering book that brings recent debates about the religious-secular divide, deprivatization, and the global resurgence of religion into the center of international relations, challenging in the process the core secularist assumptions of the field of IR.

Norris, Pipa, and Ronald Inglehart, *Sacred and Secular: Religion and Politics Worldwide.* New York: Cambridge University Press, 2004.

A spirited, though not fully convincing, defense of the traditional theory of secularization based on extremely rich and interesting data from the World Values Surveys that seem to confirm a positive strong correlation between religious beliefs and socioeconomic insecurity. An invaluable source of information, full of original analytical insights, within an oversimplified theory of religion and history.

Taylor, Charles, *A Secular Age.* Cambridge, MA: Harvard University Press, 2007.

The best analytical, phenomenological, and genealogical account we have of our modern, secular condition by one of the most important philosophers of our time. It challenges equally all the received positions on secularization, secular modernity, and secularism, making every oversimplification look simplistic.

3 }

The Politics of Secularism
Elizabeth Shakman Hurd

Introduction

In 2008, *New York Times* columnist Roger Cohen observed that "the fight for Turkey's soul is not about to abate.... The West should do all it can to safeguard that openness—which may involve an occasional dose of 'secular fascism.'"[1] Cohen's statement attests to the belief in the need to privatize religion, using force if necessary, and to the perception of threat posed by public religion. As a founding principle of modern politics, secularist settlements of the relation between religion and politics are closely bound up with notions of the public interest, democracy, freedom, justice, and legitimacy. Given this impressive pedigree, it should come as no surprise that international relations theorists have operated on the assumption that secularism and religion are clear and unproblematic concepts that may be relevant for social theorists or anthropologists but have little to do with the central concerns of late modern international politics. This assumption reflects the extraordinary power of secularist authority in the Western political imagination. As it turns out, secularisms (in the plural) are not fixed and final achievements of European-inspired modernity but social constructs and patterns of political rule with diverse and contested histories and important global and comparative implications. Failure to see this has led to a selective blindness in the study of world politics. The unreflective blanket usage of the categories of the secular and the religious has masked the diversity, history, and politics surrounding claims to secularism, secularization, secular democracy, and a host of related concepts.

This chapter calls for a thorough reappraisal of the category of the secular: how it has been used, understood, and applied in the analysis of world politics.[2] Secularism refers to a matrix of discourse and practice that involves defining, managing, and often remaking religion in public space. There are many forms of secularism.[3] In the language of international relations (IR), secularisms are productive modalities of power that work "through diffuse constitutive relations" to contribute to the "situated social capacities of actors."[4] They are vehicles through which shared interests and identities involving religion and politics developed at the domestic, regional, and transnational levels become influential at the global level. Secularisms are not reducible to material power but play a constitutive role in creating agents and the normative structures in which these agents interact.

This essay describes two influential trajectories of secularism and explains why they are important to contemporary world politics: laicism, from the French *laïcité*, which distills a particular understanding of religion and bans it from politics, and Judeo-Christian secularism (JCS), which defines religion as a source of unity and identity within societies and civilizations and conflict between them. Variations on these ideal-types have been influential in and between countries that inherited, borrowed, or had imposed on them the political and religious traditions of historical Latin Christendom, including Europe and its settler colonies (United States, Canada, Australia), Turkey, Iran, and India, among others. Practitioners, theorists, and ordinary people organize and orient their responses to questions of religion and politics, including world politics, through these forms of secularism. Yet absent critical, philosophical, and historical scrutiny, received categories and practices of secularism appear natural and inevitable. It is hard to imagine them otherwise. This essay discusses two ideal-types of secularism that have become so powerful that they go often unseen, appearing as part of the normal background context of international relations. It draws attention to how secularism is constituted differently in different times and places, the contestation and challenges that surround and inhabit the various forms of secularism, and the lives they take on in the world as they shape both analytic perspectives in social science and practical projects in politics and international affairs.

The Politics of Laicism

In *The Secular City*, Harvey Cox suggested that "it will do no good to cling to our religions and metaphysical versions of Christianity in the hope that one day religion or metaphysics will once again be back. They are disappearing forever...."[5] In *Empire*, Hardt and Negri observe that "every metaphysical tradition is now completely worn out."[6] John Esposito notes that "the degree of one's intellectual sophistication and objectivity in academia was often equated with a secular liberalism and relativism that seemed antithetical to religion.... Neither development theory nor international relations considered religion a significant variable for political analysis."[7] Laicism is a tradition of the secular city, world empire, and Western academy that presumes that metaphysical traditions have been transcended. It is one of the founding principles of modern politics and the foundation of the separation of church and state. Derived from the Jacobin tradition of *laïcisme*, it is associated with what Chatterjee describes as "a coercive process in which the legal powers of the state, the disciplinary powers of family and school, and the persuasive powers of government and media have been used to produce the secular citizen who agrees to keep religion in the private domain."[8]

Most literature on the Protestant Reformation and the Westphalian settlement charts the decline of religion in European public life. Krasner, for instance, suggests that "the idea of sovereignty was used to legitimate the right of the sovereign to collect taxes, and thereby strengthen the position of the state, and to deny such right to the church, and thereby weaken the position of the papacy."[9] For Krasner, Westphalia "delegitimized the already waning transnational role of the Catholic Church and validated the idea that international relations should be driven by balance-of-power considerations rather than the ideals of Christendom."[10] Westphalian republicanism was organized on a modern conception of social and political order in which individual subjects assembled a society under a single sovereign authority. By challenging the arbitrary rights of kings in the name of the common good,[11] the new republicanism transformed preexisting hierarchic forms of order, as conventional accounts have it. Yet the new republicanism also reinforced a particular distinction between natural and supernatural order that came out of, and remained indebted to, a broader Christian framework.[12] Early republican order was characterized by a strong idea of providence and a pervasive sense that men were enacting a master plan that was providentially preordained. The idea of moral order underlying this arrangement would, according to Taylor, be unrecognizable to non-Westerners due to its emphasis on a providential plan to be realized by humans.[13] That early republicanism was situated within this broader Christian context fits with Krasner's argument that in the Treaty of Osnabrück (one of two treaties that made up the Peace of Westphalia, alongside the Treaty of Münster) religious toleration was limited to Lutherans, Calvinists, and Catholics.[14] Westphalia led not to privatization but to the "territorialization of religion," the "formation of polities in which territory, state, and confession were closely linked."[15]

The tradition identified here as laicism emerged gradually and fitfully, and not without rivals, out of this Christian-influenced Westphalian order. Though presenting itself as a universalizable discourse and a solution to the wars of religion, William Connolly's description of it as a "a specific fashioning of spiritual life…carved out of Christendom"[16] comes closer to the mark. Joshua Mitchell argues that even "the idea of the sovereign self, the autonomous consenting self, emerged out of Christianity…paying attention to the religious roots of consent in the West alert us to the fact, that it is in fact a provincial development, not necessarily universalizable."[17] The influence of Christianity on the original Westphalian settlement makes it difficult to subsume modern international order into realist and liberal frameworks that operate on the assumption that religion has been privatized. Particular—not universal—forms of secularism contributed to the constitution of modern forms of state sovereignty that claim their universality by *defining* the limits of state-centered politics, with religion on the outside.

Most realist and liberal approaches to international relations operate on the laicist assumption that religion has been confined to the private sphere or has disappeared.[18]

This assumption supports structuralist and materialist approaches to international relations in which religion is seen as epiphenomenal. Neorealism proceeds on the assumption that states have fixed interests and that state behavior is constrained by international structure defined by factors such as the distribution of power, technology, and geography. Historical materialism dismisses religion as "a mode of consciousness which is other than consciousness of reality, external to the relations of production, producing no knowledge, but expressing at once the anguish of the oppressed and a spurious consolation."[19] Materialist approaches neglect the productive role of norms and "tend to view rules and norms as being contingent upon, and thus reducible to, material configurations of power or resources."[20] Focusing on the interaction of preexisting state units to explain how international norms influence state interests, identity, and behavior, even constructivists treat religion as private by prior assumption.

Yet secularism cannot be reduced to material power or ideology: it is a collection of practices that plays a constitutive role in creating agents and contributing to the structures in which they interact. The problem for international relations of the attempt to expel religion from politics or assume that it has been privatized within the state is that it demands "not only the sharing of the (independent political) ethic but also of its foundation—in this case, one supposedly independent of religion."[21] Laicism defines religion by designating that which is not religious: the secular.[22] This is a form of politics that, as Pizzorno argues with reference to absolute politics, "set(s) the boundaries between itself and other activities."[23] Laicism sets the terms for what constitutes legitimate politics and legitimate religion. In modern religiously diverse societies, attempts to manage the terms through which a particular understanding of religion is defined (and confined) lead to conflict between laicists, policing the boundary of what they define as the public sphere, and their rivals, who see this policing as an extension of religion in the name of a rival (laicist) set of metaphysical assumptions.[24] As Taylor observes:

> What to one side is a more strict and consistent application of the principles of neutrality is seen by the other side as partisanship. What this other side sees as legitimate public expressions of religious belonging will often be castigated by the first as the exaltation of some peoples' beliefs over others. This problem is compounded when society diversifies to contain substantial numbers of non-Judaeo-Christian religions. If even some Christians find the "post-Christian" independent ethic partisan, how much harder will Muslims find it to swallow it.[25]

By holding fast to a definition of religion and excluding it from politics, laicism marks out the domain of the secular and associates it with public authority, common sense, rational argument, justice, tolerance, and the public interest.[26] It reserves the religious as that which it is not and associates religion with a personal God and beliefs about that God.[27] Laicism, then, is not simply the absence of religious or theological discourse. It enacts a particular kind of theological discourse in its own right. It "theologizes" the religions that it oversees, by which I mean to discourse and reason theologically, to speculate in theology.[28]

Laicism is most powerful when it appears as the natural order that emerges when there is no ideology present.[29] Laicism posits itself as public, neutral, and value-free, while positing religion, religious actors, and institutions as private, affective, and value-laden. Religion is denominated as violent, irrational, undemocratic, and other. This explains why, according to Cavanaugh, "liberal theorists...assume that public faith has a dangerous tendency to violence"[30] and accounts for Appleby's reference to the "conventional wisdom that religious fervor—unrestrained religious commitment—inevitably expresses itself in violence and intolerance."[31] Laicism is the conventional wisdom adopted by Cavanaugh's liberal theorists. The secular public sphere becomes the domain of reason, objectivity, deliberation, and justice, and the religious private sphere the realm of subjectivity, transcendence, effeminacy, and affect.

The Politics of Judeo-Christian Secularism

Judeo-Christian secularism is a discursive tradition developed in the mid-twentieth century primarily, though not exclusively, in the United States. It is distinguished, on the one hand, by the partial displacement of the dominant narrative of Protestant hegemony and, on the other, by the representation of certain moral and political values as held in common by Christianity and Judaism and connected to Western traditions of law and governance. While laicism defines and confines religion to a private sphere, this second tradition of secularism connects contemporary Euro-American secular formations to a historical legacy of Western Christian and, beginning in the mid-twentieth century and then only selectively, "Judeo-Christian" cultural and religious beliefs, historical practices, legal traditions, governing institutions, and forms of identification. The common denominator of all varieties of JCS is that Western political order is grounded in a set of values with their origins in either Christian or Judeo-Christian tradition that cannot (should not?) be diluted or denied.

Let me be clear: in referring to "Judeo-Christian" tradition, I am not suggesting that there is consensus between or within any variation of Jewish or Christian tradition about what this term means or even whether it should be used at all. There isn't. But the term has played a leading role in a powerful cultural production that relies on the conviction that there is such a thing as a Judeo-Christian tradition that serves as the fount and foundation of certain modern political values, such as liberty, equality, democracy, and secularism. Many individuals are disciplined into this worldview and rely on it to organize their approach to religion and politics. The JCS narrative connects a broad and diverse (even conflicting) set of religious traditions to Western models of secular governance and has been particularly influential in the American political imagination. My aim is to acknowledge its authority, not to legitimize the forms of politics it engenders but rather to come to terms with its global political influence.

In other words, I am not suggesting that Christian or Judeo-Christian values *actually* form the basis of Western institutions or styles of governance, but rather that the *conviction* among adherents to this narrative that they do is in itself powerful enough to warrant critical scrutiny. I am also not suggesting that the concept of Judeo-Christian is either valid or invalid; this is not for me to decide.[32] What I am suggesting is that a specific variety of civic republican tradition emphasizing the connections between moral values allegedly held in common by Judaism and Christianity (Old Testament, Ten Commandments, etc.) and particular reference points for modern governance such as liberty, equality, and the separation of church and state has become powerful and therefore merits scholarly attention. This tradition is real *because* it is imagined; I am not asserting that it is imagined because it is real. To make the latter kind of claim, as U.S. President Barack Obama said in reference to the debate over abortion rights, would be above my pay grade.

Take as an example of this narrative the religious populism of Richard John Neuhaus.[33] Neuhaus argues that Catholic moral arguments should "re-clothe the naked public square" as the basis of American identity and foreign policy. Americans for Neuhaus are a Christian people, and Catholic natural law theorizing should serve as the moral-religious foundation for American public life.[34] Catholicism in this narrative is not the enemy of liberalism but "its true source and indispensable foundation."[35] For Neuhaus and others who offer different riffs on this narrative, religion (understood as Catholicism, Christianity, and/or Judeo-Christianity) is the defining feature of Western civilization. Jelen gets at this idea by using Berger's concept of a sacred canopy: "in the United States, a 'Judeo-Christian' tradition is thought to provide a moral basis for political life—what some analysts have described as a 'sacred canopy' beneath which political affairs can be conducted. Religion is thought to perform a 'priestly' function of legitimating political authority."[36] Christian and/or Judeo-Christian–derived forms of secular order, in this view, are among the core values of Western civilization and the common ground on which Western democracy rests. Religion plays a constitutive role not outside but *within* secular politics (note the contrast with laicism), serving as "the basis of an ethical consensus without which popular government could not operate."[37]

In the laicist narrative, the Christian identity of the West has been superseded, radically transformed, and essentially rendered irrelevant. A modern, rational West was reinvented and rejuvenated by democratic tendencies inherited from its Greek and Roman predecessors. The Judeo-Christian secularist story does not share this assumption that after the Protestant Reformation and the Enlightenment, linkages between Western politics and public forms of Christianity were definitively severed. Working out of a different set of assumptions about the relationship between religion and modern politics, it draws on earlier European arrangements in which church and state were unified, each representing a different aspect of the same divine authority.[38]

It is worth recalling that the perception of a larger Christian context within which both church and state were embedded set the terms of American public discourse until quite recently, and in some places it still does. Following the influx of immigrants to the United States in the late nineteenth and early twentieth centuries, however, in most places it became politically expedient to operate in increasingly nonsectarian terms.[39] While Protestant discourse took a backseat to a more generic civic religion, a de facto Protestant establishment continued to set the ground rules.[40] The civic republican imagination of the Protestant majority informed the relation between religion and democratic politics in early America. Its influence was (and remains) palpable in legislative prayer; state acknowledgment of Easter, Christmas, Thanksgiving, and the Christian Sabbath; and the outlawing of blasphemy and punishment of atheism.[41] As Gedicks explains, Protestants "opposed a particular Protestant denomination to Protestantism in general, which later they did not equate with an establishment. The notion of prayer and worship based on the Bible accepted by all Protestants did not amount to a general establishment, but constituted an essential foundation of civilization."[42] To be secular, in this line of reasoning, meant not to privilege one Protestant denomination over another. The common ground of Protestant civilization was taken for granted, though, of course, dissenting Christians and many others were excluded from it. A similar situation prevailed contemporaneously in England. In a study of nineteenth-century debates between British evangelicals and their utilitarian rivals, van der Veer notes that despite their differences, all agreed that "civil society and the forms of knowledge on which it was based were ultimately part and parcel of Christian civilization."[43]

The Protestant claim to a common ground, though slowly eroded by increasing religious diversification and eventually (though often at glacial speed and not without contestation and confrontation) modified to incorporate both Catholic and, after World War II, Jewish influences, nonetheless retains a cultural foothold in the United States. It is out of a celebratory reading and ongoing amendment of this cultural inheritance that the JCS narrative emerged and continues to shape modern dispositions toward the secular and the place of religion within it. A narrative of Protestant hegemony was transformed into a slightly more liberalized pluralism, drawing on a deep well of tradition in which first Protestant Christianity, then Christianity more broadly, then Judaism were (again selectively and not without dissent) linked to the possibility of civilization and cited as the source of first principles for governing institutions.

While Tocqueville described this famously in reference to the United States,[44] modern scholars including Bellah, Connolly, Juergensmeyer, Taylor, van der Veer, Morone, and Pizzorno have chronicled how religion resonates in and through modern liberalism and secularism.[45] Morone paints a lively portrait of American history in which the nation develops "not from religious to secular but from revival to revival."[46] Connolly points to liberal thinkers such as J. S. Mill who extol Judeo-Christian tradition as the moral basis of civilizational unity and identity and for whom it is "through Jewish and Christian culture above all that a territorial people acquires the civilizational conditions of possibility for representative government."[47] Van der Veer charts a long tradition of combining liberalism and evangelical moralism in Anglo-American political thought, describing British Liberal leader Gladstone's (1809–98) writings as invoking a "liberal view of progress... but added to this is the notion that progress is the Christian improvement of society and that in such progress we see the hand of God."[48] Taylor describes a "common ground" mode of secularism, in which members of a political community agree on an ethic of peaceful coexistence and political order based on doctrines common to all Christian sects, or even to all theists.[49] Historically, he suggests, this represented a successful compromise in Europe for warring sects because "political injunctions that flowed from this common core trumped the demands of a particular confessional allegiance."[50] The objective was not to expel religion from politics in the name of an independent ethic, as in laicism, but to prevent the state from backing one (Christian) confession over another by appealing to that which all held in common. This evenhandedness between (Christian) confessions was the basis of the original American separation of church and state.[51]

Unlike laicism, JCS does not claim to exclude religion (as long as the latter is understood as Christianity or, perhaps, Judeo-Christianity) from modern spheres of power and authority. It diverges from laicism regarding the role of religious tradition in the maintenance of the secularist separation of church and state. While laicism assumes that religion has receded out of modern spheres of authority or diminished altogether, JCS is a form of religious "accommodationism" in which "religion (singular) is ultimately good for democratic politics, because a *shared* adherence to a common religious tradition provides a set of publicly accessible assumptions within which democratic politics can be conducted."[52] In this political imaginary, the separation of church and state is a unique Western achievement that emerged from adherence to common European religious and cultural traditions. You can't have one without the other.

In international relations, the influence of Judeo-Christian secularist assumptions are palpable in arguments in which religious traditions are portrayed as the source of particular styles and institutions of governance, forms of civilizational identity, and violent clashes between so-called civilizations. Christianity, in many versions of this narrative, or Judeo-Christianity in others has culminated in and contributes to the unique Western achievement of the separation of church and state and the development of liberal democracy.[53] As one proponent of this argument, Samuel Huntington, argues, "Western Christianity, first Catholicism and then Protestantism, is historically the single most important characteristic of Western civilization."[54] This prevailing dualism between "God and Caesar, church and state, spiritual and temporal authority... contributed immeasurably to the development of freedom in the West" and forms part of "the factors which enabled the West to take the lead in modernizing itself and the world."[55] Religion is the bedrock of this cultural inheritance, responsible for differentiating between civilizations and between individuals: "in the modern world, religion is a central, perhaps *the* central, force that motivates and mobilizes people."[56]

Huntington's argument is a political project that seeks to create the very divisions in the world that he purports to merely describe. He divides the world into two hierarchical categories: those who share the Christian or Judeo-Christian common ground and those who do not. This echoes divisions proposed in the fourteenth century by Italian jurist Bartolus de Sassoferato, who divided the world into five classes: the "populus Romanus" ("almost all those who obey the Holy Mother Church") and four classes of "populus extranei": the Turks, the Jews, the Greeks, and the Saracens.[57] Bartolus's scheme parallels Huntington's seven (or eight) major civilizations: Western, Confucian, Japanese, Islamic, Hindu, Slavic-Orthodox, Latin American, and "possibly African." Anthony Pagden describes the effects of these divisions:

> The effect of Bartolus's ethnic division is once again to limit "the world" to a distinct cultural, political, and in this case religious, community. And again it places boundaries between what may be counted as the domain of the fully human world, and those others—which because of their rejection of the hegemony of the Western Church now also included the Greeks—who have no place within the *civitas*, and so no certain claim upon the moral considerations of those who do.[58]

In international politics, the assumption that a Christian secular common ground ends abruptly at the edge of Western civilization leads to calls to defend this ground against internal and external enemies, resulting in what Connolly has described as "civilizational wars of aggressive defense of Western uniqueness."[59] These can become aggressive as the common ground is challenged and even reconfigured under the stress of a pluralistic West made up of Christians, Jews, Muslims, Hindus, Buddhists, atheists, and agnostics, among others. At this point, either the common ground is renegotiated or an assertive defense of it is undertaken. Neuhaus takes the latter position, arguing that the godless are incapable of a "morally convincing account" of the nation and concluding that "those who believe in the God of Abraham, Isaac, Jacob, and Jesus turn out to be the best citizens."[60]

This form of exclusionary religio-secular triumphalism finds expression in international relations in the idea that Western powers have a monopoly over the proper relationship between religion and politics. As Keane argues,

> The principle of secularism, which "represents a realisation of crucial motifs of Christianity itself" (Bonhoffer), is arguably founded upon a sublimated version of the Christian belief that Christianity is "the religion of religions" (Schleiermacher), and that Christianity is entitled to decided for non-Christian others what they can think or say—or even whether they are capable of thinking and saying anything at all.[61]

This reasoning normalizes particular religions and religious actors and marginalizes many non-Western and non-(Judeo-)Christian forms of philosophy and practice. If the dualism between spiritual and temporal authority is accepted as uniquely Western and (Judeo-)Christian, then non-Westerners who want to democratize have no alternative but to adopt Western forms of secularism. In this scenario, non-Westerners who do *not* support Western (Christian) forms of secularism are portrayed as children who refuse to acknowledge that they are sick and need to stay in. Yet those who do advocate such forms are charged with advancing pale imitations of a robust Western secular ideal, thereby departing from (and potentially betraying) indigenous traditions. This has the effect of delegitimizing indigenous modalities of negotiating across lines of religious difference, as they are associated with selling out to Western power and/or betraying local tradition. An example is the oppositional relationship that has developed between European and American forms of secularist politics and many forms of political Islam, such that the latter is assumed to stand in opposition to the former.[62]

Any attempt to fix the meaning of religion and define its relationship in or out of politics—any attempt to displace the politics of secularism—is inherently political. From the perspective of democratic pluralism, universal forms of politics grounded in the claim to have either transcended religio-cultural particularities (laicism) or to have located the key to democratic moral and political order in a particular religio-cultural tradition or history (JCS) are equally problematic.

Conclusion

As Michael Barnett has observed, "actors struggle over the power and the right to impose a legitimate vision of the world because doing so helps to construct social reality as much as it expresses it."[63] For many academics and practitioners, this is a secular vision of the world and a secular social reality. Most of us, perhaps unconsciously, perhaps less so, think, work, struggle against, and live within variations of the two forms of secularism described in this essay. These laws, institutions, and sensibilities do not merely reflect social reality but construct it by providing "a set of parameters, focal points, or even points of contention around which political discourse revolves."[64] They facilitate closure and agreement around received settlements of the relation between religion and politics. Secularism, it turns out, is a powerful "pattern of political rule."[65]

Secularist settlements have only recently been subject to analysis by political scientists, in part because they tend to fall just beyond the peripheral vision of conventional empiricist and rational-choice methods that have served as default approaches in the field. These settlements are sustained by a variety of unarticulated assumptions: secularization as the most recent step in the worldly realization of Christian or Judeo-Christian morality, secularization as the natural evolution toward a universal morality that transcends the need for metaphysical moorings, secularization as a commendable side effect of democratization and modernization, and secularization as the result of the globalization of a modern state system in which religion has been privatized once and for all. Though jostling for supremacy and often colliding head-on, these powerful narratives and the laws, institutions, and practices that they inform and sustain are hard at work in the world as they strive to both create and manage religious diversity; imbue state interest and identity with meaning and legitimacy; secure an image of contemporary international order as modern, secular, and democratic; and normalize particular religions and religious actors as either fit or unfit for participation in democratic politics in the twenty-first century. The entanglements between these secularist formations and the religious traditions from which they have emerged, and with which they remain intertwined, confirm Barnett's intuition that secular and religious elements in international order are not as cleanly segregated as IR theorists may have assumed.[66]

I conclude with four takeaway points. First, there are many varieties of secularism (Turkish Kemalism, French *laïcité*, American Judeo-Christian secularism), each representing a contingent yet powerful political settlement of the relation between religion and politics. Different secularisms look, feel, and live differently, particularly those that emerged out of and against Christianity, as did European and American forms of secularism, but through and against other religious traditions as well, including Islam, which has a variety of traditions of separation between political and religious authorities. Different forms of secularism exist within Europe and outside it. Multiple trajectories of secularism may co-exist in Christian-, Hindu-, Buddhist, and Muslim-majority societies.

Second, secularisms are not fixed in stone but produced and renegotiated through laws, practices, and social relations, including international relations. Questions of history, power, politics, and authority are front and center in these processes. Yet particular forms of secularism can become so entrenched that they appear to be exempt from processes of production and contestation. Like nationalism, they come to seem natural and manage to operate below the threshold of public discourse and debate. Today, for instance, challenges to secularism are often automatically designated as religious resurgence. My argument suggests that the politics of religious resurgence cannot be captured as simply a rise or return of religion taken in a predefined way but that the term points toward something bigger: an acceleration of challenges to secularist settlements and the laws, institutions, and assumptions that underpin them. What often passes as religious resurgence is a series of challenges to *particular* political settlements involving religion, politics, and the state.[67] Kemalists in Turkey and laicists in France for example are no longer able to monopolize public debate over what it means to be a secular state. Challenges to Kemalism and to republican *laïcité* are not adequately captured by the term religious resurgence. These political movements seek to redefine and refashion the secularist settlements of their respective states.

Third, the assumption that religion was rendered irrelevant to power politics after the Westphalian settlement needs to be reevaluated. As Peter Katzenstein observes, "conventional renderings of the historical origins of the modern European state system and religious politics are intellectually suspect.... Religion continues to lurk underneath the veneer of European secularization."[68] Modern forms of secularism emerged out of a Christian-influenced Westphalian order, and the influence of this order on the Westphalian settlement makes it difficult to subsume the current international order into realist and liberal frameworks that assume that religion has been privatized. In other words, modern forms of secularism contribute to the constitution of a particular practice of state sovereignty that claims to be universal by defining the limits of state-centered politics with something called religion on the outside. To delimit the terms and boundaries of the political by defining religion as a private counterpart to politics is a political move. European and American practices of secularism are thus deeply implicated in producing and normalizing historically contingent practices of sovereign authority.

Fourth, the politics of secularism cannot be understood without reference to European and global history, including colonial history. This is a point at which I part ways with Charles Taylor's rich genealogy of the European secular in *A Secular Age*—for me, it cannot be fully understood absent this global context. Secularisms have been created though actions and beliefs and cannot be abstracted from the global historical contexts in which they emerged and in which Europe has played a formative role. While on the one hand French *laïcité* emerged out of and remains indebted to both the Enlightenment critique of religion and Christian reform, on the other it has been constituted through colonial and postcolonial relationships with France's Muslim-majority neighbors.

If forms of secularism are contingent products of complex social, historical, theological, and political developments, then the question is how do particular instantiations of secularism become authoritative in particular contexts, and what are their political consequences.? The first step is to acknowledge that to define secularism authoritatively, whether as a political theorist, a government official in a development agency, a political activist, a religious authority figure, or a United Nations expert, is a powerful political move. A host of assumptions and convictions about religion are interwoven with forms of political authority that describe themselves as secular. Secularisms are not fixed and final achievements of European-inspired modernity but patterns of political rule with their own contested histories and global political implications. Failure to acknowledge this has led to a selective blindness in the study of world politics, as the blanket usage of these categories masks the politics surrounding claims to secularism, secularization, secular democracy, secular human rights, and related constructs.

This essay has sought to bring into sharper focus the tools needed to enact a shift in the study of religions and world politics. Opening up the black box of secularism that has remained closed due to the mistaken conviction that modernization theorists long ago resolved the question of religion and politics, removing the theoretical and conceptual blinders insisting that there is only one secularism and not many, and recognizing the simultaneous indispensability and inadequacy of European history, politics, and power to understanding the global politics of secularism clear a path for new answers to the vexing questions raised by the presence, and often surprising locations, of religion in contemporary world politics.

Notes

1. Roger Cohen, "The Fight for Turkey," *International Herald Tribune* (June 22, 2008). Available at www.iht.com/articles/2008/06/22/opinion/edcohen.php.

2. This essay draws on my book *The Politics of Secularism in International Relations* (Princeton, NJ: Princeton University Press, 2008). Excerpts from the book are reprinted with permission of Princeton University Press. An extended version of this essay appears as "Secularism and International Relations Theory" in *Religion and International Relations Theory*, ed. Jack Snyder (New York: Columbia University Press, 2011), 60–90.

3. See *Comparative Secularisms in a Global Age*, ed. Linell Cady and Elizabeth Shakman Hurd (New York: Palgrave Macmillan, 2010).

4. Michael Barnett and Raymond Duvall, "Power in International Politics," *International Organization* 59 (Winter 2005), 48.

5. Harvey Cox, *The Secular City* (New York: Macmillan, 1965), 4.

6. Michael Hardt and Antonio Negri, *Empire* (Cambridge, MA: Harvard University Press, 2000), cited in William E. Connolly, *Pluralism* (Durham, NC: Duke University Press, 2005), 150.

7. John L. Esposito, *The Islamic Threat: Myth or Reality?* 2nd ed. (New York: Oxford University Press, 1992), 200.

8. Partha Chatterjee, "The Politics of Secularization in Contemporary India," in *Powers of the Secular Modern: Talal Asad and His Interlocutors*, ed. David Scott and Charles Hirschkind (Stanford, CA: Stanford University Press, 2006), 60.

9. Stephen D. Krasner, "Westphalia and All That," in *Ideas & Foreign Policy: Beliefs, Institutions and Political Change*, ed. Judith Goldstein and Robert Keohane (Ithaca, NY: Cornell University Press, 1993), 238.

10. Stephen D. Krasner, "Sovereignty," *Foreign Policy* (January–February 2001), 21.

11. Craig Calhoun, *Nationalism* (Minneapolis: University of Minnesota, 1997), 70.

12. This is not to ignore the deep divisions between Christians (and others) in Europe at the time: "when we view Europeanization as a long historical process, we inevitably confront the creation of Europe as a community through, first, the extrusion of religious difference and, second, the management of religious schism within a broader Latin Christian community." Daniel Nexon, "Religion, European Identity, and Political Contention in Historical Perspective," in *Religion in an Expanding Europe*, ed. Timothy A. Byrnes and Peter J. Katzenstein (New York: Cambridge University Press, 2006), 260.

13. Charles Taylor, Seminar on Secularization, Northwestern University, Evanston, Illinois, Spring 2003. This argument is elaborated in *A Secular Age* (Cambridge, MA: Harvard University Press, 2007).

14. Stephen D. Krasner, *Sovereignty: Organized Hypocrisy* (Princeton, NJ: Princeton University Press, 1999), 81, citing Treaty of Osnabrück (1648), 240, 241, Article VII.

15. Nexon, "Religion, European Identity, and Political Contention," 277.

16. William E. Connolly, *Why I Am Not a Secularist* (Minneapolis: University of Minnesota Press), 23.

17. Joshua Mitchell, Comments presented at the Pew Forum on Religion and Public Life and the Pew Christian Scholars Program conference on *Theology, Morality, and Public Life*, University of Chicago Divinity School, Chicago, Illinois, February 25–27, 2003.

18. Scott Thomas argues that this applies equally to the English school in "Faith, History and Martin Wight: The Role of Religion in the Historical Sociology of the English School of International Relations," *International Affairs* 77:4 (2001), 926.

19. Talal Asad, *Genealogies of Religion: Discipline and Reasons of Power in Christianity and Islam* (Baltimore: Johns Hopkins University Press, 1993), 46.

20. Mlada Bukovansky, *Legitimacy and Power Politics: The American and French Revolutions in International Political Culture* (Princeton, NJ: Princeton University Press, 2002), 19.

21. Charles Taylor, "Modes of Secularism," in *Secularism and Its Critics*, ed. Rajeev Bhargava (Oxford: Oxford University Press, 1998), 38.

22. "In the discourse of modernity 'the secular' presents itself as the ground from which theological discourse was generated. . . . " Talal Asad, *Formations of the Secular: Christianity, Islam, Modernity* (Stanford, CA: Stanford University Press, 2003), 192.

23. Alessandro Pizzorno, "Politics Unbound," in *Changing Boundaries of the Political: Essays on the Evolving Balance between the State and Society, Public and Private in Europe*, ed. Charles S. Meier (Cambridge: Cambridge University Press, 1988), 28.

24. Taylor, "Modes of Secularism," 36.

25. Ibid., 36–37.

26. Connolly, *Why I Am Not a Secularist*, 21.

27. Ibid.

28. See the OED definition of *theologize* at http://ets.umdl.umich.edu/cgi/o/oed/oed-idx?q1=theologize&type=Lookup.

29. Melani McAlister makes this argument regarding gender in *Epic Encounters: Culture, Media and U.S. Interests in the Middle East* (Berkeley: University of California Press, 2001), 232.

30. William T. Cavanaugh, "A Fire Strong Enough to Consume the House: The Wars of Religion and the Rise of the State," *Modern Theology* 11:4 (October 1995), 409.

31. Scott R. Appleby, *The Ambivalence of the Sacred: Religion, Violence and Reconciliation* (Lanham, MD: Rowman and Littlefield, 2000), 5.

32. For a discussion of "secular witnesses belonging to the Judeo-Christian tradition" and the attempt to come to terms with their response to suicide bombing that is suggestive of one way in which this categorization may be helpful, see Talal Asad, *On Suicide Bombing* (New York: Columbia University Press, 2007), 91.

33. For another variation see Rodney Stark, *The Victory of Reason: How Christianity Led to Freedom, Capitalism and Western Success* (New York: Random House, 2005).

34. Damon Linker, "Without a Doubt: A Catholic Priest, a Pious President, and the Christianizing of America," *New Republic* (April 3, 2006). On Neuhaus's philosophy, see his *Catholic Matters: Confusion, Controversy and the Splendor of Truth* (New York: Basic Books, 2006), *The Naked Public Square* (Grand Rapids, MI: Eerdmans, 1984), and *The Catholic Moment* (New York: HarperCollins, 1990). For two very different critiques, see Damon Linker, *The Theocons: Secular America under Siege* (New York: Doubleday, 2006), and Cavanaugh, "A Fire Strong Enough to Consume the House," 410–412.

35. Linker, "Without a Doubt."

36. Ted Jelen, *To Serve God and Mammon: Church-State Relations in American Politics* (Boulder, CO: Westview, 2000), 11. On the sacred canopy, see Peter L. Berger, *The Sacred*

Canopy: Elements of a Sociological Theory of Religion (New York: Doubleday, 1967), and Neuhaus, *The Naked Public Square*.

37. Jelen, *To Serve God and Mammon*, 34.

38. See Frederick Mark Gedicks, "The Religious, the Secular, and the Antithetical," *Capital University Law Review* 20:1 (1991), 116.

39. Ibid., 122.

40. "Protestantism still affected public business, but implicitly, more as the source and background of political movements than as the movements themselves" (ibid., 122).

41. Ibid., 123.

42. Thomas J. Curry, *The First Freedoms: Church and State in America to the Passage of the First Amendment* (New York: Oxford University Press, 1987), 123–124; quoted in Gedicks, "The Religious, the Secular, and the Antithetical," 123, n. 30.

43. Peter van der Veer, "The Moral State: Religion, Nation, and Empire in Victorian Britain and British India," in *Nation and Religion: Perspectives on Europe and Asia*, ed. Peter van der Veer and Hartmut Lehmann (Princeton, NJ: Princeton University Press, 1999), 28.

44. "In the United States it is not only mores that are controlled by religion, but its sway extends over reason.... So Christianity reigns without obstacles by universal consent.... Thus while the law allows the American people to do everything; there are things which religion prevents them from imagining and forbids them to become.... Religion, which never intervenes directly in the government of American society should therefore be considered as the first of their political institutions." Alexis de Tocqueville, *Democracy in America*, trans. George Lawrence (New York: Harper and Row, 1969), 292.

45. See Robert Bellah's concept of American civil religion in *Beyond Belief: Essays on Religion in a Post-Traditional World* (Berkeley: University of California Press, 1991) and Juergensmeyer's argument that American nationalism blends secular nationalism and the symbols of Christianity into a form of "civil religion" in Mark Juergensmeyer, *The New Cold War? Religious Nationalism Confronts the Secular State.* (Berkeley: University of California Press, 1993), 28.

46. James A. Morone, *Hellfire Nation: The Politics of Sin in American History* (New Haven, CT: Yale University Press, 2003), 3.

47. Connolly, *Why I Am Not a Secularist*, 78.

48. Van der Veer, "The Moral State," 24.

49. Taylor, "Modes of Secularism."

50. Ibid., 33. Taylor cites Pufendorf and Locke as examples.

51. Ibid., 35.

52. Jelen, *To Serve God and Mammon*, 90.

53. Samuel P. Huntington, "Religious Persecution and Religious Relevance in Today's World," in *The Influence of Faith: Religious Groups and U.S. Foreign Policy*, ed. Elliott Abrams (New York: Rowman and Littlefield, 2001), 60.

54. Samuel P. Huntington, *The Clash of Civilizations and the Remaking of World Order* (New York: Simon & Schuster, 1996), 70.

55. Ibid., 70, 72.

56. Ibid., 63.

57. Anthony Pagden, *Lords of All the World: Ideologies of Empire in Spain, Britain and France c. 1500–c. 1800* (New Haven, CT: Yale University Press, 1995), 28.

58. Pagden, *Lords of All the World*, 28.

59. William E. Connolly, "The New Cult of Civilizational Superiority," *Theory and Event* 2:4 (1999), 4.

60. Neuhaus, cited in Linker, "Without a Doubt."

61. John Keane, "Secularism?" in *Religion and Democracy*, ed. David Marquand and Ronald L. Nettler (Oxford: Blackwell, 2000), 14.

62. Elizabeth Shakman Hurd, "Political Islam and Foreign Policy in Europe and the United States," *Foreign Policy Analysis* 3:4 (October 2007), 345–367.

63. Michael Barnett, *Dialogues in Arab Politics: Negotiations in Regional Order* (New York: Columbia University Press, 1998), 250, citing Michael Williams, "Hobbes and International Relations: A Reconsideration," *International Organization* 50:2 (Spring 1996), 213–237.

64. Bukovansky, *Legitimacy and Power Politics*, 25.

65. Asad, "Responses," in *Powers of the Secular Modern*, 219.

66. Michael Barnett, "Another Great Awakening? International Relations Theory and Religion," in *Religion and International Relations Theory*, ed. Jack Snyder (New York: Columbia University Press, 2011), 91–114.

67. This argument is developed further in my article, "Theorizing Religious Resurgence," *International Politics* 44:6 (November 2007), 647–665.

68. Peter Katzenstein, "Multiple Modernities as Limits to Secular Europeanization?" in *Religion in an Expanding Europe*, 32–33.

69. José Casanova, *Public Religions in the Modern World* (Chicago: University of Chicago Press, 1994), 20.

Annotated Bibliography

Ayoob, Mohammed, *The Many Faces of Political Islam: Religion and Politics in the Muslim World*. Ann Arbor: University of Michigan Press, 2007.
An accessible introduction to the many varieties of political Islam from Morocco to Indonesia including analysis of their implications for global politics. Argues that Islamic tradition is no different from other religious traditions in wrestling with religion and/ in politics.

Cady, Linell, and Elizabeth Shakman Hurd, eds., *Comparative Secularisms in a Global Age*. New York: Palgrave, 2010.
Collection of essays exploring the history and politics of secularism and the public role of religion in France, India, Turkey, and the United States in comparative and global perspective. Interprets the varieties of secularism as a series of evolving and contested processes of defining and remaking religion rather than static solutions to the challenges posed by religious and political difference. Contributors include leading scholars from across disciplines, secular and religious traditions, and regional expertise.

Göle, Nilüfer, and Ludwig Ammann, eds., *Islam in Public: Turkey, Iran, and Europe*. Istanbul: Bilgi University Press, 2006.
This volume examines Islam and public life in secularist Turkey, post-Islamic Iran, and Europe. It is especially valuable for those interested in the analysis of the microprocesses

surrounding the emergence of Muslim profiles and practices in public life in these contexts. Offers a powerful and grounded series of critiques of European assumptions about the public-private and secular-religious oppositions.

Hefner, Robert W., ed., *Remaking Muslim Politics: Pluralism, Contestation, Democratization.* Princeton, NJ: Princeton University Press, 2005.

Excellent collection on the rise of civil-democratic Islam across the Muslim-majority world and the clash between civil-democratic Islamists and their conservative opponents. Impossible to see "Islam," or its role in politics, as a monolithic force after reading this book.

Hurd, Elizabeth Shakman, *The Politics of Secularism in International Relations.* Princeton, NJ: Princeton University Press, 2008.

Argues that secularist divisions between religion and politics are not fixed but socially and historically constructed and explains why this matters for the theory and practice of international relations. Includes detailed case studies of how the politics of secularism has influenced relations between Turkey and the European Union and how it has conditioned relations between the United States and postrevolutionary Iran. Offers new readings of the rise of political Islam and the global religious resurgence.

Jakobsen, Janet R., and Ann Pellegrini, eds., *Secularisms.* Durham, NC: Duke University Press, 2008.

Explores local secularisms in relation to religious traditions, including Islam, Judaism, Hinduism, and Christianity in India, Iran, Turkey, Great Britain, China, and the United States. Discusses how feminism has been implicated in the dominant secularization story. In dislodging secularism's connection to the single (and singular) narrative of progress, it opens spaces for other possible narratives about secularism and religion—as well as for other possible ways of inhabiting the contemporary world.

Navaro-Yashin, Yael, *Faces of the State: Secularism and Public Life in Turkey.* Princeton, NJ: Princeton University Press, 2002.

An ethnographic analysis of the public cultures of secularism and religion and the power of the state in modern Turkey. Innovative analyses of the political economy of Islamism and the "cult of Atatürk."

Schwedler, Jillian, *Faith in Moderation: Islamist Parties in Jordan and Yemen.* Cambridge: Cambridge University Press, 2007.

A careful examination of the implications of inclusion and exclusion of Islamic parties in the democratic process in Yemen and Jordan. Offers a theoretically sophisticated discussion located at the intersection of comparative politics, Middle East studies, democratization, and religion and politics.

Scott, Joan Wallach, *The Politics of the Veil.* Princeton, NJ: Princeton University Press, 2007.

A study of the politics of *laïcité* in France focused on the *affaire du foulard* and the controversy surrounding the 2004 French law banning religious signs in public schools. Provocative analysis of what the controversy over the veil reveals about gendered practices and assumptions in French public culture involving the division between public and private, secular and religious, and permissible and impermissible.

PART II

Religion, Democracy, and Human Rights

4 }

Religion, Democracy, and
the "Twin Tolerations"
Alfred Stepan

Are all, or only some, of the world's religious systems politically compatible with democracy?[1] This is, of course, one of the most important and heatedly debated questions of our times. My goal is to contribute to this debate from the perspective of comparative politics. More specifically, as a specialist in political institutions and democratization, I intend to discuss three questions, the answers to which should improve our understanding of this critical issue.

First, what are the minimal institutional and political requirements that a polity must satisfy before it can be considered a democracy? Building on this analysis, what can we then infer about the need for the "twin tolerations"—that is, the minimal boundaries of freedom of action that must somehow be crafted for political institutions vis-à-vis religious authorities, and for religious individuals and groups vis-à-vis political institutions?

Second, how have a set of long-standing democracies—the fifteen countries in the European Union (EU) prior to the end of the Cold-War—actually met these requirements, and what influential misinterpretations of the Western European experience with religion and democracy must we avoid?

Third, what are the implications of the answers to our first two questions for polities heavily influenced by such cultural and religious traditions as Confucianism, Islam, and Eastern Orthodox Christianity—traditions that some analysts, starting from a civilizational as opposed to an institutional perspective, see as presenting major obstacles to democracy?

Before addressing these three questions, let me briefly give some quotations from Samuel P. Huntington's *The Clash of Civilizations and the Remaking of World Order*, an exceedingly influential statement of a civilizational perspective that represents a major competing perspective to my own institutional approach.

Huntington gives primacy of place to Christianity as the distinctive positive influence in the making of Western civilization: "Western Christianity...is historically the single most important characteristic of Western civilization."[2] For Huntington, Western culture's key contribution has been the separation of church and state, something he sees as foreign to the world's other major religious systems. "In Islam," Huntington says, "God is Caesar; in [Confucianism,] Caesar is God; in Orthodoxy, God is Caesar's junior partner." Huntington warns: "The underlying problem for the West is not Islamic fundamentalism. It is Islam."[3]

Clearly, a central thrust of Huntington's message is not only that democracy emerged *first* within Western civilization but also that the other great religious civilizations of the world lack the unique bundle of cultural characteristics necessary to support Western-style democracy.

If we approach the issue from an institutionalist perspective, will we arrive at a different view of the probable cultural boundaries of democracy?

Democracy and Core Institutions

All important theorists of democratization accept that a necessary condition for completing a successful transition to democracy is free and contested elections of the sort discussed by Robert A. Dahl in his classic book, *Polyarchy*. Among the requirements for democracy, Dahl includes the opportunity to formulate and signify preferences and to have these preferences weighed adequately in the conduct of government. For these conditions to be satisfied, Dahl argues that eight institutional guarantees are required: (1) freedom to form and to join organizations, (2) freedom of expression, (3) the right to vote, (4) eligibility for public office, (5) the right of political leaders to compete for support and votes, (6) alternative sources of information, (7) free and fair elections, and (8) institutions for making government policies depend on votes and other expressions of preference.[4]

My colleague Juan J. Linz and I have argued that Dahl's eight guarantees are a necessary but not a sufficient condition of democracy. They are insufficient because no matter how free and fair the elections and no matter how large the government's majority, democracy must also have a constitution that itself is democratic in that it respects fundamental liberties and offers considerable protections for minority rights. Furthermore, the democratically elected government must rule within the confines of its constitution and be bound by the law and by a complex set of vertical and horizontal institutions that help to ensure accountability.

If we combine these criteria, it is clear that democracy should not be considered consolidated in a country unless there is the opportunity for the development of a robust and critical civil society that helps check the state and constantly generates alternatives. For such civil-society alternatives to be aggregated and implemented, political society, and especially political parties, should be allowed unfettered relations with civil society.

Democracy is a system of conflict regulation that allows open competition over the values and goals that citizens want to advance. In the strict democratic sense, this means that as long as groups do not use violence, do not violate the rights of other citizens, and stay within the rules of the democratic game, *all* groups are granted the right to advance their interests, both in civil society and in political society. This is the minimal institutional statement of what democratic politics does and does not entail.[5]

What does this institutional "threshold" approach imply about religion, politics, democracy, and the "twin tolerations"? Specifically, what are the necessary boundaries of freedom for elected governments from religious groups, and for religious individuals and groups from government?

Democratic institutions must be free, within the bounds of the constitution and human rights, to generate policies. Religious institutions should not have constitutionally privileged prerogatives that allow them to mandate public policy to democratically elected governments. At the same time, individuals and religious communities, consistent with our institutional definition of democracy, must have complete freedom to worship privately. In addition, as individuals and groups, they must be able to advance their values publicly in civil society and to sponsor organizations and movements in political society, as long as their actions do not impinge negatively on the liberties of other citizens or violate democracy and the law. This institutional approach to democracy necessarily implies that no group in civil society—including religious groups—can a priori be prohibited from forming a political party. Constraints on political parties may only be imposed *after* a party, by its actions, violates democratic principles. The judgment as to whether a party has violated democratic principles should be decided not by parties in the government but by the courts. Within this broad framework of minimal freedom for the democratic state and minimal religious freedom for citizens, an extraordinarily broad range of concrete patterns of religious-state relations would meet our minimal definition of a democracy.

Let us explore this argument further by moving to our second question. Empirically, what are the actual patterns of relations between religion and the state in long-standing democracies? How have the twin tolerations of freedom for democratically elected governments and freedom for religious organizations in civil and political society been constructed in specific democratic polities?

Western Europe and the Twin Tolerations

How should one read the "lessons" of the historical relationship between Western Christianity and democracy? Here I would like to call particular attention to four possible misinterpretations. *Empirically*, we should beware of simple assertions about the actual existence of "separation of church and state" or the necessity of "secularism." *Doctrinally*, we should beware of assuming that any of the world's religious systems are univocally democratic or nondemocratic. *Methodologically*, we should beware of what I will call the "fallacy of unique founding conditions." And *normatively*, we should beware of the liberal injunction, famously argued by the most influential contemporary political philosopher in the English language, John Rawls, to "take the truths of religion off the political agenda."[6]

When discussing the prospects for democracy in non-Western, "non-Christian" civilizations, analysts frequently assume that the separation of church and state and secularism are core features not only of Western democracy but also of democracy itself. For such analysts, a religious system such as Eastern Orthodoxy—where there is often an established church—poses major problems for the consolidation of democracy. Similarly, when an Islamic-based government came to power in Turkey in 1996, there were frequent references to the threat that this presented to Western-style secular democracy. Indeed, military encroachments on the autonomy of the democratically elected government in Turkey have frequently been viewed as an unfortunate necessity to protect secular democracy. Are these correct readings or dangerous misreadings of the lessons of the relationship of church and state in Western democracies?

To answer this question, let us undertake an empirical analysis of the degree to which the separation of church and state actually exists in a specific set of Western countries, all of which for the last decade have satisfied Dahl's eight institutional guarantees and the additional conditions for a democracy that I have stipulated, and have socially and politically constructed the twin tolerations. First, we should note that, as of 1999, five of the EU's fifteen member states—Denmark, Finland, Greece, Sweden, and the United Kingdom (in England and Scotland)—had established churches.

The Netherlands does not have an established church. Yet, as a result of heated conflict among Catholics, Calvinists, and secularizing liberal governments over the role of the church in education, the country arrived in 1917 at a politically negotiated "consociational" settlement of this issue. It permits local communities, if they are overwhelmingly of one specific religious community, to choose to have their local school be a private Calvinist or a private Catholic school *and* to have it receive state support.

Germany and Austria have constitutional provisions in their federal systems allowing local communities to decide on the role of religion in education. Germany does not have an established church, but Protestantism and Catholicism are eligible for special state services. For example, German taxpayers, unless they elect to pay a 9 percent surcharge to their tax bill in the form of a church tax (*Kirchensteuer*) and thereby officially become a member of the church (*Mitglied der Kirche*), do not have the automatic right to be baptized, married, or buried in their denominational church or, in some cases, may find it difficult to gain easy access to the church hospitals or old-age homes that receive state support from the *Kirchensteuer*. Thus the vast majority of citizens in the former West Germany paid the state-collected church tax.

What do contemporary Western European constitutions and normal political practice indicate about the role of religious parties in government? Despite what Western analysts may think about the impropriety of religious-based parties ruling in a secular democracy like Turkey, Christian Democratic parties have frequently ruled in Germany, Austria, Italy, Belgium, and the Netherlands. In the twentieth century, probably the two most "hostile" separations of church and state in Western Europe occurred in 1931 in Spain and in 1905 in France. Both of these countries, however, now have a "friendly" separation of church and state. In fact, since 1958, the French government has paid a substantial part of the cost of the Catholic Church's elementary school system. Virtually no Western European democracy now has a rigid or hostile separation of church and state. Most have arrived at a democratically negotiated freedom of religion from state interference, and all of them allow religious groups freedom not only to worship privately but also to organize groups in civil society and political society. The lesson from Western Europe, therefore, lies *not* in the need for a "wall of separation" between church and state but in the constant political construction and reconstruction of the twin tolerations. Indeed, it is only in the context of the twin tolerations that the concept of separation of church and state has a place in the modern vocabulary of Western European democracy.

A similar caveat should be borne in mind concerning the concept of "secularism." Discursive traditions as dissimilar as the Enlightenment, liberalism, French republicanism, and modernization theory have all argued (or assumed) that modernity and democracy require secularism. From the viewpoint of empirical democratic practice, however, the concept of secularism must be radically rethought. At the very least, serious analysts must acknowledge, as table 4.1 makes clear, that secularism and the separation of church and state have no inherent affinity with democracy and indeed can be closely related to nondemocratic forms that systematically violate the twin tolerations.

The categories in table 4.1 are not meant to be exhaustive or mutually exclusive, but simply to convey the range of democratic and nondemocratic state-religious patterns. They show that there can be democratic and nondemocratic secularism, democracies with established churches, and even democracies with a "very unfriendly" separation of church and state. One obviously could develop many other categories. My central analytic point stands, however. If we are looking for the defining characteristics of democracy vis-à-vis religion, secularism and the separation of church and state are not an intrinsic part of the core definition, but the twin tolerations are.

More Misinterpretations

Building on our reading of the empirical context of such phrases as "separation of church and state" and "secularism," we are in a position to see why we should beware of three other major misinterpretations.

1. *The assumption of univocality.* We should beware of assuming that any religion's doctrine is univocally prodemocratic or antidemocratic. Western Christianity has certainly been *multivocal* concerning democracy and the twin tolerations. At certain times in its history, Catholic doctrine has been

TABLE 4.1 } The "Twin Tolerations" Varieties of Democratic Patterns of Religion-State Relations

Relatively Stable Patterns			Relatively Unstable Patterns
Secular but Friendly to Religion	Nonsecular but Friendly to Democracy	Sociologically Spontaneous Secularism	Very Unfriendly Secularism Legislated by Majority but Reversible by Majority
No official religion. Full separation of church and state. No state monies for religious education or organizations. Private religious schools allowed if they conform to normal academic standards. Full private and public freedom for all religions as long as they do not violate individual liberties. Religious organizations allowed to minister to their followers inside state organizations (such as the military and state hospitals). Religious groups allowed full participation in civil society. Organizations and parties related to religious groups allowed to compete for power in political society.	Established church receives state subsides, and some official religion taught in state schools (but nonreligious students do not have to take religious courses). Official religion accorded no constitutional or quasi-constitutional prerogatives to mandate significant policies. Citizens can elect to have "church tax" sent to a secular institution. Nonofficial religion allowed full freedom and can receive some state monies. All religious groups can participate in civil society. All religious groups can compete for power in political society.	Society largely "disenchanted" and religion not an important factor in political life. Democratically elected officials under no significant pressures to comply with religious dictates concerning their public policy decisions. All religious groups free to organize civil society and to compete for political power, but have little weight or salience.	Antireligious tone in most state regulations (for example, teaching of religion forbidden in state *and* non-state-supported schools; no chaplains of any religion allowed in military organizations or state hospitals). Significant percentage of believers "semiloyal" or disloyal to regime.

marshaled to oppose liberalism, the nation-state, tolerance, and democracy. In the name of Catholicism, the Inquisition committed massive human rights violations. John Calvin's Geneva had no space either for inclusive citizenship or for any form of representative democracy. For more than 300 years, Lutheranism, particularly in Northern Germany, accepted both theologically and politically what Max Weber called "caesaropapist" state control of religion.[7]

Extrapolating from these historical situations, numerous articles and books were written on the inherent obstacles that Catholicism, Lutheranism, or Calvinism places in the way of democracy because of its antidemocratic doctrines and non-democratic practices. Later, of course, spiritual and political activists of all these faiths found and mobilized doctrinal elements within their own religions to help them craft new practices supportive of tolerance and democracy.

The warning we should take away from this brief discussion is obvious. When we consider the question of non-Western religions and their relationship to democracy, it would seem appropriate not to assume univocality but to explore whether these doctrines contain *multivocal* components that are *usable* for (or at least *compatible* with) the political construction of the twin tolerations.

2. *The fallacy of "unique founding conditions."* This fallacy involves the assumption that the unique constellation of specific conditions that were present at the birth of such phenomena as electoral democracy, a relatively independent civil society, or the spirit of capitalism must be present in all cases if they are to thrive. The fallacy, of course, is to confuse the conditions associated with the invention of something with the possibility of its replication or, more accurately, its *reformulation* under different conditions. Whatever we may think about Max Weber's thesis in *The Protestant Ethic and The Spirit of Capitalism*, no one who has carefully observed South Korea, Taiwan, or Hong Kong would deny that these polities have created their own dynamic forms of capitalism.[8] We should beware of falling into the fallacy of unique founding conditions when we examine whether polities strongly influenced by Confucianism, Hinduism, Orthodoxy, or Islam can emulate or re-create, using some of their own distinctive cultural resources, a form of democracy that would meet the minimal institutional conditions for democracy spelled out earlier in this essay.

3. *Removing religion from the political agenda.* In their theoretical accounts of the development of a just society, contemporary liberal political philosophers John Rawls and Bruce Ackerman give great weight to *liberal arguing* but almost no weight to *democratic bargaining*.[9] Rawls is particularly interested in how a plural society in which the citizens hold a variety of socially embedded, reasonable, but deeply opposed comprehensive doctrines can arrive at an overlapping consensus. His normative recommendation is that, on major issues of quasi-constitutional import, individuals should be able to advance their arguments only by using freestanding conceptions of justice that are not rooted in one of the comprehensive but opposing doctrines found in the polity. Following this logic, public arguments about the place of religion are appropriate only if they employ, or at least can employ, freestanding conceptions of political justice.

Rawls's argument is both powerful and internally consistent. Yet he devotes virtually no attention to how *actual* polities have consensually and democratically arrived at agreements to "take religion off the political agenda." Almost none of them followed the Rawlsian normative map.

Politics is about conflict, and democratic politics involves the creation of procedures to manage major conflicts. In many countries that are now long-standing democracies, both Western and non-Western, the major conflict for a long period of time was precisely over the place of religion in the polity. In many of these cases, this conflict was politically contained or neutralized only after long public arguments and negotiations in which religion was the dominant item on the political agenda. Thus in the Netherlands, as noted earlier, religious conflicts were eventually taken off the political agenda of majority decision making by a *democratic—but not liberal or secular—consociational agreement* that allocated funds, spaces, and mutual vetoes to religious communities with competing comprehensive doctrines.

Achieving such an agreement normally requires debate within the major religious communities. And proponents of the democratic bargain are often able to win over their fellow believers only by employing arguments that are *not* conceptually freestanding but deeply embedded in their own religious community's comprehensive doctrine.

One can expect, therefore, that in polities where a significant portion of believers may be under the sway of a doctrinally based nondemocratic religious discourse, one of the major tasks of political and spiritual leaders who wish to revalue democratic norms in their own religious community will be to advance theologically convincing public arguments about the legitimate multivocality of their religion. Although such arguments may violate Rawls's requirement for freestanding public reasoning, they are vital to the success of democratization in a country divided over the meaning and appropriateness of democracy. Liberal arguing has a place in democracy, but it would empty meaning and history out of political philosophy if we did not leave room for democratic bargaining and the nonliberal public argument within religious communities that it sometimes requires.

Let us now turn to exploring these general arguments in the contexts of cultures heavily influenced by Islam.

Islam and the "Free Elections Trap"

There is an extensive body of literature arguing that many key aspects of democracy are lacking in the Islamic tradition. The lack of separation between religion and the state is seen as stemming from the Prophet Muhammad's fusion of military and spiritual authority. The lack of space for democratic public opinion in making laws is seen as deriving from the Qur'an, in which God dictated to the Prophet Muhammad the content of fixed laws that a good Islamic polity must follow. The lack of inclusive citizenship is seen as originating in interpretations of the Qur'an that argue that the only true polity in Islam is the fused religious-political community of the *Ummah*, in which there is no legitimate space for other religions. Certainly, with the rise of Islamic fundamentalism, these claims have been frequently asserted by some Islamic activists. Especially in the context of the Algerian crisis of 1991–92, this gave rise to scholarly assertions that Islam and democracy are incompatible and to arguments in the West's leading journals of opinion warning against falling into the "Islamic free elections trap." According to this view, allowing free elections in Islamic countries would bring to power governments that would use these democratic freedoms to destroy democracy itself.

Any human rights activist or democratic theorist must, of course, acknowledge that numerous atrocities are being committed in some countries in the name of Islam. In Algeria, both the military state and Islamic fundamentalists slaughtered innocents. Women's rights are flagrantly violated by the Taliban in Afghanistan. In the name of Islam, parts of Sudan have been turned into killing zones. At the aggregate level, a recent attempt to document political freedoms and civil rights around the world concluded that "the Islamic world remains most resistant to the spread of democracy."[10]

It is in this context that Huntington asserted that the West's problem is "not Islamic fundamentalism but Islam." Huntington's vision of Islam's future allows virtually no room for struggling democratic forces to prevail in some key Islamic countries. Indeed, democratic failure is almost "overdetermined" in his world of authoritarian "kin cultures" and unstoppable cultural wars. How should empirical democratic theorists respond?

We should first begin with some neglected facts. The two standard rankings of democracies in the world, Ted Gurr's *Polity* and that of Freedom House, regularly classify about 400 million Muslims who live in Muslim-majority countries such as Indonesia, Turkey, Senegal, Albania, Mali, and, since 2009, Bangladesh as living in "electorally competitive" systems.

To explain this, we might begin with my hypothesis that all great religious civilizations are multivocal. Although Islamic fundamentalists are attempting to appropriate political Islam, there are also other voices—in the Qur'an, in scholarly interpretations of the Qur'an, and among some major contemporary Islamic political leaders. For example, Sura (verse) 256 of the Qur'an states: "There shall be no compulsion in Religion." This injunction provides a strong Qur'anic base for religious tolerance.[11] Let us look at the world's most populous Muslim country, Indonesia.

In any attempt at democratic transition, leadership and organization are extremely important. The two largest and most influential Islamic organizations at the start of the democratic transition in Indonesia, Nahdatul Ulama (NU) and Muhammadiyah, both with more than 25 million members, were led by Abdurrahman Wahid and Amien Rais, respectively, both leaders in the struggle against the military regime of Suharto. Amien Rais played a key role in helping to keep the student protests mobilized, relatively peaceful, and focused on democratic demands. After Suharto's fall, he considered leading an existing Islamic political grouping but instead created a new political party, the PAN, that was not explicitly Islamist and included non-Muslims in its leadership.

Abdurrahman Wahid (later president of Indonesia) also created a new political party, the PKB, and throughout the 1999 electoral campaign, he argued against an Islamic state and in favor of religious pluralism. Wahid often operated in informal alliances with the most electorally powerful political leader, Megawati Sukarnoputri, and her secular nationalist party, the PDI, which includes secular

Muslims, Christians, and many non-Muslim minorities. In Indonesia, Muslim identities are often moderate, syncretic, and pluralist. Muslim women in Indonesia have significantly more personal and career freedom than those in the Middle East. In this context, there was at least some space for a leader like Wahid—despite his weakness as an administrator—to attempt to foster a transition to democracy by constantly arguing that tolerance was one of the best parts of Indonesia's religious tradition. Free elections have since been held. Given the high quality of the free elections that were held in 2004 and 2009 in Indonesia, many scholars are now beginning to think that Indonesia is a consolidated democracy.[12]

Let us now turn to Bangladesh. The 1996 election in Bangladesh satisfied all of Dahl's eight institutional guarantees. Voter turnout, at 73 percent (with women around 76 percent), was 13 percent higher than in any general election in the nation's history. Interestingly, the fundamentalist Islamic Party (JI) trailed far behind three other parties, winning only three seats. The JI seems to have polled worst among women. After a two-year military "caretaker" government, a general election was held on December 29, 2008. These elections were relatively orderly, had better than an 80 percent turnout, and were classified as free and fair by election observer teams. The JI won only two of the 300 seats.[13]

Thus Huntington's implication that elections in predominantly Islamic countries will lead to fundamentalist majorities who will use their electoral freedom to end democracy gets no support from our analysis of electoral and political behavior in two of the world's most populous Islamic majority countries, Indonesia and Bangladesh, as well as by countries such as Turkey, Senegal, Mali, and Albania.[14]

Orthodox Christianity: Not a Strong Ally but a Strong Obstacle?

What can we say about Orthodox Christianity and democracy? As an empirical democratic analyst who has followed resistance movements to nondemocratic rule in communist Europe, I believe one has to acknowledge that Roman Catholicism and Protestantism played a more powerful role in recent civil society resistance movements than did Orthodoxy. Why? And what does this mean, and *not* mean, for democracy in countries where Orthodoxy is the weightiest religion? The major explanation for this variance cannot lie in the core religious doctrine of orthodoxy, per se, because for their first millennium, Roman Catholicism and Orthodox Christianity shared the same theological doctrines. The subsequent Orthodox–Roman Catholic division was fundamentally about papal authority and papal infallibility, not about other doctrinal disputes. The critical differences concerning recent patterns of state resistance in Orthodoxy and Roman Catholicism lie more in their differing organizational forms, and in which parts of their common multivocal tradition have been given the most emphasis, than in doctrine itself.

Let us look comparatively at the question of civil society resistance. Roman Catholicism, as a transnational, hierarchical organization, can potentially provide material and doctrinal support to a local Catholic church to help it resist state oppression.[15] To the extent that the Catholic Church might resist the state, it could be considered support for a more robust and autonomous civil society. Empirically, in the resistance stage of democratization, Linz and I analyze in a recent book how the Catholic Church played a supportive role in Poland, Lithuania, Chile, Brazil, and, in the last years of Franco, Spain. Protestantism, with its emphasis on individual conscience and its international networks, can also play a role in supporting civil society's opposition to a repressive state, as in East Germany and in Estonia. In the 1970s and 1980s, Protestantism, and even more so post–Vatican II Catholicism, chose to give important weight to "the prophetic mission" that calls for individuals to speak out against worldly injustice, no matter what the consequences.

Concerning civil society and resistance to the state, Orthodox Christianity is often (not always) organizationally and ideologically in a relatively weak position because of what Max Weber called its caesaropapist structure, in which the church is a *national*, as opposed to a *transnational*, organization. In caesaropapist churches, the national state often plays a major role in the national church's finances and appointments. Such a national church is not really a relatively autonomous part of civil society because there is a high degree, in Weber's words, of "subordination of priestly to secular power."[16] Indeed, under Stalin, the role of secular power in the USSR often meant the de facto participation of the KGB in the highest religious counsels of Orthodoxy.

As Max Weber and others have emphasized, Orthodoxy places more stress on liturgy than on action and privileges quietism as a response to the world.[17] In the structural context of caesaropapism and the liturgical context of quietism, the prophetic response to injustice, while doctrinally available in Orthodoxy's multivocal tradition, is seldom voiced.[18]

Having acknowledged all of this, I do not believe that Orthodox Christianity is an inherently antidemocratic force. That is to say, if the leaders of the state and political society are committed to democracy and follow democratic practices, the caesaropapist structures and the quietist culture should lead to loyal support of democracy by the Orthodox Christian church, as in Greece since 1975. Bulgaria will be an interesting country to watch in this respect. However, if the leaders of the state and political society are antidemocratic, the democratic opposition in civil society will not normally receive substantial or effective support from a national Orthodox church.

Let me illustrate these points by discussing the Greek case. Greece, and the Greek part of divided Cyprus, are the only Orthodox-majority countries that, for the last five consecutive years, have met all the criteria for a democracy discussed earlier in this essay. Greece, from 1967 to 1974, was under authoritarian military rule. What was the role of the Orthodox Church vis-à-vis the military dictatorship and the democratic transition? Three points are worth highlighting. First, there were two military juntas, one established in 1967 and one established in November 1973. Within months of the start of both juntas, the juntas had managed to arrange the appointment of a new archbishop to head the Greek Orthodox Church.[19] This would have been impossible in Poland. Second, no past or new scholarly work on the 1967–75 Greek dictatorship accords any significant formal or informal role to Orthodox Church resistance to the dictatorship.[20] Third, once democracy was instituted in 1974, except for efforts to preserve some minor church prerogatives, the Orthodox Church did nothing significant to oppose, resist, or stall the eventual consolidation of democracy and has been broadly supportive of the democratic government. Indeed, the Greek Orthodox Church has been much less critical of left-wing democratic governments in Greece than the Polish Catholic Church has been of left-wing democratic governments in Poland.

Greece has an established church. But as we have seen, so do Iceland, Denmark, Finland, Norway, England, and until 2000, Sweden. From this comparative institutional perspective of long-standing democracies, the democratic task in Greece after 1974 did not require the disestablishment of the church, but the elimination of any nondemocratic domains of church power that restricted democratic politics. The Greek democrats have done this, and the Greek Orthodox church has accepted this. Note, not only does democracy not require a disestablished church but also democracy requires, consistent with our thoughts about an unfettered civil society, and the right of believers to express themselves individually and collectively in political society, that no constraints are put on the rights of Orthodox members to argue their case in the public arena. Greek democracies have respected this area of legitimate autonomy of religion. There have been some changes both within state-society relations and within the Orthodox Church that have made the twin tolerations easier to sustain in the post-1975 world. The constitution crafted in 1975 and ratified in a referendum is somewhat clearer than the previous Greek constitutions about democratically appropriate areas for state action vis-à-vis religion and for the established church's action vis-à-vis other religions and the elected government.[21] Also, within the Orthodox Church, there is growing sentiment that the church would be religiously more robust, and more able to play an independent role in civil society, if it were less dependent on the state.[22]

The most important change in the role of the church in Greek politics is that from 1946 to 1949, Greece experienced a civil war, and the church opted for an anti-communist exclusionary state for much of the 1946–74 period, not caring whether this state respected democratic procedures.[23] Militarily, the Greek Civil War ended in 1949; politically, the Greek Civil War ended with the creation of a democratic government in 1974; culturally, the Greek Civil War ended with the 1989 coalition between the communists and the conservative New Democracy party. With the cultural end of the civil war, the political salience of the recognized Greek Orthodox Church diminished even more, and the twin tolerations became more socially embedded in the Greek polis and in church-state relations.

Unfinished Business

All the world's major religions today are involved in struggles over the twin tolerations. In the first two decades of their independence after World War II, India and

Israel were under the political and ideological hegemony of secular political leaders and parties. By the 1990s, however, both of these secular political traditions were challenged by opposition movements that drew some of their support from forces seeking to redraw the boundaries of the twin tolerations to accommodate more fundamentalist and less tolerant visions of the polity.

In Israel, the state was originally a nationalist state for the Jewish people, but there are growing demands for it to be a religious as well as a nationalist state.[24] There are also demands to make citizenship for the Arab minority less inclusive and even to amend the Law of Return to give Orthodox rabbis the authority to determine "whom the state of Israel recognizes as a Jew."[25]

In India, the Hindu neofundamentalist party, the BJP, and their associated shock troops in (un)civil society, such as the RSS, formed the government with numerous regional parties after the 1998 and 1999 general elections. The militant factions of the RSS want to eventually utilize the majority status of Hindus to make India a state that would privilege Hindu values as they interpret them.

A major force against the BJP and the RSS is the Gandhian-Nehruvian strand of Hinduism that insists that not only Hinduism but also India are multivocal and that the deepest values of Hinduism must respect, and even nurture, the idea of India not as a nation-state of Hindus, but as a diverse, tolerant, civilizational state. Gandhi and Nehru knew that since India was de facto multicultural, multireligious, and multicommunity, "nation-state building" and "democracy building" were conflicting logics.

India, in the year 2000, was seventeen times poorer than any democracy in the Organization for Economic Cooperation and Development. The support for democracy in India under such difficult conditions cannot be understood without an appreciation of the tremendous power that Gandhi developed by using some traditional Hindu religious values and styles of action, such as satyagraha, in his peaceful struggles for independence, for democracy, for antiuntouchability, and for respect for Muslims. For Gandhi, *satyagraha* meant "truth force," a form of nonviolent resistance that seeks "the vindication of truth not by infliction of suffering on the opponent but on oneself."[26] For Gandhi, satyagraha was a means to awaken the best in the opponent. Gandhi's goals were to generate widespread recognition of the justice of the cause.[27]

If India, with its 600 million non-Hindi speakers, with its twenty-two official languages (fourteen of which are spoken by at least 10 million people), and with its "minority" population of about 140 million Muslims, is to remain a democracy, the BJP and RSS voices of India as a Hindu and Hindi nation-state must be met by an ever stronger Gandhian voice of India as a multireligious, civilizational home to a billion people.[28] In both the 2004 and 2009 elections, the BJP lost control of the central government, partly as a reaction against some of its support for Hindu fundamentalist policies in the massacre in Gujarat.

A more complete study of the themes raised by this brief essay would not only discuss religions I have omitted but also analyze, in much greater detail than I have done, the strange career of the emergence of the twin tolerations in the West.

The establishment of state-sponsored churches in Scandinavia and Britain, while initially a form of political control of the church, eventually led not only to the twin tolerations but also in the long run to the "sociologically spontaneous secularization" of the vast part of its citizens. Why?

Liberal scholars might also want to reexamine how illiberal many of the liberal anticlerical movements were in France and Spain at times. What was the political effect of this liberalism from above? In Spain in the early 1930s, did liberal and socialist anticlericalism justify tearing down walls separating civil cemeteries from Jewish cemeteries? If the 1905 French liberal model of expropriating Jesuit property had been followed in the United States, Georgetown University and many other Jesuit universities would have been expropriated. Would this have contributed to the strengthening of a liberal, or an antiliberal, discourse in the United States?

Finally, even the Western world's most solid construction of a wall separating church and state, the U.S. Constitution's First Amendment, which states that "Congress shall make no law respecting an establishment of religion, or prohibiting the free exercise thereof," is misunderstood by many contemporary U.S. citizens. The amendment did not prohibit the thirteen original states from having *their own established* religions. The First Amendment only prohibited Congress from establishing one official religion for the United States as a *whole*. In fact, on the eve of the revolution, only three of the thirteen colonies—Rhode Island, Pennsylvania, and Delaware—had no provision for an established church. Even after the revolution, the South Carolina constitution of 1778 established the "Christian Protestant Religion." Four New England states continued for some time with state-subsidized, largely Congregational, churches.[29] The eventual political construction of the West's strongest separation of church and state, combined with the social emergence of one of the West's most churchgoing and recently most fundamentalist populations, is another of the "crooked paths" of toleration and intoleration that needs more study and reflection.

Notes

This essay originally appeared in the *Journal of Democracy* (11:4, October 2000) and is reprinted here by permission of the Johns Hopkins University Press.

1. A much longer version of this essay with 106 footnotes and extensive discussions of democracies in countries with Confucian and Orthodox Christian traditions is available in Alfred Stepan, *Arguing Comparative Politics* (New York: Oxford University Press, 2001), 213–253.

2. Samuel P. Huntington, *The Clash of Civilizations and the Remaking of World Order* (New York: Simon and Schuster, 1996), 70.

3. Quotations come from ibid., 70, 217, 238, 28, and 158, respectively.

4. See Robert A. Dahl, *Polyarchy: Participation and Opposition* (New Haven, CT: Yale University Press, 1971), 1–3.

5. See Juan J. Linz and Alfred Stepan, *Problems of Democratic Transition and Consolidation: Southern Europe, South America and Post-Communist Europe* (Baltimore: Johns Hopkins University Press, 1996), chapter 1.

6. John Rawls, *Political Liberalism* (New York: Columbia University Press, 1993), 151.

7. For Max Weber's discussion of caesaropapism, see Max Weber, *Economy and Society*, ed. Guenther Roth and Claus Wittich (Berkeley: University of California Press, 1978), 1159–1163.

8. Max Weber, *The Protestant Ethic and the Spirit of Capitalism,* trans. Talcott Parsons (New York: Charles Scribner's Sons, 1958). Weber, however, is careful not to commit this fallacy himself.

9. See John Rawls, *Political Liberalism*; and Bruce A. Ackerman, *Social Justice in the Liberal State* (New Haven, CT: Yale University Press, 1980).

10. Adrian Karatnycky, "The 1998 Freedom House Survey: The Decline of Illiberal Democracy," *Journal of Democracy* 10 (January 1999), 121.

11. For examples of these voices, see the expanded version of this essay, "The World's Religious Systems and Democracy: Crafting the 'Twin Tolerations,'" in Alfred Stepan, *Arguing Comparative Politics*, 213–254, especially 234–236.

12. See *Democratization and Islam in Indonesia*, eds., Mirjam Künkler and Alfred Stepan, (New York: Columbia University Press, 2012).

13. See Yasmeen Murshed and Nazim Kamran Choudhury, "Bangladesh's Second Chance," *Journal of Democracy* 8:1 (January 1997), 70–82. For the December 2008 general elections, see *Wikipedia*.

14. For almost 40 years, there have been no democracies in Arab majority countries. In my judgment, this will change in 2012 in Tunisia. Since the Arab Spring, I have carried out research in Egypt and in Tunisia on the possibility of democratic transitions in both countries. In several Op Eds published by *Project Syndicate*, I give reasons why democratization is further along in Tunisia. If successful, this would mark the end of Arab exceptionalism. See a forthcoming article by me in the *Journal of Democracy*.

15. The resistance of the Catholic Church in Poland has, of course, been amply documented, but even under Stalin, in Lithuania, priests, and often virtually their entire parishes, would repeatedly sign individual protests against state policies. See the fascinating documentation in W. Stanley Vardys, *The Catholic Church: Dissent and Nationality in Soviet Lithuania* (Boulder, CO: East European Quarterly, distributed by Columbia University Press, 1978). Jane Ellis, in her review of the role of religions in the fifteen Soviet republics, writes: "The strongly Catholic area of Lithuania ... was virtually the only church in the USSR where bishops, clergy and faithful had remained at one, so there was little need for recrimination over compromises." See her *The Russian Orthodox Church: Triumphalism and Defensiveness* (Houndmills, England: Macmillan, 1996), 3.

16. For Max Weber's discussion of caesaropapism, see his *Economy and Society*, 2 vols., ed. Gunther Roth and Claus Wittich (Berkeley: University of California Press, 1978), 2:1159–1163; quote is from 2:1161.

17. Weber discusses two contrasting ideal-types of routes toward religious salvation. One route toward salvation he calls "world rejecting." In such a route, "concentration upon the actual pursuit of salvation may entail formal withdrawal from the world. ... One with such an attitude may regard any participation in these affairs as an acceptance of the world, leading to alienation from God." The other route he calls "inner worldly." In this route, "the concentration of human behavior on activities leading to salvation may require participation within the world (or more precisely: within the institutions of the world but in opposition to them). ... In this case the world is presented to the religious virtuoso as his responsibility. He may have the obligation to transform the world." Ibid., 1:542. For Weber,

the Russian Orthodox monastic traditions inclined more toward the world-rejecting route. Massive repression by totalitarian atheistic states under the influence of Stalin also contributed, no doubt, to the selection of quietism in much of Orthodox Europe in recent history. With less state repression and also probably less state financial support, I expect somewhat less quietism in Orthodoxy's future.

18. Orthodoxy, of course, is not completely univocal in terms of actions. Empirically, the Orthodox tradition allows for individual protests by religious leaders and their followers. The "Old Believers" in Czarist Russia were a source of some dissent.

19. For details, see Charles A. Frazee, "The Orthodox Church of Greece: The Last Fifteen Years," in *Hellenic Perspectives: Essays in the History of Greece*, ed. John T. A. Koumoulides (Lanham, MD: University Press of America, 1980), 145–180.

20. In December 1997, I participated in an international conference in Athens that analyzed the dictatorship thirty years after its inauguration. No scholar I talked to said that new evidence of church resistance has appeared. On democratization and traditional cultural values such as the quietism of Orthodoxy, see Nikiforos Diamandouros, "Cultural Dualism and Political Change in Post-Authoritarian Greece," Instituto Juan March, Madrid, Working Paper 1994/50, esp. pp. 10–12 and the exhaustive footnote 14 on pp. 58–59.

21. See A. Baskedis, "Between Partnership and Separation: Relations between Church and State in Greece under the Constitution of June 9, 1975," *Ecumenical Review* 29:1 (1977), 52–61.

22. For a spirited analysis of how orthodoxy is, contra Huntington, consistent with democracy and capable of politically significant internal change, see Elizabeth H. Prodromov, "Paradigms, Power, and Identity: Rediscovering Orthodoxy and Regionalizing Europe," *European Journal of Political Research* 30 (September 1996), 125–154.

23. For a historical analysis of the role of the Greek military that contains interesting insights about church-military relations, see Thanos Veremis, *The Military in Greek Politics: From Independence to Democracy* (London: Hurst, 1997).

24. Charles S. Liebman, Director of the Argov Center for the Study of the Jewish People at Bar-Ilan University, asserts: "Israeli Judaism [has] undergone a transformation that makes it appear less, rather than more, compatible with the precondition for a stable democratic society." One of the reasons he cites for this change was the growing role in the 1980s and 1990s of neofundamentalist religious parties in the making or breaking of minority governments, either Labor or Likud. Given this context, Liebman argues there was a "growing deference of the non-religious population to the religious elites' definition of Judaism, the Jewish tradition and the Jewish religion." He argues this has implications for the inclusiveness of Israeli democracy because on the basis of virtually all the Israeli public opinion surveys he has studied, even if he controls for education and ethnicity: "The religious Jew is more likely to harbor prejudice and less likely to respect the political rights of Arabs" [than the nonreligious Jews]. See Charles S. Liebman, "Religion and Democracy in Israel" in *Israeli Democracy under Stress*, ed. Ehud Sprinzak and Larry Diamond (Boulder, CO: Lynne Rienner, 1993), 273–292; quotes are from 277–278 and 291. In the same volume, also see the introduction by the editors, 1–20, and the article by Yaron Ezrahi, "Democratic Politics and Culture in Modern Israel: Recent Trends," 255–272.

25. Liebman, ibid., 284–285.

26. See Suzanne Hoeber Rudolph, "The New Courage: An Essay on Gandhi's Psychology," *World Politics* (October 1963), 98–117; quote is from 114.

27. For Gandhi's mobilization of satyagraha and other religious symbols for modern democratic purposes, see Lloyd I. Rudolph and Susanne Hoeber Rudolph, *The Modernity of Tradition: Political Development in India* (Chicago: University of Chicago Press, 1967). For Gandhi's overall philosophy of conflict, see Joan Bordurant, *The Conquest of Violence: Gandhi's Philosophy of Conflict* (Princeton, NJ: Princeton University Press, 1958).

28. For a critical analysis of the BJP and the RSS, see Tapan Bosu et al., *Khaki Shorts and Saffron Flags: A Critique of the Hindu Right* (New Delhi: Orient Longman, 1993). For a discussion of the new crisis of Indian secularism in the post-Nehruvian world and the rise of Hindu fundamentalism that contributed to the 1992 demolition of the Babri Mosque, see Stanley J. Tambiah, "The Crisis of Secularism in India," and Amartya Sen, "Secularism and Its Discontents," both in the previously cited Rajeev Bhargava, *Secularism and Its Critics* (New York: Oxford University Press, 2005), 418–453, 454–485.

29. For the history of the establishment of churches in America and for debates over the First Amendment, see A. J. Reichley, *Religion in American Public Life* (Washington, DC: Brookings Institution, 1985), 53–167.

Annotated Bibliography

Bhargava, Rajeev, article in this book.
Read for a powerful argument about the originality and utility of India's brand of democratic secularism.
Casanova, José, *Public Religions in the Modern World.* Chicago: University of Chicago Press, 1994.
This is the pioneering book on the secularism debate, especially on "public religions." His article in this book looks at three fundamental things that have changed about public religions in the modern world since he wrote his classic fifteen years ago. All three of these changes have implications for the twin tolerations.
Künkler, Mirjam and Alfred Stepan, eds., *Democratization and Islam in Indonesia.* (New York: Columbia University Press, 2012). For the last eight years, Indonesia has been widely evaluated to be the highest quality democracy of any of the ten countries in ASEAN, the Association of Southeast Asian Nations. This volume contains analyses of how this came about and especially how within Indonesia's two major Islamic organizations, with over 70 million members, democracy had become the consensual doctrine even before the democratic transition.
Kuru, Ahmet T., *Secularism and State Policies toward Religions: The United States, France, and Turkey.* Cambridge: Cambridge University Press, 2009.
Kuru, Ahmet T and Alfred Stepan, eds., *Democracy, Islam and Secularism in Turkey.* (New York: Columbia University Press, 2012). This book reviews the political history of Turkey, from the Ottoman Empire to Atatürk's aggressive secularism, to the appearance and evolution, since 2001, of a Islamist-inspired party (AKP) that has contributed to Turkey's emergence as a major regional power in the Middle East, a possible model moderate democratic Islamism of the sort that one of the contributors, Stathis Kalyvas, compares with Christian democracy in an earlier era.
This is an excellent book on three different versions of "separatist secularism."

Norris, Pippa, and Ronald Inglehart, *Sacred and Secular: Religion and Politics World Wide*. Cambridge: Cambridge University Press, 2004.

Read this for numerous tables related to religion and depicting attitudes throughout the world based on the University of Michigan's World Value Surveys.

Philpott, Daniel, "Explaining the Political Ambivalence of Religion." *American Political Science Review* 101:3 (August 2007), 505–525.

See this article for a major attempt to look historically and comparatively at what is involved in conflicts over religion that end in inclusive and tolerant democracies and those that do not.

Stepan, Alfred, *Arguing Comparative Politics*. Oxford: Oxford University Press, 2001, 213–254.

This text contains the much longer version of Stepan's article in this book. This "Twin Tolerations" article is part of his long-term work on the fundamental choices involved in creating and sustaining modern democracies. His related articles on key problems of democracy such as paths of democratic transition, civil society, political society, parliamentary versus presidential frameworks, varieties of federalism, the tasks of democratic opposition and democratic consolidation, and democratic control of the security apparatus are also available in *Arguing Comparative Politics*.

Stepan, Alfred, "Rituals of Respect: Sufis and Secularists in Senegal in Comparative Perspective", *Comparative Politics*, forthcoming 2012. Senegalese society has, over the last two centuries, crafted, between Sufis and French-style laicite secularists, a series of mutually reinforcing "rituals of respect," which first helped facilitate accommodation among groups in potential conflict, then facilitated toleration, and eventually, respect and democracy.

Stepan, Alfred, "The Multiple Secularisms of Modern Democracies and Autocracies," in *Rethinking Secularism*, ed. Craig Calhoun, Mark Juergensmeyer, and Jonathan VanAntwerpen. Oxford: Oxford University Press, 2011, 114–144.

In both of these, Stepan builds on Bhargava's arguments for the cases of Senegal and Indonesia.

Stepan, Alfred, with Graeme Robertson, "An *Arab* more than a *Muslim* Democracy Gap." *Journal of Democracy* 14:3 (July 2003), 30–44.

One of the major puzzles about Muslims and democracy is that on purely socioeconomic grounds, some non-Arab, Muslim-majority countries (Indonesia, Bangladesh, Senegal, Mali, Turkey, Albania) are among the world's greatest "electoral overachievers" (as is the country with the second largest Muslim population, India), whereas Arab Muslim-majority countries, as a set, are the world's greatest "electoral underachievers." For a forum that has two articles criticizing Stepan/Robertson, and their response, see *Journal of Democracy* 15:4 (October 2004), 126–146.

Walzer, Michael, *On Toleration*. New Haven, CT: Yale University Press, 1999.

Read this for a short and accessible overview of toleration by a leading political theorist.

5}

How Should States Deal with Deep Religious Diversity?

CAN ANYTHING BE LEARNED FROM THE INDIAN MODEL
OF SECULARISM?

Rajeev Bhargava

Secular states and their underlying ideology, political secularism, appear to be under siege everywhere. They were severely jolted with the establishment of the first modern theocracy in 1979 in Iran. By the late 1980s, Islamic political movements had emerged in Egypt, Sudan, Algeria, Tunisia, Ethiopia, Nigeria, Chad, Senegal, Turkey, Afghanistan, Pakistan, and even in Bangladesh.

Movements challenging secular states were hardly restricted to Muslim societies. Protestant movements decrying secularism emerged in Kenya, Guatemala, and the Philippines. Protestant fundamentalism became a force in American politics. Sinhalese Buddhist nationalists in Sri Lanka, Hindu nationalists in India, religious ultraorthodox Jews in Israel, and Sikh nationalists in the state of Punjab in India, as well as among diasporic communities in Canada and Britain, began to question the separation of state and religion.

Even the largely secular-humanist ethos of Western Europe did not remain untouched by this public challenge. The migration from former colonies and intensified globalization have thrown together in Western public spaces pre-Christian faiths, Christianity, and Islam. The cumulative result is unprecedented religious diversity, a weakened public monopoly of single religions, and a generation of mutual suspicion, distrust, hostility, and conflict. This is evident in Germany and Britain but was dramatically highlighted by the headscarf issue in France and the murder of filmmaker Theo Van Gogh in the Netherlands, shortly after the release of his controversial film about Islamic culture.

Mainstream Western Secularism: Part of the Problem

Can Western secularism reinvigorate itself and deal with the new reality of the vibrant presence of multiple religions in public life and the accompanying social   73 tensions? In what follows, I argue that available mainstream *conceptions* of Western secularism are likely to meet neither the challenge of the vibrant public presence of religion nor the challenge of increasing religious diversity. To deal with this emergent diversity, the West must modify its conception either by going back in time and looking for resources in its own past diversities or by turning its attention to other conceptions of secularism and patterns of religion-state relationships developed outside the West. The model developed in the subcontinent, especially in India, provides one such alternative conception. Without taking it as a blueprint, the West must examine the Indian conception and possibly learn from it.

The dominant self-understanding of Western secularism is that it is a *universal* doctrine requiring the strict separation (exclusion) of church and religion from state for the sake of individualistically conceived moral or ethical values. This dominant self-understanding takes two forms, one inspired by an idealized version of the American model of separation and the other by the equally idealized French model.

The idealized American self-understanding interprets separation to mean *mutual exclusion*. Neither the state nor religion is meant to interfere in the domain of the other. This mutual exclusion is believed necessary to resolve conflicts between different Christian denominations, to grant some measure of equality between them, and most crucially to provide individuals the freedom to set up and maintain their own religious associations. Mutual exclusion is necessary initially for religious liberty and then for the more general liberties of individuals. This strict or "perfect separation," as Madison termed it, must take place at each of three distinct levels: (a) ends, (b) institutions and personnel, and (c) law and public policy. Levels (a) and (b) make the state nontheocratic and disestablish religion. Level (c) ensures that the state has neither a positive relationship with religion—for example, no policy of granting aid, even nonpreferentially, to religious institutions—nor a negative relationship with it; it is not within the scope of state activity to interfere in religious matters, even when some of the values (such as equality) professed by the state are violated *within* the religious domain. Congress simply has no power to legislate on any matter pertaining to religion. This noninterference is justified on the ground that religion is a privileged, private (nonstate) matter, and if something is amiss within this private domain, it can be mended only by those who, within that sphere, have a right to do so. This, according to proponents of this view, is what religious freedom means. Thus, the freedom that justifies mutual exclusion is negative liberty and is closely enmeshed with the privatization of religion. In my view, this model of secularism encourages on the part of the state a passive respect for religion and is sensitive only to some aspects of interreligious and intrareligious domination.

The idealized French understanding interprets separation differently. The state is separated from religion at levels (a) and (b), but at level (c), it retains the power to interfere in religion. But religion is divested of any power to intervene in matters of state. In short, separation means one-sided exclusion. The state may interfere in religion to hinder or suppress it or even to help religion but in all cases only to ensure its control over religion. Religion becomes an object of law and public policy on terms dictated by the state. Since this conception arose to counter the excessive domination of the church, it encourages an active disrespect for religion and is concerned solely with preventing the religious order from dominating the secular. This focus makes it indifferent to aspects of interreligious and intrareligious dominations.

Both these versions developed in the context of a single-religion society to solve the problems of one religion, namely, Christianity. Both understand separation as exclusion and make individualistically conceived values—individual liberty, equality between individuals, or both—as the ground for separation.

It is now increasingly clear that both (liberal and republican) individualist forms of Western secularism have persistent difficulties coping with community-oriented religions such as Roman Catholicism, Islam, and some forms of Hinduism and Sikhism that demand greater public presence and even official recognition for themselves—particularly when they begin to cohabit the same society. The French have had difficulty even with Protestantism. Moreover, these forms of secularism were not designed for societies with *deep* religious diversity. This is less true of the idealized American secularism, which has some resources to fight interreligious domination but few to wage a struggle against intrareligious domination. Because the state is unable to facilitate freedoms or equality within religions, it forces people to exit from their religion rather than press for intrareligious equality. On the other hand, French secularism is quite strong in meeting the threat of intrareligious domination, when some members of a religious community dominate members of their own religion (e.g., anticlericalism in France). However, it is unable to properly meet the challenge of interreligious domination, when members of one religious community discriminate against, marginalize, or even oppress members of another religious community.

Why so? Because issues of radical individual freedom and citizenship equality arose in European societies *after* religious homogenization. The birth of confessional states was accompanied by massive expulsion of subject communities whose faith differed from the religion of the ruler. Such states found some place for toleration in their ethical space, but as is well known, toleration was consistent with deep inequalities and with humiliating, marginalized, and virtually invisible existence. The liberal democratization and the consequent secularization of many European states has helped citizens with non-Christian faiths acquire most formal rights. But such a scheme of rights neither embodies a regime of interreligious equality nor effectively prevents religion-based discrimination and exclusion. Indeed, it masks majoritarian, ethno-religious biases. This is evident in different kinds of difficulties faced by Muslims. For example, in Britain a third of all primary school children are educated by religious communities. Yet applications for state funding by Muslims were frequently turned down. Four years after they were accepted, there were only two Muslim schools, compared with 2,000 run by Roman Catholics and 4,700 run by the Church of England. Similar problems persist in other European countries. This is also manifest in the failure of many Western European states to deal with the issue of headscarves (France), demands by the Muslims to build mosques or minarets and therefore practice their own faith (Germany, Italy, Switzerland), or proper burial grounds of their own (Denmark). As Islamophobia grips the imagination of several Western societies (exemplified by the cartoon controversy in Denmark), it is very likely that Muslim citizens will continue to face disadvantage on account of membership in their religious community.

I hope I have said enough to explain the crisis of individualistic, diversity-resistant secularism and why both these forms of Western secularism have become part of the problem.

Should we turn, then, to states that are religion centered and fuse with rather than separate from religion? Not if we value freedom and equality and are sensitive to religion-related domination. Historically, such states—for example, the states that established the Anglican Church in England or the Catholic Church in Italy—valued neither freedom nor equality. Such states recognized a particular version of the religion enunciated by that church as the official religion, compelled individuals to congregate for only one church, punished them for failing to profess a particular set of religious beliefs, levied taxes in support of one particular church, and mandated instruction of the favored interpretation of the religion in educational institutions. In such cases, not only was there inequality among religions (Christians and Jews) but also there was inequality among the churches of the same religion. Societies with such states either persecuted minority religious groups or were wracked by interreligious or interdenominational wars.

States with substantive establishments have not changed with time. In Pakistan, for instance, the virtual establishment of the dominant Sunni sect has proved to be disastrous, even to Muslim minorities. For example, Ahmedis have been deemed a non-Muslim minority and therefore convicted for calling themselves Muslims or using the word *mosque* to designate their place of worship. In my view, the formal establishment of the dominant religion does little to bolster better intercommunity relations in European states.

The Indian Model of Secularism

There is another model of secularism, one not generated exclusively in the West, which meets the needs of deeply religiously diverse societies and also complies with principles of freedom and equality: the Indian model. In India, the existence of deep religious diversity has ensured a response to problems not only within religions but also between religions.

Although not available as a doctrine or theory, such a conception was worked out jointly by Hindus and Muslims in the subcontinent and can be found in the best moments of intercommunal practice in India and in the country's constitution, appropriately interpreted.

Seven features of the Indian model are striking and relevant to wider discussion.

First, multiple religions are not extras, added on as an afterthought, but present at its starting point, as part of its foundation.

Second, it is not entirely averse to the public character of religions. Although the state is not identified with a particular religion or with religion more generally (there is no establishment of religion), there is official and therefore public recognition granted to religious communities.

Third, it has a commitment to multiple values—liberty or/and equality, not conceived narrowly as pertaining to individuals but interpreted broadly to cover the relative autonomy of religious communities and equality of status in society, as well as more basic values such as peace and toleration between communities. This model is acutely sensitive to the potential within religions to sanction violence.

Fourth, it does not erect a wall of separation between state and religion. There are boundaries, of course, but they are porous. This allows the state to intervene in religions, to help or hinder them without the impulse to control or destroy them. The state has multiple roles, such as granting aid to educational institutions of religious communities on a nonpreferential basis or interfering in socioreligious institutions that deny equal dignity and status to members of their own religion or to others (for example, the ban on untouchability; the obligation to allow everyone, irrespective of caste, to enter Hindu temples; and potentially to correct gender inequalities), on the basis of a more sensible understanding of equal concern and respect for all individuals and groups. In short, it interprets separation to mean not strict exclusion or strict neutrality but rather what I call principled distance.

Fifth, this model shows that we do not have to choose between active hostility and passive indifference or between disrespectful hostility and respectful indifference toward religion. We can combine the two: have the necessary hostility as long as there is also active respect; the state may intervene to inhibit some practices, so long as it shows respect for other practices of the religious community and does so by publicly lending support to them.

Sixth, by not fixing its commitment from the start exclusively to individual or community values or marking rigid boundaries between public and private, India's constitutional secularism allows decisions on these matters to be taken either within the open dynamics of democratic politics or by contextual reasoning in the courts.

Seventh, this commitment to multiple values and principled distance means that the state tries to balance different, ambiguous but equally important values. This makes its secular ideal more like a contextual, ethically sensitive, politically negotiated arrangement (which it really is), rather than a scientific doctrine conjured by ideologues and merely implemented by political agents.

A somewhat forced, formulaic articulation of Indian secularism goes something like this. The state must keep a principled distance from all public or private, individual-oriented or community-oriented religious institutions for the sake of the equally significant (and sometimes conflicting) values of peace, this-worldly goods, dignity, liberty, and equality (in all its complicated individualistic or nonindividualistic versions). Indian secularism then is an ethically sensitive negotiated settlement between diverse groups and divergent values.

Two Features of Indian Secularism: Principled Distance and Contextual Secularism

Let me elaborate in somewhat greater detail two key features of Indian secularism, namely, principled distance and its contextualist character. Indian secularism admits fairly strict separation at the level of ends: the state has no religious ends. Separation exists at the level of personnel and institutions too; this is what distance means. But at the third level, it maintains a flexible approach on the question of inclusion and exclusion of religion and the engagement and disengagement of the state, which depends on the context, nature, or current state of relevant religions. This engagement must be governed by principles undergirding a secular state, that is, principles that flow from a commitment to its stated values. This means that religion may intervene in the affairs of the state if such intervention promotes freedom, equality, or any other value integral to secularism. For example, citizens may support a coercive law of the state grounded purely in a religious rationale if this law is compatible with freedom or equality. Equally, the state may engage with religion or disengage from it and engage positively or negatively, but it does so depending entirely on whether these values are promoted or undermined. A state that intervenes or refrains from interference on this basis keeps a principled distance from all religions. This is one constitutive idea of principled distance. This idea is different from strict neutrality, in which the state may help or hinder all religions to an equal degree and in the same manner; if it intervenes in one religion, it must also do so in others. Instead, it rests on the idea that treating people or groups as equals is entirely consistent with differential treatment. This idea is the second ingredient in what I have called principled distance.

What kind of treatment do I have in mind? First, religious groups have sought exemptions from practices in which states intervene by a promulgating a law to be applied neutrally to the rest of society. This demand for noninterference is made on the ground either that the law requires them to do things not permitted by their religion or that it prevents them from doing acts mandated by it. For example, Sikhs demand exemptions from mandatory helmet laws and from police dress codes to accommodate religiously required turbans. Elsewhere, Jews seek exemptions from Air Force regulations to accommodate their yarmulkes. Muslim women and girls demand that the state not interfere in their religiously required chador. Jews and Muslims seek exemption from Sunday closing laws on the ground that this is not required by their religion. Principled distance allows, then, that a practice that is banned or regulated in one culture may be permitted in the minority culture because of the distinctive status and meaning it has for its members. For many republican or liberal theories, this is a problem because of a simple, somewhat absolutist morality that gives overwhelming importance to one value, particularly to equal treatment or equal liberty. Religious groups may demand that the state refrain from interference in their practices, but they may equally demand that the state interfere to give them special assistance so that they are also able to secure what other groups are able to routinely get by virtue of their social dominance in the political community. It may grant authority to religious officials to perform legally binding marriages, to have their own rules or methods of obtaining a divorce, to promulgate rules about relations between ex-husband and ex-wife, to arbitrate civil disputes, and so on. Principled distance allows the possibility of such policies on the grounds that to hold people accountable to an unfair law is to treat them as unequals.

However, principled distance is not just a recipe for differential treatment in the form of special exemptions. It may even require state intervention in some religions more than in others, considering the historical and social condition of all relevant religions. For the promotion of a particular value constitutive of secularism, some religions, relative to other religions, may require more interference from the state. For example, suppose the value to be advanced is social equality. This requires, in part, undermining caste hierarchies. If this is the aim of the state, then it may be required of the state that it interferes in caste-ridden Hinduism much more than in, say, Islam or Christianity. However, if a diversity-driven religious liberty is the value to be advanced by the state, then it may have to intervene in Christianity and Islam more than in Hinduism. If this is so, the state can neither strictly exclude considerations emanating from religion nor keep strict neutrality with respect to religion. It cannot antecedently decide that it will always refrain from interfering in religions or that it will interfere in each equally. Indeed, it may not relate to every religion in society in exactly the same way or intervene in each religion to the same degree or in the same manner. To want to do so would be plainly absurd. All it must ensure is that the relationship between the state and religions is guided by nonsectarian motives consistent with some values and principles.

How is principled distance related to the imaginative idea of twin tolerations proposed by Alfred Stepan? I believe the spirit that animates them is the same, but there are crucial differences. Both reject strict separation and are more accommodative toward religions, but principled difference is less hospitable to formal establishments and appears to allow greater intervention by the state to advance equality within and between religions.

Twin toleration is ambiguous between two interpretations. According to the first, the idea of twin tolerations is a less rigid version of noninterference by religion and democratic state in one another's domain. But it retains many problems endemic to the idealized American conception. For example, it limits the state from intervening in the affairs of religion, even when it could and should. It is indifferent to conceptions of substantive equality and lacks the capacity to support religious groups that would not survive without support from the state. Moreover, it, too, is suited to contexts of predominantly single-religion societies and is less workable in societies marked by deep religious diversity. On the second, more charitable view, toleration of religion must be consistent with the fullest possible democratic conceptions of liberty and equality of all individuals and groups. In this version, it becomes indistinguishable from principled distance. If so, Stepan and I reach the same idea by taking different routes.

Contextual secularism is contextual not only because it captures the idea that the precise form and content of secularism will vary from one to another context and from place to place but also because it embodies a certain model of contextual moral reasoning. This it does because of its character as a multivalue doctrine and by virtue of its commitment to principled distance. To accept that secularism is a multivalue doctrine is to acknowledge that its constitutive values do not always sit easily with one another. On the contrary, they are frequently in conflict. Some degree of internal discord and therefore a fair amount of instability are an integral part of contextual secularism. For this reason, it forever requires fresh interpretations, contextual judgments, and attempts at reconciliation and compromise. This contextual secularism recognizes that the conflict between individual rights and group rights or between claims of equality and liberty or between claims of liberty and the satisfaction of basic needs cannot always be adjudicated by recourse to some general and abstract principle. Rather, they can only be settled case by case and may require a fine balancing of competing claims. The eventual outcome may not be wholly satisfactory to either but still be reasonably satisfactory to both. Multivalue doctrines such as secularism encourage accommodation—not giving up one value for the sake of another but rather their reconciliation and possible harmonization to make each work without changing the basic content of apparently incompatible concepts and values.

This endeavor to make concepts, viewpoints, and values work simultaneously does not amount to a morally objectionable compromise. This is so because nothing of importance is being given up for the sake of a less significant thing, one without value or even with negative value. Rather, what is pursued is a mutually agreed middle way that combines elements from two or more equally valuable entities. The roots of such attempts at reconciliation and accommodation lie in a lack of dogmatism, in a willingness to experiment and think at different levels and in separate spheres, and in a readiness to make decisions on a provisional basis. It captures a way of thinking characterized by the following dictum: Why look at things in terms of this or that, why not try to have both this and that? In this way of thinking, it is recognized that though we may currently be unable to secure the best of both values and may therefore be forced to settle for a watered-down version of each, we must continue to have an abiding commitment to search for a transcendence of this second-best condition. It is frequently argued against Indian secularism that it is contradictory because it tries to bring together individual and community rights and that articles in the Indian Constitution that have a bearing on the secular nature of the Indian state are deeply conflictual and at best ambiguous. This is to misrecognize a virtue as a vice. In my view, this attempt to bring together seemingly incompatible values is a great strength of Indian secularism.

Discerning students of Western secularism may now begin to find something familiar in this ideal. But then, Indian secularism has not dropped fully formed from the sky. It is not sui generis. It shares a history with the West. In part, it has learned from and built on it. Indian secularism may be seen as a route to retrieving the rich history of Western secularism—forgotten, underemphasized, or frequently obscured by the formula of strict separation. If so, Western societies can find reflected in it not only a compressed version of their own history but also a vision of their future.

Two objections might arise on reading this. First, it might be said: look at the state of the subcontinent! Look at India! How deeply divided it remains! What about the violence against Muslims in Gujarat and against Christians in Orissa? How can success be claimed for the Indian version of secularism? I do not wish to underestimate the force of this objection. The secular ideal in India is in periodic crisis and is deeply contested. Besides, at the best of times, it generates as many problems as it solves.

But it should not be forgotten that a secular state was set up in India *despite* the massacre and displacement of millions of people on ethno-religious grounds, and it has survived in a continuing context in which ethnic nationalism remains dominant throughout the world. As different religious cultures claim their place in societies across the world, it may be India's development of secularism that offers the most prodiversity, freedom-sensitive, and democratic way forward. In any case, this account must not be read as an apologia for the Indian state but as a reasonable and sympathetic articulation of a conception that the Indian state frequently fails to realize. My discussion is meant to focus on the comparative value of this conception and its potential for the future and not on how in fact it has fared in India. And why should the fate of ideal conceptions with transcultural potential be decided purely on the basis of what happens to them in their place of origin?

Second, it might be objected that I do not focus on the best practices of Western states and emphasize the more vocal articulations of Western secular conceptions. But that precisely is my point. The dominant conception of Western secularism is derived from an idealized self-understanding of two of its versions rather than from the best practices of Western states, including the practices of the United States and France. It is my view that this doctrinal conception (a) obstructs an understanding of alternative conceptions worked out on the ground by morally sensitive political agents; (b) by influencing politicians and citizens alike, frequently distorts the practice of many Western and non-Western states; and (c) masks the many ways in which interreligious or intrareligious domination persists in many Western societies. Moreover, it is this conception that has traveled to all parts of the world and is a continuing source of misunderstanding of the value of secular states. My objective is to displace these conceptions or at least put them in their place.

I hope to have demonstrated that there are at least two broad conceptions of secularisms, one that for convenience I have called the mainstream Western (the American and the French) and the other that provides an alternative to it as embodied in the Indian model. I do not wish to suggest that this alternative model is found only in India. The Indian case is meant to show that such an alternative exists. It is not meant to resurrect a dichotomy between the West and the East. As I have mentioned, I am quite certain that this alternative version is embedded in the best practices of many states, including those Western states that are deeply enamored by mainstream conceptions of political secularism. My objective in this chapter was to draw attention to the point that political theorists do not see the normative potential in the secular practices of these different states because they are obsessed with the normativity of just one variant, the mainstream model of secularism. Western states need to improve their understanding of their own secular practices, just as Western secularism needs a better theoretical self-understanding. Rather than get stuck on models they developed at a particular time in their history, they would do well to more carefully examine the normative potential in their own political practices or to learn from the original Indian variant.

This problem of misunderstanding secularism afflicts India, too. Both the self-proclaimed supporters of secularism and some of its misguided opponents in India could learn from examining the original Indian variant. Indeed, it is my conviction that many critics of Indian secularism will embrace it once they better understand its nature and point, something that can be done only when we loosen the grip of one model of secularism and recognize the existence of multiple secularisms.

SOME POSSIBLE IMPLICATIONS

- The state cannot avoid having or endorsing a policy toward religion or religious organizations. Religion plays an important part in the lives of many people, and religious institutions function in this world like purely secular institutions. So, separation cannot mean the exclusion of religion from the domain of the state.
- Separation of church and state should also not be interpreted as absolute or strict neutrality. No state can possibly help or hinder all religions in the same manner and to the same degree.
- The state may interfere with religion and refrain from such interference, depending entirely on which of these promotes the values of freedom and equality or undermines interreligious and intrareligious dominations.
- Values of freedom and equality must be interpreted both as rights of individuals and, wherever required, as rights of communities. Community rights are particularly important if religious groups are vulnerable or, because of their small number, have relatively little power to influence the process of decision making.
- Secularism must be neither servile nor hostile to religion. It must manifest an attitude of neither blind deference nor indifference but of critical respect toward all religions.

- Secularism that professes principled distance and is sensitive to multiple values cannot avoid making contextual judgments. Contextual judgments allow for ethically sensitive balancing and compromise.
- Those who think that they are emancipated from religion or believe that their own religion is emancipated, but not that of others, should accept with humility that none of their achievements is irreversible. They should also not fail to remember the history of oppressions within their own respective religion, as well as the repressive policies of many secular states. As more and more societies become multireligious, a sense of vulnerability about one's own religion—indeed, one's own worldview—will be crucial for a peaceful and just world order. If secularism is to survive as a transcultural normative perspective, it must be de-Christianized, de-Westernized, and deindividualized. In saying so, I do not mean that it must wholly sever its links with Christianity or the West, but its ties with them must be loosened. It should be able to draw its justifications from the conceptual resources of other civilizations and accommodate community-based rights. Only with this form of secularism and a state nourished by it can deep religious diversity be managed.

Annotated Bibliography

Bader, Veit, *Secularism or Democracy?* Amsterdam: Amsterdam University Press, 2007.
Like Bhargava, Bader argues against idealized American and French models of secularism and proposes that the best approach to governance of religious diversity is provided by what he calls associative democracy. Like Bhargava, he also argues that despite their alleged liberal-democratic character, many Western states continue to mask ethno-religious, majoritarian biases. However, he makes a strong plea that the word *secularism* be dropped from at least legal and constitutional discourse.
Bhargava, Rajeev, ed., *Secularism and Its Critics*. New York: Oxford University Press, 1998.
An invaluable collection of essays that includes both the most recent and the older debate of secularism in India and juxtaposes them with articles on political secularism in Western societies. Probably the first such collection of its kind.
Bhargava, Rajeev, "Distinctiveness of Indian Secularism," in *The Future of Secularism*, ed. T. N. Srinivasan. New York: Oxford University Press, 2007, 20–59.
This text contains a longer version of Bhargava's article in this book. The essay by Romila Thapar is also useful to understand the background of Indian secularism.
Casanova, Jose, *Public Religions in the Modern World*. Chicago: University of Chicago Press, 1994.
Probably the best recent work on secularization. Casanova deconstructs the secularization thesis and argues that it contains not one but three theses: (a) the thesis of the decline of religion, (b) the thesis of the privatization of the religion, and (c) the functional differentiation thesis. Casanova argues that only the differentiation thesis is worth

rescuing. He provides a powerful argument that religions are getting deprivatized and can play a useful role in the public sphere of modern societies consistent with liberal and democratic values.

Levey, Geoffrey Brahm, and Tariq Modood, *Secularism, Religion and Multicultural Citizenship*. New York: Cambridge University Press, 2009.

Containing several essays including Casanova, Bhargava, and Modood, with a foreword by Charles Taylor, it challenges the theory and practice of Western secularism and focuses on the experience of Muslims in a wide variety of countries that are broadly liberal and democratic (Britain, Germany, France, Denmark, United States, Australia, and India).

Stepan, Alfred, "The World's Religious Systems and Democracy: Crafting the 'Twin Tolerations,'" in *Arguing Comparative Politics* (New York: Oxford University Press, 2001), 213–254.

As the title suggests Stepan proposes the valuable notion of Twin Tolerations between religion and democracy. He argues (1) that minimal freedom for the democratic state and the minimal religion's freedom of citizens are compatible with a broad range of patterns of religions state relations and (2) that democratic states may neither be hostile to religion nor strictly separate themselves from it.

6 }

Rethinking Islam and Democracy
Robert W. Hefner

The end of the Cold War created high hopes for liberalization and democratic reforms in the Muslim-majority countries of the world. However, the break-down of the political process in Algeria during 1991–92, terrorist violence in the mid-1990s, and the 9/11 attacks in the United States led some Western analysts to conclude that Muslim countries may be the great exception to the democratizing trends of our age. As most famously captured in Samuel Huntington's *The Clash of Civilizations*, a few analysts saw an even deeper meaning in the events of the early post–Cold War era. They argued that there is a pervasive "democracy deficit" in the Muslim world, and it is the result, not of institutional impasses or momentary imbalances of power, but of an abiding civilizational incompatibility between Islam and democracy.[1]

Today, arguments like these strike many political analysts as old hat and settled. Do we really need to hear yet another exchange on Islam and democracy? Yet, if we take the pulse of broader commentaries in policy institutes, academia, and, above all, the mass media, it is clear that there has been surprisingly little progress toward a new consensus on democracy and Muslim politics. In this chapter, I suggest that it is time that this change, because there is a new body of empirical research that sheds new and important light on the question of Islam and democracy. This chapter examines the issue by way of four arguments.

First, when empirical measures rather than imagined civilizational traits are referenced, it turns out that there is no democracy deficit in the broader Muslim world; a significant number of non-Arab Muslim countries have made impressive headway toward consolidating electoral democracy. However, at least until the tumultuous transformations of February and March 2011, there did appear to be a democracy deficit in the 18 to 20 percent of the Muslim world that is ethnically Arab.

Second, survey data also indicate that in most Muslim-majority countries, even those where the government is undemocratic, the Muslim public views democratic institutions favorably, indeed at rates comparable to those in Western countries.

Third, notwithstanding their expressed support for democracy, a significant proportion of these Muslim publics has "un-liberal" ideas on women, non-Muslims, and matters of religious freedom. Whether these attitudes represent a threat to democratization or are merely variations on the quality of democracy is a question on which analysts disagree, and on which I comment toward the end of this chapter.

Fourth and last, the accumulated research suggests democratization is alive and well in the non-Arab portions of the Muslim world; as of spring 2011, it appears that the process is also making headway in parts of the Arab world. However, the evidence also suggests that, when and where democratization moves forward, its accompanying political culture may more closely resemble what some have referred to as a "civil Islamic" or "Muslim" democracy rather than the Atlantic-liberal variety familiar and favored in the United States and Western Europe. Muslim democracy will come in varied forms, but some among its most recurring characteristics may well be a reluctance to privatize religious affairs, reservations about full freedom of religious expression, and the presence of a small but well-organized activist minority opposed to democracy on the grounds that it is religiously unacceptable. Although a small minority in most Muslim societies, the presence of antidemocratic rejectionists may at times explain why, despite the great change that has taken place in public views of democracy, Muslim-majority societies are somewhat more likely to be plagued by outbreaks of "religiously"-inspired antidemocratic resistance than their non-Muslim counterparts.

A *Muslim* Democracy Deficit?

The question of whether there is, in fact, a democracy deficit in the political performance of the forty-seven or so Muslim-majority countries of the world was addressed several years ago in two articles in the *Journal of Democracy* by the political scientists Alfred Stepan and Graeme B. Robertson (Stepan and Robertson 2003, 2004). Stepan and Robertson approached the question by drawing on two of the most comprehensive data sets on democracy and civil liberties around the world: the Polity Project and Freedom House's annual surveys of political rights and civil liberties. Rather than trying to provide comprehensive measures of all aspects of democratic performance, Stepan and Robertson focused their discussion on "electoral competitiveness." They deemed a country electorally competitive if it met two conditions: "the government sprang from reasonably fair elections" and "the elected government was able to fill the most important political offices" without being second-guessed by unelected authorities (Stepan and Robertson 2003, 3).

With this measure in hand, Stepan and Robertson reviewed the Freedom House and Polity Project data on political performance in Muslim countries from 1973 to 2002. The findings from this thirty-year comparison were striking. Of some twenty-nine non-Arab Muslim-majority countries, more than a third enjoyed significant political rights for at least three years, and more than a quarter experienced at least five consecutive years (Stepan and Robertson 2003, 31). These are quite respectable scores for societies at the level of socioeconomic development at which most non-Arab Muslim societies find themselves. By contrast, among the Arab Muslim countries, not a single one experienced five consecutive years of electoral competitiveness, and only Lebanon reached the more modest threshold of three consecutive years (2003, 32). The authors concluded that "a non-Arab Muslim-majority country was almost 20 times more likely to be 'electorally competitive' than an Arab Muslim majority country" (2003, 33).

Adding to this stark contrast is the fact that the overall pattern defies oft-cited arguments on the conditions conducive to democratization. Proponents of the "developmentalist thesis" have long argued that as per capita income increases, so, too, does a country's chances for electoral democracy. Measured against this income standard, however, some 44 percent of Arab countries underachieve; no Arab country overachieves. By contrast, Stepan and Robertson discovered that 31 percent of the non-Arab Muslim-majority countries are democratic overachievers relative to their income levels.

Another way in which the non-Arab Muslim majority countries defy conventional expectations has to do with ethnolinguistic diversity. As is well known, John Stuart Mill believed that ethnolinguistic diversity was inimical to democracy. Recently, several American political theorists have tried to breathe new life into this notion. On this question, however, the contrast between Arab and non-Arab Muslim-majority countries is again striking. Many among the electorally competitive non-Arab countries—Senegal, Mali, Bangladesh, Indonesia—are characterized by high levels of ethnolinguistic diversity. By contrast, the Arab countries, which tend to be electorally noncompetitive, "began with the lowest levels of ethnolinguistic fragmentation" (Stepan and Robertson 2003, 40).

In their conclusion, Stepan and Robertson observe that, in matters of electoral competitiveness, the sixteen Arab countries comprise the single large bloc among all of the world's states that "underachieve" relative to their levels of economic development. By contrast, the thirty-one Muslim-majority but non-Arab countries make up the single largest bloc of countries of electoral "overachievers" relative to their level of economic development. The overachievers include countries as culturally diverse as Turkey, Senegal, Mali, Bangladesh, and Indonesia (Stepan and Robertson 2003, 30–35). Unlike their Arab counterparts, and contrary to the democracy-deficit thesis, these Muslim-majority countries suffer from no democracy deficit whatsoever.

Muslim Publics and Democratic Ideals

Leaving aside questions of political performance, researchers have also recently addressed the question of the breadth of public support for democracy as measured by opinion surveys in Muslim-majority countries. The assumption guiding this research is that, if the clash-of-civilization thesis really were correct, we would expect to find not only poor democratic performance in Muslim-majority societies but also widespread public antipathy for democracy on the grounds that it is contrary to Islamic teaching.

Although in the 1970s and 1980s there were almost no comparative studies of public opinion in Muslim-majority countries, since the 1990s, several far-ranging surveys have been carried out. We now have solid survey data from the Pew Public Forum, the World Values Surveys, the Gallup Organization, and a host of independent research projects (see Esposito and Mogahed 2007; Fattah 2006; Hassan 2002; Norris and Inglehart 2004, 133–156). Although most of these surveys cover diverse topics, several make direct assessments of the Muslim public's views on democratic institutions and values.

The findings from these surveys are, once again, striking. In the great majority of, but not all, Muslim countries, most people indicate that they believe that democracy is a good form of government, and one that they would like to see established in their own country.[2] Pippa Norris and Ronald Inglehart's (2003, 2004) recent analyses of World Values survey data provide one of the most comprehensive gauges of the breadth of this support. World Values teams have now carried out studies in eleven Muslim countries: Algeria, Jordan, Pakistan, Turkey, Azerbaijan, Indonesia, Bangladesh, Albania, Morocco, Iran, and Egypt (Norris and Inglehart 2003,140). Although the political regimes operative in these countries vary greatly, Norris and Inglehart report that attitudes toward democracy do not. The majority of people view democracy as a good form of government and one to which they aspire. Comparing survey data from these countries with the West, the authors note, "There were no significant differences between the publics living in the West and in Muslim religious cultures in approval of how democracy works in practice, in support for democratic ideals, and in approval of strong leadership" (2003, 146). The authors observe that "Muslim publics did display greater support for a strong societal role by religious authorities than do Western publics" (147), but they quickly add that many non-Western publics share that view.

Surveys carried out by other individuals and organizations point to similarly high levels of support for democracy (Esposito and Mogahed 2007; Fattah 2006; Hassan 2002; Hefner, 2011a). However, these survey data come with one important caveat: several states not included in the World Values Polling, including Saudi Arabia, Libya, and the Gulf States, diverge significantly from the prodemocracy norm. Survey and ethnographic data from these countries indicate that a sizable plurality or outright majority of respondents oppose democracy, usually on the grounds that it is said to be contrary to Islam. Although public opinion in the Muslim world as a whole is generally supportive of democracy, then, opinion varies across national boundaries. Equally important, some who reject democracy as un-Islamic are so passionate in their opposition that their presence in a society can present a serious challenge to civic peace and the realization of democratic ideals, even where the broader public is otherwise favorably inclined. Even where their proportion in the total population is relatively small, the presence of such antidemocratic rejectionists will remain one of the most distinctive challenges to democratization in Muslim-majority societies (as discussed later).

The second and final point concerning Muslim opinion further complicates the relatively upbeat findings on modern Muslims and democracy. In many but not all Muslim-majority countries, the public's enthusiasm for democracy coexists with an equally strong ambivalence toward issues that many Western and Muslim democratic theorists regard as necessary for a full flowering of democratic institutions (Diamond 1999, 2002). The most notable points of tension concern the question of equal rights for women and non-Muslims and the thorny issue of freedom of religious expression, including the right to convert from Islam. On all these points, some of the public in Muslim-majority countries has decidedly unliberal views. This ambivalence raises the question as to whether the support for democracy expressed in surveys is actually all that it appears to be. Space in this article does not allow a full discussion of all of these questions, but a later section highlights a few of the issues in the debate.

Muslim Democracy's Achilles' Heel?

Notwithstanding media stereotypes to the contrary, gender practices in Muslim-majority countries vary greatly from Mali to Egypt and from Pakistan to Indonesia. The variation demonstrates that neither Islam nor Islamic law is the sole determinant of Muslim gender realities. Gender "matters" in Muslim-majority societies, but it matters in complex and contextually variable ways (see Ahmed 1992; Charrad 2001; Fish 2002).

This variation acknowledged, recent studies have shown that in many Muslim-majority countries, a substantial proportion of the population, both male and female, appears reluctant to accept the idea that men and women are equal and, more specifically, that women should be able to exercise executive authority over men. This finding emerged as a central theme of Pippa Norris and Ronald Inglehart's 2003 analysis of the World Values Survey data. The authors conclude that the real clash of cultures between Muslims and the West concerns not democracy, but women and sexuality. "Any claim of a 'clash of civilizations' based on fundamentally different political goals held by Western and Muslim societies represents an oversimplification of the evidence," they observe (2003, 68). "Any deep-seated divisions between Islam and the West will revolve far more strongly around social rather than political values, especially concerning the issues of sexual liberalization and gender equality" (Norris and Inglehart 2004, 139).[3]

What are we to make of these differences? Many analysts, and certainly many Muslim scholars, feel that the legacy of Islamic law, or the shari'a, has long been the most decisive influence on public attitudes toward gender and sexuality. The status of women in the historical shari'a was handled primarily through family law, touching on matters of marriage, divorce, property, and inheritance. In all of these fields, women were accorded fuller rights than they are thought to have enjoyed in pre-Islamic Arabia, rights significantly greater than their counterparts in medieval Europe (Ahmed 1992, 9–25; Vikor 2005, 300). Nonetheless, on a number of key issues, the shari'a put women at a significant disadvantage relative to men. In religious courts, women's testimony counted as just half that of men. A woman's right to initiate divorce was severely restricted compared with her husband's. A girl's inherited share of her parents' properties was half her brother's. Most troubling of all for modern notions of citizenship, classical jurisprudence stipulated that in both domestic and public affairs women were not to exercise authority over men. Citing verse 4:34 of the Qur'an, jurists assigned men guardianship or protectorship (*qawama*) over women. Many commentators went further, severely limiting the rights of women to appear in public or to associate with men, thereby limiting women's participation in male-dominated public spheres (Ali 2006, 117–131; An-Na'im 2008, 108–109; Mernissi 1991, 151–153).

In practice, the actions and rulings of Islam's judges (*qadi*) were often more flexible than these classical provisions imply. Indeed, as a number of recent studies have shown, proceedings in Islamic courts, especially regarding questions of marriage and divorce, were often informed by local notions of gender identity and fairness as much as they were the terms of classical jurisprudence (see Bowen 2003; Hirsch 1998; Peletz 2002). Nonetheless, in modern times, Islamist calls for the implementation of shari'a have more consistently invoked, not the situated practices of judges or the nuanced arguments of classical jurisprudence, but cut-and-paste summaries of the historical shari'a, complete with gender-inequitable prescriptions for women (see Ahmed 1992, 89–207; Ali 2006; Esack 2001; Friedmann 2003; Othman 1997).

Islamic law's stipulations with regard to non-Muslims show a similarly differentiating disposition, in a manner that can be at odds with modern notions of democratic citizenship. Qur'anic revelations dating from the Medina period (622–632 C.E.) hint at a sharp distinction between Muslims and non-Muslims. Chapter 9, Sura 29 of the Qur'an, for example, urges believers to fight against and humble those to whom God has given revelation, that is, Jews and Christians, but who no longer forbid what God has forbidden.[4] From the classical period onward, many Muslim jurists interpreted this passage as evidence of enduring hostility between Muslims and non-Muslims. During Islam's middle ages, jurists extended the distinction into regulations concerning the political standing of non-Muslim "peoples of the book" (*ahl al-kitab*). As recipients of earlier divine revelations, and as the demographic majority in the central Arab lands during the first 150 years of the Muslim era, the peoples of the book were accorded an official "protected" status known as *dhimmihood* (An-Na'im 2008, 128–136; Bulliet, 1994, 39; Friedmann, 2003, 58–74). *Dhimmas* (*ahl al-dhimma*) were tolerated and given a measure of autonomy on the condition that they submit to Muslim rule and pay a special capitation tax, the *jizya*. At the same time, however, the shari'a imposed restrictions, the effect of which was to underscore *dhimma* subordination, sometimes humiliatingly. In legal principle, polytheists like Hindus, who were not included among peoples of the book, were subject to even more draconian restrictions.

In historical fact, however, many Muslim rulers took a pragmatic approach and set aside the shari'a's restrictions when dealing with polytheists and people of the book. For most of their history, for example, India's great Mughal rulers chose to dispense with the shari'a's provisions with respect to non-Muslims (Richards 1995, 39). Muslim rulers in premodern Southeast Asia were also casual with regard to the shari'a's guidelines for dealing with non-Muslims (Hooker 1984; Reid 1993). Nonetheless, although often put aside in practice, the principle of religiously differentiated citizenship was never formally effaced from Muslim jurisprudence. Its lingering presence has posed a serious challenge for today's proponents of Muslim democracy, particularly where strict-constructionist jurists have reinvoked the concept as a principle of modern Muslim politics (Hefner 2011b; cf. Awang, 1994).

A similar tension has emerged in modern times with regard to questions of religious freedom, not least of all as concerns the right to divert or apostatize from Islam. Historically, Islam had no counterpart to early modern Europe's Inquisition or anti-witchcraft campaigns, which killed tens of thousands of people. During the classical and Ottoman periods, there were occasional prosecutions for apostasy, some of which resulted in capital punishment. However, the overall rate of prosecution was far less than in Christian Europe during the same periods (Friedmann 2003, 121–159; Vikor 2005, 295). By comparison with medieval Christian jurisprudence, Muslim jurists took care not to apply the accusation of apostasy broadly and to require high standards of proof for a conviction. Those accused of apostasy were given repeated opportunities to revert back to a proper profession of Islam. If the offender persisted in his or her ways, the penalty was death or, in the case of women (according to some schools of law), indefinite imprisonment. On these points, although not as severe as the situation in Christian Europe, the historical shari'a developed a legal vigilance on matters of the faith in tension with the oft-cited injunction in Qur'an 2:26 that there is no compulsion in Islam (An-Na'im 2008, 118–120).

In sum, on all of these issues—women, non-Muslims, and Muslim nonconformists or apostates—the historical shari'a prescribed ethical strictures at odds with modern liberal democratic ideals, like those enshrined in the 1948 Universal Declaration of Human Rights. Modern Islamist thinkers like Sayyid Qutb of Egypt and Abdu'l A'la Mawdudi of Pakistan have taken strong exception to liberal formulations of human rights (Musallam 2005; Nasr 1996). Documents like the Universal Islamic Declaration of Human Rights (UIDHR) and the constitutions of the Islamic Republics of Iran and the Sudan have been more restrained in their criticisms of liberal rights schemes, but their position does not otherwise greatly differ (Mayer 2007, 123–124).

Some theorists of a modernization persuasion have suggested that it is only a matter of time before these and other obstacles to a fuller realization of citizenship ideals in Muslim countries are pushed aside. On gender, for example, Norris and Inglehart have suggested that gender differentials in Muslim-majority societies will diminish as Muslim societies make the transition from modern to postmodern societies. This view is premised on the confidence that religious realities are less decisive in shaping a modern society's values and practices than is its level of socioeconomic development. With regard to women, in particular, Norris and Inglehart have argued that modernist industrialization reduces fertility rates, educates women, and expands extrafamilial employment opportunities. In the next phase of development, postmodernization, we see "a shift toward greater gender equality as women move into higher status economic" and political roles"; the period also ushers in "a more permissive and liberal sexuality, including tolerance of divorce, abortion, and homosexuality" (Norris and Inglehart 2004, 137). Norris and Inglehart conclude that, because their societies are not yet postmodern, young Muslims' views on women and sexuality "remain unchanged, in contrast to the transformation of lifestyles and beliefs experienced among their peers living in postindustrial societies" (Norris and Inglehart 2004, 149).

Although the World Values Survey on which Norris and Inglehart base their findings has contributed enormously to our cross-cultural understanding of religion and modernity, the evidence from contemporary Muslim societies seems at odds with Norris and Inglehart's argument on two critical points. First, their characterization of Muslim women's roles as traditional and "unchanging" overlooks studies indicating that in most Muslim-majority societies women's roles are in the throes of a great transformation. The most striking features of this transformation are, first, the movement of masses of girls and women into education, including higher education, and, second, the related march of women into a *relatively* higher degree of employment and/or participation outside family settings (see Brown 2000, 127). In all but a handful of Muslim lands, gender cultures are no longer traditional but fast-changing and thoroughly contested (Charrad 2001; Mir-Hosseini 1999; White 2003).

The more critical point on which Norris and Inglehart's model errs, however, is in its tendency to discount the independent influence of religious culture and organizations on modern public life. Contrary to the situation in Western Europe (the situation in the United States is different, confounding any attempt to speak of a uniform Western modernity on matters of religion), the gender transition in Muslim lands has coincided with a historically unprecedented Islamic resurgence. Sociologists of Western religion disagree as to exactly what has happened to religion in the West since the 1960s, particularly regarding the still vital role of religion in the United States compared with Western Europe (Berger, Davie, and Fokas 2008; Casanova 1994; Davie 2000). But most agree that at least Western Europe has seen a precipitous secularization or, as the historian Hugh McLeod has put it, a far-reaching "de-Christianization" (McLeod 2003). By contrast, during this same thirty- to forty-year period, most of the Muslim world has seen a spectacular increase in religious observance, expressed in everything from mosque construction and religious education to men's beards, women's headscarves, and heightened debate over the place of religion in public life.

The political question developments like these pose is Does the resurgence mean that the undemocratic laws applied in medieval times to women, non-Muslims, and Muslim nonconformists will continue to be used today? The evidence from contemporary Muslim societies suggests that there will be no single answer to this question. Some Muslim theorists believe these social statuses fall squarely under the jurisdiction of Islamic law as classically understood; other Muslim commentators insist the details of the classical tradition no longer apply, even if the overarching "principles" (*maqasid al-shari'a*) of the law are still relevant (Hefner 2011b). Inasmuch as this foundational dispute remains unresolved, we should expect to see that the status of women, non-Muslims, and Muslim nonconformists will be the focus of debate for some time to come, even in countries that make an otherwise successful transition to electoral democracy. In this respect, modern Muslim politics in general, and Muslim democracy in particular, may develop features like the "culture wars" (Hunter 1991) seen the United States, where deep disagreements on public-ethical matters like abortion and gay rights prompt some groups to question the legitimacy of the political system as a whole.

A quick survey of political developments in several Muslim societies reveals the pervasiveness of these tensions. To take the example of women, we know that women were central players in the student-activist groups that helped to overthrow Indonesia's President Suharto in May 1998, including the Muslim Brotherhood—inspired group known as KAMMI (Hefner 2000; Madrid 1999). Women were also active in the grassroots organizations that helped to catapult moderate Islamist and conservative Muslim democratic parties to electoral victory in Turkey in the late 1990s and early 2000s (Kuru 2009, 179; White 2002). Women activists also played a key role in Iran's Islamic revolution, as well as the post-Khomeini (and 2009) movement for cultural and political reform (Adelkhah 1991; Mir-Hosseini 1999). In all of these countries, however, prominent religious conservatives have managed to use their social standing to influence the public debate as well. The *shari'a* conservatives decry gender liberalization as un-Islamic and insist that women must be barred from exercising authority over men and, indeed, from most public arenas where they might mix freely with men (see Shehadeh 2003).

Examples like these indicate that, where democracy takes root in Muslim-majority countries, the situation for women, non-Muslims, and Muslim nonconformists may continue to show the influence of certain religious authorities and ethico-legal legacies peculiar to the Muslim world. Certainly, as Norris and Inglehart have argued, there will be some common elements of gender change as well, for example, in education and aspects of familial demography. But the contrasting biography of religion in the late-twentieth-century West (at least in its European version) as opposed to Muslim-majority countries will also make for differences. In much of the Western world outside the United States, changes in women's roles have taken place against the backdrop of a galloping secularization of public life and declining religious observance (Davie 2000). The political discourse accompanying these changes has, with only a few exceptions, been a philosophically liberal and secular one, highlighting notions of individual autonomy, personal expression, and "choice." By contrast, although there are some secular Muslim feminists, the more common discourse for the reform of women's roles in Muslim lands builds on two ideals more subtly religious than the liberal principle of individual autonomy: women's equal dignity as creatures of an all-just God and the need for all believers to take a more active role in implementing the tenets their faith (see Moghadam 2002; Wickham 2003). In other words, what is distinctive about gender change in the contemporary Muslim world is that it bears the imprint of the educational, demographic, and life opportunity changes Norris and Inglehart highlight *and* an Islamic revival that has reached into the deepest recesses of public and private life.

Precisely what these developments mean for democracy will no doubt vary from society to society, but one additional point merits mention. As Moataz Fattah's survey of 31,000 Muslims in thirty-two Muslim countries has shown, the majority of educated Muslim women find Western notions of gender relations and sexuality problematic. Many insist that Western models of femininity are not liberating but irreligious and commercialized. However, Fattah's survey offers up a no less important fact: "literate Muslim women in all countries," he finds, "are more supportive of democratic norms and institutions than are Muslim men" (Fattah 2006, 44; cf. Joseph 2000). The gender revolution in Islam may not have the secularizing impact of gender change in the West, but, where combined with women's movement into higher education, it may yet have powerfully auspicious implications for democratization.

The Challenge of Intense Minorities

The cultural ambivalences seen in contemporary Muslim societies raise two final questions. First, where democratization moves forward in Muslim-majority countries, is its political culture likely to differ from that of the democratic West? Of course, the cultures of citizenship and democracy in the West are far more varied than some philosophical treatments of Western liberalism imply, not least of all as regards the place of religion and ethics in public life. The question nonetheless remains: are there likely to be basic differences in democratic culture in Western and Muslim societies? A second question follows from this first: where democracy takes hold, is it likely to face challenges peculiar to Muslim-majority societies?

On the question of the characteristics of Muslim democracy, the political scientist Vali Nasr has suggested that the democracy emerging in Muslim-majority societies is likely to differ from that of the liberal West, and for this reason, the system is best referred to as "Muslim" democracy rather than liberal. Nasr's reasoning has less to do with any distinctive cultural influences he sees as operative in Muslim countries than it does with the practical constraints of the democratization process taking place in countries like Senegal, Turkey, Bangladesh, and Indonesia. Developments in these nations, Nasr argues, are being driven by on-the-ground electoral engagements rather than master cultural narratives. As a result, Nasr argues, Muslim democracy will rest "not on an abstract, carefully thought-out theological and ideological accommodation between Islam and democracy, but rather on a practical synthesis that is emerging...in response to the opportunities and demands created by the ballot box" (Nasr 2005, 14–15).

Nasr is right to emphasize the importance of elections for reshaping modern Muslim political culture, but his argument may not go far enough. The evidence from contemporary Muslim societies suggests that where democracy takes hold, it may show the influence not just of contemporary electoral bargaining but of legacies rooted in the ethico-legal and organizational heritage of Islam itself. One consequence of such legacies may well be that as it brings more citizens into the political process, Muslim democratization may have the curious effect of not creating a greater separation of religion and state but actually increasing demands for more extensive collaboration, particularly on matters of public morality. State-mandated Islamic education in public schools and a heightened emphasis on public standards of morality—these and other collaborations across the state-society divide have already become the norm rather than the exception in the late-modern Muslim world. Demands for such collaboration are not likely to diminish as Muslim-majority countries become more democratic.

For students of comparative politics and political culture, it is important *not* to make this aspect of modern Muslim politics more exceptional than it is. First of all, the collaboration most Muslims have in mind is *not* the theocratic fusion of religion and state that revolutionary Iran has attempted and that commentators like Huntington have wrongly claimed is representative of Muslim politics as a whole. From the first centuries of the Muslim era, the main currents in Muslim politics were untheocratic; contemporary Iran is, in this regard, a radical exception to the historical rule. In most societies, religious scholars were enjoined to comment on matters of public ethical importance, but there was a significant separation of state jurisdictions from those of the *ulama* (see Brown 2000, 31–37; Vikor 2005; Zubaida 2003, 78–89).

It is also important to emphasize that modern Muslims' penchant for having some measure of state support for religion does not distinguish modern Muslims from believers in other religio-political traditions. Notwithstanding the mistaken assumptions of modernization theorists a generation ago, a high wall of separation between religion and state was *not* the norm in Western Europe during the nineteenth and twentieth centuries (see Kuru 2009; Moensma and Soper 1997). Most Western European countries countenanced extensive collaboration between church and state; indeed, most still today have established churches and/or special financial arrangements for the support of religious institutions like churches and schools (Jackson et al., 2007). These and other comparative examples suggest that, as long as a democracy extends full religious and political rights to all citizens, collaborations across the state-religion divide need not be antithetical to democracy.

In a recent study of the separation of religion and state in 152 countries, political scientist Jonathan Fox offered a comprehensive reassessment of the religion-and-state question that also helps to put the Muslim example in perspective (Fox 2006). Fox's data show that a full separation of religion and state (defined at 537 as "no state support for religion and no state restrictions on religion") is found *nowhere in the world* except the United States. A full separation of religion and state, then, "is far from the norm; rather, it is a rare exception to the more general rule that governments involve themselves in religious issues" (559). Three-quarters of all of these states "have measurable levels" of government involvement in religion (558).

Equally surprising, Fox found that, as a society undergoes economic development, there is a tendency for the state to become *more* and not less involved in religious affairs. In a conclusion that resonates with findings from Muslim countries—but demonstrates that there is no Muslim exceptionalism in this regard—Fox writes:

> It is precisely in those states where modernity has most undermined the traditional community that religious elements within the state are most likely to try to legislate religious morals and traditions that were previously enforced at the social level. Similarly, it is precisely the most modern states that have the greatest ability to interfere in the daily lives of their citizens, including the regulation of religion. (Fox 2006, 562)

Fox's data also speak to the circumstances of religion in Muslim-majority states. When compared with other cultural regions, governments in Muslim-majority countries are the most likely to sanction state support for religion. Some 76.9 percent of Muslim-majority states provide some form of institutional support to Islam; 51.3 percent have made Islam their official religion. Catholic-majority countries have almost as high a level of support for religion; however, today they are less likely to have an official religion. On these and other measures, "Muslim states are the most religious, followed by the Catholic states" (559).

Summarizing the implications of his findings for religion and democracy, Fox suggests that they contradict the conventional wisdom that democracies need a full separation of religion and state to thrive. He comments that such an arrangement "is nearly nonexistent among democracies and even marginal SRAS [separation of religion and state] does not exist in a large majority of them" (2006, 563). This finding, he concludes, is "sufficiently unequivocal and strong to warrant a major reconsideration of our assumptions regarding the role of religion in modern times in general and the role of religion in democracies in particular" (563).

If Fox and other studies on the separation of religion and state are correct, then there is no necessary contradiction between state involvement in Islamic affairs and democratic government. The critical question is not whether such engagements occur, but the precise nature of the interaction and whether it undermines the civic rights of citizens professing non-Islamic religions or of Muslims who profess their faith in a nonconformist fashion.

It is not with regard to secularism, then, but here, on the question of the precise nature of the collaboration between the state and Islam, that some of the fiercest religio-political battles are likely to rage in Muslim lands. The battle will not pit *étatizing* Islamists against secularist democrats advocating religion's abolition or privatization. Most Muslim democrats are committed to a third way between theocracy and secular democracy, in which "religious principles and democratic values coexist" (Esposito and Mogahed 2007, 63). The struggle, then, will pit proponents of Muslim democracy against what in most countries will be a ultraconservative minority who reject democracy on the grounds that it is contrary to Islam. On occasion, some in the latter camp may be so convinced of the immorality of democracy that they may escalate their opposition into violence. This pattern of a small but intense opposition to the democratic system may well remain an enduring aspect of Muslim politics, even where the system becomes electorally democratic.

Equally important, as Monica Duffy Toft has recently argued (Toft 2007), where such intensely committed rejectionists exist, political elites may be tempted to embellish their conservative credentials and engage in religious "outbidding" in an effort to recruit the rejectionists to their side (103). As Toft shows, outbidding of this sort played a central role in the rise to power of the radical Islamist leadership in the Sudan. Threatened by the military advances of non-Muslims in the country's south, Sudan's rulers "tendered competing bids to enhance their legitimacy" and thereby "forced religion to the center of what had started as a conflict over the distribution of offices and economic resources" (Toft 2007, 125). A similar but not quite so lethal process of outbidding has taken place in other modern Muslim countries, including Zia ul-Haq's Pakistan (Nasr 1996), Sadat's Egypt (Wickham 2003), and Soeharto's Indonesia in the 1990s (Hefner 2000).

Where it achieves its desired aim, outbidding of this sort increases the likelihood that women and religious minorities will be assigned a second-class status, consistent with narrowly formalist interpretations of Islamic law. Outbidding elites are also more likely to allow Islamist supporters to invoke classical legal stipulations on apostasy to attack secular, freethinking, or nonconformist Muslims. As in contemporary Iran, the neoconservatives' political theology legitimates their defiance of the democratic aspirations of the Muslim majority. Control of the repressive machinery of state in turn provides the neoconservatives with the leverage to make good on that defiance.

A distinctive feature of Muslim democracy, then, is likely to be that its proponents will have to dedicate considerable religious and political capital to containing challenges from those who reject democracy as un-Islamic. The proponents of Muslim democracy will also have to be on guard against Islamist outbidding by political elites. A central feature of both initiatives will in turn involve the effort not to create a full separation of Islam and state but to demonstrate that Islamic law is best understood not as an unchanging blueprint for theocratic governance but as a source for general principles and ethical guidance compatible with Muslim democracy.

Conclusion

Recent research on Muslim politics suggests four conclusions on the question of Islam and democracy. First, there is no democracy deficit in the broader Muslim world, but, for reasons I could not fully explore in this chapter, there has been until recently just such a deficit in Arab Muslim lands. Second, notwithstanding variation in political performance, public opinion in most Muslim lands favors democratic government. Third, notwithstanding the public's prodemocracy disposition, certain values identified in the modern West with democracy and liberalism, such as gender equality and religious tolerance, may continue to encounter opposition from a portion of the Muslim public (the size of which will vary by country and political circumstance). Fourth, Muslim democracy may be accompanied by considerable state support for religion, as well as efforts by prodemocracy Muslims to contain the energies of a minority convinced that democracy is antithetical to Islam.

In Muslim democracies, then, we can also expect to see significant public support for the idea that religious ethics are not purely private matters. But the idea behind this support is not all that different from the views of much of the European public in the late nineteenth and early twentieth century. As in Western Europe in that era, the collaborations of religious organizations with the state will not always generate cultural currents conducive to individual religious freedom. Some believers may be encouraged to adopt intolerant views toward non-Muslims and Muslim nonconformists.

However, if the radicals can be held at bay and political elites restrained from engaging in religious outbidding, the consequences of state support for religion need not at all be dire. Like Western European democracies in the late nineteenth and early twentieth centuries, some Muslim societies may strike an evolving balance between state support for religion and expanding democratic participation. They will be able to do so only if the antidemocratic stream within Muslim politics and society can be effectively contained, not least of all through their demonstration of the political and ethical benefits of Muslim democracy itself.

Western observers and policy analysts can assist democratization in the Muslim world by recognizing two simple facts: first, that a momentous shift in Muslim political culture toward support for the idea of democracy is indeed underway and, second, that its outcome will not be made in the West but will bear the unmistakable and enduring imprint of Islamic concerns and powers.

Notes

1. Huntington sharpened this point by observing that one of the most important preconditions for democracy in the West was Christianity's separation of church and state. By contrast, he asserted, "In Islam," there is no such separation; "God is Caesar" (Huntington 1996, 70). As Huntington saw it, the refusal to separate religion and state had far-reaching political implications. Among other things, it meant that in Muslim countries, there was no check on political power, no space for forging public opinion, and no possibility for a concept of citizenship inclusive of non-Muslims, as well as Muslims.

2. As an aside to this discussion, the fact that many respondents in Arab Muslim countries share this favorable view of democracy with their non-Arab Muslim counterparts indicates that it is not public opinion that is holding back democratic progress in the Arab-Muslim world, but certain structural and institutional obstacles.

3. Steven Fish adds another layer of empirical detail to Norris and Inglehart's findings. He notes that in measures of female literacy, sex ratios, and the percentage of women active in government, Muslim-majority countries perform rather poorly when compared with countries at a comparable level of socioeconomic development (Fish 2002, 25).

4. Passages like these have led modern reformists to argue that the Suras in question apply only to heated contests taking place in seventh-century Medina, not to Muslim relations with Christians and Jews for all time. This is a highly controversial thesis among Islamic scholars, to say the least. See An-Na`im 1990 and 2008 and Taha 1987.

Works Cited

Adelkhah, Fariba. 1991. *La révolution sous le voile: Femmes Islamique d'Iran*. Paris: Karthala,1991.

Ahmed, Leila. 1992. *Women and Gender in Islam: Historical Roots of a Modern Debate*. New Haven, CT: Yale University Press.

Ali, Kecia. 2006. *Sexual Ethics and Islam: Feminist Reflections on Qur'an, Hadith, and Jurisprudence*. Oxford: One World.

An-Na`im, Abdullahi Ahmed. 1990. *Toward an Islamic Reformation: Civil Liberties, Human Rights, and International Law*. Syracuse, NY: Syracuse University Press, 1990.

An-Na`im, Abdullahi Ahmed. 2008. *Islam and the Secular State: Negotiating the Future of Shari`a*. Cambridge, MA: Harvard University Press, 2008.

Awang, Abdul Rahman. 1994. *The Status of the Dhimmi in Islamic Law*. Kuala Lumpur: International Law Book Services.

Berger, Peter, Grace Davie, and Effie Fokas. 2008. *Religious America, Secular Europe? A Theme and Variations*. Burlington, VT: Ashgate.

Bowen, John R. 2003. *Islam, Law and Equality in Indonesia: An Anthropology of Public Reasoning*. Cambridge: Cambridge University Press.

Brown, Carl. 2000. *Religion and State: The Muslim Approach to Politics*. New York: Columbia University Press.

Bulliet, Richard W. 1994. *Islam: The View from the Edge*. New York: Columbia University Press.

Casanova, José. 1994. *Public Religions in the Modern World*. Chicago: University of Chicago Press.

Charrad, Mounira M. 2001. *States and Women's Rights: The Making of Postcolonial Tunisia, Algeria, and Morocco*. Berkeley: University of California Press.

Cook, Michael. 2000. *Commanding Right and Forbidding Wrong in Islamic Thought*. Cambridge: Cambridge University Press.

Davie, Grace. 2000. *Religion in Modern Europe: A Memory Mutates*. Oxford: Oxford University Press.

Diamond, Larry. 1999. *Developing Democracy: Toward Consolidation*. Baltimore: Johns Hopkins University Press.

———. 2002. "Elections without Democracy: Thinking about Hybrid Regimes." *Journal of Democracy* 13:2:21-35.

Diamond, Larry, Marc F. Plattner, and Daniel Brumberg, eds. 2003. *Islam and Democracy in the Middle East*. Baltimore: Johns Hopkins University Press.

Eickelman, Dale F., and James Piscatori. 1996. *Muslim Politics*. Princeton, NJ: Princeton University Press.

El Fadl, Khaled Abou. 2004. *Islam and the Challenge of Democracy*. Princeton, NJ: Princeton University Press.

Esack, Farid. 2001. "Islam and Gender Justice: Beyond Simplistic Apologia." In *What Men Owe to Women: Men's Voices from World Religions*, ed. John C. Raines and Daniel C. Maguire. Albany: State University of New York Press, 187–210.

Esposito, John L., and Dalia Mogahed. 2007. *Who Speaks for Islam: What A Billion Muslims Really Think*. New York: Gallup, 2007.

Fattah, Moataz A. 2006. *Democratic Values in the Muslim World*. Boulder, CO: Lynne Rienner.

Fish, M. Steven. 2002. "Islam and Authoritarianism." *World Politics* 55, 4–37.

Fox, Jonathan. 2006. "World Separation of Religion and State into the 21st Century." *Comparative Political Studies* 39:5, 537–569.

Friedmann, Yohanan. 2003. *Tolerance and Coercion in Islam: Interfaith Relations in the Muslim Tradition*. Cambridge: Cambridge University Press.

Hassan, Riaz. 2002. *Faithlines: Muslim Conceptions of Islam and Society*. Karachi: Oxford University Press.

Hefner, Robert W. 2000. *Civil Islam: Muslims and Democratization in Indonesia*. Princeton, NJ: Princeton University Press.

———. 2004. "Muslim Democrats and Islamist Violence in Post-Soeharto Indonesia," in *Remaking Muslim Politics: Pluralism, Contestation, Democratization*, ed. Robert W. Hefner. Princeton, NJ: Princeton University Press, 273–301.

Hefner, Robert W.2011a.. "Human Rights and Democracy in Islam: The Indonesian Case in Global Perspective." In *Religion and the Global Politics of Human Rights*, ed. Thomas Banchoff and Robert Wuthnow. Oxford: Oxford University Press. 39-69.

———. 2011b. "Shari'a Politics: Law and Society in the Modern Muslim World." In *Shari'a Politics: Islamic Law and Society in the Modern World*, ed. Robert W. Hefner. Bloomington: Indiana University Press, 1-54

Hirsch, Susan F. 1998. *Pronouncing and Persevering: Gender and the Discourses of Disputing in an African Islamic Court*. Chicago: University of Chicago Press.

Hooker, M. B. 1984. *Islamic Law in South-East Asia*. Singapore: Oxford University Press.

Hunter, James Davison. 1991. *Culture Wars: The Struggle to Define America*. New York: Basic Books.

Huntington, Samuel P. 1996. *The Clash of Civilizations and the Remaking of the World Order*. New York: Simon & Schuster, 1996.

Inglehart, Ronald and Pippa Norris. 2003. "The True Clash of Civilizations." *Foreign Policy* 135 (March-April), 62-70.

Joseph, Suad, ed. 2000. *Gender and Citizenship in the Middle East*. Syracuse, NY: University of Syracuse Press.

Kuru, Ahmet T. 2009. *Secularism and State Policies toward Religion: The United States, France, and Turkey*. Cambridge: Cambridge University Press.

Madrid, Robin. 1999. "Islamic Students in the Indonesian Student Movement, 1998–1999: Forces for Moderation." *Bulletin of Concerned Asian Scholars* 39:3, 1–24.

Mayer, Ann Elizabeth. 2007. *Islam and Human Rights*, 4th ed. Boulder, CO: Westview.

McLeod, Hugh. 2003. "Introduction." In *The Decline of Christendom in Western Europe, 1750–2000*, ed. Hugh McLeod and Werner Usorf. Cambridge: Cambridge University Press, 1–26.

Mernissi, Fatima. 1991. *Women in Islam: An Historical and Theological Enquiry*. Oxford: Basil Blackwell

Mir-Hosseini, Ziba. 1999. *Islam and Gender: The Religious Debate in Contemporary Iran*. Princeton, NJ: Princeton University Press.

Mir-Hosseini, Ziba, and Richard Tapper. 2006. *Islam and Democracy in Iran: Eshkevari and the Quest for Reform*. London: I. B. Tauris.

Moensma, S., and C. Soper. 1997. *The Challenge of Pluralism: Church and State in Five Democracies*. Oxford: Rowman and Littlefield.

Moghadam, Valentine M. 2002. "Islamic Feminism and Its Discontents: Toward a Resolution of the Debate." *Signs: Journal of Women in Culture and Society* 27:4, 1135–1171.

Musallam, Adnan A. 2005. *From Secularism to Jihad: Sayyid Qutb and the Foundations of Radical Islamism*. Westport, CT: Praeger.

Nasr, Vali Seyyed Reza. 1996. *Mawdudi and the Making of Islamic Revivalism*. Oxford: Oxford University Press.

Nasr, Vali Seyyed Reza. 2005. "The Rise of 'Muslim Democracy,'" *Journal of Democracy* 17:2, 13–27.

Norris, Pippa, and Ronald Inglehart. 2004. *Sacred and Secular: Religion and Politics Worldwide*. Cambridge: Cambridge University Press.

Othman, Norani. 1997. "Grounding Human Rights Arguments in Non-Western Cultural Terms: Shari'a and the Citizenship Rights of Women in a Modern Nation-State." Bangi, Malaysia: IKMAS Working Paper Series, No. 10, Malaysian National University.

Peletz, Michael G. 2002. *Islamic Modern: Religious Courts and Cultural Politics in Malaysia*. Princeton, NJ: Princeton University Press.

Reid, Anthony. 1993. *Southeast Asia in the Age of Commerce, 1450–1680*, vol. 2, *Expansion and Crisis*. New Haven, CT: Yale University Press.

Richards, John F. 1995. *The Mughal Empire*. Cambridge: Cambridge University Press.

Sachedina, Abdulaziz. 2001. *The Islamic Roots of Democratic Pluralism*. Oxford: Oxford University Press.

Shehadeh, Lamia Rustum. 2003. *The Idea of Women in Fundamentalist Islam*. Gainesville: University of South Florida.

Soroush, Abdolkarim. 2000. *Reason, Freedom, and Democracy in Islam*. Oxford: Oxford University Press.

Stepan, Alfred, and Graeme B. Robertson. 2003. "An 'Arab' More than a 'Muslim' Electoral Gap," *Journal of Democracy* 14:3, 30–44.

Stepan, Alfred, and Graeme B. Robertson. 2004. "'Arab' Not 'Muslim' Exceptionalism," *Journal of Democracy* 15:4, 140–146.

Taha, Mahmoud Mohamed. 1987. *The Second Message of Islam*. Syracuse, NY: Syracuse University Press.

Toft, Monica Duffy. 2007. "Getting Religion? The Puzzling Case of Islam and Civil War." *International Security* 31:4, 97–131.

Vikor, Knut S. 2005. *Between God and the Sultan, between God and the Sultan: A History of Islamic Law*. Oxford: Oxford University Press.

White, Jenny B. 2003. *Islamist Mobilization in Turkey: A Study in Vernacular Politics*. Seattle: University of Washington Press.

Wickham, Carrie Rosefsky. 2003. *Mobilizing Islam: Religion, Activism, and Political Change in Egypt*. New York: Columbia University Press.

Zubaida, Sami. 2003. *Law and Power in the Islamic World*. London: I. B. Tauris.

Annotated Bibliography

An-Na`im, Abdullahi Ahmed, 1990. *Toward an Islamic Reformation: Civil Liberties, Human Rights, and International Law*. Syracuse, NY: Syracuse University Press, 1990.

A now-classic essay on the Islamic grounds for a modern reformation of Muslim politics to make the tradition compatible with pluralist democracy and international standards of human rights.

An-Na`im, Abdullahi Ahmed, 2008. *Islam and the Secular State: Negotiating the Future of Shari`a*. Cambridge, MA: Harvard University Press.

A sweeping historical and analytic survey of the origins of Islamic law, paying particular attention to the implications of the law for non-Muslims, women, and religious freedom in the modern world.

Brown, Carl, 2000. *Religion and State: The Muslim Approach to Politics*. New York: Columbia University Press.

A historical and comparative overview of the development of Muslim politics in the Middle East and South Asia. The book's early chapters are notable for their comparison of politics in premodern Christendom with that in the Muslim world. The study also provides a clear discussion of the major differences between Shi`a and Sunni politics. The book concludes with an incisive analysis of the forces giving rise to radical Islamism in modern times, which Brown demonstrates is a departure from the main historical currents of Muslim politics.

Cook, Michael, 2000. *Commanding Right and Forbidding Wrong in Islamic Thought*. Cambridge: Cambridge University Press.

Written by one of today's most highly regarded specialists of Islamic thought, this book provides a comprehensive intellectual history of one of the most important principles of Muslim public ethics.

Esposito, John L., and Dalia Mogahed, 2007. *Who Speaks for Islam: What a Billion Muslims Really Think*. New York: Gallup, 2007.

A short but incisive reflection on survey data from around the Muslim world, demonstrating the widespread commitment to both democratic government and implementation of general principles of Islamic law.

Joseph, Suad, ed., 2000. *Gender and Citizenship in the Middle East*. Syracuse, NY: University of Syracuse Press.

An important collection of essays on the status and rights of women in the contemporary Middle East.

Mir-Hosseini, Ziba, 1999. *Islam and Gender: The Religious Debate in Contemporary Iran*. Princeton, NJ: Princeton University Press.

A richly researched study of public arguments over the rights and status of women in a country where the gender debate has achieved a cacophony and intensity greater than in most Muslim countries.

Shehadeh, Lamia Rustum, 2003. *The Idea of Women in Fundamentalist Islam.* Gainesville: University of South Florida.

A balanced treatment of conservative Islamist thinkers' views on the place of women in a Muslim society.

Stepan, Alfred, and Graeme B. Robertson, 2003. "An 'Arab' More Than a 'Muslim' Electoral Gap," *Journal of Democracy* 14:3, 30–44; and 2004. "'Arab' Not 'Muslim' Exceptionalism," *Journal of Democracy* 15:4, 140–146.

Elegantly written, these two essays review the data on electoral competition in modern Muslim-majority countries, showing that claims of the existence of a democratic gap in the Muslim world apply quite clearly to Arab-majority countries but not very well to the 75 percent of the world's Muslims who are non-Arab.

Vikor, Knut S., 2005. *Between God and the Sultan, between God and the Sultan: A History of Islamic Law.* Oxford: Oxford University Press.

This book offers a comprehensive overview of the historical development and politics of Islamic law from the early Islamic period to today. The book is notable for the author's ability to summarize complex aspects of the law in a manner that shows their relevance for Muslim politics today.

7 }

Religious Freedom, Democracy, and International Human Rights

John Witte Jr. and M. Christian Green

In January 2008, news headlines and human rights Web sites around the world broadcast the story of a death sentence handed down by a local Afghan court to a twenty-three-year-old journalism student, Sayed Perwiz Kambakhsh, for committing the crime of blasphemy.[1] The student had downloaded and distributed an article from the Internet after annotating it with words deemed to be an insult to the Prophet Muhammad. The article in question was critical of certain Islamic beliefs and practices that were seen as oppressive to women. Kambakhsh had allegedly added to the text some of his own criticisms of Muhammad's teachings on women's rights. The death sentence drew criticism from journalists, human rights activists, and political leaders around the world, inspiring European Parliament President Hans-Gert Pöttering to protest to Afghan President Hamid Karzai: "The alleged 'crime' of this person would appear to be that he has distributed publications aimed at improving the situation of Afghan women."[2]

At the appeals court, Judge Abdul Salam Qazizada, a holdover from the Taliban era, was reportedly antagonistic toward Kambakhsh.[3] In support of the blasphemy charge against Kambakhsh, the court considered as evidence anecdotal reports that the young man was a socialist, was impolite, asked too many questions in class, and swapped off-color jokes and messages with friends. In October 2008, an Afghan appeals court overturned Kambakhsh's death sentence and sentenced him instead to twenty years in prison, presumably due to the considerable international attention to his case and international pressure on the Afghan government.[4] Kambakhsh began his prison term in March 2009, the same month in which Afghan President Hamid Karzai signed a law specifying circumstances in which Afghan women of the Shia Muslim tradition must have sex with their husbands under Muslim family law.[5] Interpretations of Islamic law that sanction marital rape may well have been among the abuses of women's rights that the young journalist Kambakhsh was seeking to address in his writing.

Such has been the state of religious liberty and human rights in an Afghanistan newly democratic and purportedly liberated from Muslim extremists. This kind of story recurs in endless variations in the Middle East, Africa, the Balkans, and various former Soviet nations and provinces in Eastern Europe and Central Asia. Clearly, religion and freedom do not yet coincide in many countries, however rosy their new constitutional claims to religious rights and freedoms for all. Apostasy, blasphemy, conversion, and defamation—these are the new alphabet of religious rights violations in a number of regions around the world. Occurring at the intersection of religion and international human rights, they are also challenges to the universality of human rights and the democratic institutions that generate and affirm them.

The Human Rights Revolution and Global Awakening of Religion

The new concerns about religious rights and religious offenses come at a time when religion has been a key beneficiary of a human rights revolution often viewed as universal, global, and democratic in normative aspiration, if not always in practical effect. Cresting in the last third of the twentieth century, the modern human rights revolution has helped to catalyze a great awakening of religion around the globe. One cause and consequence of this religious resurgence is that the ambit of human rights protections for and by religions has been substantially expanded. In part because of the global "third wave" of democratization, more than 200 major new statutes and constitutional provisions on religious rights have been promulgated since 1975—many replete with generous protections for liberty of conscience and freedom of religious exercise; guarantees of religious pluralism, equality, and nondiscrimination; and several other special protections and entitlements for religious individuals and religious groups.[6] These national guarantees have been matched with a growing body of regional and international norms building on foundational guarantees contained in the 1948 Universal Declaration of Human Rights[7] and successor instruments on religious freedom. With their legal and political status thus guaranteed, religious groups have enjoyed greater capacity to ease the plights and expand the rights of women, children, and refugees in many parts of the globe and have been particularly effective in addressing matters related to what are increasingly referred to as the "third generation" of human rights, having to do with health (particularly HIV/AIDS), the environment, disaster relief, globalization, peacemaking, and conflict transformation.

At the same time, however, this very same world human rights revolution has coincided with intensifying religious and ethnic conflict, oppression, and belligerence. In Yugoslavia, Rwanda, and Sudan, ethnic nationalism and religious extremism have conspired to bring violent dislocation or death to hundreds of rival religious believers each year and persecution, false imprisonment, forced starvation, and savage abuses to untold thousands of others. In France, Belgium, Germany, and Austria, political secularism, laicization, and nationalism have combined to threaten civil denial and deprivation to a number of believers, particularly "sects" and "cults" of high religious temperature or of low cultural conformity. And in many parts of the world today, barbaric Islamist terrorists have waged a destructive jihad against all manner of religious, cultural, and ethnic enemies, real and imagined. Other European nations, such as the Netherlands, Sweden, and Denmark, have also seen increased tensions concerning their rapidly growing Muslim minorities. In communities across Asia and into the Middle East and North Africa, Christians, Jews, and Muslims have faced sharply increased restrictions, repression, and more than occasional martyrdom.

Indeed, in many areas of the world, a new "war for souls" has broken out—a battle to reclaim the traditional cultural and moral fabric of these new societies and a struggle to retain adherence and adherents to indigenous faiths. In part, this is a theological war, as rival communities have often cast each other in religious terms. The ecumenical spirit of previous decades—characterized by the participation of the world's nations and religious groups in the creation of the United Nations and the near-unanimous approval of the 1948 Universal Declaration[8]—is giving way to sharp new forms of religious balkanization. In part, this is a legal war, as local religious groups conspire with political leaders to adopt statutes and regulations restricting the constitutional rights of their foreign religious rivals. Several countries of late have passed firm new antiproselytism laws, imposed cult registration requirements, tightened visa controls, and instituted various other discriminatory restrictions on new or newly arrived religions. Several parts of the non-Western world seem to be in a new dawn of fundamentalist Islamic and Christian religious establishments. These tensions exist under the surface of shiny constitutional veneers of international human rights instruments and despite the overall success of the human rights revolution.[9]

"On Condition No One Asks Us Why"

HUMAN RIGHTS AS UNIVERSAL *IUS GENTIUM* AND *LINGUA FRANCA*

Questions concerning religious freedom, democracy, and human rights are not new in international law. They confronted the drafters of the international bill of rights from the very beginning. Some Muslim nations, particularly Pakistan, Egypt, and Saudi Arabia, objected to provisions of the 1948 Universal Declaration of Human Rights dealing with marriage and family and guaranteeing the right to change one's religion.[10] In the end, however, Saudi Arabia was the lone dissenter on the religious freedom provision and the only Muslim nation to withhold its full support through abstaining from the final vote.[11] The declaration was adopted with forty-eight votes in favor, eight abstentions, and no nations opposed.

In the sixty years since the Universal Declaration, human rights, including religious rights, have emerged as part of the common law, the *ius gentium*, of an emerging world culture. Historically, the *ius gentium* was the set of principles and customs that were common to several political communities and often the basis for treaties and other diplomatic conventions. The *ius gentium* was stable, but not static; it changed over time and across cultures—as new interpretations of law were offered and became increasingly conventional. Thus, the *ius gentium* provided a transtemporal, transcultural, and more or less universal set of norms and a consistent body of principles by which a person and a people could govern themselves.

What gave the *ius gentium* enduring authority in the history of the West was that it drew heavily from all manner of legal and cultural traditions. The *ius gentium* provided the foundation on which the international human rights apparatus emerged—haltingly in the eighteenth and nineteenth centuries and more fully in the twentieth, in the aftermath of two devastating world wars. Universal and global inquiries into common laws and common principles of right living, in fact, predate the current calls for cosmopolitanism and globalization by many centuries.

In recent years, discussions of "Asian values" and Islamic human rights have revived earlier questions about the universality of human rights, particularly human rights grounded in or having to do with religion. The charge has been that human rights are the hegemonic creatures of Western Christianity, Enlightenment liberalism, or some admixture of the two. For some, these debates have raised questions about the foundations, even the existence, of human rights per se, regardless of whether the rights in question pertain to or involve religion. To the extent that these debates have prompted religious traditions to reconsider and retrieve their own traditions of and commitment to human rights, they are worthwhile conversations to have. But inquiries into the relationship between religion and human rights need not be so foundationalist in their character and consequence.

Philosopher Jacques Maritain, one of a group of philosophers summoned by UNESCO to consult on the Universal Declaration of Human Rights, when asked how proponents of different ideologies could agree to a list of fundamental rights, replied, "Yes, we agree about the rights *but on condition no one asks us why.*"[12] The goal, he elaborated, was to agree "not on the basis of common speculative idea, but on common practical ideas, not on the affirmation of one and the same conception of the world, of man, and of knowledge, but upon the affirmation of a single body of beliefs for guidance in action."[13] Philosophers and jurists since have also found value in nonfoundational, practical, anthropological, hermeneutical, and discursive approaches to human rights.[14] Whatever their foundation, religious or otherwise, it is increasingly the case that "human rights are accepted as a transcultural language"[15] and that "the language of human rights has become a moral *lingua franca.*"[16]

The human rights norms that underlie much of the emerging international common law are not a static belief system born of Western Christendom and Enlightenment liberalism. They are fluid, elastic, and open to challenge and change. The human rights regime is not a fundamental belief system. It is a relative system of ideas and ideals that presupposes the existence of fundamental beliefs and values that will constantly shape and reshape it. Human rights norms have grown in international law out of long-standing religious and cultural traditions. They have traditionally provided a forum and a focus for subtle and sophisticated philosophical, theological, and political reflections on the common good and our lives. They are derived from and dependent on the transcendent principles that religious traditions, more than any other groups, continue to cultivate. But they are aimed universally at the common good of all peoples. The human rights regime is neither the child of Christianity and the Enlightenment, nor a ward under exclusive guardianship of either.

Human rights norms are the *lingua franca* and the *ius gentium* of our times, the common law of nations, the "middle axioms" in our moral and political discourse between the traditions and practices of the past and our aspirations and goals for the future. Human rights have emerged today as one of the richest products of the interaction of religion and international law—the common law and common power of the emerging cosmopolitan world order. But the progress has not always been smooth, and there have been many obstacles and detours along the way.

The International Law Framework of Religion and Human Rights

If the 1948 Universal Declaration provided the foundation for religious freedom as a human right, subsequent documents provided the framework. Four international instruments contain the most critical protections of religious rights and liberties: (1) the International Covenant on Civil and Political Rights (ICCPR),[17] (2) the United Nations Declaration on the Elimination of All Forms of Intolerance and Discrimination Based on Religion or Belief ("1981 Declaration on Religion and Belief"),[18] (3) the Concluding Document of the Vienna Follow-up Meeting of Representatives of the Participating States of the Conference on Security and Cooperation in Europe ("1989 Vienna Concluding Document"),[19] and (4) the Declaration on the Rights of Persons Belonging to National or Ethnic, Religious, and Linguistic Minorities ("1992 Minorities Declaration").[20]

The ICCPR largely repeats the capacious guarantee of religious rights and liberties first announced in the 1948 Universal Declaration. Article 18, the key religion provision, protects the "right to freedom of thought, conscience, and religion," defined to include "freedom to have or to adopt a religion or belief of [one's] choice, and freedom, either individually or in community with others and in public and private, to manifest [one's] religion or belief in worship, observance, practice and teaching." Permissible restraints on religious freedom are limited to instances that pose a risk to the "public safety, order, health, or morals or the fundamental rights and freedoms of others." Additional provisions of the ICCPR call on state parties to prohibit "any advocacy of national, racial, or religious hatred that constitutes incitement to discrimination, hostility, or violence," require equal treatment of all persons before the law, prohibit discrimination based on religion, and guarantee religious minorities "the rights to enjoy their own culture" and "to profess and practise their own religion."[21]

The 1981 Declaration on Religion and Belief elaborates the religious liberty provisions that the ICCPR adumbrated. It sets forth a lengthy, illustrative catalogue of freedoms that illustrates more concretely the ICCPR's guarantees.[22] Specifically enumerated rights include the rights to worship and assemble, to maintain charitable and humanitarian institutions, to acquire and use ritual objects and materials, to produce and disseminate publications, to teach religion, to solicit and receive financial and other charitable contributions, to designate religious leaders, to celebrate holy days and days of rest, and to communicate to those within and without the faith both nationally and internationally. It also includes more elaborate prohibitions than the ICCPR on religious discrimination and intolerance, barring religious "discrimination by any State, institution, group of persons, or person" and defining discrimination as "any distinction, exclusion, restriction or preference based on religion or belief, and having as its purpose or as its effect nullification or impairment of the recognition, enjoyment, or exercise of human rights or fundamental freedoms on an equal basis."

The 1989 Vienna Concluding Document extends the religious liberty norms of the 1981 Declaration, particularly for religious groups. It prohibits religious discrimination against both "individuals and communities...in all fields of civil, political, economic, social and cultural life."[23] It recommends "norms of mutual tolerance and respect between believers of different communities as well as between believers and non-believers" and includes a number of specific free exercise grants that recognize and balance throughout the rights of "individual believers and communities of believers." A number of its religious group rights provisions reflect the international right to self-determination of peoples, long recognized as a basic norm of international law.

The 1992 Minorities Declaration recognizes even more fully the right to self-determination of groups within pluralistic societies. It guarantees a religious community the right to practice its religion, an ethnic community the right to promote its culture, and a linguistic community the right to speak its language without undue state interference or unnecessary legal restrictions. The declaration recognizes "the promotion and protection of the rights" of religious, cultural, and linguistic minorities as "an integral part of the development of a society as a whole and within a democratic framework based on the rule of law."[24] So conceived, the right to religious self-determination provides religious groups some of the same strong protections afforded to religious individuals under the freedom of conscience guarantee. It also expands group rights beyond the usual parameters of language, ethnicity, and geography to include groups based on religious affiliation.

In recent years, two Islamic declarations on human rights have drawn attention for their distinctive views of religious freedom. The 1981 Universal Islamic Declaration of Human Rights, as its title suggests, is framed in highly universal terms. Its foreword proclaims it to be a "declaration for mankind," invoking a classic Qur'anic passage describing the creation of humanity "into nations and tribes, so that you might come to know one another."[25] It guarantees "freedom of belief, thought, and speech" and, more specifically, a person's "right to freedom of conscience and worship in accordance with his religious beliefs." It condemns actions that "hold in contempt or ridicule the religious beliefs of others or incite public hostility against them" and declares that "respect for the religious feelings of others is obligatory on all Muslims." Above all, it declares, that the "Qur'anic principle 'There is no compulsion in religion' shall govern the religious rights of non-Muslim minorities" and "in a Muslim country religious minorities shall have the choice to be governed in respect of their civil and personal matters by Islamic Law, or by their own laws."[26] The Universal Islamic Declaration would appear to be a clear indication that notions of universal human rights do exist in Islam, including the right to religious freedom.

The more recent 1990 Cairo Declaration on Human Rights, by contrast, contains no articles specifically devoted to religious freedom, but it does cite "race, color, language, sex, *religious belief*, political affiliation, [and] social status" as impermissible bases of discrimination.[27] Religious rights are mentioned in a provision on educational rights, as well as in the context of the believer's right "to live in security for himself, his *religion*, his dependents, his honor, and his property."[28] At the same time, a provision on free speech limits the applicability of free speech guarantees in cases where such speech would "arouse nationalistic or *doctrinal* hatred or do anything that may be an incitement to any form of racial discrimination."[29] In its linkage of religion to race and other categories of identity, the Cairo Declaration is a precursor to the more recent connections made among religion, race, and ethnicity in the "combating defamation of religions" resolutions that have been introduced by the Muslim member states of the Organization of the Islamic Conference (OIC) at the United Nations in recent years. As we shall see, the conflation of religion, race, and ethnicity in those resolutions suggests a potentially narrower ambit of religious freedom than the earlier Universal Islamic Declaration. But it is equally important to recognize that the Cairo Declaration does affirm the fundamental nature of religious rights, even as it hints at the grounds for their restriction.

The New Alphabet of Religious Freedom

POINTS OF TENSION AND A CHALLENGE FOR UNIVERSALITY

The various international human rights instruments set forth in the previous section highlight and address a number of the hottest legal issues surrounding religion that have confronted national and international tribunals over the past half century: How to protect religious minorities within a majoritarian religious culture. How to place limits on religious and antireligious and cultural discrimination or on religious and antireligious exercises and expressions that cause offense or harm to others. How to adjudicate challenges that a state's proscriptions or prescriptions run directly counter to a party's core claims of conscience or cardinal commandments of the faith. How to negotiate the complex needs and norms of religious groups without according groups too much sovereignty over their members or individuals too little relief from secular courts. How to adjudicate intrareligious or interreligious disputes How to determine the proper levels of state cooperation with and support of religious officials and institutions in the delivery of vital social services. These have been the perennial issues that have long taxed the international human rights apparatus, as well as the courts and legislatures of many nation-states.

More recently, international attention and international law has come to focus on three particularly controversial issues: (1) proselytism (or evangelization in Christian terms), (2) conversion (especially when conceived as apostasy), and (3) blasphemy (recently reconceived as "defamation of religion"). Each of these three issues deserves further adumbration, as they are among the most hotly contested religious freedom issues today and arise particularly when religious traditions and religious believers confront each other in the current global resurgence of religion.

PROSELYTISM, OR EVANGELIZATION

Proselytism is a feature and result of the democratic revolution of the modern world. New religious freedom has brought many new religious conflicts to tender new democracies. In addressing instances of proselytism, states must balance one community's right to exercise and expand its faith versus another person's or community's right to be left alone to its own traditions. The state must protect the juxtaposed rights claims of majority and minority religions and of foreign and indigenous religions. And in the end, the state must craft a general rule to govern multiple theological understandings of conversion—the contemplated result of successful proselytism.

On the issue of proselytism and its regulation, the international human rights instruments provide ample direction. The ICCPR protects a person's freedom to "manifest" religion or belief through "teaching" but prohibits outright any "coercion" that would impair another's right "to have or adopt a religion or belief." At the same time, it allows legal restrictions that are necessary for "respect of the rights and reputation of others; for the protection of national security or of public order (ordre public) or of public health or morals" and guarantees to religious minorities "the right to enjoy their own culture" and "to profess and practise their own religion."[30] The ICCPR thus protects the general right to proselytize for the sake of peaceably seeking the conversion of another. It provides no protection for coercive proselytism, at a minimum barring physical or material manipulation of the would-be convert and in some contexts even subtler forms of deception, enticement, and inducement. It also casts serious suspicion on any proselytism among children or among adherents to minority religions. But, outside of these contexts, the religious expression inherent in proselytism is no more suspect than political, economic, artistic, or other forms of expression and should have at minimum the same rights.

The problem of proselytism and retaliation has gotten worse rather than better in many regions in the world in the last decade. The clashes between foreign and local faiths, particularly between and among Christian and Islamic groups and subgroups, has also spread to other regions of the world that have been newly opened to foreign mission by democratization, warfare, terrorism, or force majeure. The problem of proselytism has taken a further ironic turn in the past decade with the establishment of aggressive new state policies of laicization and secularization in Europe and the growing antisect movement in both Western Europe and the United States. This has given the modern proselytism issue a strong new pluralistic dimension: how to protect the rights of religious minorities even while maintaining the peace, order, and integrity of the modern nation-state and national society. The expulsion of Korean Christian missionary groups in Afghanistan in 2006 and charges by Muslims that Christians were dispensing religion along with humanitarian aid in tsunami-stricken Indonesia in 2005 are recent examples of the kinds of concern that proselytism and allegations of it can arouse in some of the most vulnerable, conflict-ridden, and disaster-torn areas of the world.

CONVERSION AND APOSTASY

Just as one person or group's proselytism may interfere with another person or group's liberty of conscience, one person's freedom to convert from one faith to another may amount to apostasy in the eyes of the faith left behind. Today, the issue of religious conversion has become more divisive than ever, in legal, theological, and diplomatic circles alike. Most Western Christians have easy conversion into and out of the faith. Most Jews have difficult conversion into and out of the faith. Most Muslims have easy conversion into the faith but allow for no conversion out of it, at least for prominent members. Orthodox, Hindu, Jewish, and indigenous groups around the world tie religious identity not to liberty of conscience and voluntary choice, but to birth and caste, blood and soil, language and ethnicity. This conflation of religion with race, ethnicity, nationality, and other markers of identity generally taken to be given rather than chosen, while common to these religions and cultures, has, as we shall see, become problematic in recent debates over defamation of religions.

On the issue of religious conversion, the major international human rights instruments largely accept the insistence on religious voluntarism common among Western Christian and other proselytizing groups. The 1948 Universal Declaration included an unequivocal guarantee, despite the objections of some Muslim delegations and organizations, that religious freedom includes a person's "right to change his religion or belief."[31] Subsequent international instruments largely repeated this language. But by the time of the 1981 Declaration on Religion and Belief, the dispute over the right to conversion had become more prominent. The controversy over conversion has continued, to this day, to prompt many state delegations to dissent from any move toward creating a binding covenant on the topic of religious rights and freedoms.

Christians and Muslims share in common a predilection for proselytism but differ profoundly on the propriety of conversion. The question of conversion forces Christians to confront their own often violent histories of inquisition and heresy, in which banishment or execution were viewed as the only way to deal with heretics and in which Jews, Muslims, and other non-Christians were at best tolerated in Christian society. While Muslims historically treated Jews, Christians, and Zoroastrians as fellow people of the book (the *dhimmi*) who could enjoy a modicum of rights and autonomy, this tolerance has given way in some Muslim communities today to growing hostility.[32] Moreover, charges of heresy or its stronger form, apostasy, have been increasing in recent years in the Muslim world against those who seek to convert from the Muslim faith or resist conversion into it. This new trend has elicited the concern and condemnation of many state governments and human rights organizations, particularly in cases where the charges of heresy and apostasy are made against people who were born, married, or coerced into the faith and who later, upon opportunity for mature reflection, choose to leave. Such charges seem to conflict directly both with human rights ideals of religious liberty and the Qur'anic injunction that "there can be no coercion in matters of faith."[33] Nevertheless, the question of conversion persists in the war for souls taking place in many regions of the world today.

BLASPHEMY AND "DEFAMATION OF RELIGIONS"

In an era in which the publication of a cartoon in Denmark depicting the prophet Muhammad as a terrorist can incite religious riots around the world, charges of blasphemy, seemingly as premodern as charges of heresy or apostasy, are making their way back into the headlines. Concerns about blasphemy are vividly illustrated in the Kambakhsh case in Afghanistan. They are also reflected in antiblasphemy provisions that continue to remain on or have only recently been repealed from the criminal law of a number of Western European nations.[34] Many Western European countries that outlaw denial of the Holocaust and "hate speech" also have in their midst thriving neo-Nazi and right-wing nationalist groups whose ideologies draw on religion, particularly Christianity, to entice and incite their constituencies.[35] What blasphemy is—critique of an established church, Holocaust denial, remarks that are anti-Semitic, anti-Christian, Islamophobic, or offensive to other religious, ethnic, and cultural groups—and whether it should be prosecuted remain open questions in many parts of the world.

Over the last decade, the issue of blasphemy has surfaced at the United Nations and other international bodies under the rubric of "defamation of religions." Beginning in 1999, when they were first proposed at the United Nations, and picking up steam after the terrorist attacks of September 11, 2001, resolutions for "Combating Defamation of Religions" have been generating increasing controversy.[36] These resolutions have been proposed at both the United Nations Commission on Human Rights (renamed the Human Rights Council in 2006), where they have been approved each year since 1999,[37] and at the larger General Assembly, where they have been approved since 2005.[38] The Human Rights Council's decision in March 2011 not to take up the most recent proposed resolution may, however, signal an end or an evolution of the "deffamation of religions" concept. Early drafts of the resolutions were controversial for singling out Islam and Muslims for particular protection.[39] Subsequent versions were broadened to include respect for "cultural, ethnic, religious, and linguistic diversity" and for "people belonging to different cultures, religions, and beliefs."[40] Despite this more religiously plural formulation, the United States, several European nations, and religious freedom organizations have continued to object to the defamation of religions resolutions as a violation of freedoms of religion and speech. The resolutions, while not having the force of law, demand respect for Islam but contain language that could be used to justify persecution of religious minorities, particularly in Muslim countries. Indeed, the resolutions have already been invoked to justify harsh blasphemy laws in Pakistan, Egypt, Sudan, and Afghanistan.

In recent years, the defamation of religions resolutions have been drawing on not only international laws governing religious freedom but also international resolutions against racism. The result has been a particularly provocative mixture of religion, ethnicity, and race that, rather than advancing growing moderation and pluralism in the movement against defamation of religions, has, arguably, had the effect of exacerbating the controversy further. These race and ethnicity arguments hark back to the 1965 International Convention on the Elimination of All Forms of Racial Discrimination.[41] The convention was largely directed at discrimination based on "race, colour, descent, or national or ethnic origin."[42] But the preamble also contemplated religious groups as beneficiaries of its nondiscrimination provisions in affirming "human rights and fundamental freedoms for all, without distinction as to race, sex, language, or *religion*" and in including "freedom of thought, conscience, and religion" in its list of fundamental freedoms.[43] As we have seen, the 1992 Declaration on the Rights of Minorities, coming just before two of the bloodiest recent conflations of religion and ethnicity in Bosnia and Rwanda, made similar connections between religion and other markers of group identity and minority status.

The connections between religion, race, and ethnicity were made even more explicit in the Durban Declaration and Programme of Action that emerged from the World Conference against Racism, Racial Discrimination, Xenophobia and Related Intolerance, held in Durban, South Africa, in 2001.[44] The Durban Conference adjourned just three days before the cataclysmic events of September 11, 2001, and only after considerable rancor over the extent to which the Israel-Palestine conflict dominated conference proceedings and news headlines. At Durban, issues of "race, colour, descent, or national or ethnic origin" were combined with issues of "sex, language, *religion*, political or other opinion, social origin, property, birth or other status" in fiery denunciations of "racism, racial discrimination, xenophobia and related tolerance."[45] The U.S. and Israeli delegations pulled out of the conference midway because of draft platform language linking Zionism to racism, and the European Union refused to accede to demands by Arab nations that Israel be criticized for practices that they deemed racist. The United States also boycotted the Durban Conference's sponsoring organization, the United Nations Commission on Human Rights, as a "sham" for the remainder of the Bush administration. The introduction of defamation of religions resolutions at the United Nations, particularly since 2001, has carried echoes of the Durban discord.

More recent versions of the defamation of religions resolutions approved by the U.N. General Assembly in December 2008 and December 2009—the resolutions before and after the eight-year review of the 2001 Durban Confernce—might be presumed to be the most moderate after having been the subject of criticism and modification for nearly a decade, Such a presumption would, however, be a mistake. The December 2008 resolution began by reaffirming "universal respect for and observance of all human rights and fundamental freedoms without distinction as to *race,* sex, language, or *religion.*"[46] The resolution affirmed that human rights are "universal, indivisible, interdependent, and interrelated." Despite this initial appeal to universal harmony, the opening portions of the resolution are sprinkled with numerous references to racism, xenophobia, and the controversial proceedings and program of the 2001 Durban Conference. The resolution concluded by speculating on the "possible correlation" between defamation of religions and "the upsurge in incitement, intolerance and hatred in many parts of the world." This correlation, borne out empirically by such incidents as the Danish cartoon controversy, carried the ominous implication that, if the resolution were not to pass, further violence would ensue.

Just three months after the approval of the December 2008 "defamation of religions" resolution at the General Assembly, a new resolution was approved by the Human Rights Council in March 2009.[47] The March 2009 version called for combating defamation of religions in much the same manner as previous iterations but with the addition of more positive and pluralistic language. The resolution called not only for opposition to defamation of religions but also for "greater harmony and tolerance in all societies," for "respect and understanding of religious and cultural diversity throughout the world," and for recognition of the "valuable contributions of all religions to modern civilization and the contribution that dialogue among civilizations can make towards improved awareness and understanding of common values shared by all mankind." If the 2008 resolution was radical for its particular conflation of racial and religious categories, the 2009 resolution was radical for its pluralism. Even with these pluralistic additions, the March 2009 resolution in the Human Rights Council was the first such resolution to be adopted with more countries voting against or abstaining than voting in favor.[48] This narrow approval was interpreted by some as an indication that the movement against religious defamation had been largely repudiated by the international community. It is also likely that those voting against or abstaining may also have been anticipating and seeking to ward off further controversy in April 2009 at the Durban Review Conference ("Durban II").

Even as the General Assembly and Human Rights Council were debating the 2008 and 2009 defamation of religions resolutions, preparations were being made for Durban II, which took place in Geneva in late April 2009. The OIC states lobbied, initially successfully, for the insertion of defamation of religions language into the Durban II draft platform. The United States, Israel, Canada, Australia, New Zealand, Germany, Italy, Poland, and the Netherlands withdrew their participation in the conference when Israeli-Palestinian issues again threatened to dominate, but the insertion of defamation of religions language into the draft platform became an additional reason for withdrawal. The defamation of religions language was withdrawn in the weeks prior to the conference, but it remained to be seen whether the objecting countries would reconsider their withdrawal. The United States ultimately reaffirmed its nonparticipation but also signaled a potential shift in policy with the announcement of its intent to seek a place on the Human Rights Council with a view toward improving the body's reputation through its participation.

Though Durban II began bombastically with an opening speech by Iranian President Mahmoud Ahmadinejad denying the Holocaust and denouncing the state of Israel, it ended with an outcome document that, even while controversially affirming the Durban I platform, also omitted the defamation of religions language that had made it into earlier drafts. In its provisions addressing religion, the Durban II document officially deplored the "global rise and number of incidents of racial or religious intolerance and violence, including Islamophobia, anti-Semitism, Christianophobia and anti-Arabism," as well as the "derogatory stereotyping and stigmatization of persons based on their religion or belief."[49] It reaffirmed the prohibition of "advocacy of national, racial or religious hatred that constitutes incitement to discrimination, hostility or violence."[50] It further condemned "acts of incitement to hatred, which have targeted and severely affected racial and religious communities and persons belonging to racial and religious minorities, whether involving the use of print, audio-visual or electronic media or any other means" and called on the international community to "fully and effectively prohibit any advocacy of national, racial, or religious hatred that constitutes incitement to discrimination, hostility or violence."[51] Throughout the document, religion was more frequently analogized to more fluid and interpretive communities based on language and culture than to the more fixed and embodied categories of race, ethnicity, and nationality based on blood and land.[52] Overall, the Durban II outcome document sought to protect persons over religions and to prohibit objectively verifiable acts of incitement over the subjectively felt assaults of defamation in a way that is more congruent with extant and emerging international norms. The Durban II document–for all the fraught negotiations over the defamation of religions resolutions that preceded it—did finally signal what would seem to be an overall movement away from the defamation of religions concept.

In December 2010, another defamation of religions resolution was approved by the U.N. General Assembly by the narrowest margins ever.[53] In March 2011, the Human Rights Council decided not to take up the defamation of religions issue. In July 2011, the U.N. Human Rights Committee, the U.N. body charged with oversight and ongoing interpretation of the ICCPR possessing both a broader mandate and a less controversial history than the Human Rights Council, issued General Comment No. 34 "Article 19: Freedoms of opinion and expression," taking note of the connection between defamation of religions and blasphemy laws. Therein, the Committee maintained, "Prohibitions of displays of lack of respect for a religion or other belief system, including blasphemy laws, are incompatible with the Covenant... Thus, for instance, it would be impermissible for any such laws to discriminate in favor of or against one or certain religions or belief systems, or their adherents over another, or religious believers over nonbelievers. Nor would it be permissible for such prohibitions to be used to prevent or punish criticism of religious leaders or commentary on religious doctrine and tenets of faith."[54] Thus, for now, the connection between freedom of religion and freedom of expression has put a halt to the incursion of defamation of religions and blasphemy concepts in international human rights pertaining to religion.

Religion, Democracy, and the *Ius Gentium* of Human Rights

The "defamation of religions" resolutions may seem to be a trend that has peaked or the narrow province of the OIC states. At the same time, defamation of religions and hate speech issues continue to roil certain countries and regions—most notably in Africa, where postcolonial, multiethnic states have drawn the attention of Christian and Muslim missionaries and have been prone to genocidal conflicts, and in Western Europe, where democratic, largely secular, and putatively liberal and tolerant societies have increasingly had to confront the status of religious minorities in their midst. In those contexts, allegations of defamation of religion and incitement of hatred may be less a cause than a symptom of deeper conflicts and controversies at the intersection of religion, race, sex, ethnicity, nationality, language, culture, and other markers of individual and group status.[55]

A truly democratic approach to religion and international human rights may require both normative distinctions and practical disentanglement. Rather than reducing religious rights to other civil and political rights, on the one hand, or analogizing religion to other aspects of individual and group identity, on the other, proponents of religious freedom may want to insist on the distinctness of religious rights as something more than the amalgamation of rights to speech, press, and association or just another identity category that can be conflated with race, ethnicity, and other criteria. Religious rights have been construed largely individualistically and voluntaristically in the world's secular, liberal democracies. A more robust notion of religious rights may better capture their communal and identity-based dimensions—often experienced as given, not chosen—in ways that protect the true core of religion.[56] That said, the most difficult conflicts in years to come will be between individuals and societies for whom religion is a matter of choice in where one worships on the weekend and those for whom it is a matter of submission affecting all facets of life, both communally and comprehensively.

Religion may also need to be separated, as much as possible, from issues of race, ethnicity, and other givens of individual and group identity. These categories of identity may be better addressed individually. The ratcheting up of religious claims through connection to the more fundamental, unassailable, organic, blood-and-soil categories of race and ethnicity serves to insulate religion from valid and civil forms of external and internal critique but at the risk of inciting even more virulent and violent forms of conflict. In such contexts, religion itself is diminished, becoming a pretext for and instrument of conflict, rather than a repository of wisdom and reconciliation, much less a defender of truth and justice. Again, a better understanding of religion, its power and its peril, might eliminate the need to bootstrap religion to greater prominence by connecting it to race, ethnicity, and other categories. In certain cases and conflicts, the correlations between religion and race or ethnicity are too strong to be ignored. But connecting religion to race risks ontologizing it and naturalizing it in a way that eclipses or elides the nonfoundational and hermeneutical understandings of religion that are more conducive to the intrareligious and interreligious dialogues and discourses that are necessary to realize a common law, *ius gentium* culture of international human rights that includes religious freedom.

The defamation of religions movement, from the local level of the Kambakhsh case to the international wrangling at the United Nations and Durban II, may be seen as a particularly pointed challenge to the universality of human rights, especially those pertaining to religion. It is illustrative of some important tensions that exist when law and religion play out in international affairs, particularly when it comes to the universality of human rights. The defamation debate has served both to illustrate and to reaffirm some principles that do seem to be part of the *ius gentium* of international religious freedom. First, international religious freedom provisions protect persons, and by extension groups of persons, not ideas, ideologies, or even religions per se. Religious freedom must be realized in the open and mutually self-critical dialogue of religious believers and religious bodies, not caricatured in insulation from the critique and encounter of the religious other. Clashes of believers and bodies may be adjudicated through criminal laws against incitement of violence, but they should not be construed as or allowed to devolve into clashes of civilizations.[57] Second, the justification and framework of international human rights are strongly biased toward the protection of minorities. Where defamation of religions arguments are used to defend majority traditions and established religions, they are inherently suspect. When asserted to protect ideas and beliefs, rather than the people and communities who hold them, and particularly when asserted to protect religious majorities from religious minorities without or from dissenters within, defamation of religion arguments are objectionable and antidemocratic.

The universality of human rights has held up "as long as no one asks why," in Maritain's famous phrase. The various covenants and conventions of international human rights law, as concerns religion, while not always unanimous in their acclamation or uniform in their application, have generally been taken to be universal in their aspiration. What happens when increased globalization, communication, and internationalism in the legal sphere brings to light uncomfortable differences of opinion, orientation, and ontology in the religious sphere? Most religions have a stake in asserting the truth of their own beliefs against the apparent falsehood of the beliefs of others. At the level of normative interreligious engagement, refraining from asking the "why" questions may be difficult if not disingenuous, if one purports to want to truly understand and respect religious beliefs and religious diversity. How to have these conversations in a way that is both critical and constructive amid descriptive and doctrinal pluralism remains a crucial challenge for the international sphere.

Notes

1. "Afghanistan: Journalist Given Death Sentence for 'Blasphemy,'" Radio Free Europe, January 23, 2008; Abdul Waheed Wafa and Carlotta Gall, "Death Sentence for Afghan Student," *New York Times*, January 24, 2008; Nora Boustany, "Afghan Reporter's Death Sentence Draws Wide Condemnation," *Washington Post*, January 25, 2008; "Afghan Senate Backs Death Penalty," *BBC News*, January 30, 2008.

2. "EU Parliament President Calls for Life of Afghan Student to Be Spared," theparliament.com, January 21, 2008; see www.eupolitix.com/EN/News/200801/def9afd4-1ad8-4763-acd4-75b5b316c6e4.htm.

3. Jean MacKenzie, "Saving Parwez Kambakhsh," RAWA News, June 16, 2008; www.rawa.org/temp/runews/2008/06/16/saving-parwez-kambakhsh.html.

4. "No Death Sentence for Afghan Journalist," *New York Times*, October 21, 2008.

5. Carlotta Gall and Sangar Rahimi, "Karzai Vows to Review Family Law," *New York Times*, April 4, 2009.

6. See analysis in Natan Lerner, *Religion, Secular Beliefs, and Human Rights: 25 Years after the Declaration* (Leiden: Martinus Nijhoff, 2006), with sample documents collected in Ian Brownlie and Guy Goodwin-Gill, eds., *Basic Documents on Human Rights*, 5th ed. (Oxford: Oxford University Press, 2006); Tad Stahnke and J. Paul Martin, eds., *Religion and Human Rights: Basic Documents* (New York: Center for the Study of Human Rights, Columbia University, 1998); and Tore Lindholm et al., *Facilitating Freedom of Religion or Belief: A Deskbook* (Leiden: Martinus Nijhoff, 2004).

7. G.A. Res. 217A, at 71, U.N. GAOR, 3d Sess, 1st plen. mtg., U.N. Doc A/810 (December 12, 1948). [hereinafter "1948 Universal Declaration"]

8. See esp. the account of this ecumenism contained in John Nurser, *For All Peoples and All Nations: Christian Churches and Human Rights* (Washington, DC: Georgetown University Press, 2005).

9. Anthony Gill, *The Political Origins of Religious Liberty* (New York: Cambridge University Press, 2007).

10. Mary Ann Glendon, *A World Made New* (New York: Random House, 2001), 154, 168, 222.

11. Ibid., 168.

12. Ibid., 77 (emphasis added).

13. Ibid., 77–78.

14. See Abdullahi A. An-Na'im, "Toward an Islamic Hermeneutic of Human Rights," in *Human Rights and Religious Values: An Uneasy Relationship?* ed. Abdullahi A. An-Na'im et al., (Grand Rapids, MI: Eerdmans, 1995); Robert A. Schapiro, "The Consequences of Human Rights Fundamentalism," 54 *Emory Law Journal* (2005): 171–185; John Kelsay and Sumner B. Twiss, "Universality vs. Relativism in Human Rights," in *Religion and Human Rights*, ed. John Kelsay and Sumner B. Twiss (New York: Project on Religion and Human Rights, 1994).

15. Jürgen Habermas, *Religion and Rationality* (Cambridge, MA: MIT Press, 2002), 153.

16. Michael J. Perry, *Toward a Theory of Human Rights* (New York: Cambridge University Press, 2007), 4.

17. G.A. Res. 2200A (XXI), 21 U.N. GAOR Supp (No. 16) at 52, U.N. Doc. A/6316, 999 U.N.T.S. (December 16, 1966). [hereinafter "ICCPR"]

18. G.A. Res. 36/55, U.N. GAOR Supp. (no. 151), U.N. Doc. A/RES/36/55 (November 25, 1981). [hereinafter "1981 Declaration on Religion and Belief"]

19. 28 I.L.M. 527. [hereinafter "1989 Vienna Concluding Document"]

20. G.A. Res. 47/135, Annex, U.N. Doc. A/Res/47/135/Annex, December 18, 1992. [hereinafter "1992 Minorities Declaration"]

21. ICCPR provisions cited in this paragraph include Arts. 18, 20.2, 21, 26, and 27. It should be noted that the ICCPR has been ratified by 162 of the 192 countries that are members of the United Nations, including almost all of the Muslim states who are members of the Organization of the Islamic Conference (OIC).

22. 1981 Declaration on Religion and Belief, Arts. 1 and 6.

23. All references in this paragraph are to 1989 Vienna Concluding Document, Principle 16.

24. 1992 Minorities Declaration, Preamble.

25. Universal Islamic Declaration of Human Rights (London: Islamic Council, 1981), foreword quoting Qur'an, Sura 49:13. See www.alhewar.com/ISLAMDECL.html.

26. Ibid., Arts. 13, 12, 14, 10

27. Cairo Declaration on Human Rights in Islam, August 5, 1990, U.N. GAOR, World Conf. on Hum. Rts., 4th Sess., Agenda Item 5, U.N. Doc. A/CONF.157/PC/62/Add.18 (1993) [English translation], Art. 1 (emphasis added).

28. Ibid., Art. 22 (emphasis added).

29. Ibid., Art. 18 (emphasis added).

30. Art. 18, 19, and 27 are quoted in this paragraph.

31. 1948 Universal Declaration, Art. 18.

32. Donna E. Arzt, "*Jihad* for Hearts and Minds: Proselytizing in the Qur'an and the First Three Centuries of Islam," and Richard C. Martin, "Conversion to Islam by Invitation: Proselytism and the Negotiation of Identity in Islam," in *Sharing the Book: Religious Perspectives on the Rights and Wrongs of Proselytism*, ed. John Witte Jr. and Richard C. Martin (Eugene, OR: Wipf & Stock, 2008), 89–91, 110.

33. Qur'an, Surah 2:256.

34. See Jeroen Temperman, "Blasphemy, Defamation of Religions and Human Rights Law," *Netherlands Quarterly of Human Rights* 26:4 (2008), 519–522, for a summary of blasphemy laws in the United Kingdom, Ireland, Greece, and the Scandinavian countries.

35. Recent United States State Department International Religious Freedom reports catalogue many such incidents and movements in European countries under the category of "societal abuses and discrimination."

36. For a critique of these resolutions, see Becket Fund for Religious Liberty, "Combating Defamation of Religions." Issues Brief Submitted to the UN Office of the High Commissioner of Human Rights (Washington, DC: Becket Fund for Religious Liberty, June 2, 2008). See www.becketfund.org/files/a9e5b.pdf.

37. See UNCHR Res 1999/82, "Defamation of religions," adopted April 30, 1999, without a vote; UNCHR Res 2000/84, "Defamation of religions," adopted April 26, 2000, without a vote; UNCHR Res 2001/4, "Combating defamation of religions as a means to promote human rights, social harmony and religious and cultural diversity," adopted April 18, 2001 by roll-call vote, 28 to 15, with 9 abstentions; UNCHR Res 2002/9, "Combating defamation of religion," adopted April 15, 2002, by a recorded vote, 30 to 15, with 8 abstentions; UNCHR Res 2003/4, "Combating defamation of religions," adopted April 14, 2003, by a recorded vote, 32 to 14, with 7 abstentions; UNCHR Res 2004/6, "Combating defamation of religions," adopted April 13, 2004, by a recorded vote, 29 to 16, with 7 abstentions; UNCHR Res 2005/3, "Combating defamation of religions," April 12, 2005, adopted by a recorded vote of 31 to 16, with 5 abstentions; UNHRC Res 4/9, "Combating defamation of religions," adopted March 31, 2007, by a recorded vote of 24 to 14, with 9 abstentions, adopted by a recorded vote of 21 to 10, with 14 abstentions; UNHRC Res 7/19, "Combating defamation of religions," adopted March 27, 2008; UNHRC Res 10/22, "Combating defamation of religions," adopted March 26, 2009, with a recorded vote of 23 to 11, with 13 abstentions; UNHRC Res 3/16, "Combatting defamation of religions," adopted by a recorded vote of 20 to 17, with 8 abstentions. Significant here is the progression from adoption without a vote, to roll-call votes, and then recorded votes. Also significant is the steadily decreasing number of votes in favor and the increasing number of negative votes and abstentions.

38. UN GA 60th Sess, Res 60/150, "Combating defamation of religions," U.N. Doc A/Res/60/150, adopted December 16, 2005; UN GA 61st Sess., Res 61/164, "Combating defamation of religions," U.N. Doc. A/Res/61/164, adopted December 19, 2006; UN GA 62 Sess, Res 62/154, "Combating defamation of religions,' U.N. Doc. A/Res/62/154, adopted December 18, 2007; UN GA, 63rd Sess, Res 63/171, "Combating defamation of religions," adopted December 18, 2008; UN GA, 64th Sess, Res 64/156, "Combatting defamation of religions," adopted December 18, 2009; UN GA, 65th Sess, Res 65/224 "Combatting defamation of religions," adopted December 21, 2010.

39. See UN GA 60th Sess, Agenda Item 71(b), "Yemen Draft Resolution: Combating defamation of religions," U.N. Doc. A/C.3/60/l.29, October 31, 2005.

40. UN GA Res 62/154.

41. Specifically, the International Convention on the Elimination of All Forms of Racial Discrimination G.A. res. 2106 (XX), Annex, 20 U.N. GAOR Supp. (No. 14) at 47, UN Doc. A/6014 (1966), 660 U.N.T.S. 195, *entered into force* January 4, 1969.

42. Ibid., Art. 1.

43. Ibid., Preamble and Art. 5(vii).

44. See Durban Declaration and Programme of Action adopted by the World Conference against Racism, Racial Discrimination, Xenophobia and Related Intolerance, held in

Durban, South Africa, from August 31 through September 8, 2001. See www.unhchr.ch/pdf/ Durban.pdf.

45. Ibid., Preamble.

46. UN GA Res 63/171, "Combating defamation of religions," approved December 18, 2008 (emphases added).

47. UN HRC Res 10/22 "Combating defamation of religions," adopted March 26, 2009.

48. The vote proceeded along the usual lines—with supporting votes coming largely from OIC members and opposition coming mostly from Canada and various European nations represented on the council. Those *voting in favor* included Angola, Azerbaijan, Bahrain, Bangladesh, Bolivia, Cameroon, China, Cuba, Djibouti, Egypt, Gabon, Indonesia, Jordan, Malaysia, Nicaragua, Nigeria, Pakistan, Philippines, Qatar, Russian Federation, Saudi Arabia, Senegal, and South Africa. Those *voting against* included Canada, Chile, France, Germany, Italy, Netherlands, Slovakia, Slovenia, Switzerland, Ukraine, and United Kingdom of Great Britain and Northern Ireland. Those *abstaining* included Argentina, Brazil, Bosnia and Herzegovina, Burkina Faso, Ghana, India, Japan, Madagascar, Mauritius, Mexico, Republic of Korea, Uruguay, and Zambia.

49. Office of the United Nations High Commissioner for Human Rights, "Outcome Document of the Durban Review Conference," Art. 12. See www.un.org/durbanreview2009/ pdf/Durban_Review_outcome_document_En.pdf.

50. Ibid., Art. 13.

51. Ibid., Arts. 68, 69.

52. Ibid., Arts. 14, 70, 82, 99, 102, 106, 109, 110, and 127.

53. UN GA Res 65/224 "Combatting defamation of religions," approved December 21, 2010.

54. UN Human Rights Committee, "General Comment No. 34: Article 19: Freedoms of opinion and expressionm," July 21, 2011, par. 48.

55. For a discussion of how recent Shari'a-based allegations of blasphemy, defamation, and apostasy by Muslims are "embedded within a larger discourse on identity, community, and difference," see Anver M. Emon, "On the Pope, Cartoons, and Apostates: Shari'a 2006," *Journal of Law and Religion* 22 (2007), 303–321.

56. There is an ongoing discussion in legal and jurisprudential circles concerning whether religious rights are "special" or "distinctive." See, e.g., Steven G. Gey, "Why Is Religion Special? Reconsidering the Accommodation of Religion under the Religion Clauses of the First Amendment," *University of Pittsburgh Law Review* 52:75 (1990–1991); Christopher L. Eisgruber and Lawrence G. Sager, "The Vulnerability of Conscience: The Constitutional Basis for Protecting Religious Conduct," *University of Chicago Law Review* 61:1245 (1994); Douglas Laycock, "Religious Liberty as Liberty," *Journal of Contemporary Legal Issues* 7 (1996); Michael W. McConnell, "The Problem of Singling Out Religion," *DePaul Law Review* 50:1 (2000–2001); Ira C. Lupu and Robert Tuttle, "The Distinctive Place of Religious Entities in Our Constitutional Order," *Villanova Law Review* 47:37 (2002); Andrew Koppelman, "Is It Fair to Give Religion Special Treatment," *University of Illinois Law Review* 571 (2006).

57. For a detailed critique of laws prohibiting incitement to religious hatred in the European human rights system, see Susannah C. Vance, "The Permissibility of Incitement to Religious Hatred Offenses under European Convention Principles," *Transnational Law and Contemporary Problems* 14 (2004–2005), 201–251.

Annotated Bibliography

An-Na'im, Abdullahi A., et al., eds., *Human Rights and Religious Values: An Uneasy Relationship?* Grand Rapids, MI: Eerdmans, 1995.

This collection of essays examines the relationship between religion and human rights, including juridical and religious perspectives from Hinduism, Buddhism, Judaism, Christianity, and Islam. It argues that human rights can be justified and supported within these various religious traditions and the "common morality" to which they give rise.

Bucar, Elizabeth A., and Barbara Barnett, eds., *Does Human Rights Need God?* Grand Rapids, MI: Eerdmans, 2005.

Philosopher Jacques Maritain, consulting with a UNECSO committee on the development of the Universal Declaration of Human Rights, famously observed that participants from various religious and philosophical traditions could agree on universal human rights, provided that they did not ask why. This collection of essays addresses the "why" of human rights in chapters covering religious and philosophical perspectives (Christian, Jewish, Islamic, and Confucian), secular responses, and regional perspectives from Palestine, the Czech Republic, South Africa, and the United States.

Gill, Anthony, *The Political Origins of Religious Liberty*. New York: Cambridge University Press, 2007.

This historical study examines the political underpinnings of religious liberty, arguing that religious regulation, in the hands of various political interests, is an instrument of secularization. The book challenges views of religious liberty as sui generis and universal and thus insulated from politics

Glendon, Mary Ann, *A World Made New*. New York: Random House, 2001.

This book, by a leading international human rights scholar, provides a highly detailed and engaging history of the development of the Universal Declaration of Human Rights at the United Nations in 1947 and 1948. In particular, it accounts for the key role played by Eleanor Roosevelt in ensuring that the declaration produced substantial agreement, if not always outright consensus, across various religious and political lines.

Kelsay, John, and Sumner B. Twiss, eds., *Religion and Human Rights*. New York: Project on Religion and Human Rights, 1994.

This book, edited by two leading religious ethicists, provides a comparative religious perspective on human rights across the world's religions. It accounts for why various religions accept some, but not all, human rights, and it pays particular attention to the role of religious fundamentalism; the religious oppression of women; case studies in the Middle East, North America, and China; and the positive role that religion can play in human rights and conflict resolution.

Lerner, Natan, *Group Rights and Discrimination in International Law*. Leiden: Brill Academic, 2001.

The question of whether groups based on religion, race, ethnicity, and other criteria deserve special rights has been an ongoing challenge in international law grounded in a political liberalism that tends to focus on relationships between the individual and the state. This book examines the problem, with particular focus on religious and racial intolerance.

Lerner, Natan, *Religion, Secular Beliefs, and Human Rights: 25 Years after the Declaration*. Leiden: Martinus Nijhoff, 2006.

This book examines the legal meaning of religion and belief as reflected in the body of international law on religious freedom that has developed since the Universal Declaration of

Human Rights. Topics include the work at the United Nations on religious freedom, the status of religious minorities, proselytism, religion and terrorism, use and abuse of religious symbols, international criminal law, and particular issues related to the relationship between the state and religious communities in Israel and between Israel and the Holy See.

Nurser, John, *For All Peoples and All Nations: Christian Churches and Human Rights*. Washington, DC: Georgetown University Press, 2005.

Largely through a biographical presentation of the work of leading World Council of Churches figure O. Frederick Nolde, Nurser describes the considerable efforts of the Christian ecumenical community in drafting the Universal Declaration of Human Rights. It is a highly detailed case study of the role that religion did and can play in supporting human rights.

Perry, Michael J., *Toward a Theory of Human Rights*. New York: Cambridge University Press, 2007.

Written by a leading jurisprudential philosopher and constitutional and human rights scholar, this book considers various religious and nonreligious grounds for a morality of human rights. From this highly normative framework, it examines the application of human rights morality to the issues of abortion, capital punishment, and same-sex relationships—each one an international as well as a domestic flashpoint in human rights discourse.

John Witte, Jr. and Frank S. Alexander, eds., *Christianity and Human Rights: An Introduction*. New York: Cambridge University Press, 2011.

With contributions from leading scholars, including a foreword by Archbishop Desmond Tutu, this book provides an authoritative treatment of how Christianity shaped human rights in the past, and how Christianity and human rights continue to challenge each other in modern times.

John Witte, Jr. and M. Christian Green, eds., *Religion and Human Rights: An Introduction*. New York: Oxford University Press, 2011.

With contributions by a score of leading experts, this book provides authoritative and accessible assessments of the contributions of Judaism, Christianity, Islam, Hinduism, Confucianism, Buddhism, and Indigenous religions to the development of the ideas and institutions of human rights. It also probes the major human rights issues that confront religious individuals and communities around the world today, and the main challenges that the world's religions will pose to the human rights regime in the future.

Witte, John, Jr., and Richard C. Martin, eds., *Sharing the Book: Religious Perspectives on the Rights and Wrongs of Proselytism*. Eugene, OR: Wipf & Stock, 2008.

This book takes up, in robust form, the issue of religious proselytism, which, along with blasphemy and apostasy, remains a crucial issue for international religious human rights in the twenty-first century. Essays compare and contrast views of proselytism in Judaism, Christianity, and Islam.

PART III

Religion, Conflict, and Peacemaking

8 }

Religion, Terrorism, and Civil Wars
Monica Duffy Toft

Religion and Organized Violence

Religion is not dead, nor is it dying. In fact, religion has experienced a resurgence, and with that resurgence has come an increase in violence, war, and terrorism. Al Qaeda premised its attacks of September 11, 2001, on religious principles; further, civil wars raged between Buddhists and Hindus in Sri Lanka, between Hindus and Muslims in India, and among Muslims in Iraq and Christian and Muslims in Nigeria.

Since the end of the Cold War, the subject of religion and organized violence has been increasingly prominent in international politics.[1] Religion, however, has always played a role in violent contests, ranging from individual duels to mass conflicts between empires or states. But what is that role? And what general principles and policies may we derive from a greater understanding of the link between civil war, terrorism, and religious belief, practice, and identity?

Before proceeding, it must be said that religion is not dangerous; violence is the exception when it comes to faith traditions. History no doubt demonstrates that religion is capable of serving as the source of large-scale and organized violence, as do the religious civil wars and terrorist groups of today. Nonetheless, religion is ambivalent;[2] it has also mobilized millions of people to oppose authoritarian regimes, inaugurate democratic transitions, support human rights, and relieve human suffering. In the twentieth century, religious movements helped end colonial rule and usher in democracy in Latin America, Eastern Europe, sub-Saharan Africa, and Asia. The post–Vatican II Catholic Church played a crucial role by opposing authoritarian regimes and legitimating the democratic aspirations of the masses. Such examples of the positive effects of faith confirm that religion is not, in itself, harmful. Still, religion can, under the right circumstances, serve as a ready alternative to other forms of identification, a source of political power, and a key to authority among a community of believers. At times, the ambivalence of religion allows political actors to utilize it as a legitimizing force when carrying out campaigns of aggression.

This article has four main sections. I begin by discussing five anecdotes that highlight the role of religion in two types of large-scale violence: civil wars and terrorism. I then introduce key concepts, followed by important empirical facts about religious civil wars from 1940 to 2010. Finally, I examine religiously inspired terrorism. Regarding both civil wars and terrorism, I note that religiously inspired violence is, by and large, more deadly than violence justified by other means. In addition, I show that Muslim communities have come to play a disproportionate role in violence: more than 80 percent of religious civil wars involve Muslims, and religiously motivated incidents of terrorism involve adherents of Islam more than any other faith.[3]

Why Now?

Why has religious violence risen to the fore at this point in history? By and large, the secularist ideologies that seemed destined to triumph have faltered. In the 1960s, secularism dominated world politics, asserting that modernization would inevitably extinguish religion's hold on private lives, as well as public politics.[4] But if 1966 was the peak of secularism's rule, the next year marked the beginning of the end of its global hegemony. In 1967, the leader of secular Arab nationalism, Gamal Abdel Nasser, suffered a humiliating defeat at the hands of the Israeli Army. By the end of the 1970s, Iran's Ayatollah Khomeini, avowedly "born-again" U.S. President Jimmy Carter, television evangelist Jerry Falwell, and Pope John Paul II had all become prominent figures on the world stage. A decade later, Catholic members of the Solidarity movement in Poland and jihad-promoting mujahideen in Afghanistan helped defeat atheistic Soviet Communism. A dozen years later, nineteen hijackers who saw their attacks as a religious mission transformed world politics.[5]

In addition, with increasing globalization and democratization, more populations are demanding a greater say in governance, including a desire to have religion play an increasingly public role. The spread of democracy has enhanced the reach of religiously based political movements, many of which have emerged from democratic processes with a good deal of legitimacy and organization that are capable of challenging existing political orders. Democracy has thus given voice to religious actors and institutions and has led to demands for greater political representation of religion in the public sphere.

The modern world has proven remarkably hospitable to a public presence of religious belief. Today, people enjoy more political freedom, more democracy, and more education than perhaps at any time in history.[6] Greater wealth, more education, and more political freedom were supposed to usher in a more secular world. They did not. In fact, the period in which economic and political modernization has been most intense—the last thirty to forty years—has witnessed a resurgence in religious practice and an intensification of religious faith around the world. The world's largest religions have expanded at a rate that exceeds global population growth.[7] According to scholars Ronald Inglehart and Pippa Norris, "The world as a whole now has more people with traditional religious views than ever before— and they constitute a growing proportion of the world's population."[8]

Religious growth has challenged secularism in no small part due to the global expansion of freedom and democracy. Thanks to the "third wave" of democratization between the mid-1970s and early 1990s, and smaller waves of freedom since, citizens in dozens of countries have become empowered to shape their public lives in ways that were inconceivable in the 1950s and 1960s. A new pattern emerged as citizens exercised these new political freedoms. Politically empowered groups began to challenge the secular constraints imposed by the first generation of modernizing, postcolonial leaders. Often, as in Communist countries, secularism and enforced atheism had been imposed by sheer coercion; in other cases, as in Atatürk's Turkey, Nehru's India, and Nasser's Egypt, secularism retained legitimacy because elites relied on it for national integration and modernization and because of the powerful charisma of these countries' founding fathers. In Latin America, right-wing dictatorships, sometimes in coordination with the Catholic Church, imposed restrictions that limited grassroots religious influences, particularly from liberation theology and Protestant "sects." But with the liberalization of politics in countries such as India, Mexico, Nigeria, Turkey, and Indonesia in the late 1990s, religion and politics became increasingly intertwined.

In Afghanistan, decades of violence pitted the Cold War blocs against one another, but the end of the Cold War allowed the rise of an extremist and isolated government that harbored terrorists bent on destroying those it viewed as enemies to its beliefs and traditions. The global war on terrorism is rooted in what was once a local fight that became international, then local, and then international again. As Afghanistan and other cases show, activist Islamic political figures, groups, and individuals have been at the source of a new eruption of "Muslim rage." In reality, their campaigns are only the most recent outbreaks of a deep undercurrent that has been gathering force for decades and extends far beyond the Muslim world. Global politics is increasingly marked by what might be called "prophetic politics" that sometimes turn violent.

Religion and Violence in Context

Whether in the form of civil war or terrorism, religious violence takes into account theological convictions as well as pragmatic, contextual issues. Together, these reflect the "political theology" of a given time. The cases available to us show that the influence of religious beliefs in politics is not confined to a single religious tradition and that it arises in an array of forms and situations.

IRAN

For the Islamic Republic of Iran, Shia history figures large in social and political thought; with a population that is 98 percent Muslim, and with 89 percent of that Muslim populace being Shia, arguments rooted in this strand of Islam have traction.[9] Here, the tradition of martyrdom is one point where religion and violence intersect, and it has been a particularly prominent issue since Iran's Islamic Revolution of 1979. During that period, Ayatollah Ruhollah Khomeini stressed the Shia connection to the idea of martyrdom—embodied in Imam Hussein, grandson of the Prophet Muhammad. In Shiism, Hussein is a sort of hero-martyr: fighting and dying in the name of the faith at Karbala, he serves as a model for justice in the face of oppression.[10] Khomeini, however, is thought to have engaged in what Fouad Ajami has called an "overly political and unyielding interpretation" of Imam Hussein's seventh-century death.[11] Rather than noting the nuances of Hussein's political struggle against the Umayyad Caliph Yazid, Khomeini depicted Hussein as an eager martyr. When the symbolism of Hussein's martyrdom became central to the demonstrations that filled Tehran's streets in the late 1970s,[12] influential religious voices encouraged Muslims to recall Hussein as they rose up against the Shah and to refuse to be passive victims.

The point here is that the reinterpretation of a religious figure's role from that of passive to active victim resulted in a new political theology that legitimated the seizure of power and made possible a *religious* revolution.

BOSNIA AND HERZEGOVINA

The period between 1981 and 1992 marked the disintegration of the former Yugoslavia and the strengthening of nationalist movements in the Balkan region.[13] Central to this period was Slobodan Milosevic, who became head of the Serbian Communist Party in May 1986.[14] To enhance his power, Milosevic incorporated nationalist language into his rhetoric and emphasized religious-national myths,[15] successfully exploiting the emotions tied to those myths: "He understood the power of the Kosovo myth for most Serbs. Serbs regard Kosovo as their Jerusalem."[16] According to the mythology of Kosovo, Serbs are encouraged to avenge the Ottoman defeat that took place on June 28, 1389.[17]

Michael Sells holds that religion was the leading factor in the war, in that ethnic cleansing "was based upon religiously informed ideologies and constructions of difference"[18] and "victims were selected largely on the basis of their formal religious affiliation as Croat, Serb, or Muslim—that is, on the basis of their affiliation with Catholicism, Serb Orthodoxy, or Islam."[19] That individuals would be targeted solely because of their religion remains problematic, however, for they ranged from being strictly observant believers to being only nominally religious.[20] Today, reports issued by the U.S. Department of State show that religiosity has remained low among all groups in Bosnia and Herzegovina, although "religious leaders claim that it is increasing among the young as an expression of increased identification with their ethnic heritage."[21] With religion still being tied so closely to ethnicity, conflict among ethnic groups often wreaks havoc on religious targets seen as representative of ethnic interests, such as religious buildings and clerics.[22]

TAJIKISTAN

In Tajikistan, religion appears to hold sway in the political realm much more so than in the personal lives of the citizenry. Trends in the country, and in Central Asia as a whole, have held steady in favor of this balance since the breakup of the Soviet Union, and although "religion has become part of the search for identity," individual religious practice remains low.[23]

The civil war in Tajikistan (1992–97) began when the Islamic Renaissance Party (IRP), led by Said Abdullo Nuri, voiced its opposition to the country's postindependence government. Its agenda was characterized primarily by nationalism; it did not seek to create an Islamic state. As one *Economist* study notes, the form of Islamism seen in Tajikistan has lacked the type of steady backing that would allow it to bring about a major shift in government structure:

> Central Asian politics are shaped more by tribal and ethnic allegiances than by ideology, so Islamic movements in the region are likely to remain fragmented. During the civil war in Tajikistan, for example, mullahs from the Kulab region supported the government, whereas former communist apparatchiks from the Gharm region overwhelmingly joined the IRP-dominated [United Tajik Opposition]. Moreover, there seems to be little genuine popular support for setting up Islamic states in the region.[24]

The IRP has solidified a form of moderate Islamism in Tajikistan.[25] While this moderation must be attributed in part to the underlying religious ideology of the IRP, it can also be traced to the manner in which the government dealt with the party following the war. The state's decision to accommodate the IRP and assign it a place in the political process, as T. Jeremy Gunn has written, carries the potential to transform the party into a much less radical entity[26] and offers a model for dealing with religious extremism.[27] Unlike other former Soviet states of Central Asia, Tajikistan is unique in allowing religious parties to participate in politics.[28]

ALGERIA

In another case that pits Islamists against secularists, Algeria's civil war is instructive in a different sense. Violence was sparked there in the first days of 1992, after the government annulled a December 1991 general election in which the Islamic Salvation Front (FIS) was poised to defeat the National Liberation Front.[29] As a result of the backlash against Islamist forces in early 2002, FIS leaders and activists were pushed underground.

In 1996 The *New York Times* characterized Algeria as posing "the increasingly widespread quandary of how to sift moderate political Islam from Islamic militancy and terrorism."[30] And unlike the IRP, the FIS stated its goal as turning Algeria "into an orthodox Islamic state."[31] With the Islamists and the secular political elite both being portrayed as uncompromising,[32] the best option at present might be to move the country forward on an entirely new slate. That is, if both sides are deadlocked regarding the past, the healing of old wounds will have to be set aside in favor of what is practical now. The 2004 reelection of President Abdelaziz Bouteflika, by all accounts legitimate, to a second term in office could be a step in this direction. In March 2004, Bouteflika established a new amnesty program to deal with residual tensions from the civil war; although the program did not probe into past events, the amnesty offered reconciliation to parties "with blood on their hands," including terrorists.[33] As with Tajikistan, moderation by both sides might usher in a period of accommodation; however, here the question remains whether the FIS, a popularly supported and once elected political organization, will moderate its objective of establishing an Islamic state.

INDIA

For India, a state seeking a more prominent role in the international community, achieving societal religious tolerance is essential, and continued high levels of communal violence are "a major embarrassment."[34] In its postpartition form, Hindu-majority India generally experiences conflict between Hindu forces and either its Christian, Sikh, or Muslim minority. Whereas the western state of Gujurat tends to see the most Hindu-Muslim violence in the country, Orissa in the east saw a bout of fighting in 2008 when twenty people were killed after the murder of a well-known Hindu priest. In early 2002, Hindu-Muslim violence caused 1,000 mostly Muslim deaths and led to a September attack on the Akshardham Cultural Complex—a Hindu temple complex in Delhi. In letters left behind by the gunmen, it was suggested that they intended to exact revenge for Muslim casualties.[35]

For India's current political climate, then, religion matters. When the Bharatiya Janata Party (BJP) gained power in the 1990s and brought its support of Hindu nationalism to center stage,

> religion became an essential part of a voter's political identity. The party emphasized "cultural nationalism," and its campaign themes included several items that are anathema to Muslims, like the temple construction in Ayodhya and the institution of a uniform civil code that would outlaw many Muslim practices.[36]

Elsewhere, the BJP has come under fire for policies that favor Hindus and "has been accused of being complicit in violence against both Muslims and Christians to win votes."[37] Since 2005, when bombings by groups such as the Indian muja-hideen began to increase throughout the country, voices of moderate Islam in India have spoken out against terrorism.[38]

Key Concepts: Religion and Violence

There are thousands of religions worldwide, each with practices and beliefs that distinguish it from other religions and from other systems of practices and beliefs, such as political and economic activity. Religion is therefore a lumpy and complex concept or variable.[39] Textbook definitions of religion typically include some or all of the following elements: a belief in a supernatural being (or beings); prayers and communication with that being; transcendent realities that might include some form of heaven, paradise, or hell; a distinction between the sacred and the profane and between ritual acts and sacred objects; a view that explains the world as a whole and a person's role in it; behavior and a prescribed moral conduct in line with that worldview; and a group of people bound to one another on the basis of these elements.[40]

While extreme religious ideology is a leading motivation for most transnational terrorist activity and a growing number of civil wars, we must also remember that the complexity of religion is tremendous. Functionalist definitions, much as the one just given, can be helpful in framing basic issues and outlining religion as a system of beliefs and institutions that are at the disposal of actors. Thanks to such definitions, a more straightforward understanding can be gained of how those actors bring religion into the public sphere as a resource. At the same time, discussing "religion" as a concept is of little help unless we also examine the religious persons, actors, and institutions whose beliefs and practices breathe life into the study of religion. As Harjot Oberoi writes, religious practices can be a rich source of information about the formative ideas and traditions of religious communities: "Ritual enactments are a condensed statement of the most deeply held values of a society."[41] In practice, a dialectic bond connects the orthodox beliefs of a religion and the rituals that reflect and reinforce those notions of truth. Only by examining both aspects of religion will the motivations of religious individuals, groups, and organizations be understood.

In the West, when one thinks of religion and violence, one generally focuses on religions of peoples of the book (Christianity, Judaism, and Islam), as well as on Buddhism and Hinduism. It is what these religions may have in common that makes them of such interest to scholars of violence, as well as to policy makers grappling with ending or preventing religious civil wars and terrorism. In particular, as practiced today, these religions share two key aspects relevant to the likelihood that conflict between competing groups may escalate into violence. First, religion tends to be uncompromising. That is, even given some liberty in translation and interpretation over time, the texts of the Hebrew Bible, New Testament, and Qur'an limit the conduct of followers in important ways.[42] Each of these three texts serves as a guide to conduct approved or mandated by a supreme being. Conduct departing from these guidelines puts a follower at risk of losing God's favor. The end result is that when followers believe they are being asked to violate the key tenets of their faith as laid down in holy scripture, they are less likely to do so, even when it might result in what most would consider a better outcome, such as peace.

Second, as a rule, religion encourages followers to discount their physical survival.[43] The logic is simple. The physical self is mortal and hence temporary, but the religious self is potentially immortal and eternal. If belief is strong enough, therefore, sacrificing the temporary and mortal to obtain the eternal and immortal may seem rational.[44] In the Christian and Muslim traditions, self-sacrifice in religiously prescribed conduct is believed to yield the reward of eternal, superphysical existence in a heaven or paradise.

Taken together, aspects of religion as they relate to violence chip away at bargaining and self-preservation, two key pillars of the state system established in the Treaty of Westphalia of 1648.[45] A rational person (or state) is expected to assess the tangible costs and benefits of action or inaction and then maximize his or her utility by choosing the course of action that will result in the highest likelihood of benefit with the lowest risk or cost.[46] But religious actors will often act differently, choosing instead to sacrifice tangible benefits for intangible ones, even to the point of sacrificing their own lives.[47] Thus a secular actor (or state) can be coerced or deterred by the threat of destruction, whereas a religious actor (or theocracy) may be impossible to coerce or deter in the same way.[48]

Statistics show that Muslim societies and ideas based in Islam are key factors in contemporary terrorism and civil war. While religion in general has increasingly become a factor in civil wars, such conflicts also involve Islam more so than other faiths; among religious civil wars occurring between 1940 and 2010, for example, Islam was a factor in over three-fourths of the wars (36 wars or 82 percent). To provide a comparison, Christianity was involved in 52 percent of these cases (23 wars), and Hinduism was part of the dynamic in 16 percent of such cases (seven wars).[49] Among civil wars as a collective, a conflict is more likely to become a *religious* civil war if the actors identify with Islam rather than another religious tradition.[50]

How does one account for the striking frequency of Islam in civil wars? Analyses of how much sway a religious tradition has among a state's populace or within its political authority structure do not go very far in explaining this phenomenon. In addition to influential transnational strands of Islam, three factors help to explain why Islam has played a larger role in contemporary religious civil wars than other faiths. The first factor is historical: the timing of the emergence of the state system and the subsequent development of an international system that made industrialized states the most lethal form of political association. The second is geographical: the colocation of Islamic holy sites and concentrated petroleum reserves. (Significantly, until recently, petroleum as a strategic resource was closely identified with the Arabian Peninsula.) The third is structural: a component of Islam known as jihad that has been interpreted and practiced since ancient times.[51]

Toward the end of the nineteenth century and through two world wars, Western advanced industrial states, with their secular governments and highly developed killing technology, came into increasingly (and increasingly violent) contact with the Middle East.[52] In their interstate depredations and later export of the concept of nationalism as a high form of legitimacy, the West became a force for inadvertently unifying and radicalizing Islam. The colonial and postcolonial periods, marked by the paradoxical mix of good intentions, on one hand, and exploitation, on the other, helped to re-create the concept of Arab (and Islamic) unity.[53] In addition, both Arab nationalism and Islamic fundamentalism received a strong boost from the establishment—with some Western help—of a Jewish state in 1948 on territory predominantly populated by Arabs and Muslims. More important, Mecca, Islam's holiest site, is located on the Arabian Peninsula. It follows that the West's increasing dependence on petroleum and the growing antipathy between Jews, Muslims, Arabs, and Persians after World War II would combine to make conflict more likely in this region and that as a result of faith and resource collocation, Islam would play a disproportionately greater role.

In addition, violence of an Islamic sort was incubated in Afghanistan when, throughout the 1980s, those opposing the Soviet-backed regime saw the external, aggression-oriented sort of jihad (as opposed to the internal sort that focuses on personal struggle) as a fitting weapon. Called by this battle, young Muslims traveled great distances to Afghanistan to defend Islam by killing Soviet troops and the Soviet Union's local allies. This effort was thus characterized by a sense of religious obligation; combined with a never-ending stream of cash and weapons across Afghanistan's notoriously porous borders, these young men—the mujahideen—prevented the Soviets from achieving their political objectives at an acceptable cost. Although military analysts in the West were apt to credit high technology (specifically, U.S.-made Stinger surface-to-air missiles) with the Soviet defeat in Afghanistan, to Islam's more conservative clerics and to many Muslims, jihad's external aspect was responsible for defeating a nuclear-armed, advanced-industrial Christian state.[54] This accounts for why, since the end of the Cold War, external jihad has become the legitimizing principle of choice for Islam's most conservative clerics—many of whom either personally satisfied their religious obligation to defend the faith from "godless communists" or sanctioned others to do so. This explains why the term *jihad*, as used today in both the West and the Islamic world, tends to be reduced to this external aspect.

For the current piece, which aims to show why organized religious violence has taken its current form, the developments described here are significant. By contrast, a similar appeal to take up arms in a contemporary Christian context is highly unlikely,[55] not because Christianity is free of its own versions of jihad—the Crusades are only the most notorious reminder that it is not—but because as inheritors of the state system that came out of the Thirty Years' War, Western elites have long since secularized their political leadership.[56] On the whole, religious motivation is responsible for the largest proportion of terrorist attacks with known perpetrators from 1998 to 2004. Of these, 98 percent involved Islamic ideas as a cause for violence.[57] Thanks to the chain of events that began in earnest in the 1970s, the current trajectory of religiously motivated aggression indicates that it will prove difficult to decrease the prevalence of religion—and especially Islam—in the arena of large-scale violence.

An Empirical Assessment of Religion and Civil Wars, 1940–2010

DISTRIBUTION OF CIVIL WARS ACROSS TIME

An examination of the occurrence of civil wars across the decades reveals an increase in the proportion of civil wars with religion as a feature of the fight. From the 1940s to the 1950s, the figure rose from 19 to 30 percent. The 1960s witnessed a modest decline to 22 percent, but the figure grew in the 1970s to 36 percent and continued to climb in the 1980s to 41 percent and into the 1990s to 45 percent. Religious civil wars also make up a disproportionate number of ongoing wars after 2010. There were sixteen ongoing wars as of 2010. Of these, eight (or 50 percent) had a religious dimension.

DISTRIBUTION OF CIVIL WARS ACROSS SPACE

Most religious civil wars have occurred in four regions: Asia and the Pacific, the Middle East, Europe, and Africa. From 1940 to 2010, Latin America and North America have experienced no religiously based civil wars. Asia and the Pacific experienced twenty religious civil wars (45 percent of all religiously based civil wars), while the regions of the Middle East, Africa, and Europe experienced eight wars each.

Of the total of forty-four religious civil wars from 1940 to 2010, only twenty-four states were responsible for them. Table 8.1 provides the distribution of wars across states.

Three states experienced three or more wars. India experienced six, followed by Indonesia and Yugoslavia with three each. An additional eleven states experienced two of the forty-four religious civil wars, and the remaining ten wars occurred within other states.

INTRAFAITH VERSUS INTERFAITH RELIGIOUS CIVIL WARS

Is there a difference in how often a given religion is involved in a civil war in which a religious schism (i.e., intrafaith) or a different religion (i.e., interfaith) is

TABLE 8.1 } Distribution of Religious Civil Wars across States, 1940–2010

State and Combatant	Start Year
Afghanistan Mujahadeen/Taliban	1978
Afghanistan Taliban	2004
Algeria Fundamentalists	1992
Azerbaijan/USSR Nagorno Karabakh	1988
Bangladesh Chittagong Hill	1972
Burma Karens	1948
Burma Kachins	1960
Chad National Liberation Front	1965
China Tibet	1950
China Tibet	1954
Cyprus Greek/Turk clashes	1963
Cyprus Coup/ Turk invasion	1974
Ethiopia Ogaden	1977
Georgia Abkhazia	1992
India Partition	1946
India Hyderabad	1948
India Naga revolt	1956
India Kashmir	1965
India Sikh insurrection	1982
India Kashmir	1988
Indonesia Ambon/Moluccans	1950
Indonesia Aceh revolt	1953
Indonesia Timor-Leste	1975
Iran Revolution	1978
Iran National Council of Resistance	1981
Iraq Shiite insurrection	1991
Iraq Insurgency	2003
Israel/Palestine Independence	1945
Lebanon First civil war	1958
Lebanon Second civil war	1975
Nigeria Biafra	1967
Nigeria Maitatsine	1980
Philippines Moro rebellion	1972
Philippines Moro rebelliion	2000
Russia First Chechen war	1994
Russia Second Chechen war	1999
Sri Lanka Tamil insurgency	1983
Sudan Anya-Nya	1955
Sudan Sudan People Liberation Movement	1983
Syria Sunnis versus Alawites	1979
Tajikistan Civil War	1992
Yugoslavia Croatian secession	1991
Yugoslavia Bosnian civil war	1992
Yugoslavia Kosovo	1998
Total	44

a central issue of conflict? An examination of the relationship of religion to violence across civil wars reveals that Islam is most involved in intrareligious wars. Both Islam and Christianity dominate the distribution of interfaith civil wars. Table 8.2 provides the data.

There were twelve intrafaith civil wars from 1940 to 2010. Islam was involved in eleven of these (a striking 90 percent). Of these twelve cases, six involved religious fundamentalists who sought to overthrow a secular state (e.g., Afghanistan). The remainder involved movements for self-determination (e.g., the Achinese of Indonesia) or communal violence (e.g., the Maitatsine of Nigeria).

Interreligious wars made up the remaining thirty-two cases (73 percent).[58] Of the interfaith civil wars, Islam was again well represented, but so was Christianity. Islam was involved in twenty-six of these wars (83 percent), and Christianity was involved in twenty-one (66 percent). Moreover, of the religious pairings in a war, Islam and Christianity were engaged most often. Significantly, however, twice as many wars emerged when Christianity was the dominant state religion. War broke out in thirteen cases where Christianity dominated, in six where Islam was dominant, and six where Hinduism was dominant. The remaining interreligious wars involved Buddhism (six cases), Taoism (two cases), and Judaism (one case).

SUMMARY

Three important facts about religion and civil wars emerge from this analysis. First, religious civil wars made up more than a third of all civil wars fought from 1940 to 2010, and there is little sign that this trend will wane any time soon.

TABLE 8.2 } **Intrareligious and Interreligious Civil Wars, 1940–2010**

Type of war	Number of Cases
Intrafaith	12
Islam	11
Christianity	1
Interfaith state-opposition	32
Christianity-Islam	13
Islam-Christianity	6
Hinduism-Islam	4
Hinduism-Christianity	1
Hinduism-Sikhism	1
Taoism-Buddhism	2
Islam-Buddhism	2
Buddhism-Christianity	1
Buddhism-Hinduism	1
Judaism-Islam	1
Total	44

Second, the increase in the proportion of civil wars with a religious tint occurred first in the 1970s and continued into the 1980s. Third, among the world's major religions, Islam was involved in just over 80 percent of these civil wars.

The Role of Religion in Terrorism

DISTRIBUTION OF TERRORIST ACTIVITIES ACROSS TIME

The rate of terrorism, too, has climbed steadily since 1970, with a marked increase occurring after September 11, 2001.[64] The use of suicide missions has escalated in recent years as well, especially since 2005.[65] Statistics further show that while suicide attacks by secular groups have fallen off, the rate of religious suicide missions has increased.[66] Compared with all other terrorist organizations, the task of ending religiously motivated groups is more difficult. Since 1968, whereas 62 percent of terrorist organizations have been terminated, only 32 percent of religious terrorist organizations have come to an end.[67] Regarding termination types, religious terrorist groups are unique in that not one such organization has achieved victory since 1968.[68] A 2008 study by the RAND Corporation finds that among all 648 terrorist groups in its data set, 7 percent end through military force, 10 percent end by victory, 40 percent end through policing, and 43 percent end through processes of politicization.[69] Of the 648 groups, 41 percent have ended, 38 percent remain active, and 21 percent ended because their members joined other terrorist organizations.[70] As regards the forty-five religious terrorist groups that have ended, twenty-six (or 57.8 percent) splintered, thirteen (or 28.9 percent) succumbed to policing efforts, three (or 6.7 percent) fell to military force, and three (again, 6.7 percent) shifted toward political activity.[71]

DISTRIBUTION OF TERRORIST ACTIVITIES ACROSS SPACE

According to the Global Terrorism Database, for the period 1998–2004, 991 terrorist incidents of a total of 4,824 (or 20.5 percent) had a religious perpetrator. It is striking that among terrorist attacks carried out by groups classified as religious, Islamic ideology was a factor 98.1 percent of the time (in 972 of 991 incidents). The data in table 8.3 demonstrate this, with statistics provided for each country (thirty-seven in all) that experienced a religiously motivated terrorist attack during this time span.[72]

Alongside this data on the influence of Islam, Bruce Hoffman has reported that thirty-one of the thirty-five terrorist groups that have used suicide attacks as a tactic are Islamic. In addition, of the suicide attacks that have been carried out since September 11, 2001, 81 percent were perpetrated by organizations with an Islamic ideology.[73]

TABLE 8.3 } Religious Terrorist Incidents by Country, 1998–2004

Country	Total Incidents	Religious Incidents Total	Where Islamic ideology a factor (%)
Afghanistan	199	94	94 (100)
Algeria	426	91	91 (100)
Bangladesh	64	3	3 (100)
Egypt	6	2	2 (100)
Ethiopia	7	1	1 (100)
India	784	114	110 (96)
Indonesia	215	61	61 (100)
Iran	35	14	14 (100)
Iraq	317	39	39 (100)
Israel	191	77	76 (99)
Italy	47	2	0 (0)
Jordan	9	1	1 (100)
Kenya	10	3	3 (100)
Kuwait	5	1	1 (100)
Kyrgyzstan	9	2	2 (100)
Lebanon	87	55	55 (100)
Malaysia	3	1	1 (100)
Morocco	5	5	5 (100)
Nepal	143	1	1 (100)
Nigeria	47	1	1 (100)
Pakistan	236	35	35 (100)
Palestine	209	56	56 (100)
Philippines	380	235	234 (100)
Russian Federation	435	1	1 (100)
Saudi Arabia	32	14	14 (100)
Somalia	20	1	1 (100)
South Africa	43	1	1 (100)
Spain	284	6	6 (100)
Sudan	22	1	1 (100)
Syria	2	1	1 (100)
Tanzania	2	1	1 (100)
Thailand	71	1	1 (100)
Turkey	224	18	18 (100)
Tunisia	2	1	1 (100)
Uganda	121	38	27 (71)
United States of America	80	4	4 (100)
Yemen	52	9	9 (100)
Total	4824	991	972 (99)

A key debate in scholarship on religious terrorism is the question of whether occupation, not religion, best or better explains the phenomenon of suicide attacks. Robert A. Pape has supported this idea,[74] arguing that resentment of foreign occupation is a significant incentive for suicide terrorism: "Since 1980, there has not been a suicide terrorist campaign directed mainly against domestic opponents or against foreign opponents who did not have military forces in the terrorists homeland."[75] Assaf Moghadam cites three reasons this cannot be the case at the present time. First, it has become clear that "suicide attacks increasingly occur where there is no discernible occupation."[76] In addition, countries that are host to occupation do not always see suicide attacks directed toward the occupying power.[77] Finally, "many suicide attacks, even if they do target the occupation forces, are not carried out by those individuals who, theoretically, should be most affected by the occupation."[78]

For organizations such as al Qaeda, a decrease in occupation of key territories—whether real or perceived—is likely to have little bearing on the organization's terrorist activities: "On the contrary, all signs indicate that Al Qaeda views the struggle as a protracted, third world war of cosmic proportions."[79] Here, religion again trumps occupation as a motivation for terrorism.

THE DEADLINESS OF RELIGIOUSLY INSPIRED TERRORISM

One reason religious terrorism is particularly destructive is that terrorists motivated by religion tend to see the indiscriminate use of violence as acceptable or necessary, if used in the pursuit of a higher cause.[80] At present, most studies of the lethality of religious terrorism focus on suicide missions. One study, conducted by Peter S. Henne, suggests a correlation between religious ideology in general and the increased severity of a suicide attack. Henne posits "ideology" here as a mode of interpretation; religion must be factored into the equation, but only through an organization's ideology, which considers doctrine alongside context. According to his data set, religious suicide attacks cause more deaths even though they constitute a minority of total suicide missions—"a difference that is statistically significant."[81] Within this framework, he argues that the link between religious ideology and lethality exists independently of both the religion in question and additional socioeconomic factors.[82] In light of debates on the actual importance of religion to terrorism (versus the instrumental use of religion), this study is useful in demonstrating that we "can thus neither deny the importance of religion in religious terrorists' actions nor place the blame for their violence on an entire religious tradition."[83]

Another essay by Assaf Moghadam shows a notable correlation among an increase in suicide attacks, an increase in casualties and injuries caused by such attacks, and an increase in the number of suicide missions motivated by Salafi-Jihadist ideology. These figures have been climbing steadily since 1981, with the largest spike since 2001. Moghadam's data allow us to see that the rise in lethal suicide attacks has not been driven merely by religion, but rather by a particular religious ideology: that of the Salafi Jihad.[84] Moghadam also shows that Salafi-Jihadist suicide missions rose sharply from 2001 to 2007, followed only distantly in numbers by missions that were motivated by other ideologies. Taken together, these data suggest that the increase in deaths resulting from suicide attacks is linked to the heightened presence of Salafi-Jihadist thought among responsible groups.

Three key points are worth summarizing. First, religious terrorism has intensified in recent years, with a marked increase in the number of religiously motivated suicide missions. Second, Islamic ideology appears in a disproportionately high number of religious terrorist incidents. And third, religious terrorism tends to be more lethal than terrorism inspired by other factors. There is thus reason to be concerned when actors are motivated by religious tenets and beliefs and are willing to act on them.

Conclusion

In the study of contemporary violence and international order, religion stands out as an issue demanding attention. Religion not only contributes to a strikingly high proportion of civil wars and incidents of terrorism but also renders such violence deadlier and more difficult to bring to a lasting end. Bearing this in mind, it seems significant that Islamic ideology appears as a motivating factor in such violence more often than other religious traditions. These are issues that are not on the verge of being resolved; rather, they will continue to require close study—not only of religion but also of socioeconomic and political factors that contribute to the decision to resort to violence. Where do such factors lead to using religion as a justification for conflict? In contrast, which doctrinal and discursive shifts are taking place within religious communities that might help to underpin the use of force?

Notes

1. Cf. Douglas Johnston, *Religion: The Missing Dimension of Statecraft* (Oxford: Oxford University Press, 1994); the special issue of *Millennium: Journal of International Studies* 29:3 (December 2000); and Daniel Philpott, *Revolutions in Sovereignty: How Ideas Shaped Modern International Relations* (Princeton, NJ: Princeton University Press, 2001). For some recent works that assess the resurgence of religion into public life, see Gilles Kepel, *The Revenge of God* (University Park, PA: Pennsylvania State University Press, 1994); David Westerlund, ed., *Questioning the Secular State: The Worldwide Resurgence of Religion in Politics* (New York: St. Martin's, 1996); Peter L. Berger, ed., *The Desecularization of the World* (Grand Rapids, MI: William B. Eerdmans, 1999); and Susanne H. Rudolph and James Piscatori, *Transnational Religion and Fading States* (Boulder, CO: Westview, 1997).

2. For more on this particular point, see, for example, R. Scott Appleby, *The Ambivalence of the Sacred: Religion, Violence, and Reconciliation* (New York: Rowman and Littlefield, 1999).

3. Of the world's population in 2007, 33 percent adhered to Christianity, 21 percent to Islam, 13 percent to Hinduism, 6 percent to Buddhist, and about 12 percent to other religions (including 0.4 percent and 0.2 percent to Sikhism and Judaism). Nonreligious constituted about 12 percent, and atheists made up about 2 percent. *CIA World Factbook*, https://www.cia.gov/library/publications/the-world-factbook/geos/xx.html.

4. Much of this section draws on my coauthored article with Timothy Samuel Shah, "Why God Is Winning," *Foreign Policy* (July–August 2006), 38–43. Much of this thesis about why religion, why now is developed more fully in our book (with Daniel Philpott), *God's Century: Resurgent Religion and Global Politics* (New York: Norton, 2011).

5. For more on the assertion that the September 11 attacks were based in Islam, see Ben Fox, "9/11 Defendants: 'We Are Terrorists to the Bone,'" *Associated Press Online* (March 10, 2009).

6. According to Freedom House, the number of "free" and "partly free" countries jumped from 93 in 1975 to 147 in 2005. UNESCO estimates that adult literacy rates doubled in sub-Saharan Africa, Arab countries, and South and West Asia between 1970 and 2000. The average share of people in developing countries living on less than a dollar a day fell from 28 percent to 22 percent between 1990 and 2002, according to World Bank estimates.

7. Consider the two largest Christian faiths, Catholicism and Protestantism, and the two largest non-Christian religions, Islam and Hinduism. According to the *World Christianity Encyclopedia*, a greater proportion of the world's population adhered to these religious systems in 2000 than a century earlier. At the beginning of the twentieth century, a bare majority of the world's people, precisely 50 percent, were Catholic, Protestant, Muslim, or Hindu. At the beginning of the twenty-first century, nearly 64 percent belonged to these four religious groupings, and the proportion may be close to 70 percent by 2025. The World Values Survey, which covers 85 percent of the world's population, confirms religion's growing vitality.

8. Pippa Norris and Ronald Inglehart, *Sacred and Secular: Religion and Politics Worldwide* (New York: Cambridge University Press, 2004), 235.

9. Adherents to Shi'i Islam are a minority of the world's Muslims, making up between 10 and 15 percent. Sunnis are the majority at 85 to 90 percent. Iran and Iraq (and likely Bahrain) are the only states in which Shia are in the majority, 89 and 60 to 65 percent, respectively (Bahrain, more than 70 percent). Muslims make up the majority of their state's population in Afghanistan, Albania, Algeria, Azerbaijan, Bahrain, Bangladesh, Brunei, Burkina Faso, Chad, Comoros, Djibouti, Egypt, Gambia, Guinea, Guinea-Bissau, Indonesia, Iran, Iraq, Jordan, Kuwait, Kyrgyzstan, Lebanon, Libya, Malaysia, Mauritania, Morocco, Niger, Nigeria, Oman, Pakistan, Qatar, Senegal, Sierra Leone, Somalia, Sudan, Syria, Tajikistan, Tunisia, Turkey, United Arab Emirates, Uzbekistan, and Yemen. Most Muslims, eight of ten, do not live in the Middle East (Egypt and Turkey are the only two states that make it into the top ten states with the largest Muslim populations; Indonesia, Pakistan and Bangladesh are the top three), and most Muslims are not Arab (again, Indonesia, Pakistan and Bangladesh top the list). *CIA World Factbook*, https://cia.gov/library/publications/the-world-factbook/fields/2122.html.

10. Fouad Ajami, "Iran: The Impossible Revolution," *Foreign Affairs* 67:2 (Winter 1988), 135–155, 148. See also Manochehr Dorraj, "Symbolic and Utilitarian Political Value of a Tradition: Martyrdom in the Iranian Political Culture," *Review of Politics* 59:3, Non-Western Political Thought (Summer 1997), 489–521.

11. Ajami, "Iran," 148.

12. See, for example: Karen Armstrong, "The Iranian Revolution Was the Ultimate Passion Play," *Times (London)*, February 9, 2009, 26.

13. Branka Magas, *The Destruction of Yugoslavia: Tracking the Breakup 1980–1992* (London: Verso, 1993); and Susan Woodward, *Balkan Tragedy: Chaos and Dissolution after the Cold War*(Washington, DC: Brookings Institution, 1995).

14. Adam LeBor, *Milosevic: A Biography* (London: Bloomsbury, 2002), 71.

15. Misha Glenny, *The Fall of Yugoslavia*, rev. ed. (New York: Penguin, 1996); Michael Ignatieff, *Blood and Belonging* (New York: Farrar, Straus and Giroux, 1993).

16. LeBor, *Milosevic*, 79.

17. Celia Hawkesworth, *Religious Quest and National Identity in the Balkans* (New York: Palgrave, 2001), 221. Also see Monica Duffy Toft, *The Geography of Ethnic Violence: Identity, Interests and Issue Indivisibility* (Princeton, NJ: Princeton University Press, 2003), especially chapter 2.

18. Michael Sells, "Crosses of Blood: Sacred Space, Religion, and Violence in Bosnia-Hercegovina," *Sociology of Religion* 64:3 (Autumn 2003), 309–331, 310.

19. Ibid., 309.

20. Michael A. Sells, *The Bridge Betrayed: Religion and Genocide in Bosnia* (Los Angeles: University of California Press, 1996), 14.

21. "Bosnia-Herzegovina: International Religious Freedom Report 2002," U.S. Department of State, Bureau of Democracy, Human Rights, and Labor, www.state.gov/g/drl/rls/irf/2002/13930.htm.

22. Ibid.

23. "Allah's Shadow," *Economist* 368:8334 (July 26, 2003).

24. Ibid.

25. Hizb-ut-Tahrir (www.hizbuttahrir.org/) has been outlawed in Tajikistan, Uzbekistan, and Kyrgyzstan.

26. T. Jeremy Gunn, "Shaping an Islamic Identity: Religion, Islamism, and the State in Central Asia," *Sociology of Religion*, 64:3 (Autumn 2003), 389–410, 399–400, 402–403.

27. Fabio Oliva, "Between Contribution and Disengagement: Post-Conflict Elections and the OSCE Role in the Normalization of Armed Groups and Militarized Political Parties in Bosnia and Herzegovina, Tajikistan, and Kosovo," *Helsinki Monitor: Security and Human Rights* 18:3 (2007), 192–207, 206.

28. See, for example, Gunn, "Shaping an Islamic Identity."

29. Judith Miller, "The Islamic Wave," *New York Times*, May 31, 1992, sec. 6, p. 23.

30. Roger Cohen, "State of Fear: A Special Report," *New York Times*, December 28, 1996, 1.

31. Caryle Murphy, "Algeria's Secular Army, Islamic Militants Battle for Power," *Washington Post*, January 25, 1994, A14.

32. Ibid.

33. Craig Whitlock, "Algerian Program Offers Amnesty, but Not Answers about Past," *Washington Post*, September 17, 2006, A17.

34. Kim Barker, "India, a Nation of Many Religions, Struggles to Overcome Sectarian Strife," *Chicago Tribune*, October 1, 2008.

35. Amy Waldman, "In Massacre of Hindus, A Grim Omen for All India," *New York Times*, September 26, 2002, 12.

36. Barry Bearak, "Muslims Fear India's Voting Will Erode Their Tiny Stake," *New York Times*, September 19, 1999, 1.

37. Barker, "India, a Nation of Many Religions."

38. Rama Lakshmi, "India's Moderate Muslims See Peril In Growth of Stricter Form of Islam," *Washington Post*, June 29, 2008, A16.

39. As philosopher of religion William Alston illustrates, defining *religion* is difficult and controversial. It is not my task to come up with a definitive example—just one that helps to clarify the arguments advanced here. William P. Alston, "Religion," *Encyclopedia of Philosophy*, vol. 7 (New York: Macmillan, 1972), 140–145.

40. This definition follows Alston's definition (ibid.).

41. Harjot Oberoi, *The Construction of Religious Boundaries: Culture, Identity and Diversity in the Sikh Tradition* (Chicago: University of Chicago Press, 1994), 66.

42. Logically, we should therefore expect theocracies to be much more authoritarian than nontheocracies, because when church and state are fused, opposition to state policy becomes tantamount to opposition to God. On the other hand, a recent study of the alleged relationship between Islam and "authoritarianism" found only one causal link between the antidemocratic character of Islamic states and Islam as a religion: the subordination of women. See M. Steven Fish, "Islam and Authoritarianism," *World Politics* 55:1 (October 2002), 4–37. On religion, political values, and women, see also Norris and Inglehart, *Sacred and Secular*.

43. Again, readers should keep in mind that my discussion of religion, religious practice, and religious motivations is ideal-type and not meant to stand as descriptive even of the practice or motivation of a majority of the followers of any particular religion.

44. Religion is not the only system of beliefs that can have this effect: nationalism also shares it. See especially Benedict Anderson, *Imagined Communities: Reflections on the Origin and Spread of Nationalism* (London: Verso, 1991), 9–12.

45. See Stephen Krasner, *Sovereignty: Organized Hypocrisy* (Princeton, NJ: Princeton University Press, 2003); Philpott, *Revolutions in Sovereignty*; and Philpott, "The Challenge of September 11 to Secularism in International Relations," *World Politics*, 55:1 (October 2002), 66–95.

46. On the history of the rational state more generally, see Stephen Toulmin, *Cosmopolis: The Hidden Agenda of Modernity* (Chicago: University of Chicago Press, 1990); and Albert O. Hirschman, *The Passions and the Interest: Political Arguments for Capitalism before Its Triumph* (Princeton, NJ: Princeton University Press, 1977).

47. Note that according to prominent neorealists such as Kenneth N. Waltz, the domestic preferences of substate actors disappear at the interstate system level. See Waltz, *Theory of International Politics* (New York: Macmillan, 1979), 76–78. Policy makers in the real world appear less sanguine, however, as the debate over Iranian nuclearization makes clear. See also John J. Mearsheimer, *The Tragedy of Great Power Politics* (New York: W. W. Norton, 2001).

48. See Monica Duffy Toft, "Issue Indivisibility and Time Horizons as Rationalist Explanations for War," *Security Studies* 15:1 (January–March 2006), 34–69.

49. Toft, "Getting Religion? The Puzzling Case of Islam and Civil War," *International Security* 31:4 (Spring 2007), 97–131, 113.

50. Ibid., 97.

51. For more on these issues, see ibid., 107–112.

52. This is not to say that the Middle East can be conflated with Muslim society. As we know, most of the world's Muslim population lives outside of the Middle East. However, in terms of the development of contemporary political Islam, certain regions of the Middle East are particularly relevant because many leading ideologues developed and spread their schools of thought there. For example, with regard to the development of current jihad movements and the pivotal role of Abdullah Azzam, see Thomas Hegghammer, "Introduction: Abdallah Azzam, Imam of Jihad," in *Al Qaeda in Its Own Words*, Gilles Kepel and Jean-Pierre Milelli (Cambridge, MA: Belknap Press of Harvard University Press, 2008), 81–101.

53. This is a concept that predates the advent of the European state system and has endured ever since. For early manifestations of nationalism against first the Ottomans

and then the British, see George Antonius, *The Arab Awakening: The Story of the Arab National Movement* (New York: Simon, 2001); and T. E. Lawrence, *The Seven Pillars of Wisdom: A Triumph* (New York: Anchor, 1991). For a more scholarly account, see Rashid Khalidi, Lisa Anderson, Muhammad Muslih, and Reeva S. Simon, eds., *The Origins of Arab Nationalism* (New York: Columbia University Press, 1991). See also Ernest Gellner, ed., *Islamic Dilemmas: Reformers, Nationalists, and Industrialization* (New York: Mouton, 1985); Bernard Lewis, *Islam and the West* (New York: Oxford University Press, 1994); and Bernard Lewis, *What Went Wrong? Western Impact and Middle Eastern Response* (New York: Oxford University Press, 2002).

54. On Islamic strategic thinkers' views on how to defeat the West, see Jarret M. Brachman and William F. McCants, "Stealing al-Qa'ida's Playbook," *Studies in Conflict and Terrorism* 29:4 (June 2006), 309–321.

55. On the contrary, the most useful type of argument a beleaguered combatant—be it an incumbent government or a rebel group—could make to gain Western support today is that of any ally in the war against Islamic fundamentalist terror. There is nothing, however, to prevent Christianity, or even Judaism, from reactivating this aspect of faith and practice. In Judaism's case, because only a single state is Jewish, when threatened, Jewish elites will not tender religious bids for external support because no other state exists that could come to Israel's aid on religious grounds. Nevertheless, when powerful states have significant numbers of nationals living outside the state (or when in powerful states they have a strong lobby—for example, the Jewish-Israel lobby in the United States), religious appeals may make more sense. See John Mearsheimer and Stephen Walt, "The Israel Lobby," *London Review of Books*, March 23, 2006, 3–12.

56. This is not a teleological argument. Christianity could again become the focus of internecine fighting, but today (especially in Europe) this remains unlikely.

57. Examination of the data supplied in the Global Terrorism Database 2 (GTD2) indicates that Islamic ideology was a factor in 98.1 percent (or 972 of 991) of terrorist incidents carried out by perpetrators classified as religious from 1998 to 2004. See "Global Terrorism Database," National Consortium for the Study of Terrorism and Responses to Terrorism (START), University of Maryland and U.S. Department of Homeland Security, www.start.umd.edu/data/gtd/.

58. This finding contradicts Fox, who discovers that the majority of ethno-religious conflicts he studied occurred within religions. The reason might be because he examined both low-level conflict and rebellion using the "Minorities at Risk" data set, and this analysis examines only full-scale civil war. See Jonathan Fox, *Religion, Civilization and Civil War: 1945 through the Millennium* (Lanham, MD: Lexington, 2005), 59–67.

64. "Global Terrorism Database," National Consortium for the Study of Terrorism and Responses to Terrorism (START), University of Maryland and U.S. Department of Homeland Security, www.start.umd.edu/data/gtd/.

65. Assaf Moghadam, "Suicide Terrorism, Occupation, and the Globalization of Martyrdom: A Critique of *Dying to Win*," *Studies in Conflict and Terrorism* 29:8 (May 2006), 707–729.

66. Ibid., 718.

67. Seth G. Jones and Martin C. Libicki, *How Terrorist Groups End: Lessons for Countering al Qa'ida* (Pittsburgh, PA: RAND, 2008), 36.

68. Ibid., xiv.

69. Ibid., 19.

70. Ibid., 35.

71. Ibid., 36–37.

72. "Global Terrorism Database." These data make use of the "religious perpetrator type" classification used by the GTD.

73. Bruce Hoffman, *Inside Terrorism* (New York: Columbia University Press, 2006), chapter 5. This has been noted by Assaf Moghadam in "Suicide Terrorism," 718–719.

74. See Robert A. Pape, "The Strategic Logic of Suicide Terrorism," *American Political Science Review* 93:3 (August 2003), 343–361; and Robert A. Pape, *Dying to Win: The Strategic Logic of Suicide Terrorism* (New York: Random House, 2005).

75. Pape, "The Strategic Logic of Suicide Terrorism," 349.

76. Moghadam, "Suicide Terrorism," 719.

77. Ibid., 719–720.

78. Ibid., 720.

79. Ibid., 718.

80. See, for example, Bruce Hoffman, "'Holy Terror': The Implications of Terrorism Motivated by a Religious Imperative," *Studies in Conflict and Terrorism* 18:4 (October–December 1995), 271–284, 273.

81. Peter S. Henne, "The Ancient Fire: Religion and Suicide Terrorism," PhD Candidate, Government Department, Georgetown University, 2009, 6.

82. Ibid., 4, 27.

83. Ibid., 29.

84. Moghadam describes the Salafi Jihad as "the guiding ideology of Al Qaeda"—an ideology that groups use as the basis for "a self-declared 'holy war' in the name of a distorted view of Islam." See Moghadam, "Al Qaeda, Salafi Jihad, and the Proliferation of Suicide Attacks," *International Security* 33:1 (Winter 2008–2009), 4, 16. See also Mohammed M. Hafez, *Suicide Bombers in Iraq: The Strategy and Ideology of Martyrdom* (Washington, DC: United States Institute of Peace, 2007).

Annotated Bibliography

Appleby, R. Scott. *The Ambivalence of the Sacred: Religion, Violence, and Reconciliation.* New York: Rowman and Littlefield, 2000.

This book provides an excellent overview of how religion is related to violence but also peace and reconciliation. It is a meaty tome with lots of theoretical insights and examples drawn from an array of important historical and contemporary events (despite being published before September 11, 2001).

Hoffman, Bruce. *Inside Terrorism.* New York: Columbia University Press, 2006 (rev. and expanded ed.).

This book provides one of the best and most comprehensive understandings of terrorism. It is theoretically insightful, tracing the different logics for the various types of terrorism we have witnessed and are likely to witness in the future.

Huntington, Samuel P. *The Clash of Civilizations and the Remaking of World Order.* New York: Simon and Schuster, 1996.

This books advances perhaps one of the most famous theses of the late twentieth and early twenty-first centuries: no longer will states clash, but civilizations that have different cultures. Although the thesis has undergone tremendous scrutiny, the basic insight seems to ring true as religious actors, ideas, and institutions seem to be playing a greater role in global affairs. An article version first appeared in *Foreign Affairs* in the 1993 summer edition.

— Juergensmeyer, Mark. *Terror in the Mind of God: The Global Rise of Religious Violence.* Berkeley: University of California Press, 2000 (updated ed.).

Provides an excellent treatment of how religion motivates people to use violence for political ends. It also includes a number of case studies on how Buddhist, Christian, Jewish, Muslim, and Sikh actors theologically justify their violence.

Pape, Robert. *Dying to Win: The Strategic Logic of Suicide Terrorism.* New York: Random House, 2005.

A theoretical and empirical treatment of suicide terrorism, it argues that suicide terrorism is not the result of religion or religious extremism, but of occupation: self-determination movements are largely responsible for most suicide terrorist actions from 1980 to 2003. It includes data of all suicide attacks for this period. (Many of the results were published in article form as "The Strategic Logic of Suicide Terrorism." *American Political Science Review* 97:3 (August 2003), 343–361.)

Toft, Monica Duffy. "Getting Religion? The Puzzling Case of Islam and Civil War." *International Security* 31:4 (Spring 2007), 97–131.

This article provides an overview of the role of religion in civil wars since 1940. It finds that the proportion of civil wars with religion as a core issue has been increasing over time and that adherents to Islam are disproportionately engaged in religious civil wars. It makes the case that the reasons are not intrinsic to Islam, but an artifact of the contemporary historical structure in which Islam is operating.

9 }

What Religion Offers for the Politics of Transitional Justice

Daniel Philpott

On April 26, 1998, officers of the Guatemalan army bludgeoned to death Catholic Bishop Juan Gerardi in the garage of his home in Guatemala City.[1] Two days earlier, in the Metropolitan Cathedral of the same city, he had delivered the report of the Recovery of Historical Memory Project (REMHI), an initiative that he had formed and launched in 1995 to expose the atrocities of Guatemala's generation-long civil war, which was finally settled only in 1996. In its goal of telling the truth about the past, REMHI resembled truth commissions in other countries. But unlike other truth commissions, it was not a government, but the Catholic Church, that launched it, indeed out of the very conviction that the government's efforts were far too weak. REMHI was also unique for its style of taking testimony, training several hundred *animadores*, or volunteers, to fan out across the countryside to hear the stories of guerrillas, government soldiers, and ordinary peasants and to offer them spiritual and psychological support. Reconciliation, repentance, forgiveness, and acknowledgment of the truth were major themes in REMHI's operation—and in Gerardi's final address. That he was assassinated was ironic, for REMHI, like Guatelama's transition to peace in general, was weak precisely for its lack of accountability for human rights violators. But reconciliation, too, it seems, comes at a steep price.

Over the past generation, a global wave of countries have undertaken what has come to be known as transitional justice—efforts to address the injustices of a past period of civil war, genocide, or dictatorship, whether through trials, truth commissions, reparations, apologies, forgiveness, or the building of memorials and monuments. Underappreciated in academic analysis, though sometimes generating a buzz in the popular media, is the role of the religious in these doings: Anglican Archbishop Desmond Tutu in South Africa, Catholic Bishop Carlos Belo in East Timor, Bishop Gerardi in Guatemala, and all of the pastors and priests, rabbis and imams who have organized efforts to heal the wounds of past injustices in villages, cities, and their own religious communities. But what difference have the religious made? They have led the way, I shall argue, in developing an alternative to the liberal human rights paradigm that has dominated transitional justice, with its stress on accountability, punishment, rights, and the rule of law. That alternative is reconciliation, which does not reject rights or even necessarily punishment but combines these with a much wider array of restorative practices, including apology, forgiveness, reparations, acknowledgment, and civil society efforts to bring about healing. Proffering this more holistic approach, the religious have shaped and conducted such practices not only in Guatemala, South Africa, and East Timor but also in Chile, Brazil, El Salvador, Iraq, Northern Ireland, Germany, Sierra Leone, Brazil, and elsewhere. But the religious are neither reconcilers nor even influential everywhere. What motivates, enables, and distinguishes those who are—and what their influence has been—is what this essay seeks to explain.

Two Paradigms

Perpetrators ought to be punished and victims vindicated—so can be summarized the core commitments of the liberal human rights paradigm, the approach to transitional justice voiced most commonly by human rights activists, international lawyers, United Nations officials, several nongovernmental organizations (NGOs) that support transitional justice, and many scholars.[2] Usually coupled with human rights, democracy, and free markets, these commitments find a central place in the liberal tradition of political thought. The gradual but cumulatively successful prosecution of Chilean generals during the 1990s and 2000s; other successful prosecutions through national courts; the establishment of international tribunals in Yugoslavia and Rwanda and, ultimately, a permanent International Criminal Court; and reparations settlements—such are this paradigm's signature triumphs. The blanket amnesties common to the Latin American transitions of the 1980s and all other failures of accountability—these elicit the paradigm's signature cry, "Never Again!"

Leading intellectuals in the liberal human rights school have called into question core features of religious arguments for reconciliation. At times, the religious have linked reconciliation with amnesty or reductions in punishment. Tutu, for instance, defended the conditional amnesty of South Africa's Truth and Reconciliation Commission not only as a pragmatic alternative to civil war but also as an element of an altogether different form of justice from retributivism—restorative justice, a close cousin of reconciliation.[3] Liberal human rights voices are skeptical. Abrogating punishment, they argue, is always a sacrifice of justice, ought never to be reenvisioned as justice, and should be permitted only when demonstrably necessary for peace or democracy.[4] They are also skeptical that goals of religious reconciliation like healing, overcoming enmity, and forgiveness are achievable or even morally appropriate in politics, for they violate individual autonomy, disrespect liberalism's plurality of values, and undermine central democratic virtues of argument and deliberation.[5] Finally, intellectuals of the liberal human rights paradigm are chary of religious language in the politics of transitional justice, holding to some version of philosopher John Rawls's argument that political arguments, at least in constitutional matters, ought to be expressed in secular or public language.[6]

Despite these criticisms from the liberal human rights paradigm, it is too simple to equate this paradigm with secularism and the reconciliation paradigm with religion. There are secular voices who both criticize the liberal paradigm and advocate reconciliation. Few of today's leading religious perspectives on transitional justice reject human rights or democracy; historically, Judaism and Christianity have provided vital intellectual foundations for human rights.[7] Human rights activists have worked closely with religious leaders and communities for accountability in Chile, Brazil, Timor-Leste, post-Communist Germany, and elsewhere.

Still, theologians and religious activists, in their theorizing and in their political involvements, have led the way in fashioning an approach to transitional justice with a distinct center of gravity and important consequences for politics. Reconciliation is their axial idea. Christians have offered the majority of religious arguments for political reconciliation in the past generation, but Jews and Muslims have proposed versions, too. In all three Abrahamic faiths, reconciliation as a public, political practice is a recent addition to an ancient scroll. Protestant theologians like Albrecht Ritschl, Dietrich Bonhoeffer, and Karl Barth floated the idea in the late nineteenth and early twentieth centuries, while, in the Catholic Church, Pope Benedict XV urged reconciliation and forgiveness upon Europe's great powers at the end of the First World War. Reconciliation's explosive crescendo in Christian thinking, though, arose from the contemporary global outbreak of political transitions, which provided the demand for the idea, and from Tutu's leadership of South Africa's Truth and Reconciliation Commission, which articulately supplied the idea. Some Jewish thinkers have advanced political reconciliation as well, most prominently American Rabbi Marc Gopin, whose life's project is to retrieve Jewish concepts like *teshuva* (turning back, repentance) and *aveilus* (a form of mourning) for peace building and reconciliation in modern states. Gopin's Islamic counterpart is Mohammed Abu-Nimer, also an American intellectual and activist, who has tapped ideas and rituals from Islamic scripture and tradition for similar purposes.[8]

In all of these traditions, reconciliation broadly means restoration of a broken relationship to a state of right relationship. But relationship in what sense? In the liberal human rights paradigm, right relationship means that citizens come to respect and recognize one another's human rights and deliberative capacities. Religious concepts may well endorse these dimensions of right relationship, but they envision a fuller restoration, also involving apology, forgiveness, empathetic acknowledgment of suffering, and the transformation of enmity between both groups and individuals. These restorations are intrinsically important, increasing human flourishing in itself, but important also for leavening, diluting, and sometimes transforming the emotions of hatred, resentment, and revenge that frustrate stable and just political orders, sometimes for several generations, as in Bosnia, Northern Ireland and Rwanda.[9]

It is in their foundations that religious perspectives differ most from the liberal human rights paradigm. Liberal arguments about transitional justice rely on reason alone, usually a Kantian or utilitarian sort. Religious rationales for reconciliation, at least those in the Abrahamic traditions, derive their prescriptions for horizontal relationships within political communities from the vertical relationship that God forges with humanity. In Jewish perspectives, reconciliation mirrors God's covenant with Israel, to which God is faithful and willing to restore even after repeated strayings. Christian theologians root reconciliation in God's own reconciliation with humanity through Jesus Christ. In Islamic writings, reconciliation flows from the mercy of Allah, his willingness to forgive the repentant, and Qur'anic injunctions to reconcile.

Distinctive, too, is these traditions' way of thinking about justice, the most fundamental political virtue. Most striking is the claim of some theologians that reconciliation does not merely complement or supplement justice, but in fact is itself justice.[10] They point to the Hebrew words that translate to the English *justice* in the Jewish scriptures—*sedeqah* and *mishpat*—and point out that these also translate into righteousness, the thoroughgoing right relationship prescribed in God's covenants. Christian theologians point out precisely the same dynamic in the New Testament Greek words for *justice*, the several words that begin with the stem *dik-*, most prominently *dikaiosune*. Something much like right relationship is also the meaning of the Arabic *'adl*, the word that the Qur'an most commonly uses for justice. If right relationship is at the core of the meaning of reconciliation, and if justice means comprehensive right relationship, then it follows that reconciliation is itself a concept of justice. Such a restorative understanding pervades the array of practices through which reconciliation is realized in political orders. It offers a distinctive grounding to the punishment of human rights violators, one based on reintegration rather than abstract retribution. It also grounds what is perhaps the most innovative and controversial practice that religious traditions have to offer—forgiveness.

Religious arguments for reconciliation typically define *forgiveness* quite differently than philosophers and other modern thinkers have defined it since the Enlightenment—that is, as far more than a relinquishment of claims owed by perpetrators, an action that involves the victim's own will to restore and that often helps him to recover his own sense of agency. The Abrahamic faiths differ somewhat in their teachings on forgiveness. In Judaism and Islam, forgiveness is meant to be conditional upon the prior repentance of perpetrators, whereas Christian theologians are more willing to commend unilateral forgiveness on the part of victims, though they are divided over the issue.[11] Like public reconciliation, the practice of forgiveness in politics is a relatively new entry in the Abrahamic theological traditions. Accounts of transitional justice tell us that forgiveness is also a far rarer political practice than truth telling, trials, reparations, and even apologies. Nelson Mandela is one of the few statesmen to practice forgiveness publicly in a transitional setting. Religious leaders have practiced forgiveness and commended it to victims of political injustices more often, though, in South Africa, Rwanda, Sierra Leone, Chile, El Salvador, Northern Ireland, Timor-Leste, Colombia, Yugoslavia, and Germany.

Forgiveness, along with acknowledgment, restorative punishment, apologies, and the like, add up to an approach to transitional justice that addresses the broad range of wounds that political injustices inflict. This is the promise of reconciliation for political orders. Realizing this promise depends on how well reconciliation can command a consensus in any given political setting. Since world religions differ in their approaches to past evil, as do theological strands within religions, building consensus will in turn depend on how well reconciliation can be articulated in the terms of local beliefs. Helping to bridge differences among beliefs is in part the possibility of articulating the core concepts of reconciliation in secular language. The contemporary theory of restorative justice, for instance, resonates closely with reconciliation and has been articulated powerfully in secular terms. In this respect, reconciliation is much like other political and moral concepts that garner both religious and secular justifications: human rights, the laws of war, and natural law.

Reconciliation's application to politics also requires further conceptual development, particularly in response to the criticisms that the liberal human rights paradigm has raised. How can forgiveness be compatible with punishment? Does reconciliation interfere improperly in matters of the soul or violate moral autonomy? Such questions constitute an intellectual agenda for this alternative paradigm.

Religion and Reconciliation in Practice

The religious, then, have played a pivotal role in developing and spreading a paradigm for transitional justice—reconciliation—that they espouse disproportionately though not exclusively. But what kind of influence have the religious and the paradigm of reconciliation actually had in the politics of transitional justice? And what factors make certain religious actors influential? Across the world, religious actors have sought to shape transitional justice both at the level of official policy and in civil society, where they perform trauma healing, conflict resolution, reconciliation practices, and other forms of peace building in communities.

Here, I look closely only at religious actors' efforts to shape official policies, especially governments' choices for truth commissions or trials. These shaping activities show up, to greater and lesser degrees, in fifteen prominent cases of political transitions away from civil war and authoritarianism. Representative of transitional justice during the past generation, they involve a mixture of punitive measures, including trials and vetting policies, and institutions designed to bring about other dimensions of restoration, including truth commissions, reparations policies, memorials, apologies, and forgiveness, combining these in various proportions. In eight of these cases, religious leaders and communities exercised an important influence on transitional justice: Guatemala, Brazil, Chile, South Africa, Sierra

Leone, Timor-Leste, Peru, and Germany. In all of these cases, they promoted truth commissions. They did so in two ways: first, they shaped the decision for truth commissions through speaking out publicly, lobbying, and sometimes even organizing efforts to investigate past injustices themselves. Second, they shaped the actual functioning of truth commissions by influencing the selection of commissioners, sometimes actually serving as commissioners, providing logistical support for organizing and conducting hearings, locating and supporting victims and witnesses, and providing counseling in the wake of hearings. In two of these eight cases, Germany and Timor-Leste, at least some religious figures also publicly advocated punitive justice—trials, vetting policies, and other forms of accountability—although these same figures also endorsed truth commissions. In the remaining seven of the fifteen cases, though, the influence of religious actors was weak to nonexistent. The entire set, then, shows that religious actors have overwhelmingly promoted truth commissions where they are influential but have been influential in only a little over half of the cases.

What characterizes those religious actors who proved influential? Broadly, two factors.[12] The first is their political theology—their core doctrine of political authority and justice. Almost all of them carried a political theology of reconciliation, one resembling closely the paradigm described in the previous section. Even the proponents of punitive justice—Bishop Carlos Belo in Timor-Leste and former dissident pastor Joachim Gauck in Germany, for instance—articulated the language of reconciliation, though they stressed punishment and accountability comparatively strongly. Indeed, their arguments fortify the possibility that punishment can be justified compatibly with reconciliation.

But political theology describes only what animates and informs the stances of religious actors toward transitional justice, not what empowers them. A second factor behind their influence is one that contemporary sociologists of religion have described in some detail, though Hegel and Tocqueville also explored it far earlier—differentiation, or institutional autonomy from the state. Those religious actors who strongly influenced transitional justice enjoyed autonomy from their state during the period of war or authoritarianism and maintained autonomy during the transition period. Many of them preserved this autonomy only by fending off predatory states, maintaining for themselves what George Weigel has called a sphere of "moral extraterritoriality," in which they could deliberate and advocate, though always riskily.[13] During the transition to peace, democracy, or both, their autonomy then conferred on them a moral authority to shape their state's approach to transitional justice.

Religious actors who influenced their governments' institutions of transitional justice held both a political theology of reconciliation and institutional autonomy. Arguably, the strongest case of religious influence on transitional justice was that of Guatemala's Catholic Church, whose activities were described earlier. In the 1980s, the hierarchy and grassroots of this church had united and asserted autonomy from the state, becoming a strong critic of the military regime's human rights abuses during Guatemala's civil war. Reconciliation resounded through REMHI, both in its method and in its findings.[14]

In Brazil and Chile, churches conducted investigations of their military regimes' injustices. The Chilean Catholic Church, along with Catholic President Patricio Aylwin, became an influential advocate for Chile's Commission on Truth and Reconciliation during the transition to democracy following General Augusto Pinochet's departure from the presidency in 1990. The Catholic Church had established and preserved autonomy from the authoritarian Chilean state from the mid-1970s on; oppositional Catholic and Presbyterian sectors in Brazil had done the same from the late 1960s. The Chilean Catholic Church preached a message of reconciliation, especially in the aftermath of Pinochet's exit.[15]

The Chilean commission was a prototype for the South African Truth and Reconciliation Commission (TRC), whose harrowing and tearful hearings rendered it the world's most famous truth commission to date. Chairman Archbishop Tutu and other religious leaders and laypeople who held a theology of reconciliation strongly shaped the TRC, though far more its implementation than its formation. In conducting the TRC hearings, Tutu spoke the language of faith, forgiveness, and reconciliation while churches provided staff, publicity, and spiritual and psychological support for victims and perpetrators; encouraged their own followers to take part; and participated in hearings for faith communities. The South African churches who played this role were the same ones that had sustained determined resistance to the apartheid state—oppositional activity that was enabled by their relative autonomy from the state and often articulated in the language of reconciliation.[16]

Following civil war in three other countries—Sierra Leone, Timor-Leste, and Peru—religious leaders and communities contributed strongly to robust truth commissions, whose architects imitated and sought to improve on South Africa's TRC. Methodist Bishop Joseph Humper chaired Sierra Leone's Truth and Reconciliation Commission, with Islamic leaders also playing prominent roles. The Catholic Church in Timor-Leste publicly promoted Timor-Leste's Commission for Reception, Truth, and Reconciliation, provided two of its seven commissioners, and supported its Community Reconciliation Panels. In Peru, Protestant and Catholic churches advocated and supported that country's Truth and Reconciliation Commission, furnishing three of seven commissioners. True to the pattern, all of these religious actors had remained autonomous from the state during the civil war and carried a political theology of reconciliation that led them to advocate and participate in the truth commission. A consistent but slightly more complex pattern can also be found in postunification Germany. There, Protestant pastors who had been dissidents (i.e., autonomous) from the Communist East German government were influential in fashioning measures to deal with the past, often using the language of reconciliation, while the hierarchy of the national Protestant Church, who had been far more complicit with the regime, played little role in these measures at all.[17]

By contrast, in other equally dreadful sites of injustice and atrocity, religious actors acquiesced to tyranny, civil war, and genocide and were impotent in the aftermath, exercising little influence at all on institutions for transitional justice. These cases confirm the argument in a darker way. Most of these actors were integrated with their state—that is, they lacked institutional autonomy—during the time of authoritarianism or civil war, carried no political theology of reconciliation, or both.

Following Rwanda's genocide of 1994, in which some 800,000 died, Rwanda's established churches—Catholic, Anglican and Presbyterian—exercised little influence on the international tribunals, the national-level trials, or the local *gacaca* courts through which the Rwandan government sought to deal with the crimes committed. At best, they have issued statements of repentance, encouraged their members to participate in *gacaca*, and conducted reconciliation efforts within civil society. During the genocide itself, the hierarchies of these churches were largely silent toward the killings while some of their lower level clergy even participated in them, thus denuding the churches of their moral authority. Behind this infirmity lay a close integration between these churches and the Rwandan state, dating back to colonial times, as well as a dominant political theology that stressed individual salvation at the expense of social change, human rights, or social reconciliation.[18]

Nor did the Argentine Catholic Church shape either national trials or the work of the National Commission on the Disappearance of Persons (CONADEP) following Argentina's Dirty Wars of 1976 to 1983. Except for a handful of dissidents, this church's eighty bishops were closely tied to the military regime that disappeared, tortured, and killed its political opponents, while they rarely deployed a political theology of reconciliation.[19]

In the Czech Republic, Catholic and Protestant churches likewise played little role in shaping either the trials or the lustration that followed the country's transition away from Communism in 1989. These were churches that had been largely dominated by their Communist regime and failed to speak out against it until the 1980s, and then only weakly in comparison with defiant churches in Poland, South Africa, and elsewhere.[20]

The former Yugoslavia, where a civil war took 200,000 lives and created a million refugees between 1991 and 1995, is also a weak case of religious influence on transitional justice. Here, religious leaders and communities—the Croatian Catholic Church, the Serbian Orthodox Church, and the Islamic community in Bosnia—did little to bring about the International Criminal Tribunal of Yugoslavia or trials within the successor states of the disintegrated federation, Bosnia-Herzegovina, Croatia and Serbia, or to advocate truth commissions, which failed to occur in all three of these states. In this war fought between nations with identities defined primarily by religion, some leaders and lower level clerics in all three communities called for an end to fighting and later urged reconciliation, but many others aligned themselves with nationalist politicians. Such a mixed record left religious communities with little moral authority to influence official transitional justice efforts following the conflict.[21]

Another religious actor that wielded little clout over official transitional justice institutions, though a far more puzzling case, is the Polish Catholic Church.

Though a model of autonomy under authoritarianism whose defiance was instrumental to the Communist regime's downfall in 1989 (recent allegations that some Polish church leaders collaborated with the Polish Communist secret police somewhat detract from this description, but leave it largely intact), this church did little to advocate a truth commission, which never occurred, or the piecemeal punitive justice of the Head Commission for the Examination of Crimes against the Polish Nation. What was missing in this church was a widely shared political theology of reconciliation. Though as late as 1966 the Polish bishops were practicing forgiveness of Germany for its crimes against the Polish nation, after 1989 the church's message was dominated by abortion, the family, sexuality, and other issues it considered vital to the new post-Communist society.[22]

Two other puzzling cases of religious actors that failed to influence transitional justice are the Catholic Church of El Salvador and the Catholic, Anglican, Methodist, and some factions within the Presbyterian churches in Northern Ireland. Like the Guatemalan church, the Salvadoran Church remained autonomous during its country's civil war, helped mediate an end to it, and contained prominent clerics who preached reconciliation. The Northern Irish churches contained leaders who remained independent of governments and liberation movements alike and espoused reconciliation. What these cases illustrate is that while differentiation and a political theology of reconciliation may be necessary to a religious actor's influence on transitional justice, they are not sufficient. In El Salvador, the politics behind the truth commission was dominated by the United Nations, which included few other organizations, including even human rights groups, in its work. Here, the Catholic Church was only weakly involved. In Northern Ireland, several factors, including the reluctance of the British government to participate, have prevented truth commissions, trials, or any other sort of transitional justice effort from emerging thus far.[23]

Conclusion

The foregoing analysis suggests that the thinkers as well as the doers who have promoted the concept of reconciliation in transitional justice have been predominantly Christian. Is reconciliation, then, primarily a Christian paradigm? Its centrality in the Christian narrative, where it is accomplished through the death and resurrection of Jesus Christ, offers theological grounds for thinking so. But the concept might also travel more widely. The strength of Christianity in the politics of transitional justice is due also to the prevalence of Christianity among the populations that experienced the past generation's transitions to democracy and civil war settlements. A wider occurrence of political transitions among other religious populations might also spread the paradigm of reconciliation further. As I have argued, contemporary Jewish and Muslim thinkers have articulated and commended political reconciliation. In 2004 and 2005, Morocco became the first almost uniformly Muslim country to hold a truth commission, while Sierra Leone's robust Truth and Reconciliation Commission took place among a population that is 60 percent Muslim. Support for truth-telling processes is strong in both Afghanistan and Iraq as well. Reconciliation's close kin, restorative justice, finds parallels in other world religions.[24] The cultures of Maori tribes in New Zealand, First Nation tribes in Canada, native peoples in the United States, and the Bantu peoples in southern Africa all contain rich concepts and practices of reconciliation as well. It is not my claim that reconciliation will carry the same meaning and content everywhere it is found. It is rather that comparative analysis reveals the presence of a political theology or culturally rooted concept of reconciliation, with variations in its propositions and its warrants, in an impressively wide array of religions and cultures. Therein lie some grounds for optimism that as long as countries are still becoming democracies—and there are plenty that still might—and as long as settlements to wars are still being negotiated—and plenty of wars are still raging—reconciliation might come to offer its restorative potential to broken political orders.

Notes

This chapter is adapted from an earlier article, "What Religion Brings to the Politics of Transitional Justice," originally published in the *Journal of International Affairs* 61:1 (Winter 2007), 93–110.

1. For support in the research and writing of this essay, I am grateful to the Religion in Global Politics project at Harvard University, supported by the Weatherhead Center for International Affairs and the Smith Richardson Foundation, the Edmond J. Safra Foundation Center for Ethics at Harvard University, and the Alexander von Humboldt Foundation. For valuable research reports and assistance, I thank Robert Dowd, Julia Fitzpatrick, Colleen Gilg, Ben Kaplan, Dana Lee, Kevin Loria, Kevin McCormick, Robert Portada, John Skakun, Jonathan Smith, Carolyn Sweeney, and Erin Urquhart.

2. Good examples of the tradition can be found in Diane F. Orentlicher, "Settling Accounts: The Duty to Prosecute Human Rights Violations of a Prior Regime," *Yale Law Journal* 100:8 (June 1991); and Carlos Santiago Nino, *Radical Evil on Trial* (New Haven, CT: Yale University Press, 1996).

3. See Desmond Tutu, *No Future without Forgiveness* (New York: Doubleday, 1999).

4. See Timothy Garton Ash, "True Confessions," *New York Review of Books* 44 (July 17, 1997); and Kent Greenawalt, "Amnesty's Justice," in *Truth v. Justice: The Morality of Truth Commissions*, ed. Robert I. Rotberg and Dennis Thompson (Princeton, NJ: Princeton University Press, 2000).

5. Ash, "True Confessions," 37–38; Rajeev Bhargava, "Restoring Decency to Barbaric Societies," in Rotberg and Thompson, *Truth v. Justice*, 60–63; David A. Crocker, "Retribution and Reconciliation," *Philosophy and Public Policy Quarterly* 20:1 (Winter–Spring 2000), 1–6; Michael Ignatieff, "Articles of Faith," *Index on Censorship* 25:5 (1996), 112–113; and Amy Gutmann and Dennis Thompson, "The Moral Foundations of Truth Commissions," in Rotberg and Thompson, *Truth v. Justice*, 32–33.

6. Much more could be said about arguments for public reason, both Rawls's and others', and the nuances and conditions that they contain. Kent Greenawalt, for instance, criticizes the commission's religious language but elsewhere articulates a nuanced conception of public reason that is in some respects wider than Rawls's. See Greenawalt's "Amnesty's Justice," in Rotberg and Thompson, *Truth v. Justice*, 199. Thompson and Gutmann also voice concern about the religious language of the TRC in "The Moral Foundations of Truth Commissions."

7. See, for instance, Nicholas Wolterstorff's *Justice: Rights and Wrongs* (Princeton, NJ: Princeton University Press, 2008).

8. For examples of recent Christian writings on reconciliation, see Donald W. Shriver, *An Ethic for Enemies: Forgiveness in Politics* (New York: Oxford University Press, 1995); Robert Schreiter, *The Ministry of Reconciliation: Spirituality and Strategies* (Maryknoll, NY: Orbis, 1998); Miroslav Volf, *Exclusion and Embrace: A Theological Exploration of Identity, Otherness, and Reconciliation* (Nashville, TN: Abingdon, 1996); and John W. De Gruchy, *Reconciliation: Restoring Justice* (Minneapolis, MN: Fortress, 2003); and the essays in *The Politics of Past Evil: Religion, Reconciliation, and Transitional Justice*, ed. Daniel Philpott (Notre Dame, IN: University of Notre Dame Press, 2006). For Gopin's thought, see his *Between Eden and Armageddon: The Future of World Religions, Violence, and Peacemaking* (Oxford: Oxford University Press, 2000) and his *Holy War, Holy Peace* (Oxford: Oxford University Press, 2002). For Abu-Nimer's thought, see his *Nonviolence and Peace Building in Islam* (Gainesville: University Press of Florida, 2003).

9. On the role of emotions in fueling conflict, especially ethnic and nationalist conflict, see Roger D. Peterson, *Understanding Ethnic Violence: Fear, Hatred, and Resentment in Twentieth-Century Eastern Europe* (Cambridge: Cambridge University Press, 2002).

10. See, for instance, Christopher D. Marshall, *Beyond Retribution: A New Testament Vision for Justice, Crime and Punishment* (Grand Rapids. MI: Eerdmans, 2001); and N. T. Wright, *Evil and the Justice of God* (Downers Grove, IL: InterVarsity, 2006).

11. See L. Gregory Jones, *Embodying Forgiveness* (Grand Rapids, MI: Eerdmans, 1993); Carol Schersten LaHurd, "So That the Sinner Will Repent: Forgiveness in Islam and Christianity," *Dialog* 35: 4 (1996); and Louis E. Newman, "The Quality of Mercy: On the Duty to Forgive in the Judaic Tradition," *Journal of Religious Ethics* 15:2 (1987).

12. My theoretical argument here is drawn from Daniel Philpott, "Explaining the Political Ambivalence of Religion," *American Political Science Review* 101:3 (2007).

13. George Weigel, *The Final Revolution: The Resistance Church and the Collapse of Communism* (Oxford: Oxford University Press, 1992), 151.

14. Michael Hayes and David Tombs, eds., *Truth and Memory: The Church and Human Rights in El Salvador and Guatemala* (Leominster, England: Gracewing, 2001), 34, 104–108, 111, 125; Paul Jeffrey; "Telling the Truth," *Christian Century* (1995), 28–63; and Jeffrey Klaiber, *The Church, Dictatorship, and Democracy in Latin America* (Maryknoll, NY: Orbis, 1998), 216–238.

15. Alexandra Barahona de Brito, *Human Rights and Democratization in Latin America: Uruguay and Chile* (Oxford: Oxford University Press, 1997), 106–113, 155–160; Michael Fleet and Brian H. Smith, *The Catholic Church and Democracy in Chile and Peru* (Notre Dame, IN: University of Notre Dame Press, 1997), 160–166.

16. Lyn Graybill, "South Africa's Truth and Reconciliation Commission: Ethical and Theological Perspectives," *Ethics and International Affairs* 12 (1998), 103–123.

17. Beth Dougherty, "Searching for Answers: Sierra Leone's Truth and Reconciliation Commission," *African Studies Quarterly* 8:1 (2004); Jeffrey Klaiber, "Peru's Truth Commission

and the Churches," *Bulletin of Missionary Research* 28:4 (2004); Arnold S. Kohen, "The Catholic Church and the Independence of East Timor," in *Bitter Flowers, Sweet Flowers: East Timor, Indonesia, and the World Community*, ed. Richard Tanter, Mark Selden, and Stephen R. Shalom (Lanham, MD: Rowman and Littlefield, 2001); A. James McAdams, "The Double Demands of Reconciliation: The Case of Unified Germany," in *The Politics of Past Evil*, 127–149; and McAdams, *Judging the Past in Unified Germany* (Cambridge: Cambridge University Press, 2001), 23–54.

18. Timothy Longman, "Church Politics and the Genocide in Rwanda," *Journal of Religion in Africa* 31:2 (May 2001), 166, 171, 180.

19. Klaiber, *The Church, Dictatorship, and Democracy*, 75–91.

20. Weigel, *The Final Revolution*, 159–190; Sabrina P. Ramet, *Nihil Obstat: Religion, Politics, and Social Change in East-Central Europe and Russia* (Durham, NC: Duke University Press, 1998), 112–119.

21. David A. Steele, "Christianity in Bosnia-Herzegovina and Kosovo: From Ethnic Captive to Reconciling Agent," in *Faith-Based Diplomacy: Trumping Realpolitik*, ed. Douglas Johnston (Oxford: Oxford University Press, 2003), 126–129.

22. Andrzej S. Walicki, "Transitional Justice and the Political Struggles of Post-Communist Poland," in *Transitional Justice and the Rule of Law in New Democracies*, ed. A. James McAdams (Notre Dame, IN: Notre Dame University Press, 1997); Tina Rosenberg, *This Haunted Land: Facing Europe's Ghosts after Communism* (New York: Random House, 1995), 178–222.

23. Margaret Popkin, *Peace without Justice: Obstacles to Building the Rule of Law in El Salvador* (University Park: Pennsylvania State University Press, 2000); Daniel Santiago, *The Harvest of Justice: The Church of El Salvador Ten Years after Romero* (New York: Paulist, 1993), 169–180; Stephen J. Pope, "The Convergence of Forgiveness and Justice: Lessons from El Salvador," *Theological Studies* 64 (2003), 812–835; David Porter, Interview, November 17, 2005.

24. Hadley, Michael L., ed., *The Spiritual Roots of Restorative Justice*, Albany: State University of New York Press, 2001.

Annotated Bibliography

Abu-Nimer, Mohammed. *Nonviolence and Peace Building in Islam*. Gainesville: University Press of Florida, 2003.
Though not precisely on transitional justice, this is a rich and creative source of Islamic thought on peace building that has important implications for transitional justice.
Brudholm, Thomas, and Thomas Cushman, eds. *The Religious in Response to Mass Atrocity: Interdisciplinary Perspectives*. Cambridge: Cambridge University Press, 2009.
This is an excellent interdisciplinary exploration of the role of religion in peace building; several of the chapters touch directly on transitional justice. It is also notable for its diversity of views on the role of religion in transitional justice and on concepts like reconciliation and forgiveness, some of the chapters being quite skeptical.
De Gruchy, John W. *Reconciliation: Restoring Justice*. Minneapolis, MN: Fortress, 2003.
This is one of the best theological arguments for reconciliation with strong application to transitional justice, especially the South Africa case. Its emphasis is Christian, but it also includes a chapter on the house of Abraham.

Gopin, Marc. *Between Eden and Armageddon: The Future of World Religions, Violence, and Peacemaking*. Oxford: Oxford University Press, 2000.

Gopin's book is a landmark in the area of religious peace building, also with rich implications for transitional justice. Gopin is a Jewish rabbi and gives deep attention to the Jewish tradition but also discusses Christian and Muslim approaches.

Philpott, Daniel. *The Politics of Past Evil: Religion, Reconciliation, and the Dilemmas of Transitional Justice*. Notre Dame, IN: University of Notre Dame Press, 2006.

This book seeks to directly explore the role of religion in transitional justice, including theological, philosophical, and social scientific perspectives. Though its center of gravity is Christian, it also includes perspectives on transitional justice in interreligious contexts.

Shriver, Donald W. *An Ethic for Enemies: Forgiveness in Politics*. New York: Oxford University Press, 1995.

A significant treatment of the ethics of reconciliation and forgiveness—and one of the first in the past generation of literature. It draws from religious traditions, finds strong common ground with secular perspectives, and contains case studies.

Vinjamuri, Leslie, and Aaron P. Boesenecker. "Religious Actors and Transitional Justice" In *Religious Pluralism, Globalization, and World Politics* ed. Thomas Banchoff. Oxford: Oxford University Press, (2008), pp. 155-194

This chapter is one of the few efforts to explore empirically and create a comparative typology of the role that religion plays in transitional justice, and it is therefore a vital addition to the social science literature on transitional justice.

Volf, Miroslav. *Exclusion and Embrace: A Theological Exploration of Identity, Otherness, and Reconciliation*. Nashville, TN: Abingdon, 1996.

One of the deepest and most intellectually profound of the theological treatments of reconciliation, this book does not directly consider transitional justice but has much to say about it. Like Shriver's, it was an early but enduring influence on the current generation's thinking about reconciliation and transitional justice.

PART IV

Religion, Humanitarianism, and Civil Society

10 }

Where Is the Religion?

HUMANITARIANISM, FAITH, AND WORLD AFFAIRS

Michael Barnett

After years of researching humanitarianism without giving much attention to religion, two observations caused me to wonder what I had been missing. The first was the significance the humanitarian community attached to the distinction between faith-based and secular organizations. The presumption was that religion "mattered" in some way, but identifying precisely how became an elusive undertaking. Did this mean, for instance, that religious and secular organizations differed in terms of the populations they served, what they did on the ground, and the kinds of programs they ran? Many Christian and Islamic aid agencies attempt to convert those they assist, but some of the biggest faith-based agencies, including Islamic Relief, Catholic Relief Services, and Lutheran World Relief, appeared to keep their religious beliefs to themselves. And some of the biggest proselytizers were those from secular organizations who were trumpeting human rights. Moreover, faith and secular agencies often had comparable footprints; there were rarely any identifying marks to determine whether a latrine or well had been dug by a faith-based or a secular organization.

If a distinction could not be easily drawn by what they did, perhaps a difference could be found by what they believed. Certainly, many of those who chose to work in a faith-based institution did so because of their religious commitments and their desire to act with fellow believers. When I visited the headquarters of World Vision International in Monrovia, California, staff excused themselves in the morning for prayer. Many of the staff I met at the Islamic Relief office in Helwan, Cairo, told me how their religion had influenced their decision to seek a career in the charitable sector. However, were staff of secular agencies without faith? In response to a question regarding his personal beliefs, a former head of Médecins Sans Frontières (MSF) spoke at length about his engagement with Catholicism (including a very serious consideration of the priesthood) and the profound influence of the twentieth-century Jewish Hassidic philosopher Martin Buber, especially his classic *I and Thou*, on his thinking. Most aid workers I have met appear to treat humanitarian action as a way to connect the immanent to the transcendent and vice versa.

Moreover, whatever differences that might have existed between faith and secular agencies appeared to be dissolving in the face of international pressures. Many of today's religious agencies are shadows of their former selves. In the nineteenth century, many religious agencies, especially those with a missionary component, desired to save souls as their main or primary goal; by the end of the century, though, some downplayed this dimension in preference for saving lives and changing societies. Think of the YMCA, the Young Men's Christian Association, which was founded to evangelize the millions of young men migrating to America's urban centers in the nineteenth century but doesn't betray much of an evangelical tendency today. Sometimes these changes were premised on the rising importance Christians gave to witnessing by deed rather than by word. World Vision International is still an evangelical organization, but it no longer runs church revivals. Why have religious organizations taken on more of the characteristics associated with secular agencies? Global pressures are one possible answer. Faith-based and secular organizations confront the same environment: they tackle the same complex emergencies; they often compete for the same funds from the same donors; they increasingly espouse an ethic of consequences; they use the same metrics to provide evidence that they are delivering results; they have been jointly constructing new professional standards, sectorwide principles, and codes of conduct that apply to all agencies, religious and secular alike; and they use the same discourse.[1] In general, because they confront the same environment and respond in fairly similar ways, secular and faith-based agencies are growing more alike all the time.

Not only was I unable to clearly mark the boundaries between faith-based and secular organizations but also the broad relationship between religion and humanitarianism posed comparable challenges. This was the second observation that left me perplexed. Today, most contemporary international institutions of compassion, including international refugee and human rights law, appear thoroughly secular, citing principles of humanity and not religion, referring to an international and not a religious community, and acting on principles of impartiality and not difference based on religious identity. Yet many of them were founded on religious discourses and religiously inspired action. Modern humanitarianism's origins date back to the nineteenth century, when evangelicals began to create specialized institutions of compassion, sometimes working with and through the state but more often working entirely through voluntary, bottom-up activism.[2] Devout Christians organized the first international campaigns against slavery, forced labor, and human trafficking.[3] The desire by missionaries and similarly religiously committed individuals to bring attention to various abuses in the colonial world helped to build momentum for new forms of humanitarian intervention and awareness of unspeakable crimes committed by Westerners against colonial peoples, including King Leopold's "humanitarian" activities in the Congo Free State.[4] International humanitarian law owes a debt to Christianity. The founders of the International Committee for the Red Cross (ICRC) saw themselves as part of Christian Europe and hoped that that the organization would help instill what they perceived to be the uniquely Christian values of compassion, charity, and mercy.[5] The modern human rights movement began with religious rights (that is, religious freedom), religious forces helped to expand international human rights, and religious activists contributed to the creation of many international human rights covenants.[6]

Reading the history of humanitarianism with an eye for its religious dimensions, then, led to something of an optical illusion: when I began with the present and backtracked through history, the secular became increasingly overshadowed by the religious, and when I began at the beginning and marched forward the religious seemed to disappear into a secular sky. Rather than reaching for a standard secularization story line to make sense of this narrative, I found myself asking questions that made a sharp distinction between the religious and the secular impossible to maintain. Perhaps humanitarianism retains a religious quality and only appears (to secular humanists) secular. Perhaps religion, namely, Christianity, has found a way to convert the world without a religious conversion. Is this why so many narratives of humanitarianism are sprinkled with Christian symbolism, with references to sacrifice, redemption, offering, witnessing, atonement, and salvation? Is this why so many Islamic populations are suspicious of Western aid organizations, including those that deny any sort of religious affiliation but are still suspect because they come bearing the cross (such as the ICRC)? Are religious organizations using humanitarian institutions to launder religious values? Or perhaps humanitarianism is universal and ecumenical, reflecting the commitment of most if not all major religions to the reduction of human suffering. Values once associated with Christianity, including charity, love, and compassion, are not specific to Christianity but are truly cross-cultural. In general, the relationship between humanitarianism and religion resembled Alice's Cheshire cat, able to change appearances, sometimes before my very eyes.

This chapter uses humanitarianism's androgynous quality—its possession of both religious and secular attributes—to explore two issues regarding the contemporary world order. First, the distinction between the religious and the secular is more deceptive than informative. There is no fixed boundary between humanitarianism and religion any more than there is a fixed boundary between the secular and the religious; instead, these boundaries are an act of human creation and re-creation. The concept of "faith" is one way of collapsing the boundaries between religion and secularism in humanitarianism. I will argue that most of those who populate the humanitarian sector express different forms of faith—for some, it is associated with organized religion and pivots around God, and for others it is a form of cosmopolitanism and pivots around humanity. Despite their differences, each connects their actions to a version of the transcendent. In short, the label "faith-based" obscures the variety of faith traditions—the forms of transcendentalism, if you will—that are part of humanitarianism.[7]

Second, contemporary Western religious tradition and humanitarianism are equally wary of the "political." On the one hand, both work to maintain an autonomy from politics: Western tradition holds that God and humanitarianism occupy a space separate from politics, that religion and humanitarianism can survive only if politics stays out, and that religious and humanitarian organizations must respect the state's authority. On the other hand, both religious and humanitarian practices are constantly encroaching on politics because they find it nearly impossible to feed the poor and heal the sick without also tackling the underlying causes of suffering. The shifting terrain between religion and secularism within humanitarianism, and the political and the religious in humanitarianism, points to a faith-based world order.

Religions, Faith, and Humanitarianism

Students and practitioners of humanitarianism routinely distinguish between religious and secular aid agencies, and the former are typically labeled "faith-based organizations." Treating religion and faith as synonymous has important implications for how we understand faith in the modern world. There is the assumption that the only kind of faith is religious faith. This distinction also assumes that the world can be neatly divided into religious and secular elements (a position that few advance today). Faith-based means religious, and nonfaith implies secular. Secular agencies, then, cannot be motivated by faith because the only kind of faith that exists is religious. Yet, as I just noted, many staff of secular agencies routinely claim to be religious. Indeed, it is not uncommon for staff of religious agencies to belong to a religious community other than the one that names the aid agency; not everyone who works for Catholic Relief Services is Catholic, and you don't have to be Jewish to work for the American Joint Jewish Distribution Committee.

Whether and how we sort out the role of religion and faith in humanitarianism depends on how we define each. There is, of course, no single, accepted definition of religion. Instead of trying to settle what will always be unsettled, scholars have favored formulations that identify "family resemblances," allowing them to identify a set of beliefs, commitments, and institutionalized practices that combine to produce an entity that can be defined as more or less religious.[8] So, for instance, religions have various characteristics—including appeal to supernatural entities, conversion experiences, doctrines, rituals, understandings of the meaning of suffering, distinctions between the sacred and profane, and so on—but not all of these characteristics need to be present for the given entity to count as a religion.

Arguably more important for my argument is the distinction between religion and religious experience. Using the work of William James as his starting point, John Dewey insisted that we not confuse the two. Religion, according to Dewey, constitutes a special body of beliefs and practices that recognizes an unseen higher power that controls human destiny and deserves obedience, reverence, and worship and has some kind of institutional organization, loose or tight.[9] Religious experience, on the other hand, is when the "self is…directed toward something beyond itself and so its own unification depends upon the idea of shifting scenes of the world into that imaginative totality we call the Universe."[10] In other words, individuals can have religious experiences without belonging to a religion or associating the experience with a religion. Along similar lines, Charles Taylor has asserted that humans have a constant need to find "something beyond or transcendent to their lives."[11] Dewey and Taylor are capturing something quite real—the need of people to find meaning in their lives and to anchor that meaning in something that is bigger than they are.[12] In this way, those who have a religious experience also can develop a belief in the divine that does not depend on the existence of a God.[13]

What is common to the religious experience that is and is not associated with religion? There is no single answer, but in my conversations with those in the humanitarian community, I have become deeply impressed by the recurring importance of what can only be called the transcendent, in line with Charles Taylor's suggestion. The transcendent should not be confused with more familiar concepts, such as cosmopolitanism. When international relations scholars and political theorists refer to a global, transnational, or cosmopolitan society, they typically have in mind a belief that we have obligations to others regardless of their identity or their location.[14] The discourse of humanitarianism connects to cosmopolitanism through the principles of impartiality and nondiscrimination. The transcendent, however, refers not to the material but to the metaphysical or supernatural. Transcendentalism goes beyond cosmopolitanism—from the willed belief that we have obligations to those who live in distant lands to include the unwilled belief that stems from an "imaginative totality." Because it is unwilled belief and does not depend on empirical evidence, it is faith based. The capacity of individuals to link their everyday actions to the transcendent, to find meaning and enchantment in practical and worldly activities, is closely connected to the distinction between the immanent and the transcendent. There are various ways to think about their relationship, but for my purposes, Charles Taylor's view works well:

> The great invention of the West was that of an immanent order in Nature, whose working could be systematically understood and explained on its own terms, leaving open the question whether this whole order had a deeper significance, and whether, if it did, we should infer a transcendent Creator beyond it. This notion of the "immanent" involved denying—or at least isolating and perhaps problematizing—any form of interpenetration between the things of Nature, on the one hand, and the "supernatural" on the other, be this understood in terms of the one transcendent God or of Gods or spirits, or magic forces or whatever.[15]

Processes associated with the enlightenment, modernity, and secularization have caused considerable disenchantment, but human beings nevertheless demonstrate a remarkable talent for discovering enchantment in their daily lives and maintaining a faith in the divine. And people find that meaning outside of religion.[16]

Many who are part of the human rights movements speak of the Universal Declaration of Human Rights as their bible.[17] Although MSF might appear to be the quintessentially secular organization, it has many of the characteristics normally associated with a religious order.[18] The United Nations is frequently referred to as the international community's church.[19] There are ways in which humanitarianism appears to have the quality of a theodicy, providing a way to maintain a belief in some form of progress in a world in which unbearable suffering exists and unspeakable crimes are committed.[20]

Although I have used the concepts of faith and the transcendent to collapse the distinction between the religious and the secular in the context of humanitarian action, I now want to consider the possibility that these are distinctions with a difference. After all, these are categories that those in the aid community use to help them organize the world, not categories imposed by scholars to help them analyze the aid community. I proceed warily, however. We do not know much about how religious commitment differs from other kinds of commitments. Much of what we think we know about religious agencies derives from scattered studies and observations of Christian organizations. Moreover, we know very little about religiously inspired organizations outside of Christianity. This ignorance is especially noteworthy in the cases of Islamic charitable and philanthropic organizations, where hyperbole often substitutes for reason and firsthand analysis.[21] The general presumption is that Islamic aid agencies differ from their Western and Christian counterparts, but this observation seems largely based on speculation and suspicion and not on hard-boiled evidence. What about Jewish traditions, most notably the growing popularity of *tikkun olam*, that is, a desire to use good acts to "repair the world" that, according to Jewish Kabbalah tradition, was shattered at the point of creation?[22] What of Hindu traditions of relief, charity, and giving?[23] Relatedly, most generalizations are based on anecdotes, rumors, and cases that are picked because they prove the point, not empirical analysis. Also, because religion, religious practice, and religious interpretation are themselves in constant flux, any proposition will find the historical ground shifting and unstable, to say the least. Furthermore, many of the differences attributed to religion might be due to other factors, including the organization's age, size, nationality, and funding patterns. These caveats notwithstanding, because the humanitarian community distinguishes between religious and secular organizations, I want to suggest several ways in which religious beliefs might affect the meaning and practice of humanitarianism.

Most if not all the major religions have admonitions to care for the weakest members of the community, to demonstrate compassion for those who are suffering, and to demonstrate their own religious convictions through public and private acts of charity. These anchoring beliefs can have various kinds of effects. Religious beliefs might encourage greater stoicism. Nicholas Kristof, the *New York Times* columnist who has traveled the world bringing attention to silent suffering and neglected injustices, has remarked that the farther he travels from any given capital city, the greater the likelihood that the aid worker he meets will be from a religious organization. Not only might the religiously motivated be more willing to endure greater hardship and isolation but also they might be willing to do so for longer periods of time. Religious orders are often known for their lifelong commitment to the marginalized and the vulnerable, believing that by serving the poor, they are serving God. In general, the humanitarian imperative might look different, depending on whether the imperative derives from religious or secular faith traditions.

Religious beliefs might also affect whose suffering matters—that is, the boundaries of the moral community. Following on the beliefs that all human beings are created in God's image, have the capacity to accept Jesus Christ as their savior, and enjoy the possibility of being saved, Christian-based organizations distinguish themselves by going wherever they are needed. Although this suggests that the community is defined in a borderless manner, many Christian agencies in fact operate with the desire to expand the boundaries of the community, that is, to bring nonbelievers into the flock. Consequently, the idea of "needs" is given a spiritual inflection. In contrast, a frequent observation is that Islamic agencies do not venture outside the *umma*, the Islamic community, and, like many of their Christian counterparts, treat charitable activities as a way to strengthen the self, the body and spirit of the sufferer, and the Islamic community.[24] In short, because religions operate with different (and variegated) conceptions of community, religious organizations are likely to have different considerations in mind when deciding where to practice and whom to treat.

The claim that religions contain moral boundaries raises the equally controversial observation that humanistic faith is more likely to lead to a morally flat world. The argument, in short, is that liberal, humanistic beliefs make it difficult to sustain, at least rhetorically, the claim that some lives are worth more than others; a humanistic tradition is more likely than religious beliefs to lead to principles of impartiality and nondiscrimination. I am not suggesting that somehow the secular Enlightenment has created a superior human being. This is a position that Kant himself argued could be sustained only by an "overheated mind" and that the political theorist and religious scholar Nicholas Wolterstorff countered on the grounds that liberal humanism might shrink the moral community because it privileges only those people with developed capacities for rationality and autonomy.[25] However, humanistic discourses might have expanded the boundaries of the community.[26] Along these lines, Richard Rorty argues that (liberal) education, wealth, and security have caused societies to develop broader definitions of the moral community that are related to the centrality of the autonomy and liberty of the individual; the moral community rests on helping even the weakest person, a person valued because of her humanity.[27]

Religious beliefs might also shape the organization's understanding of the social purpose of humanitarian action. Some religious organizations see charitable activity as a precursor to conversion. Some Christian aid organizations hope that providing food, medicine, education, and other basic needs will create an opportunity for them to spread their religious message, and some Islamic agencies engage in comparable activities. For many staff of religious agencies, humanitarian action is a way to express their religious beliefs; Christian agencies often call such activity "witness-ing." (In a fascinating twist, this is a term adopted by the thoroughly secular MSF, which it calls *témoignage*). Similarly, there is historical and cross-cultural variation regarding whether aid is supposed to keep people alive and nothing more or whether it is designed to help remove the causes of suffering, today defined in the West as social justice. As a longtime member of World Vision International put it, "we are constantly taking our temperature" to see whether and how we are Christian, and such reflections caused them to become more concerned with issues of social justice. Over the 1990s, Catholic Relief Services explored how Catholic social teaching might inform its activities, and it, too, emerged with a greater commitment to social justice. The Islamic world appears to be moving from "charity" to "philanthropy," roughly paralleling the shift among Western aid agencies from relief to root causes.[28] In gen-eral, religious agencies demonstrate considerable variation in terms of what they believe is the purpose of aid and what individuals need to become "fully human," variations that can derive from different interpretations of their religion.

Last, religious organizations might be more accountable to their beneficiaries than are secular organizations.[29] One of the distinguishing features of many reli-gious organizations is the extent to which they are firmly embedded in the local com-munity. Sometimes this is the result of missionary activity, in which the individual lives for years in one place, or because activities are organized through the local, indigenous church. In either case, the argument goes, they are more likely to be inte-grated into the local community and thus be more responsive to its needs. Funding patterns might also play an independent or intervening role. Religious organiza-tions are reported to be less dependent on government financing because they have a built-in source—the faithful—and this independence might give them the luxury of not having to be overly attentive to the interests and agendas of the state.

Efforts to uncover how religion affects humanitarian action will confront con-siderable conceptual, theoretical, and methodological hurdles. There is the dan-ger of assuming that an unchanging religious sphere is neatly cleaved off from an unchanging secular sphere. There is the danger of attempting to move from highly conditioned, historically bounded, and context-dependent claims to broader gen-eralizations regarding the difference that religion makes. There is the danger of assuming that religion is somehow distinctive from the other kinds of faith tradi-tions that aid workers use to give meaning and significance to their actions. These and other dangers aside, there are grounds for exploring how religious beliefs might differ from other kinds of faith traditions and how this variation might shape the practices of humanitarian action.

Religion, Humanitarianism, and the Political

Historically speaking, humanitarianism and religion have somewhat identi-cal views on politics, namely, "Keep away!" Humanitarian agencies defined themselves in opposition to politics.[30] Certainly, they recognized that humanitarianism is the offspring of politics, that their activities bear political consequences, and that they are inextricably part of the political world. Yet the widely accepted definition of humanitarianism—the impartial, independent, and neutral provision of relief to those who are in avoidable danger of harm—emerged in opposition to a particular meaning of politics and helped to depoliticize relief-oriented activities.

The foundational purpose of humanitarian action—the provision of assistance to those at immediate risk—removed it from politics. Many activities might alleviate suffering and improve life circumstances, including human rights and development, but these are political because they aspire to restructure underlying social relations. Humanitarianism provides relief; it offers to save individuals but not to eliminate the underlying causes that placed them at risk. Humanitarians' original principles also were a reaction to politics. The principle of humanity commands attention to all humankind and inspires cosmopolitanism. The principle of impartiality demands that assistance be based on need and not discriminate on the basis of nationality, race, religious belief, gender, political opinions, or other considerations. The principles of neutrality and independence also helped inoculate humanitarianism from politics. Relief agencies are best able to perform their lifesaving activities if, and only if, they are untouched and unhindered by state interests and partisan agendas. Neutrality involves refraining from taking part in hostilities or from any action that either benefits or disadvantages the parties to the conflict. Neutrality is both an end and a means to an end because it helps relief agencies gain access to populations at risk. Independence demands that assistance should not be connected to any of the parties directly involved in the conflict or who have a stake in the outcome. Accordingly, many agencies either refused government funding or limited their reliance on it. The principles of humanity, impartiality, neutrality, and independence served to depoliticize humanitarian action and create a "humanitarian space"—a space insulated from politics.

Western religious tradition—that is, primarily Christianity and secondarily Judaism—also wants to keep a space for itself, insulated from politics. As Mark Lilla has argued, religious scholars have wrestled with how to distinguish themselves from politics, and liberal political theorists have attempted to contain religion's potential excesses. Best captured by Matthew 22:21—"Render unto Caesar the things that are Caesar's and unto God the things that are God's"—the church asserts its religious authority over the sphere of belief and worship while respecting the state's authority over the public sphere of society as a whole. As in all generalizations, there are important exceptions and shadings—not least because the religious and political spheres overlap on many contested moral issues, including "humanitarian" issues such as war and peace and the treatment of criminals and prisoners of war—but this general doctrinal orientation has had an important effect on the mind-set of religious aid agencies. In particular, it has caused many of them to worry that if they violate the state's domain, then the state might interpret this breach as an invitation to interfere in religion.[31] Illustrative of this desired divide are these snapshots from different historical periods.

The World Missionary Conference (WMC), one of the world's largest gatherings of missionaries, in Edinburgh, Scotland, in 1910, was a highly self-conscious and scientific effort to consider how best to Christianize the world. The many topics it covered included the relationship between missionaries and political power. The conference gave credit to colonialism for opening new territories to missionary work and also emphasized that because colonial powers were Christian powers that the power of the state could and should be used to spread a Christian civilization. Importantly, the conference reflected on how missionaries should best interact with colonial powers and identified a set of rules that resemble contemporary humanitarian principles. They expressed a principle of humanity: that all individuals had the right to hear the gospel and have the opportunity to convert. They expressed a principle of neutrality, insofar as it discouraged missionaries from confronting colonial governments because doing so might jeopardize access to populations in need. They attempted to maintain a line between themselves and politics. Matters of governance were the domain of the state, matters of religion were the domain of the church, and both the government and the church needed to recognize each other's sphere of authority. In addition, missionaries must not engage in "political agitation" and have a duty to teach and practice obedience to "settled government." As in all matters, there were considerable gaps between ideology and practice, and what conferees decided in Scotland might not have translated into sermons in outposts in the Sudan. However, the conference proceedings, given the considerable input from missionaries around the world, represented the determination of missionaries to communicate to political authorities that they knew their place.

World Vision International (WVI), founded in 1950 by the evangelist Dr. Bob Pierce, grew from modest beginnings to worldwide prominence in the 1980s, all the while trying to stay on the other side of politics. Its rapid rise was owed in part to Pierce's pioneering message that combined evangelism with social action. Until Pierce's time, most Protestant fundamentalists, much like many of their coreligionists, believed that religion and the state should stick to their assigned roles—religion saves souls, and governments perform social action. Moreover, fundamentalists looked down on what they believed were the excesses of liberal church organizations, which, beginning at the turn of the century, seemed to be more passionate about humanitarianism than salvation. And there were divisions within evangelicalism, most importantly between the fundamentalists and the new evangelicals. In addition to doctrinal differences, the new evangelicals broke with the fundamentalists because the former wanted to emphasize social concerns. Prior to Pierce, though, they had not crossed the line from emphasizing social concerns to doing social action—but Pierce dared them to do so.

Doing social action included evangelism but excluded politics. The new evangelicals were as respectful of traditional state-church boundaries as any other Protestant group. Even when World Vision was struggling to pay the bills during its first few decades, it refused to seek government funding because it worried about state interference. As it moved from its original focus on orphanages to children's welfare to community development, it tried to steer clear of politics as it defined it. Consequently, many of its activities became defined in technocratic terms. For instance, World Vision would teach people to fish, but it would not consider whether they had access to the lake or could get a license from the state to open a fish market. Over time, in fact, it de-emphasized the purely religious content of its programs and proselytization in favor of a somewhat more "modernist" view that there are differences between the spiritual and the material world. It was becoming more like—though still quite distinguishable from—secular development and relief agencies.[32]

Yet humanitarianism and religion both have political ambitions and frequently want to transform the world. Notwithstanding the constant claims that it is apolitical, humanitarianism always has been political. Individuals join aid agencies because they want to make a difference. They travel to sites of suffering to bear witness and protest an international sacrificial order that demands its quota of victims.[33] They lobby governments to respect international humanitarian law. Most dramatically, they are more deeply involved in trying to tackle the root causes of suffering, transporting them deep into politics as they try to create a better environment for human rights, democracies, and responsible states. Humanitarians might complain about politics encroaching on their turf, but humanitarians have always defined their turf in political terms.

Religious organizations also have difficulty respecting, or even knowing, where the boundaries exist between themselves and politics. Religious organizations and movements have frequently targeted questions of social justice, certainly in the Abrahamic traditions. Christian, Jewish, and Islamic texts make frequent reference to the need for charity and the urgency of fighting for social justice, which invariably blurs settled boundaries between religion and the state. Those who joined the antislavery societies of the early nineteenth century also justified forms of colonialism because of its civilizing properties. European powers were defined as Christian powers, making it difficult to take the religious identity out of the state. This meant that missionaries believed that they should have a friend in the colonial administrator, but it also meant that they sometimes held dissenting views concerning how "good" Christian administrators should treat local populations. If missionaries experienced tension with political authorities, it was because they often found the colonial powers failing to comport themselves in a Christian manner and needing reminders of what constituted sinful behavior.[34] Those in attendance at the WMC included a who's who from the worlds of diplomacy, letters, religion, and government, including the world-renowned diplomat Lord Alfred Balfour and the highly decorated soldier and military strategist Admiral Alfred Thayer Mahan, and the conference received letters of encouragement from many politicians, including President Theodore Roosevelt, who acknowledged the tightly braided relationship between colonialism, civilization, and Christianity. At the conclusion of the WMC, the participants pronounced their right to "exercise their influence for the removal of gross oppression and injustice, particularly where the government is in the hands of men of their own race...provided that in so doing they keep clear of association with any political movement." In this respect, they foreshadowed the contemporary distinction used by many in the humanitarian community between being political and being partisan.

This long history of drawing and redrawing the boundaries between religion, humanitarian action, and politics continues today. World Vision International and Catholic Relief Service, for instance, have become more involved in issues of social justice, including debt relief and poverty reduction, all the while claiming that they are still apolitical because they do not engage in partisan politics. Moreover, WVI's decision to turn toward an explicit consideration of social justice, inequality, access to power, and poor people's movements was the result of disappointments with its programs' effectiveness, a concern that its programs needed to reclaim their spiritual and religious character, and religious debates.[35] In addition, like much of the aid community, WVI began to consider the relationship between relief and reconstruction and how to get at the root causes of violence, injustice, and hardship. In general, WVI had broken away from its traditional religious confines and moved into the political world as it explicitly addressed issues of power, governance, and justice. Although it avoided the language of politics because of its long-standing discomfort, favoring euphemisms like "advocacy," WVI's humanitarianism now included practices that were once defined as political.

Recognizing the difficulty that Christian aid agencies face in defining the boundaries between religion and politics casts a slightly different light on Islamic humanitarianism. While there is considerable variation and complexity in the relationship between Islam and politics worldwide, themes that are explored elsewhere in this book, a sharp distinction between religion and the state is less familiar and accepted in many parts of the Muslim-majority world than in the Christian-majority societies of the West. Consequently and conceptually speaking, Islamic agencies have greater difficulty identifying where the boundaries might be drawn and even debate whether it is legitimate to try to do so.[36] However, while there are characteristic differences between Islamic and Christian aid agencies in terms of where to draw the line between religion and politics, it has by no means been easy for Christian agencies to negotiate this shifting and tense boundary.

Conclusion

Humanitarianism suggests that the relationship between religion and world order is more complicated than many students of international relations might believe. Whereas international relations theorists tend to see religion as the source of much evil and secularism as the source of stability, religiously based humanitarianism has been a source of considerable "moral progress." Whereas international relations theorists have tended to accept a secularization thesis, particularly as they observed a nineteenth-century world order that was once unabashedly labeled Christian morph into a world order organized around humanity, religion continues to shape world affairs. Whereas international relations theorists tend to try to reduce the role of religion to the role of explicitly motivated religious actors, including states and nonstate actors, the very principles of world order might themselves be constituted by religious principles. Whereas international relations theorists have been comfortable dividing the world between the secular and the religious, the boundaries between the two are constantly shifting because of real-world realities and actors.

In sum, our contemporary world order might have a religious dimension in visible and veiled ways. Whereas humanitarian organizations replicate the ever-changing distinction between the religious and the secular, the possibility that all aid agencies are faith based in one form or another suggests that perhaps we should be directing our attention away from the difference that faith makes and toward the differences between faith traditions, including secular ones. Perhaps, in the end, all humanitarianism is faith based. If so, this would make it very much a part of the contemporary world.

Notes

1. Michael Barnett, "Humanitarianism Transformed," *Perspectives on Politics* 3:4 (2005), 723–740.

2. Robert Woodberry and Timothy Shah, "The Pioneering Protestants," *Journal of Democracy* 15:2 (April 2004), 47–61; and Michael Young, "Confessional Protest: The Religious Birth of U.S. National Social Movements," *American Sociological Review* 67:5 (2002), 660–688.

3. Adam Hochschild, *Bury the Chains: Prophets and Rebels in the Fight to Free an Empire's Slaves* (New York: Mariner, 2006). Kevin Grant, *A Civilised Savagery: Britain and the New Slaveries in Africa, 1884–1926* (New York: Routledge, 2004).

4. Adam Hochschild, *King Leopold's Ghost* (New York: Mariner, 1999).

5. John Hutchinson, *Champions of Charity* (Boulder, CO: Westview, 1997), 203.

6. José Casanova, "Secularization Revisited: A Response to Talal Asad," in *Powers of the Secular Modern: Talal Asad and His Interlocuters*, ed. David Scott and Charles Hirshkind (Stanford, CA: Stanford University Press, 2006), 24–28; Dominique Marshall, "Children's Rights in Imperial Political Cultures: Missionary and Humanitarian Contributions to the Conference on the African Child of 1931," *International Journal of Children's Rights* 12 (2004), 273–318; John Nurser, *For All Peoples and Nations: The Ecumenical Church and Human Rights* (Washington, DC: Georgetown University Press, 2005); Mary Glendon, *A World Made New: Eleanor Roosevelt and the Universal Declaration of Human Rights* (New York: Random House, 2001); and David Lumsdaine, *Moral Vision in International Politics* (Princeton, NJ: Princeton University Press, 1993).

7. This chapter, and much of my thinking on the subject, was deeply influenced by a Luce-funded grant to study the relationship between religion, humanitarianism, and world order. The project's findings will be published in Michael Barnett and Janice Stein, eds., *Sacred*

Aid (NY: Oxford University Press, 2012). For a recent and good example of this exercise, see Jonathan Benthall, *Returning to Religion: Why a Secular Age Is Haunted by Faith* (London: I. B. Taurus, 2008).

9. John Dewey, *A Common Faith* (New Haven, CT: Yale University Press, 1934), 3, 9.

10. Ibid., 19. The original sentence stated "self is always directed."

11. Charles Taylor, *A Secular Age* (Cambridge, MA: Harvard University Press, 2007).

12. Consistent with these claims, the Pew Forum on Religion and Public Life reports that a healthy percentage of the people it polled claimed to be both atheist and believe in some form of the "divine." (See http://religions.pewforum.org/reports.) Also see the very poignant statement by a self-identified atheist on Africa's need for God and evangelism: Matthew Paris, "As an Atheist, I Truly Believe Africa Needs God," *Times of London* (December 27, 2008). Thanks to Timothy Shah for bringing both items to my attention.

13. There are a bevy of other concepts that are used to signify nonreligious faith, including spirituality and hope. For a similar analysis of the concept of hope, see Patrick Deneen, "The Politics of Hope and Optimism: Rorty, Havel, and the Democratic Faith of John Dewey," *Social Research* 66:2 (Summer 1999), 578–598; Richard Rorty, "Hope and the Future," *Peace Review* 14:2 (2002), 154.

14. For statements on cosmopolitanism, minimal and otherwise, see *The Political Philosophy of Cosmopolitanism*, ed. G. Brock and H. Brighouse (Cambridge: Cambridge University Press, 2005); *For Love of Country?* ed. Martha Nussbaum and Joshua Cohen (Boston: Beacon, 2002); and *Another Cosmopolitanism*, ed. Seyla Benhabib and Robert Post (New York: Oxford University Press, 2006). For a good discussion of the relationship between cosmopolitanism and the "harm principle," see Richard Sharpcott, "Anti-Cosmopolitanism, Pluralism, and the Cosmopolitan Harm Principle," *Review of International Studies* 34:2 (April 2008), 185–204.

15. Taylor, *A Secular Age*, 15–16.

16. For a terrific discussion of the secular and the sacred in modern international relations, see Stephen Hopgood, "Moral Authority, Modernity and the Politics of the Sacred," *European Journal of International Relations* 15:2 (2009), 229–255.

17. See Nicholas Guilhot, "Secularism, Realism, and International Relations," *The Immanent Frame* (October 31, 2007): www.ssrc.org/blogs/immanent_frame/2007/10/31/secularism-realism-and-international-relations/; and Elizabeth Shakman Hurd, "The Other Shore," *The Immanent Frame* (October 31, 2007): www.ssrc.org/blogs/immanent_frame/2007/12/18/the-other-shore/.

18. Benthall, *Returning to Religion*, chapter 4.

19. David Reiff, *Slaughterhouse: Bosnia and the Failure of the West* (New York: Touchstone, 1996), 20.

20. Michael Barnett, "The UN Security Council, Indifference, and Genocide in Rwanda," *Cultural Anthropology* 12:4 (1997), 551–578.

21. However, see Carlo Benedetti, "Islamic and Christian Inspired Relief NGOs: Between Tactical Collaboration and Strategic Diffidence?" *Journal of International Development* 18:6 (2006), 849–859; Jonathan Benthall, "The Red Cross and Red Crescent Movement and Islamic Societies, with Special Reference to Jordan," *British Journal of Middle Eastern Studies* (1997, 24, 2, 157–77; M. Cizakca, *A History of Philanthropic Foundations: The Islamic World from the Seventh Century to the Present Day* (Istanbul: Bogazici University Press, 2000); Jonathan Benthall and Jerome Bellion-Jourdan, *The Charitable Crescent: Politics of Aid in the Muslim World* (London: I. B. Tauris, 2003); Bruno De Cordier, "Faith-Based Aid, Globalisation and

the Humanitarian Frontline: An Analysis of Western-Based Muslim Aid Organisations," *Disasters* (2009 33, 4, 608-628).

22. Elliott Dorff, *The Way into Tikkun Olam: Repairing the World* (New York: Jewish Lights, 2007).

23. Erica Bornstein, "No Return: A Brief Typology of Philanthropy and the Sacred in New Delhi," in *The Politics of Altruism: Caring and Religion in a Global Perspective*, ed. Keishin Inaba and Ruben Habito (Cambridge: Cambridge Scholars Press, 2006), 165–179.

24. There seems to be little disagreement that Islamic agencies, empirically speaking, do not frequent non-Islamic areas; some defend this bias, though, on the grounds that Islamic societies are in considerable need, that Islamic organizations have a comparative advantage in Islamic societies, and that non-Islamic societies tend to be hostile and suspicious toward Islamic agencies.

25. Immanuel Kant, "On the Common Saying: This Might Be True in Theory, but It Does Not Apply in Practice," in *Kant: Political Writings*, ed. Hans Reiss (New York: Cambridge University Press, 1970), 188; Nicholas Wolterstorff, *Justice: Rights and Wrongs* (Princeton, NJ: Princeton University Press, 2008), 323–341.

26. See Sharpcott, "Anti-Cosmopolitanism, Pluralism, and the Cosmopolitan Harm Principle"; and Andrew Linklater, "Towards a Sociology of Global Morals with an 'Emancipatory Intent,'" *Review of International Society* 33 (April 2007), 135–150.

27. Richard Rorty, "Who Are We? Moral Universalism and Economic Triage," *Diogenes* 173 (Spring 1996), 13; Richard Rorty, "Human Rights, Rationality, and Sentimentality," in *Truth and Progress: Philosophical Papers* (New York: Cambridge University Press, 1998), 167–185.

28. Jon Alterman, S. Hunter, and A. L. Phillips, *The Idea and Practice of Philanthropy in the Muslim World*. The Muslim World Series. No. PN-ADD-444. Bureau for Policy and Program Coordination, United States Agency for International Development (Washington, DC: USAID, 2005); and conversations with Barbara Ibrahim, Director, John D. Gerhadt Center for Philanthropy and Civic Engagement, American University in Cairo, June 2008.

29. This possibility was suggested to me by Nicholas Stockton.

30. For discussions, see Michael Barnett and Thomas Weiss, "Humanitarianism: A Brief History of the Present," in *Humanitarianism in Question*, ed. M. Barnett and T. Weiss (Ithaca, NY: Cornell University Press, 2008); Jean Pictet, *The Fundamental Principles of the Red Cross* (Geneva: Henry Dunant Institute, 1979); David Forsythe, *The Humanitarians: The International Committee of the Red Cross* (Cambridge: Cambridge University Press, 2005); Fiona Terry, *Condemned to Repeat? The Paradox of Humanitarian Action* (Ithaca, NY: Cornell University Press, 2002); Thomas G. Weiss, "Principles, Politics, and Humanitarian Action," *Ethics and International Affairs* 13 (1999), 1–22; and Larry Minear, *The Humanitarian Enterprise* (Bloomfield, CT: Kumarian, 2002).

31. Bruce Nichols, *The Uneasy Alliance: Religion, Refugee Work, and U.S. Foreign Policy* (New York: Oxford University Press, 1988).

32. Interviews with WVI officials; and Bryant Myers, *Walking with the Poor: Principles and Practices of Transformational Development* (Maryknoll, NY: Orbis, 1999).

33. Jean-Herve Bradol, "The Sacrificial International Order," in *In the Shadow of Just Wars: Violence, Politics, and Humanitarian Action*, ed. Fabrice Weissman (Ithaca, NY: Cornell University Press, 2004).

34. For good overviews of the conflicts between colonial authorities and missionaries, see Brian Stanley, *The Bible and the Flag: Protestant Missions and British Imperialism in*

the Nineteenth and Twentieth Centuries (London: Appolos, 1990); and Robert Woodberry, *The Shadow of Empire: Christian Missions, Colonial Policy, and Democracy in Post-Colonial Societies* (Ph.D. diss., University of North Carolina, Chapel Hill, North Carolina, 2004).

35. Much of the intellectual history and theological foundations for the move toward transformational development is covered in Myers, *Walking with the Poor.*

36. M. A. Mohamed Salih, "Islamic NGOs in Africa: The Promise and Peril of Islamic Voluntarism," in *Islamism and Its Enemies in the Horn of Africa*, ed. Alex de Waal (London: Hurst, 2004), 146–181; *Understanding Islamic Charities*, ed. Jon Alterman and Karin von Hippel (Washington, DC: CSIS, 2007).

Annotated Bibliography

Barnett, Michael. *Empire of Humanity: A History of Humanitarianism.* Ithaca, NY: Cornell University Press, 2011.
A history of the changing forms of humanitarianism, from the late 18th century to the present. The concluding chapter examines the relationship between faith and humanitarianism.
Benthall, Jonathan, *Returning to Religion: Why a Secular Age Is Haunted by Faith.* London: I. B. Taurus, 2008.
A provocative attempt by a cultural anthropologist and long-time student of religion and humanitarian action to understand whether and how religious meaning matters.
Benthall, Jonathan, and Jerome Bellion-Jourdan, *The Charitable Crescent: Politics of Aid in the Muslim World.* London: I. B. Tauris, 2003.
A very good overview of Islamic humanitarianism, without the standard post-2001 hysteria.
Bornstein, Erica, and Peter Redfield, "Genealogies of Suffering and the Gift of Care," a Working Paper on the Anthropology of Religion, Secularism, and Humanitarianism (SSRC Working Paper), 2008.
An excellent overview of how anthropologists have and might wrestle with forms of compassion, religious and otherwise.
de Cordier, Bruno, *Faith-Based Aid, Globalization, and the Humanitarian Front Line: An Analysis of Western-Based Muslim Islamic Aid Organizations.* London: Overseas Development Institute, 2009.
Excellent introduction to the kinds of dilemmas that an Islamic agency faces in a humanitarian sector that is largely secular and Christian.
Ferris, Elizabeth, "Faith-Based and Secular Humanitarian Organizations," *International Review of the Red Cross* 87:858 (2006), 311–325.
A cut into the question of whether religious agencies differ from their secular brethren.
Humanitarian Forum: www.humanitarianforum.org.
Started by the founder of Islamic Relief, the Humanitarian Forum is dedicated to trying to build trust between Northern and Southern NGOs and between Muslim and non-Muslim agencies.
Myers, Bryant, *Walking with the Poor: Principles and Practices of Transformational Development.* Maryknoll, NY: Orbis, 1999.
Authored by a longtime staff member of World Vision International, this book provides an

interesting account of the kinds of intellectual debates and global pressures that led the world's largest religiously anchored aid agency to rethink the relationship between evangelism and aid.

Porter, Andrew, *Religion versus Empire? British Protestant Missionaries and Overseas Expansion, 1700–1914*. Manchester, England: Manchester University Press, 2004.
Excellent and detailed study of the complex relationship between religion, missionary work, colonialism, and humanitarianism.

Rozario, Kevin, *The Culture of Calamity: Disaster and the Making of Modern America*. Chicago: University of Chicago Press, 2007.
A fascinating study of the relationship between disasters, religion, and the development of the modern American state.

Stanley, Brian, *The World Missionary Conference, Edinburgh 1910*. Grand Rapids, MI: Eerdmans, 2009.
The definitive account of a major missionary conference that illuminated the crosscurrents of humanitarianism, imperialism, and religion.

11 }

Faith, Gender, and International Affairs
Katherine Marshall

Policy Debates in Practice: Human Faces

Aicha Ech-Channa, a gutsy Moroccan woman, has worked for five decades with young unmarried mothers—women who are, from many perspectives, at the bottom of the social heap, condemned as prostitutes even if their pregnancies resulted from rape, thrown out by their families, their babies stigmatized as bastards. In 1985, Mrs. Ech-Channa founded Association Solidarité Féminine, an organization that welcomes these women, teaches them skills, helps them care for their children, and works to find them jobs. She is a tireless advocate for treating all women with dignity and for respecting their rights. She sees her work as inspired by the values of equality, human dignity, and compassion that underpin the Muslim faith, but she would not describe her organization as faith based. In the early years of her career, her determination to advance women's rights and to empower unmarried mothers clashed forcefully with the established Muslim order. Even today, she and her organization are subjected to critiques and attacks from some Muslim clerics and other Muslim Moroccans. Over time, however, Morocco's royal family has actively supported her work. A new family code (the *Mudawana*) was enacted after an active and open public debate that engaged religious and secular bodies across Moroccan society. The new code advances women's rights in important areas and is noteworthy for its effort to combine the positive values and social benefits of religion and tradition with changing social norms. Gender roles and relationships are part of a sensitive and complex environment in which religion, culture, and politics are woven together. Working from within the society and also taking into account evolving international best practice, traditional ideas about gender roles and family structures have been challenged and are changing in Morocco. People like Aicha Ech-Channa are propelling such change in positive and effective ways.

Thoraya Obaid's appointment in 2001 as head of the United Nations Population Fund (UNFPA) raised eyebrows because she came from Saudi Arabia, a society known for its harsh treatment of women. She addressed the spoken and unspoken questions of her opponents in her first official address. She was, she said, proudly Muslim. She was also all that the 1994 Cairo (International Conference on Population and Development) declaration set out as its hopes for women: her father had supported her education, and she chose her husband, when to have children and how many, and where to work. "In many ways, I am what the ICPD Programme of Action is all about: ensuring that parents, brothers, and husbands are supportive, understanding and act as full partners. I am, distinguished delegates, an example of what governments and NGOs in each country are striving to achieve through the implementation of ICPD recommendations. . . . I am . . . a very positive and concrete result of a relevant, well-managed, and effective social agenda." During a decade at the UN, Obaid more than any other UN leader, asserted that without taking account of religion in all its dimensions—as a part of culture and as a system of belief—development and progress for women globally cannot succeed. The changes that modernization promises in women's traditional roles are so tightly linked to religion that engagement with religion, about rights and realities, is more needed on women's issues than on any others.

This chapter addresses the relationship between faith and gender in international affairs. Women's roles in religion have been the topic of considerable research and debate, yet analysis of and reflection on the relationships among the three—faith, gender, and international affairs—are quite meager. This chapter draws on scholarship on the various dimensions of the topic and on the author's own experience; its focus is on the policy implications of the issues raised more than on the broader questions about how religion affects gender relations and vice versa. Its starting point is to ask what we know and what we do not and to highlight emerging issues and debates.

Introducing the Themes and Framing the Issues

Religion is an important factor in shaping communities' norms and aspirations, and this has special significance for women and girls. Religion can serve as a catalyst for action to improve women's lives, or it can constitute a source of conflict and a brake on change. Modernization challenges traditional expectations and practices in profound ways, none so significantly, perhaps, as the relationship between men and women. The changes that result challenge religious institutions, practices, and beliefs. Among the most significant changes of modernization are the new approaches to international affairs that conceptualize changing gender relations as a high-priority goal worthy of debate and action as part of international development and diplomacy.

Three assumptions serve as the foundation for the following discussion. First, women play vital and unique roles in the process of social change. Because women and issues affecting women are still marginalized in many ways, specific and sharper attention to these roles can help societies overcome disadvantages and improve women's welfare. Second, notwithstanding the clear dominance of religious hierarchies by men, women play critical, though underappreciated, roles in maintaining religious traditions and in championing progress within religious institutions and communities. Women's roles in religious institutions and the complex images and expectations surrounding them affect social choices and action across many issues. Third, no issue concerning social change is as sensitive and significant as those that revolve around relations between men and women. These relationships are essential to understanding the distinctive culture of any society. They also affect individuals at a personal level, sparking emotions that many carry into debates, even at the global level. Religion also evokes strong passions, so the topic of altering traditional gender norms, which are often deeply entwined with religious justifications, can be combustible.

Contemporary global trends make this discussion particularly relevant. Growth in religious adherents appears to be outpacing population growth in much of the world, and conflicts that involve religion wrack different world regions. Some movements claiming a religious justification lie behind the increased terrorism that has shaken the global community. Culture and religion are increasingly prominent in discussions about the directions and significance of globalization. These trends thrust religion increasingly onto international agendas. Gender issues also challenge traditional approaches within many societies and especially faith traditions, as women (and sometimes men) seek to change gender relations, notably men's traditional dominance in leadership and the priorities and agendas they set. The tensions sparked by the focus on women's roles in many societies and by challenges to accepted norms of male leadership have particular significance for poorer communities and those affected by conflict, because religious beliefs and institutions are so important there and women's leadership roles often so restricted.

Faith and Gender: International Standards and Public Debate

The traditional stance in international relations fora was that relations between men and women and specific matters affecting women's rights and welfare were best addressed through international standard setting and through national laws and their application. However, this picture is changing, and issues of gender relations feature increasingly on diplomatic as well as international development agendas. Pressures for change come both from human rights activism and the leadership of prominent individuals and committed governments. Issues like the legal status of women in Afghanistan, rape during conflict, and international trafficking in women and children are far more prominent today, at least in rhetoric, than they were in the past. Issues of gender and religion often reflect a complex blend of domestic and international politics, as, for example, in recent turmoil in France about Muslim women's dress or affirmative action aimed to assure women's political representation where large international aid commitments are at issue and women's roles are perceived as constrained by religious and cultural traditions. And the roles that religion plays in specific positions taken in diplomatic settings are often complicated by layers of unstated assumptions. In sum, the topic is particularly complicated.

The broad framework for international action and dialogue about gender issues remains the Universal Declaration on Human Rights, adopted by the General Assembly of the UN in 1948 and the Convention on the Elimination of All Forms of Discrimination against Women (CEDAW), that the General Assembly adopted in 1979 (the United States has signed but not ratified CEDAW). The year 2000 Millennium Development Goals (MDGs) explicitly highlight various dimensions important for women's empowerment in the drive toward the elimination of abject poverty. Major UN conferences (detailed later), the World Economic Forum's (WEF) annual Davos meetings, and regional WEF meetings serve as settings where progress on women's issues can be measured and evaluated. The United Nations Development Programme (UNDP) issues regular updates of country rankings for progress on women's issues, including the Gender Inequality Index (GII).[1] The highest ranking countries (of 135 ranked) on the Gender Inequality Index based on 2008 data were the Netherlands, Denmark, and Sweden; ranking lowest on the same index were the Democratic Republic of the Congo, Niger, Mali, and Afghanistan.[2] The competitive spirit that these reports provoke, or naming and shaming, exerts pressure on public and private actors alike. The formation of UN Women as a new UN agency in July 2010 marked an important recognition of the need for more coordinated and assertive action on gender equality and empowerment of women.

The United Nations International Conference on Population and Development, held in Cairo, Egypt, in September 1994 was an important milestone in the process of bringing an international focus to women's empowerment issues. The Programme of Action that the conference produced still serves as the basic guiding document for the United Nations Population Fund (UNFPA) and, more broadly, as a point of reference for international discussions about women's welfare, particularly their reproductive health. Some 20,000 delegates from governments, UN agencies, non-governmental organizations, and the media gathered to discuss a wide-ranging agenda, including issues such as immigration, infant mortality, birth control, family planning, education of women, and protection of women from unsafe abortion services. Disputes about reproductive rights during the conference attracted keen media attention, and the ensuing debates continue to serve as a point of reference in dialogue concerning religion and human rights. The Holy See and several predominantly Muslim nations were staunch critics of several proposals, and their views and the debates in which they engaged received wide publicity. Despite the deep divisions so evident during the meeting, the conference achieved a consensus on four major goals: (1) to achieve universal education in all countries by 2015, (2) to reduce infant and child mortality, (3) to reduce maternal mortality, and (4) to improve access to reproductive and health services, including family planning. The conference explicitly endorsed family planning counseling; prenatal care; safe delivery; postnatal care; the prevention and appropriate treatment of infertility; the prevention of abortion; the management of the consequences of unsafe abortion; the treatment of reproductive tract infections, sexually transmitted diseases, and other reproductive health conditions; and education and appropriate counseling on human sexuality, reproductive health, and responsible parenthood. The conference also established that services for reproductive health should be made readily available. The conference focused on discouraging female genital cutting (FGC or FGM), a first in such an international setting.

The Fourth World Conference on Women, held by the UN in Beijing the following year (1995), focused more broadly on the agenda for women's issues. Similar tensions surfaced there as to what women's equality really entailed, and again they involved both the Catholic Church and several Muslim-majority nations. The agreements that emerged from the conference in the form of the platform for action, as well as areas where consensus could not be achieved, are a continuing reference point in the discourse on religion and gender equality. The Beijing Conference had another lasting effect: it focused the attention of several conservative religious groups in the United States on women's issues in an international framework, accentuating what has become known in U.S. politics as the "culture wars" in the international sphere. The force of these groups has affected international family planning, as this topic is directly related to the contested issue of abortion. These debates have had direct consequences, notably for the Mexico City policy, whereby the United States has swung back and forth, according to the Democratic or Republican identity of its administrations, in its stance on supporting any foreign groups involved with abortion. Similarly, support for UNFPA has been controversial in the United States because, inaccurately, it was perceived to support abortion, especially in China. The effects of these debates have gone well beyond the immediate topic, influencing the image of the United States as a progressive nation that supports women's rights and imprinting strong images for international publics of the role that religious institutions play, especially in American politics.[3]

An important and complex dimension of contemporary international debates arises from the currently intense focus on Muslim societies and the relationships between Muslim and non-Muslim communities; in these debates, issues for women have figured prominently. A noteworthy landmark in this ongoing debate was the 1985 Arab Human Development Report (a UNDP-sponsored effort prepared by an independent team). It was forthright in linking gender relations to disappointing economic and social progress in Arab countries (most of which are majority Muslim) and has prompted continuing discussion. More recently, President Obama's June 2009 speech in Cairo highlighted how far the politics of gender, with their complex linkages to religion, can figure on the international agenda:

> The struggle for women's equality continues in many aspects of American life, and in countries around the world. I am convinced that our daughters can contribute just as much to society as our sons. Our common prosperity will be advanced by allowing all humanity—men and women—to reach their full potential. I do not believe that women must make the same choices as men

in order to be equal, and I respect those women who choose to live their lives in traditional roles. But it should be their choice. And that is why the United States will partner with any Muslim-majority country to support expanded literacy for girls, and to help young women pursue employment through micro-financing that helps people live their dreams.[4]

Women and Faith: Complex Intersections

It is striking how little of the work about women and international relations touches on questions of religious organizations or beliefs, except to highlight what are perceived as negative dimensions. There is, however, a rich vein of scholarship that can be brought to bear. For example, much work about women and religion focuses on questions about social change at the core of development programs and processes. Work on the topic of gender and religion spans many disciplines (theology, sociology, history, anthropology, and philosophy, for a start). This discussion aims to provide a glimpse into the rich array of relevant writing and research.

Women's movements frequently argue that religious leaders and institutions cannot support the dignity and welfare of women until women are recognized as full members of the religion and are allowed access to decision-making roles. Exclusion of women from leadership roles in world religions is tied to long-standing tradition (though many would argue that scriptures rarely support these practices). Further, women rarely participated in religious education, especially higher religious education, in many parts of the world, not to speak of the gaps many women have in basic education and thus basic literacy. There is also wide, and of course much contested, agreement among women's organizations that women who do not control their bodies can have no sense of independent identity or true responsibility for their overall lives, and thus no true aspiration for equality. This issue is most commonly associated with decisions on childbearing and thus on contraception and abortion. The right to control one's body can be real only if women also enjoy economic rights—the right to earn a wage to support oneself and one's children and to manage one's property. Basic physical security, meaning protection against abuse, violence, and rape, is fundamental to dignity and welfare. The full dignity and welfare of women are, in many ways, seen as tightly linked to the elimination of abject poverty, because the world's poorest people are women.

Religious perspectives on a similar range of topics are far more diverse and more difficult to characterize, though a fairly broad agreement on the importance of the family as one of society's foundational institutions does exist. There is little real disagreement on that issue in principle, though there are large differences about what it means in practice. Focus on family can translate into many different approaches, ranging from one that gives priority to women's nurturing and motherhood roles to less traditional notions of family that encompass the array of arrangements that characterize modern family realities. Widely differing families have always existed, but the ideal conception of family is an important part of most religious traditions, whether it is based around a monogamous husband and wife and children, an extended family with several generations, or a polygamous household.

Perhaps the most clearly articulated view of the family can be found in Catholic social teaching. Given its special global position, the Catholic Church's perspectives on women elicit wide attention. The July 2004 letter issued by Cardinal Ratzinger (now Pope Benedict XVI), "Letter to the Bishops of the Catholic Church on the Collaboration of Men and Women in the Church and in the World," provides an articulated religious analysis of gender roles and includes concrete recommendations for how women should engage the world.[5] Ratzinger's letter notes fundamental differences, both mental and physical, between men and women in the church and in the world. He takes direct issue with "modern feminism," suggesting that it causes antagonism between the sexes and attempts to eliminate the differences between men and women. He calls for active collaboration between the sexes in "recognition of the difference between man and woman." He underscores the fundamental nature of women according to the feminine attributes of nurturing, life giving, caring, and a "capacity for the other." Ultimately, the letter encourages women to participate in public life and to have positions of responsibility in politics, economics, and social affairs.

Reactions to the letter reflect two polarized viewpoints on the issue of gender and religion. Some commentators described the document as a groundbreaking beginning for a dialogue between people of faith and the church about the role of women. Some critics reacted to what they described as a misreading of the feminist movement. One such commentator was Sister Joan Chittister, who argued in the *National Catholic Reporter* that what the letter describes as feminism in general only applied to a certain fraction of the movement in the 1970s.[6] The women's movement today, she argued, does not center on women dominating men or behaving exactly like them but rather on providing equal opportunities in the public and private sphere for both men and women. Arguing for women as "existing for others" reinforces women's subordinate role. Collaboration between men and women requires men as well, and the letter, she argued, says very little about what men can do to create a world of equals.

José Casanova, a Georgetown sociologist of religion, paints a stark picture of the two "sides" that this debate reflects: On one side

> the unholy alliance of patriarchy and altar... provokes... the secularist response of feminists, particularly in the West, who tend to view religious fundamentalism, indeed religion itself, as the main obstacle to the global advance of women's rights and the progressive emancipation of women, and therefore tend to advocate the secularization of state, politics, law and morality.

On the other,

> traditional religious establishments tend to view feminist agendas and, particularly, the very notion of gender as... the greatest threat not only to their

religious traditions and their moral authoritative claims, but to the very idea of a sacred or divinely ordained natural order, inscribed either in natural law, *shari'a*, or some "right way" universally valid for all times.[7]

Thus, "the religious politics of gender has become one of the most important issues facing humanity worldwide and is likely to remain an issue of increasing relevance for the foreseeable future." Gender has become the preeminently contested social question, with religion thrown, willingly or unwillingly, into the vortex of the global contestation.

It is striking that although women lack access to leadership positions in many of today's major faiths, women are often more engaged with religious practice than men. Explanations for women's religiosity are varied, and they frequently intersect with analyses that delve into questions of ethnicity, culture, and social class. Many people look to how women are socialized as a partial explanation for their relatively high religiosity. Some hold that women are socialized early on to be passive, submissive, obedient, and self-sacrificing. Other explanations center on socially constructed gender roles. In Western societies, religion is often seen as relegated to the private sphere and separate from the masculine, public sphere of the economy and wage labor. Religious participation is then seen as a part of family life and as an extension of a woman's role as nurturer and caregiver. Considerable research suggests that conventional wisdom can be misleading or at best simplistic. For example, a 2008 study highlights data from the World Values Survey indicating that the reality of gender-linked religiosity is quite complex and varies by society.[8] An interesting line of inquiry associates aspects of religious practice with perceptions of risk and security. To summarize a complex debate very succinctly, gender gaps in religiosity may be less about sex and more about the many vulnerabilities and uncertainties that women suffer.

Again, the role of women in Muslim societies is the focus of much international attention. A central theme of scholarly research on the topic is that the popular images of female Muslim subservience represent an oversimplification of complex realities that vary widely from society to society and even family to family.[9] Zainab Salbi, founder and president of Women for Women International, an advocacy organization for women, offers an interesting explanation of why Muslim women might find religious fundamentalism more appealing than the alternative. She objects to images of Muslim women as docile or complacent, suggesting that they work through traditional religious systems to benefit from "patriarchal bargains." Many women find more protection from traditional systems than from the modern state. She argues, however, that for such protection to be of real benefit, religious laws and traditions need to be redefined. Ingrid Mattson, a scholar at the Hartford Seminary and a Muslim leader, addresses a tension that many have noted in negative responses by Muslim women to seemingly well-meaning interventions from Western women and women's organizations. She highlights the difficulties that arise when Western scholars purport to speak for Muslim women. On the one hand, people in the West can give voice to the concerns of women living under oppressive regimes. On the other hand, outsiders are often quick to label something oppressive without fully considering the importance of the tradition or practice in the lives of the women they seek to help.[10]

In several contexts, religious justifications can lead to violence against women. The issue of son preference has special importance today as it is driving major changes in sex ratios in several societies. Estimates of "missing girls" (that is, aborted female fetuses or infanticide) run to well above 100 million worldwide. Son preference is strong in Hindu societies, in Chinese religions, and others, though this is an area where the boundaries between religion and culture are particularly difficult to trace. Similarly, female genital cutting, which affects some 130 million women today, especially in Africa, is defended as religious by some African tribal religions, African Muslims, and some African Christians, despite extensive analysis showing that the practice derives from forms of sexual seclusion attributed specifically to the Egyptian pharaohs, who used clitoridectomy or genital infibulation on their women to lessen the temptation of adultery.

There are, however, also numerous religious groups that have illustrated a strong commitment to the empowerment of women. Morocco's bold reformation of family law was enacted following elaborate negotiations and collaboration between secular and religious groups. Several global faith-based organizations also work to combat human trafficking, especially in women. Several Christian denominations, for example the Society of Friends, and the Bahá'í faith have long been strong advocates, from global to community levels, for women's equality.

Religious institutions have oppressed women, but religion can also serve as a liberating force. Women's roles are debated actively within most religious traditions today, though positive advances in the treatment of women have come more often from reformations of civil law (generally through the application of human rights theory) than from religion. Yet religious and civil law do not necessarily maintain different agendas for the liberation of women; in different contexts, the same reforms appear (ending polygamy or giving women the right to property) either as internal religious reforms or as amendments to civil law.

Paths Forward?

Against this backdrop of richly varied research, policy debate, and action, the significance of the combined issues of women, religion, and international affairs emerges clearly. These topics, broad and complex, vary from place to place and by religious tradition. No issue attracts more passion, anger, excitement, and confusion, in debates about social justice, than gender. Harsh debates about reproductive rights, women's freedom to work in various professions, rules applied to dress, and abortion have divided communities. Differing views about what is moral and just, what is most beneficial for those involved (mothers, unborn children), and what different approaches imply for values and the welfare of society have contributed to communication and operational gaps among organizations that see themselves on opposite sides of the culture wars. The consequences are serious, as the tensions shape perceptions and impede cooperation in addressing critical issues. This is apparent, for example, in some of the debates surrounding HIV/AIDS, such as how to engage with sex workers, teach young people about protection against HIV/AIDS, and design maternal and child health care programs.

Encouraging different groups, even when they hold sharply diverging views, to work together on topics where they can agree might allow tangible progress on, say, sanitation programs and thus dampen tensions. Another approach is to engage in purposeful and carefully planned and facilitated dialogue. The path of avoidance carries important risks, even though in practice it may allow a live-and-let-live scenario.

The examples of Aicha Ech-Channa and Thoraya Obaid, highlighted at the chapter's opening, highlight the prominent role that leadership plays in the complex process of translating agreed principles of human rights into practice and in navigating the complex shoals between respecting cultural norms and diversity and international norms of equality between men and women. Both women over long careers have witnessed the powerful principles of their faith, their commitment to the welfare of all human beings, and their courage to work for change for women and girls.

Notes

1. The Gender Inequality Index (GII) reflects women's disadvantage in three dimensions—reproductive health, empowerment and the labor market—for as many countries as data of reasonable quality allow. The index shows the loss in human development due to inequality between female and male achievements in these dimensions. It ranges from 0, which indicates that women and men fare equally, to 1, which indicates that women fare as poorly as possible in all measured dimensions.. See United Nations Human Development Reports, http://hdr.undp.org/en/media/HDR_2010_EN_TechNotes_reprint.pdf.

2. http://hdr.undp.org/en/media/HDR_2010_EN_Table4_reprint.pdf[3] A fascinating discussion of these developments is in Michelle Goldberg, *The Means of Reproduction: Sex, Power, and the Future of the World* (New York: Penguin, 2009), especially chapter 4.

4. Barack Obama, "Remarks by the President on a New Beginning," Cairo University, Cairo, Egypt (June 4, 2009). See www.whitehouse.gov/the_press_office/Remarks-by-the-President-at-Cairo-University-6-04-09/.

5. Available at www.vatican.va/roman_curia/congregations/cfaith/documents/rc_con_cfaith_doc_20040731_collaboration_en.html.

6. Joan Chittister, "To the Experts in Humanity: Since When Did Women Become the Problem?" *National Catholic Reporter*, February 8, 2004, www.nationalcatholicreporter.org/update/bn080204.htm.

7. José Casanova, "Religion, Politics, and Gender Equality: Public Religions Revisited," in José Casanova and Anne Philips, *A Debate on the Public Role of Religion and Its Social and Gender Implications. Programme on Gender and Development*. Paper No. 5, September 2009. UNRISD. Geneva, pp. 1–33.See www.unrisd.org/80256B3C005BCCF9/(httpAuxPages)/010F 9FB4F1E75408C12575D70031F321/$file/WEBCasvadrftII.pdf.

8. Pippa Norris and Ronald Inglehart, "Existential Security and the Gender Gap in Religious Values" Unpublished manuscript, for SSRC conference in New York, February 2008, cited at http://www.hks.harvard.edu/fs/pnorris/Main%20Pages/What's%20New.htm

9. See, for example, Roksana Bahramitash, "Globalization, Islamization, and Women's Empowerment in Indonesia," in *God, Guns, and Globalization: Religious Radicalism and International Political Economy* (International Political Economy Yearbook 13), ed. Mary Ann Tétreault and Robert A. Denemark (Boulder, CO: Lynne Rienner, 2004), 219–232.

10. These views are set out in greater detail in Katherine Marshall and Alisha Baghat, *Challenges of Change: Faith, Gender, and Development* (Report of the Berkley Center for Religion, Peace, and World Affairs, Georgetown University).

Annotated Bibliography

Kristof, Nicholas and Sheryl Wudon. *Half the Sky: Turning Oppression into Opportunity for Women Worldwide.*New York: Knopf, 2009.

This important book highlights the continuing challenges facing women in many parts of the world and includes both positive and challenging stories about and analysis of the roles played by religious beliefs and institutions.

Marshall, Katherine. "Development, Religion, and Women's Roles in Contemporary Societies." *The Review of Faith and International Affairs*. Vol. 8, Number 4, Winter 2010, 35–42.

This article focuses on development dimensions of women's engagement in development efforts, another neglected area.

Marshall, Katherine and Susan Hayward. *Women in Religious Peacebuilding*. United States Institute of Peace, Washington DC, May, 2011. Available at http://repository.berkleycenter.georgetown.edu/11USIPWFDDBCPW71WomenReligiousPeacebuilding.pdf

This report draws on research conducted jointly by USIP, the Berkley Center at Georgetown University, and the World Faiths Development Dialogue, to fill the large gap in knowledge and understanding of women's engagement in wide-ranging work for peace, through faith institutions or inspired by religious faith.

12 }

Religion and Development
Katherine Marshall

The avenues by which religion influences development activities in
different faiths and regions are haunting in their complexity.
—Sabina Alkire[1]

Setting the Scene: Disconnects on the Ground

A technical team met at the World Bank's Washington, D.C., headquarters for
an in-house review of a a social assessment for a southern African country. The
survey, conducted by a local team of social scientists, was part of the preparatory
work for an ambitious multidonor nationwide malaria program. State-of-the-art
participatory survey techniques were showcased, as was the effort to reach traditional leaders, local elected and appointed officials, and civil society organizations. The discussion focused among other topics on practical implications of the
study's findings. For example, the survey found widespread informal polygamy,
so the question was whether the bed nets, which are a pivotal element of anti-
malaria strategies, should be given to men or women. If the traditional path of
targeting men was followed, it could be difficult to assure that all children would
sleep under the life-saving nets that would protect them against mosquitoes. The
complex social implications were thrashed out.

What was the view of the local pastors, a participant asked? Church communities were omnipresent and active in the country and were deeply concerned about
child mortality. What had the survey learned from their responses and experience?
There was an awkward silence. It transpired that the study had failed to include
churches or pastors because religious institutions of all kinds did not form part
of the accepted definition in that country's professional development circles of
"social." This had raised no flags for the World Bank.

A workshop for interfaith teams from several African countries, held in Ethiopia,
included a field visit in Addis Ababa to a Christian organization that provided
home-based care to families who were affected by HIV/AIDS. The diverse interfaith group was discussing the broad implications of the program—its views on

orphan care, possible incentives for testing for HIV, and the community impact of the disease and the organization's response. A complex chart on the wall attracted attention. The director explained that the chart allowed him to track the complex flows from financial commitments from external organizations that supported the organization's work. No one organization could or would support their overall program, so the reality took the form of an uncertain patchwork arrangement. He found that donors tended to tire of programs after a time, moving on to meet new priorities and strategies, so a constant renewal of donors was also essential. He spent a large part of his own time mobilizing and coordinating the financing that kept the organization alive.

The visitors keenly felt the irony of this picture. The organization's work offered rich lessons about the pandemic and represented important avenues for response, for example, on orphan care and attitudes on HIV/AIDS testing. But it seemed quite disarticulated from national strategies because the organization worked independently. The financing picture was still more ironic. That very morning the workshop discussion had focused on the fact that far more international funding was available for HIV/AIDS programs than could be disbursed. There was lip service recognition that HIV/AIDS programs must be a long-term marathon, that there are no quick fixes; an essential element in success is persistence and steady learning from experience. But the reality on the ground looked very different as this program director struggled to cobble together an imperfect and uncertain financing plan for his essential work.

The common threads in these two "parables" are, first, the impressive common ground that unites very different organizations that are working to address international development and fight poverty and, second, the practical gaps between rhetoric and on-the-ground realities, both in approach and in that essential tool, financial flows. All the players involved, whether secular or faith inspired, grappled with the complex issues involved in reaching poor communities, in this instance, to fight the pandemics of HIV/AIDS and malaria. They shared a common genuine motivation to help bring about change. But effective intellectual and organizational ways to link their ideas and their practice were lacking. Both examples suggest that better understanding, communication, and coordination could well make the programs work better, grounding them more directly in community realities and offering a better chance for lasting results over the longer term.

The links between both ideas and practice that touch on religion and development are legion, but exploration of what that really means, intellectually and in practice, is still tentative and quite fragmented. The limitations in systematic investigation of the topic have several explanations. A prime reason is the breadth and complexity of the institutions and issues involved. Special sensitivities around the religion development nexus is another. Perhaps most significant is the historically shaped segmentation of language, relationships, and perspectives among different types of institutions. Despite much overlap and many synergies, the two worlds (development and faith) have largely operated in separate universes, with different institutional, intellectual, and ideological frames. The resulting disconnects and frictions matter. They can result in wasted resources and in the kind of tensions that sap will and operational efficiency. Still more, they dampen the potential energy and ingenuity that can come from creative partnerships among these different institutions. They matter above all because they represent missed opportunities in the global effort to confront the challenges of global poverty and inequity.

Framing the Question and Definitions

The Millennium Declaration that emerged from the summit of world leaders at the United Nations in the year 2000 was hailed as a reason to celebrate a near-universal, truly global commitment to achieve ancient ideals of ending poverty. The framework embodied in the Millennium Development Goals (MDGs), despite its many imperfections, defines tangible goals in eight areas, from poverty and hunger through mobilization of financial support, with deadlines and specific benchmarks designed to hold all to account. It acknowledges the complex partnerships needed to achieve results. Public and private, secular and religious, all are called to action.

The Millennium framework highlights the complexity of contemporary relationships among secular and faith-inspired actors and the way they play out in international affairs. The process of engagement in what is termed *development* is dynamic and highly interdisciplinary, and it involves an extraordinary array of different partnership arrangements. These partnerships take place at the most global and most local levels, and they vary by region, faith, nation, community, and even individual. The engagement spans virtually all sectors of activity, from AIDS to zebras. And it often sparks emotions ranging from unbridled enthusiasm to vehement opposition. Thus Sabina Alkire's observation, cited earlier, about the extraordinary complexity of the topic is an apt reminder not to indulge in overgeneralization.

Three basic questions to ask are, therefore, "What is meant by development?" "What is meant by religion?" and "What have the two to do with one another?"

As to what is meant by development, beyond a reasonable degree of consensus that absolute poverty is tragic and even evil, and on a broad definition that includes all basic human needs, the sands of understanding about what constitutes development are shifting. Especially since the end of the Cold War, the equation of three worlds is rendered largely meaningless. Grouping the world into developed and developing also has little sense, given the wide variations in country situations, changing trajectories, and disparities within any notional bloc. Today's global reality involves widely different country and regional situations, wide welfare gaps within countries, and considerable dynamism that shifts groupings over time. Côte d'Ivoire was a dynamo of development at one point, then a failing state, and now seems to be creeping back toward emerging low-income nation.

The goals of development efforts are complex, and in that sense the Millennium Development Goals represent a deceptive oversimplification. Contrasted with the straightforward notions set out by early development economists and practitioners that posited a steady progression toward modernity, fueled largely by investment projects, the scene today looks rather different. Development is well understood to involve different paths and often different ends. Human development—education and health in the first instance, social capital beyond that—is well appreciated as both a priority goal and means. Participation by communities and individuals in every aspect of the process of change is an accepted prerequisite for successful programs and is linked to what is nearly a mantra today: local ownership. That often differently defined term *equity* is taking on new importance as an objective, as it becomes increasingly clear that the goals of development go far beyond simply ending avoidable misery. Equity underscores the commonsense point that what is desired is not equality in the sense of the same outcomes and paths. Equity suggests balance, access, and opportunity. Complicating an already complex picture is a blending, in argument and strategy, of rights-based thinking, compassion, and fear of terrorism. All three strands lead to a focus on what are variously termed least-developed countries, low-income countries under stress, failing states, or the bottom billion among the world's population.

Social justice and progress have long been and remain contested space. What is new is the real prospect of a world where a decent life is expected and should be feasible for all people. The questions are how to get there and what constitutes a decent life. Here again, warring intellectual gladiators offer rather different diagnoses and prescriptions: Jeffrey Sachs argues passionately that the poorest countries have had a raw deal from geography, history, and contemporary global economic systems; they need large financial flows to get on the ladder of progress. Meanwhile, William Easterly cautions that much of the resources flowing to development have gone to questionable ends with limited results to show for vast efforts. Development is one topic where that much bandied phrase "'it's complicated" applies well. Veterans of the field (myself included) have learned reams of lessons from experience and appreciate well that simple diagnoses and remedies are perilous. Humility and awareness of the complexity of the challenge are among the most significant lessons of more than sixty years of experience.

Turning to the second challenge, defining what we mean by religion, that phrase "it's complicated" applies still more. Religion is hugely complex, and any definition, starting with the words *religion, faith*, and *spirituality*, are hotly contested. The terms are understood differently and often in ways that are quite contradictory: for example, is spirituality the essence or the opposite of religion? It should hardly be surprising that the world of religion opens a Pandora's box of information, insight, contradictions, conflicts, and wisdom, given millennia of history and the essential roles that religious belief play in human history, psychology, and welfare. But there is nonetheless a tendency for many to pigeonhole their perceptions about religion and to seek simple explanations of what it means and does.

And what do religion and development have to do with one another? For start-ers, the boundaries between religion and development are far fuzzier than most recognize. At a recent meeting, for example, one participant highlighted that all human action is motivated by faith (with economics a prominent example, with its faith in unseen hands); the question is what kind of faith? The role that religion plays in motivations, in the ordering of lives, and in organizations of many kinds is rarely straightforward or simple.

How development issues and institutions relate to religion thus varies widely. There are some clear, practical intersections: for example, where faith-inspired organizations run schools and universities, health services, HIV/AIDS work, or microfinance programs. Trickier and more elusive are questions about how religion is linked to social tensions and conflict, as well as conflict resolution and peace building. And the deepest questions turn around how religious and spiritual moti-vations affect social change and social welfare. In sketching the arena within which contemporary interactions between development and faith-inspired actors take place, there is merit in looking at different levels of engagement, with their evi-dent implications for scale: the community level, affecting day-to-day lives; national approaches, including in particular legal and policy dimensions; transnational faith organizations like the Catholic Church, which exercise particular sway; and inter-faith initiatives linked to development, a growing area of interaction.

In short, an array of caveats: approaching the topic with any prospect that the answers will be simple is unrealistic. Development and religion have far more to do with each other than most treatments of either topic would suggest, but the links are a blizzard of different pieces, a kaleidoscope of changing parts interacting, and not a single picture or mosaic.

Journeys toward Development-Religion Engagement

The path to exploring this kaleidoscope of relationships among religious and secular perspectives on development has different parts. Different stages of the journey provide a historical time dimension and also illustrate some of the issues that have emerged as the different communities and approaches have come increasingly into contact. The journey of international development—in many respects, the journey toward human social and economic progress—in a concrete way can be seen as starting in the post–World War II period, which saw the cre-ation of many of the institutions that are the most active players today: the World Bank, most United Nations specialized agencies, the Marshall Plan, and major relief agencies that evolved toward broader development roles: Catholic Relief Services, CARE, and others.

For decades, the story of engagement was largely one of ships passing in the night. With exceptions (and there are exceptions to every statement on this topic), the common working assumption was that religion belonged in the private sphere while the focus of formal development work labeled as such was on public institutions and on private investment. Knowledge and systematic exchange was limited. The World Bank library, to take a concrete example, has had no category for religion. Major faith-inspired organizations did come to serve as essentially executing arms of some development programs, particularly where humanitarian relief was concerned, but they were rarely at the policy table as fully engaged partners in those early years. Civil society, so visible and significant today, was overall rarely seen as a critical element in the development equation. Religion, if seen as part of civil society, was treated in roughly the same fashion—out of sight and out of mind.

A first element that opened up communications was the growing appreciation described earlier among development professionals that development would not come by applying simple recipes. It was rarely linear, still less often predictable. A deeper appreciation of what poverty meant, that it went far beyond low incomes, worked as a deep intellectual current that changed approaches and assumptions at many levels. For example, the Voices of the Poor studies led by the World Bank in the mid-1990s evoked keen interest and were and are widely quoted. These large and participatory surveys brought individual voices of poor people into discussions and showed the complexity of poverty, how risk and uncertainty played out, and how human development was tightly linked to opportunity. Research and operational experience combined to paint a far more complex and nuanced picture of what development truly entailed, its links to culture, the central role of gender relations, how governance changed outcomes, and many other dimensions. The new appreciations opened doors to more participation, subtler understandings of events, and more hunger for understandings that began at the community level and helped explain complex behavior and responses to circumstances and incentives.

But the newly opened understandings and doors came at a time not of harmony but of mounting tensions and critiques of development work. From the late 1970s, development work was traveling some bumpy paths. The expected steady upward trajectory and the hopes that accompanied new independence for many nations, especially in Africa, were dashed, not everywhere but in many regions and countries. Oil price increases shocked economies, development projects launched with fanfare foundered, and growing populations and especially large cities swamped plans to enroll all children in school and assure health care in poor communties. The World Bank and other development organizations shifted their focus to national policies and to programs aimed at large changes, often termed *structural adjustment*. Faith institutions, largely informed by what they were hearing from communities where the disappointments were playing out, responded with mounting criticism that went from core policies and approaches to attitudes and behavior.

Development, willy-nilly, was emerging from the shadows of technocracy into politics. Rather ill prepared for the spotlight and onslaughts, most actors responded clumsily. The tensions between a civil society movement that was revolutionized by both changing politics and technology and official institutions mounted. When protests erupted into violent confrontations, especially played out on a world scene as in Seattle in 1999 and Genoa in 2001, the future path seemed increasingly dangerous and uncertain.

Meanwhile, geopolitics had experienced the revolution of 1989 and 1990, with the fall of the Berlin Wall, the disintegration of the former Soviet Union, and the rather abrupt close of the long Cold War chapter of world history. These seismic shifts affected development thinking and organization profoundly. The political standoffs and alliances that had importantly if indirectly affected approaches to many poor countries played out over time. The longtime support for regimes like Mobutu's Zaire could no longer be justified. New so-called transition economies in east and southeast Europe and Central Asia became part of the development equation but with fundamentally different challenges. Raw and long-standing conflicts took new forms.

Amid these momentous changes at least on the development scene, the roles of religion were not at all apparent and, indeed, were largely ignored. But over time, deep-running social forces were also changing the religious landscape and, together with civil society's revolutionary explosion in activity, brought new forces to bear in many corners of the world. Debates about how to approach HIV/AIDS, awareness of the muscle and rapid spread of Pentecostal churches, the growing influence of Wahhabism in Muslim societies but also of Sufi movements, and the growing environmental movement that engaged faith actors were among the vital currents shaking the world of religion that increasingly impinged on the "space" and agendas that development institutions had seen as their *chasse gardée*.

Nowhere did this play out as clearly, in terms especially of the religion-development link, as on the issue of poor-country debt. The approaching turn of the millennium in the year 2000 marked an important watershed as both development and faith actors took stock and, often, did not like what they saw. Reflections about promises made and not kept at summit after summit generated the Millennium Development goals, while the focus on "what went wrong" for poor countries crystallized about the issue of debt.

On the MDGs, the deliberations played out largely at a state level, with heavy inputs from international nongovernmental organizations; only recently have faith communities taken on the enormous challenges that they represent. By 2010, Religions for Peace and the Micah Challenge offered examples of express focus on building alliances to translate millennium ideals into reality. Before the year 2000, however, the Jubilee 2000 movement that clearly emerged out of religious thinking and institutions, broke new ground in drawing on biblical wisdom to call for debt cancellation for poor countries. The mobilization around Jubilee 2000 turned a technocratic issue, where few truly understood the elaborate mechanics of the moving financial world consensus on debt relief, into a moral imperative. World leaders listened, and the glacial movement on debt picked up momentum. Sadly, debt was only part of the problem, and the year 2000 passed by, but the lessons of Jubilee are significant.

Partly with these openings but spurred by other forces, the alliances of religious groups took new and often startling forms and alliances. The common cause of poverty, and sometimes common frustration with official discourse and action, lay behind an array of strange-bedfellow alliances and popular mobilizations. The most striking was the alliance in the United States that generated the ambitious President's Emergency Plan for AIDS Relief (PEPFAR) program. Concerted action to end sex trafficking is another example.

This history of gradual engagement between faith and development actors, moving from indifference and ignorance to tension to something approaching rapprochement, has many more chapters. But what we see today is a growing interest in partnerships generally and with faith institutions more specifically.

Bumps along the Road

The journey outlined here has echoes in parallel histories of civil society more broadly and, for example, trade unions. The history of religious encounters in the development field, however, have some special elements. As the World Bank, under presidential leadership, sought to engage with faith institutions starting in 1998, an unexpected array of tensions and objections emerged. Some were peculiar to that institution and moment in history, but they offer a cautionary tale nonetheless. Some tensions were related to lack of knowledge—read "mutual ignorance"—others from differences in approach and language. But they were also illustrative of significant reservations, especially among secular institutions, that have stood in the way of more active engagement and cooperation.

Put briefly and almost as a caricature, country representatives, as the World Bank's governors, expressed keen reservations about engaging with religion because they saw religion as *divisive* (interfaith and intrafaith tensions, personal jealousies, church-state tensions). They were doubtful that the essential objectives of religious actors were compatible with the development mission because they saw faith institutions as supporting the status quo in many situations and read their motivations as more about future worlds or converting new members than about transforming society. Especially on topics like gender equity and reproductive health, they saw religious views and politics as *dangerous* for development. And crudely put, many saw religion as a global force as essentially *defunct* and thus of low priority.

Extensive dialogue has tempered and informed these views, and far more doors are open. The dialogue has also elicited and helped to define the hesitations of faith actors about the development world. But it would be disingenuous to suggest that the dialogue among development and faith actors is smooth or technically driven. The history and emotions around both topics are an essential part of the scene.

Today's Scene

Religion and development share large common ground. Experience and exploration highlight four particular areas of emphasis.

Faith and religious beliefs and practice are an important element in shaping the values and incentives that drive social change and social relations. Disentangling the faith element is obviously fraught with difficulty. At the broadest level, faith is part of the human endeavor to define the ideals of society and the path to achieving them. More concretely, the calls to conserve resources, save money, and attend school all have faith links. Different faiths may (or may not) approach these questions differently, coloring the path of social change accordingly. This essential backdrop is largely about understanding (not, obviously, seeking to convert or change values). Better knowledge and appreciation can inform design of programs at many levels. Poor knowledge has led to countless blunders and suboptimal programs and policies. Among live issues for exploration today are faith roles in generating, preventing, and resolving conflict, the impetus and impact of the spread of Pentecostal churches in poor communities, and the contemporary social roles that spreading Sufi movements are playing in Muslim societies.

Faith institutions shape ideas and values, but they are also very practically engaged in service delivery. Education and health, the most important are directly linked to the Millennium Development goals. The imperfect knowledge of what faith institutions are doing in these two critical sectors is an obvious knowledge gap to fill. Another is the large and largely unmapped role of faith-inspired organizations involved in virtually every aspect of development work: microfinance, water, garbage and sanitation, tree planting, and so on. Faith institutions are engaged in supporting migrants, providing safety nets for the destitute, working with the disabled, and caring for orphans. These, in turn, are high-priority topics for development institutions. There is a vast field for investigation of both quantity and quality of this work, as well as ample room for coordination and common engagement.

The bumpy road of partnerships among religious and secular partners on important development policies suggests that priority should go to thoughtful dialogue. Reproductive health and gender roles are by far the most contentious and the most important topics. Approaches to corruption and governance more broadly are another.

The engagement of faith and development institutions has often turned around practical and immediate issues. Stepping back, the engagement has also posed for all concerned a set of underlying challenges about the very objectives of development: what are the visions of an ideal society? How can traditions and traditional beliefs and cultures survive with the catapulting changes of the contemporary world? How much diversity can be sustained within a framework of common human rights and ideals of equity and equal opportunity?

Common Sense and Dialogue in an Area of Shifting Sands

A common statement in development circles is that religion is part of the problem and part of the solution. The statement is echoed by many thoughtful religious leaders, even as others find it offensive. The assessment is obviously simplistic, but it highlights three important dimensions. First, in approaching this topic, perceptions matter, and perceptions of what religion is, does, and should be are deeply held and varied. They are not abstract when they translate into real action (for example, when a public health official dismisses faith voices from a planning session because he says their approach is not evidence based). Nor is it abstract when faith leaders denigrate what they describe as the crass material motivations of dedicated development professionals. Second, highlighting the positive and negative facets of faith roles underscores the obvious point of enormous diversity in experience and approach. Few would contest that various religious sects, among them the Lord's Liberation Army, which has torn northern Uganda asunder, are evil and imperil human progress. Some religious views that call women to obey their husbands are contentious and seem incompatible with human rights. In contrast, the love of learning that is nurtured by many religious institutions and their dedicated roles as inspired teachers give meaning to goals of universal education. Thus, there is a call to a nuanced approach to the topic of religion and development, one that acknowledges the enormously significant roles and potential for good and also acknowledges where there are true differences and problems.

To conclude, the religious dimensions of development offer more a lens than a special field of study. These dimensions are so embedded in an enormous range of topics that disembedding seems nigh impossible. It is hard, looking through this lens, to see how development work could have progressed without understanding the many religious dimensions. Yet the topic, in all its complexity, has been largely neglected by both academics and operational actors, with important negative consequences. The neglect has led to missteps and, above all, missed opportunities. It has curtailed efforts to understand what have proved to be complex processes and challenges. But the neglect is not without reasons, and as always, those reasons have their history. The most obvious turn on lack of knowledge, above all a divorce of fields of study and institutions. Mapping of relevant religious work is still very partial, and mutual knowledge is often lacking. But the separations of worlds also arise from tensions on specific issues like gender and reproductive rights. Acknowledging the tensions and working to find more common ground (for example, seeking ways to cut child and maternal deaths) might help in bridging gulfs.

Note

1. Sabina Alkire, "Religion and Development," in *The Elgar Companion to Development Studies*, ed. David Alexander Clark (Cheltenham, England: Edward Elgar, 2006), 502.

Annotated Bibliography

Alkire, Sabina, Review of Religion and Development for *The Elgar Companion to Development Studies*, ed. David Alexander Clark. Cheltenham, England: Edward Elgar, 2006.
This pithy survey of issues and literature was prepared some years ago but serves as an excellent introduction to all dimensions of the question, from theology to practice on the ground. Topics covered include values, personal visions, faith-based institutions, professionals, dialogue/encounters, religion versus global development, and religious forces in civil society.

Berkley Center Web site, Georgetown University. http://berkleycenter.georgetown.edu/programs/religion-and-global-development
The Religion and Development program at the Berkley Center is active and involves partnerships with several institutions and two Henry Luce Foundation-supported projects, one reviewing faith-inspired work by region, the second reviewing development topics. In-depth interviews with practitioners (over one hundred and fifty) describe experience and insights.

Clarke, Gerard and Michael Jennings. *Development, Civil Society and Faith-Based Organisations: Bridging the Sacred and the Secular*. Basingstoke, England: Palgrave, 2008.

Haynes, Jeffrey, *Religion and Development: Conflict or Cooperation?* Basingstoke, England: Palgrave, 2007.
This book surveys the landscape largely from the perspective of conflicts.

Marshall, Katherine, and Lucy Keough, *Mind, Heart and Soul in the Fight against Poverty*. Washington, DC: World Bank, 2004.

Marshall, Katherine, and Marisa Van Saanen, *Development and Faith: Where Mind, Heart and Soul Work Together*. Washington, DC: World Bank 2007.
These two books are both a narrative of experiences in the global encounter of religion and development (for example, Jubilee 2000, the Fes Festival of Global Sacred Music, and the Fes Forum on Globalization) and more specific experiences of faith development partnerships.

Religions and Development Research Programme, University of Birmingham (UK). http://www.religionsanddevelopment.org/index.php?section=1
An ambitious five-year program supported by the British DfID, focused on four countries, India, Pakistan, Nigeria, and Tanzania. The website has a rich array of working papers and policy briefs resulting from the research.The program has concluded.

Religion and Global Development.*A special issue of The Review of Faith and International Affairs*. Vol. 8, Number 4, Winter 2010.
This special issue includes articles by renowned scholars and addresses topics ranging from the Protestant Ethic and its functional equivalents to religion and public opinion on economic globalization and anti-corruption campaigns and the evangelical tradition.

World Faiths Development Dialogue: http://berkleycenter.georgetown.edu/wfdd
This website frames the large body of information on WFDD and broader faith development links in the MDG context. It includes in-depth information on the country study of Cambodia, undertaken as an example of a country level exploration of faith development links.

There is a substantial and growing literature on specific topics, notably peace and conflict, and HIV and AIDS. There are also histories of faith-inspired organizations (for example, Habitat for Humanity International).

13 }

Interreligious Dialogue and International Relations

Thomas Banchoff

In September 2006, a retired German professor was invited back to Regensburg University to address his former colleagues. "It is a moving experience for me to be back again in the university," he began, "and to be able once again to give a lecture at this podium." His presentation, "Faith, Reason, and the University: Memories and Reflections," explored the relationship between religion and philosophy in an extended academic manner. His erudition, interspersed with reminiscences, delighted his audience. But his words reverberated far beyond the lecture hall. The retired professor was Pope Benedict XVI, and his lecture included unflattering references to the Prophet Muhammad and Islam. Condemnations and protests erupted within the Muslim world. Relations between the world's two largest religious communities entered a crisis. It took two years before high-level dialogue between the Vatican and Muslim leaders resumed.[1]

Benedict's Regensburg address and its aftermath pose the question of how interreligious dialogue relates to international relations. When people of different faiths exchange views and engage in dialogue, they typically seek to identify differences and commonalities and build greater understanding. But they are not doing politics as traditionally understood: the pursuit of interests, the building of coalitions, and the struggle over office. Still less do they appear to be conducting international relations. States dominate the economic and security agenda in a secular world of national interests, markets, and international law and institutions. Religions may have a transformative effect on individuals and communities and no doubt encounter one another within an increasingly global civil society. But how does interreligious dialogue shape international relations, and vice versa?

Much turns on one's definition of interreligious dialogue. It refers here to communication and interaction with other religious traditions in a cooperative spirit. Dialogue, in this understanding, is not solely or even primarily about theological matters. It involves members of different religious communities speaking out of their own traditions in an effort to better understand and more effectively navigate inevitable cultural, ethical, and political differences. Dialogue can have a strategic dimension; it can serve to preserve and extend the size of one's own community. But its primary aims are not to prevail over the other but to reduce conflict and promote understanding and cooperation across issues of common concern.

With this definition in mind, this essay explores both sides of a critical relationship—the impact of interreligious dialogue on international relations and vice versa. It then returns to the Regensburg controversy as an illustration of both.

How Interreligious Dialogue Shapes International Relations

At the start of the twenty-first century, interreligious dialogue shapes interstate relations primarily through national societies and foreign policies. Catholic-Jewish relations and U.S. policy toward Israel provide a first example. For almost two thousand years, through the Second Vatican Council of 1962–65, the Roman Catholic Church did not recognize Judaism as a fully legitimate religious community. In the official view, the Jews were a people who had not recognized their own Messiah; they did not understand that the New Covenant had superseded the Old. There were, of course, fruitful cultural contacts between Jews and Catholics through the centuries. But the church's official anti-Jewish stance served to legitimate discrimination, conversion drives, and political persecution. There could be no recognition of theological error, no acceptance of the equal dignity and worth of the religious other, no meaningful dialogue. Up through the 1950s, Jewish-Catholic relations around the world and in the United States were hindered by this legacy.

Pope Paul VI's 1965 declaration *Nostra Aetate* (In Our Age) proved a turning point. While insisting on the truth of Christianity, it stated that the church "cannot forget that she received the revelation of the Old Testament through the people with whom God in His inexpressible mercy concluded the Ancient Covenant." It concluded that "since the spiritual patrimony common to Christians and Jews is thus so great," one must "foster and recommend that mutual understanding and respect which is the fruit, above all, of biblical and theological studies as well as of fraternal dialogues." In keeping with the council's full embrace of universal human rights, *Nostra Aetate* highlighted the broader social and political importance of interreligious dialogue. "Mindful of the patrimony she shares with the Jews and moved not by political reasons but by the Gospel's spiritual love," the church now decried "hatred, persecutions, displays of anti-Semitism, directed against Jews at any time and by anyone."[2] Nearly two millennia after the birth of Christianity and two decades after the Holocaust, this was a momentous turning point. As Rabbi David Rosen has remarked, *Nostra Aetate* "was profoundly influenced by the impact of the Shoah and transformed the Catholic Church's teaching concerning Jews and Judaism."[3]

This remarkable break with tradition did not put an end to all Catholic-Jewish animosity or suspicion, globally or in the United States. Controversy continued to swirl over the relationship between the Old Covenant and the New, the church's role in the Holocaust, the Good Friday liturgy, and other topics. But *Nostra Aetate* set in motion a remarkable rapprochement between both communities. An official dialogue was inaugurated between the Vatican and Jewish leaders and institutionalized at a national level in many countries, particularly within the United States. Across American society, Jewish-Catholic initiatives sprang up, in contexts ranging from scriptural study to civil rights struggles. The Catholic opening coincided with and encouraged a rapprochement between Jews and Protestants, powerfully symbolized by the collaboration between Dr. Martin Luther King Jr. and Rabbi Abraham Joshua Heschel. The idea of a shared Judeo-Christian heritage as foundational for American democracy took hold as a component of U.S. national identity over the postwar decades. This movement toward a more inclusive identity had many causes, including economic and social prosperity and the shift toward a consumer society. But the Catholic Church's opening to Judaism—and the interreligious dialogue and engagement that followed—was a significant contributing factor.

The improvement of Christian-Jewish relations had an impact on U.S. foreign policy as well. Strong American support for Israel in the decades after the 1967 Six-Day War had complex roots. It grew out of national security interests, the cultural affinity between two democracies, and the political mobilization of Jewish Americans. But it would not have been as strong if not for Catholic-Jewish and Protestant-Jewish rapprochement and the solidarity with Israel as an expression of Judeo-Christian identity that it engendered. Pope John Paul II was in line with a broad consensus of U.S. Catholics, mainline Protestants, and Evangelicals when he established diplomatic relations between the Vatican and Israel in 1993. He also indicated his sympathy with Israel and the Jewish people through symbolic gestures, including a historic visit to the Holy Land in March 2000. There he placed the following prayer in the Wailing Wall: "God of our fathers, You chose Abraham and his descendants to bring your Name to the Nations: we are deeply saddened by the behaviour of those who in the course of history have caused these children of yours to suffer, and asking your forgiveness we wish to commit ourselves to genuine brotherhood with the people of the Covenant."[4] These sentiments of solidarity, the outcome of decades of constructive, if sometimes difficult dialogue and engagement, appear to have strengthened international support for Israel and its security, particularly in the United States. A 2006 Pew Survey found that Catholic support for Israel in the United States was above the American average.[5]

A second example of the linkage between interreligious dialogue and international relations concerns the European Union and Turkey. Over the past two decades, the Muslim population in Europe has grown as a result of migration flows, mainly from Turkey, North Africa, and South Asia. This European Islam is internally diverse, divided by ethnicity, country of origin, country of destination, and levels of piety and practice. Nevertheless, in European society and politics, Islam is increasingly construed as the religious other. Anti-Muslim prejudice is rife, evident in public opinion and popular association between Islam and religious extremism, stoked in the wake of the Madrid and London bombings of 2004–05. A survey published in September 2008 confirmed this trend. Half of Spanish (52 percent) and German respondents (50 percent) articulated a negative view of Muslims, for example. The rate was lower in France (38 percent) and in the United Kingdom, where the percentage admitting to unfavorable views of Muslims was the same as in the United States (23 percent).[6]

High-level efforts to promote Muslim-Christian and Muslim-secular dialogue proliferate in Europe, including an ongoing Islam Conference in Germany and the French Council of the Muslim Faith. However, those efforts have not penetrated much to the level of civil society and have not eroded the widespread view that Islam represents a threat to Europe's Christian and democratic heritage. Political leaders, while insisting on the importance of dialogue and toleration, have tended to cater to the anxieties of the Christian and secular majority. Far right parties are, not surprisingly, at the forefront of this trend. According to the British National Party, for example, "all of Europe stands on the brink of being overrun and colonised by masses of Third World Muslim invaders."[7] But some centrist parties, too, have sought to defend the secular state against a perceived Muslim threat. A prominent example was the 2004 French law, passed by a large cross-party majority, that prohibited headscarves and other conspicuous religious symbols in public schools in an effort to better integrate Islam into French society.

The fractious state of intercultural and interreligious relations in key European countries has had a negative impact on relations with a critical neighbor, Turkey. Over the past decade, alarm about a growing Muslim minority, spawned by fear of terrorism, racism, and ignorance of Islam and its tenets, has contributed to a shift in the tenor of debate over eventual European Union (EU) membership for Turkey. Support for Turkish accession, never strong to begin with, declined during the early years of the new century in two of the most powerful EU countries, France and Germany. By 2005, 74 percent of Germans opposed Turkish EU membership, as did 70 percent of French citizens. Across Europe, this decline was linked to anxieties about Turkey's Muslim heritage. In a 2005 Eurobarometer survey, 55 percent of respondents agreed that "the cultural differences between Turkey and the EU Member States are too significant to allow for this accession." Most did not view dialogue and interaction within the EU context as a way to improve relations. When asked whether "Turkey's accession to the EU would favor the mutual comprehension of European and Muslim values," only 39 percent of EU respondents agreed, while 46 percent disagreed.[8]

Following public opinion, French and German leaders have dampened their enthusiasm for eventual Turkish accession, even as they profess a desire for closer ties. They have put forward economic and political arguments for caution: the size of Turkey's economy and its agricultural sector, for example, and the fragility of its democratic institutions. But Turkey's character as a Muslim-majority nation and the perceived threat to a Christian and secular European identity are probably just as decisive in domestic political and foreign policy calculations. German

Chancellor Angela Merkel has been diplomatic but firm in suggesting a "privileged partnership" for Turkey but opposing its eventual accession. French President Nicolas Sarkozy has been blunter. As he put it in February 2007 during his successful run for the presidency, "Turkey, which is not a European country, does not have its place within the European Union." Sarkozy's hard line on Turkish accession, a departure from former President Jacques Chirac's more flexible position, coincided with the growth of anti-Muslim sentiment in French society.[9]

Patterns of interreligious dialogue and engagement—or their absence—are not the major drivers of U.S. policy toward Israel or EU policy toward Turkey. But they are significant and often overlooked in analyses of foreign policy and international affairs. Domestic politics and foreign policies are inextricably linked. And how societies manage religious pluralism internally—whether successfully through dialogue and integration or unsuccessfully through confrontation and polarization—can shape relations with other states and societies. Other international examples include strictures on religious freedom in Russia and Saudi Arabia that undercut those countries' international standing, Christian-Muslim tensions in Nigeria and Sudan that undermine civil order and those countries' efforts to tap international flows of investment and development assistance, and positive examples of peaceful interreligious and religious-secular coexistence in Muslim-majority Senegal and Malaysia, which have promoted civil peace and helped to strengthen both countries' access to investment and aid.

How International Relations Shape Interreligious Dialogue

Turning the question around: How do international relations affect interreligious dialogue? From a state-centric perspective, the question might seem unimportant. If world affairs are conceived as a struggle for power and resources, transnational religious engagement is insignificant by definition. But if one approaches the international system more broadly as an emergent global civil society, in which states remain key players but are embedded within and shaped by transnational economic, cultural, and social forces, faith communities acquire new importance. Religion and interreligious dialogue become critical components in the international system in their own right. What from a state-centric perspective appears marginal—the increasing interaction of religious communities over the past 150 years—comes to matter, as it potentially affects the worldviews, ethics, and actions of billions of religious adherents. A key question becomes: How do international and interstate relations affect the scope, content, and evolution of transnational interreligious dialogue over time?

This is not a new issue; interreligious contacts are as old as religion itself. Our current international interreligious configuration, however, emerged out of European colonial expansion during the past several centuries. Imperialism in the Middle East and South and East Asia increased interaction with Muslim, Hindu, and Buddhist societies. By the end of the nineteenth century, more and more diverse traditions—including so-called primitive religions of Africa, Asia, and the Americas—were incorporated into an increasingly global economic, political, and cultural space. Encounters with this diversity aroused curiosity and interest in Europe and the United States, where nineteenth-century pioneers in the study of comparative religions sought to make sense of it by positing five world religions with similar structural characteristics. "Hinduism" and "Buddhism"—newly invented terms—were now ranged alongside Judaism, Christianity, and Islam. The 1893 World's Parliament of Religions imprinted this new multireligious and interreligious world on the popular mind. Held in Chicago on the occasion of the World Columbian Exposition, and covered in the American press, the parliament featured religious representatives from around the world (many self-appointed) in a combination of theological exchange, social and political dialogue, and exotic spectacle.

The parliament was not institutionalized, as many of the participants had hoped. International contacts across religious communities multiplied in the era of globalization that preceded World War I, but there was no structured space for genuine dialogue. The main interest in world religions in the United States and Europe remained strategic—how best to support the colonial and missionary enterprise and to (finally) realize Jesus' command to spread the gospel to the ends of the earth. The World Missionary Conference in Edinburgh in 1910, widely considered the dawn of the ecumenical movement, reflected this strategic impetus. Missionary activity by U.S.-based Evangelical groups and European churches backed by colonial governments intensified interaction with other religious communities—on an unlevel playing field. During the first half of the twentieth century, colonialism spawned a backlash that included an assertion of religious communities and identities against Christian expansionism. In British-dominated Egypt and India, Islam and Hinduism emerged as markers of national resistance to outside rule. In China, the Boxer Rebellion (1899–1901) saw a violent reaction against foreign missionaries and their indigenous converts. International relations in a world divided between colonial powers and their subjects was not fertile ground for meaningful interreligious dialogue.

The same could be said of a world at war in 1914–18 and again in 1939–45. Instability and violence, fed by economic disaster, rabid nationalism, and racist hatreds, engulfed both Europe and the wider world, providing little respite for interreligious engagement. One can date some important ecumenical and Christian-Jewish activities to the interwar period, however. For example, a second World Mission Conference, held in Jerusalem in 1928, included some positive affirmation of non-Christian traditions. And the comparative study of religion matured within universities and seminaries, where an interest in domination was eclipsed by a desire for understanding. Only after the dust had settled from World War II and economic reconstruction had begun, however, did these trends fully take hold. Social peace in Europe and the United States; decolonization in Africa, Asia, and the Middle East; the construction of the UN system; and the 1948 Universal Declaration of Human Rights all favored the peaceful reengagement of the world's traditions.

As previously noted, Vatican II and the 1960s were a key juncture. The decision of the Roman Catholic Church to open to the modern world and to embrace democracy and universal human rights had a catalytic effect on its relationship with other religious traditions. Horror at the Holocaust provided a special impetus for a new approach to Judaism. But the *Nostra Aetate* declaration also addressed Muslims, Hindus, and Buddhists, acknowledging the positive value of each faith tradition. The ensuing Catholic dialogues with leaders from these religious traditions, often halting and difficult, marked a new departure for interfaith dialogue more broadly. The Protestant World Council of Churches, founded in 1948, turned its attention to interreligious dialogue from the late 1960s onward, while remaining internally divided on its implications for the Christian imperative to spread the gospel. The World Jewish Congress stepped up its interreligious activities in the 1970s and 1980s, as did a range of diverse Muslim, Buddhist, and Hindu organizations. The World Conference of Religions for Peace, an influential forum for dialogue, first convened in Kyoto, Japan, in 1970.

The Cold War configuration of international relations limited the range and significance of this interreligious dialogue during the postwar decades. With some exceptions, religious communities in the Soviet Union, Eastern Europe, and China were excluded. Ideological competition between democratic capitalism and one-party socialism overshadowed and limited transnational engagement among cultures and religions in general. The collapse of Communism in the late 1980s and early 1990s marked the advent of renewed interreligious engagement. The dissolution of bipolarity and a new era of globalization intensified interreligious contacts on a worldwide scale. A coalition of interreligious organizations came together to stage the second Parliament of the World's Religions in 1993 on the centenary of the first, and three more Parliaments ensued, in South Africa (1999), Spain (2004), and Australia (2009). Not only was participation more global than during the Cold War but also the range of topics addressed was broader. The 1993 Parliament endorsed a *Declaration on a Global Ethic* that underlined shared commitments to peace, justice, equality, freedom, and solidarity. Its slogan: No peace among the nations without peace among the religions, and no peace among religions without dialogue among them.

The most recent historical juncture marking the current era of interreligious dialogue was the attacks of September 11, 2001. The destruction wrought by Muslim extremists in New York, Washington, and Pennsylvania and later in Bali, Madrid, London, and Bombay sparked a new wave of interreligious initiatives. The United Nations created an Alliance of Civilizations and the World Economic Forum gathered a Council of 100 Leaders on West and Islam Dialogue. The Kingdom of Jordan launched the Amman Message in 2004, and Saudi Arabia launched its Initiative on Inter-Faith Dialogue in 2008. At the national and local levels, innumerable other dialogue efforts have sprung up to bring Muslims and non-Muslims together to articulate a shared commitment to nonviolence and the peaceful resolution of disputes. While recent scholarship has demonstrated that the vast majority of Muslims oppose terrorism, the equation of Islam with violent extremism in the West and the frustration in Muslim-majority countries with the wars in Afghanistan and Iraq and the plight of the Palestinians have complicated good-faith efforts to promote more respect and understanding. As in earlier eras, the course of international relations and world politics has constrained the scope and content of interreligious dialogue.

The Regensburg Speech and Catholic-Muslim Relations

The Regensburg speech and its aftermath illustrate the mutual impact of international relations and interreligious dialogue. During his long career in the church leadership, including two decades at the right hand of John Paul II, then Cardinal Josef Ratzinger had expressed some skepticism of interfaith dialogue. He voiced concerns that discussions of theological questions, in particular, had the potential to relativize and therefore undermine the fundamentals of the Catholic faith. Interfaith dialogue, in his view, should focus not on theology but on common approaches to global ethical, social, and policy challenges. Given his pragmatic approach to interfaith dialogue and his generally cautious approach after his assumption of office in 2005, the Regensburg speech was doubly surprising. Its effects, however unintended, were profound.

Toward the beginning of his address, at the outset of an extended discussion of faith and its perversion for violent ends, Benedict cited Manuel II Paleologus, a fourteenth-century Byzantine emperor: "Show me just what Mohammed brought that was new, and there you will find things only evil and inhuman, such as his command to spread by the sword the faith he preached." The pope did not endorse the statement; he even said it was startling. But he also did not repudiate it. In the days that followed, demonstrations erupted in Egypt, Pakistan, India, and elsewhere. Violence was limited—the only confirmed death was that of an Italian nun murdered in Somalia—but passions ran high. The Organization of the Islamic Conference, a grouping of fifty-seven Muslim-majority countries, accused the pope of "character assassination of the Prophet Mohamed" and noted that it had "refrained from indulging in polemics concerning the crusades and religious wars prosecuted by the church in Europe, in addition to the persecution of Muslims in inquisition courts in the name of Christ's peaceful and tolerant message." The pope did not apologize directly but expressed regret that Muslims had taken offense. An extended chill in Catholic-Muslim relations ensued.[10]

The confrontation between the pope and his critics—including those Catholics and other non-Muslims who feared for the future of interfaith relations—had a broader, if diffuse effect on politics and international relations in Europe. The Vatican was on record in opposition to Turkish accession to the EU, largely because Turkey was not part of the continent's Christian heritage. By evoking connections between Islam and violence—and omitting any mention of the church's own

212 { Religion, Humanitarianism, and Civil Society

checkered history—Benedict may have contributed to the polarization between European Muslims and their fellow citizens. Coming on the heels of the 2005–06 Muhammad cartoon controversy, his speech and the reaction lent political ammunition to hardliners on both sides. This was not Benedict's intention. But what had begun as a homecoming speech to fellow academics with a high level of erudition and abstraction became a public intervention in a running European debate with international political consequences.

The speech and its aftermath also illustrate the reciprocal impact of international relations on interreligious dialogue. Because of the tense state of West-Islam relations in 2006, a seemingly academic lecture by the pope contrasting Europe's Christian and rationalist heritage with the supposed irrationalism of Islam, and quoting an obscure medieval emperor on Muhammad in passing, had a significant international impact. Coming just weeks after the Israeli war against Hezbollah in Lebanon and amid the ongoing U.S. wars in Afghanistan and Iraq, Benedict's intervention was widely interpreted in light of the geopolitical situation as part of a wider Western offensive against Islam. His expressions of regret might have defused the crisis in a more positive international atmosphere. In the global constellation of 2006–07, they had little initial impact. As in earlier eras—European colonialism, the interwar period, and the Cold War—interstate relations complicated interfaith relations and threw up barriers to dialogue.

The crisis occasioned by Benedict's remarks has had one salutary and long-term effect: a new impetus for deeper Catholic-Muslim dialogue. One month after the speech, thirty-eight leading Muslim clerics and scholars endorsed an open letter pointing out that Christianity and Islam together constitute "more than 55% of the world's population, making the relationship between these two religious communities the most important factor in contributing to meaningful peace around the world." Another letter followed in October 2007, *A Common Word between Us and You*. Signed by 138 Muslim leaders, it emphasized theological and ethical commonalities shared by Islam and Christianity as a basis for far-reaching dialogue and engagement. After some hesitation, the Vatican responded positively to these overtures; a formal, high-level dialogue was initiated in late 2008.[11]

Interreligious dialogue is bound to grow more, not less, significant in the decades ahead. With globalization and the end of the Cold War, interreligious contacts have proliferated. Faith communities have stepped up their engagement in civil society and politics—a trend particularly evident in the United States and throughout the developing world. And those communities increasingly find themselves engaged in international political issues ranging from war and peace to human rights, global development, and the Israeli-Palestinian conflict. How religious groups engage one another—whether in dialogue in a spirit of mutual respect directed toward common global challenges or in confrontation over access to power, resources, and adherents—will shape world affairs in the decades ahead. The interreligious terms of engagement will continue to be constrained by interstate relations and the overall geopolitical constellation. But religious communities are better positioned than at any time before in history to have a global cultural, social, and political impact through their interaction with one another and the wider world.

Notes

1. Pope Benedict XVI, "Faith, Reason, and the University: Memories and Reflections," September 12, 2006, www.vatican.va/holy_father/benedict_xvi/speeches/2006/september/documents/hf_ben-xvi_spe_20060912_university-regensburg_en.html.

2. Pope Paul VI, "*Nostra Aetate*" [In Our Age], October 28, 1965, www.vatican.va/archive/hist_councils/ii_vatican_council/documents/vat-ii_decl_19651028_nostra-aetate_en.html.

3. David Rosen, A. James Rudin, and Lisa Palmieri-Billig, *Pope John Paul II: In Memoriam*, (New York: American Jewish Committee, 2005), 5.

4. Pope John Paul II, "Prayer of the Holy Father at the Western Wall," March 26, 2000, http://www.vatican.va/holy_father/john_paul_ii/travels/documents/hf_jp-ii_spe_20000326_jerusalem-prayer_en.html.

5. Pew Center for the People and the Press, "Americans' Support for Israel Unchanged by Recent Hostilities: Domestic Political Distemper Continues," July 26, 2006. http://people-press.org/reports/pdf/281.pdf.

6. The Pew Global Attitudes Project, "Unfavorable Views of Jews and Muslims on the Increase in Europe," September 17, 2008), 1, http://pewglobal.org/reports/pdf/262.pdf.

7. BNP News, "Controlled Media Admits That Europe Is Being Overrun by Islam," August 13, 2009, http://bnp.org.uk/2009/08/controlled-media-admits-that-europe-is-being-overrun-by-islam/.

8. European Commission Public Opinion Analysis, *Eurobarometer*, 2005, cited in Meltem Müftüler-Bac, "Turkey's Accession to the European Union: The Impact of the EU's Internal Dynamics," *International Studies Perspectives* 9 (2008), 201–219.

9. "La Turquie dans l'EU. C'est toujours non!" *Le Monde*, January 28, 2008.

10. Pope Benedict XVI, "Faith, Reason, and the University"; Organization of the Islamic Conference, "On the Pope's Recent Statements on Islam," press release, September 14, 2006), www.oic-oci.org/oicold/press/english/2006/september%202006/pope.htm.

11. For an overview of these texts and developments, see the official A Common Word Web site, www.acommonword.com/.

Annotated Bibliography

Banchoff, Thomas, ed., *Religious Pluralism, Globalization and World Politics*. Oxford: Oxford University Press, 2008.
An edited book that explores the intersection of religious pluralism and world affairs, with attention to the impact of interreligious competition and dialogue.
Godard, Hugh, *A History of Christian-Muslim Relations*. Edinburgh, Scotland: Edinburgh University Press, 2000.
A useful survey of the trajectory of Christian-Muslim interaction, both violent and peaceful, that places current interreligious dialogue efforts within a broader historical perspective.

Kung, Hans, *Christianity and World Religions: Paths of Dialogue*. Maryknoll, NY: Orbis, 1993.

A leading Catholic theologian reflects on the church's turn to interfaith dialogue since the Second Vatican Council and the obstacles and opportunities that remain, in particular with respect to Christianity's relationship to Islam, Hinduism, and Buddhism.

Patel, Eboo, *Acts of Faith: The Story of an American Muslim, the Struggle for the Soul of a Generation*. Boston: Beacon, 2007.

An interfaith leader recounts his personal journey and reflects on the challenges and opportunities for dialogue in the United States and around the world.

Smock, David R., ed., *Interfaith Dialogue and Peacebuilding*. Washington, DC: United States Institute of Peace, 2002.

Leading representatives from across faith traditions examine the prospects for and practice of interfaith dialogue. The book also includes a series of case studies outlining interreligious engagement in the service of peace around the world.

Ucko, Hans, ed., *Changing the Present, Dreaming the Future: A Critical Moment in Interfaith Dialogue*. Geneva: World Council of Churches, 2006.

The book highlights the work of the World Council of Churches in promoting interreligious dialogue since the 1960s, including its theological, cultural, social, and political dimensions.

Witte, John, Jr., and Richard C. Martin, *Sharing the Book: Religious Perspectives on the Rights and Wrongs of Proselytism*. Maryknoll, NY: Orbis, 1999.

Leading scholars analyze an issue that has complicated interreligious dialogue through the centuries: the missionary impulse that is prominent in Christianity and Islam in particular. The authors examine the difficult trade-offs between respecting other faiths and seeking to spread the truth of one's own.

Religion and the Media

14 }

Islam and the Promenades of Global Media
Mehrzad Boroujerdi and Nichole J. Allem

On the street, Malika El Aroud is anonymous in an Islamic black veil covering all but her eyes... but it is on the Internet where Ms. El Aroud has distinguished herself [as] one of the most prominent Internet jihadists in Europe. She calls herself a female holy warrior for Al Qaeda [and] bullies Muslim men to go and fight and rallies women to join the cause. "It's not my role to set off bombs—that's ridiculous....I have a weapon. It's to write. It's to speak out. That's my jihad. You can do many things with words. Writing is also a bomb."

This description contains a number of characteristic and striking words and phrases: "anonymous," "prominent Internet Jihadist," "bullies men," "weapon," and "writing." Together these elements of the subject's identity point to three important features of modernity and the information age: (1) that an individual obscure in the physical streets of a European capital could be a key figure in a controversial movement in the promenades of the virtual world, (2) that a male-dominated sphere of violence is sufficiently impacted by modern gender roles to enable a female proselytizer, and (3) that in the instantaneous online world of communication, writing is again powerful as a weapon.

In *The Consequences of Modernity*, Anthony Giddens argued that the "advent of modernity increasingly tears space away from place by fostering relations between absent others, locationally distant from any given situation of face-to-face interaction" (1990, p. 18). He argued that "globalization" was associated with the phenomenon of global processes powerfully affecting local happenings (p. 64). James Lull has stressed that the computerized revolution in communications, along with the rise of a knowledge economy, is the key distinguishing feature of globalization (2007, p. 7).[1] Meanwhile, Benedict Anderson (1992) and Arjun Appadurai (1997) have respectively analyzed how long-distance nationalism and "mediascapes"[2] impact the identity formation and political demands of exiled and diasporic communities. Anderson and Appadurai both emphasize how imagination crosses boundaries and how old and new media[3] facilitate the creation of imagined ethnic and religious communities that make modernity a more contested enterprise, the nation-state a feebler "dictator of modernity," and identity a more intricate mixture.[4] In tune with

217

the constructivist school of thought in international relations—with its emphasis on agency, contingency, ideas, language, and meaning—they maintain that imagination is central to all forms of agency.

So our Islamic female warrior is the beneficiary of an age when identity is no longer place based and geographical proximity is not a prerequisite for spreading ideas. Indeed, the Internet has made it possible for her to transcend place and enter a new agora (public space) uninhibited by the traditional handicap of gender. Yet for most Muslims, the effects of globalization and information technology have brought a great deal of cultural confusion.

The virtual agora has a Janus face. On one side, the omnipresence and incessancy of new media allow for unprecedented effects: an uninhibited promotion of faith that reaches audiences previously inaccessible, the ability to empower crowds and citizen journalists, the creation of new religious-cultural communities, and aggressive reconstructions of religious identity. But on the other face, these ubiquitous media embody a move away from the power of traditional religious authority toward the decentralized state of enabling anyone with an Internet connection to have an impact on religious discourse. These effects are manifest in the diminution of the power of experts, the fracturing of religious discourse, the questionings of religious orthodoxies, and the persistent, malignant malice of religious bigotry. New media pose a unique challenge for the religious authority of muftis and prebendary literati. A religious order accustomed to its ability to reign supreme over a captivated audience is now faced with the disruptive effects of globalization and information technology. Religious authorities now compete with the constant irreverent remarks of casual Web surfers, inquisitive commentaries of lay religious thinkers, and ontological rebuttals of secularists.

These contradictions have generated a whole host of epistemological, theological, and political questions, and even existential angst, among Muslims. Are new media strengthening a global Muslim identity? Or are they putting theology and jurisprudence deeper into the bounds of politics and the chaos of skepticism? Should Muslims have a dystopian vision of new media as a site of debauchery or an optimistic view of media as the protagonist of a new type of esprit de corps?

Before we begin to sort through these questions, a few words of caution are in order. First, stereotypes regarding the homogeneity of Muslim thought, the ecumenism of Islamic denominations, the undifferentiated nature of the "Muslim world," and the crude binary of secular West–religious Islamic world must be discarded. After all, Al-Azmeh (1993) has aptly questioned the uniformity of the Muslim world by pointing out that there is not one "Islam" but rather "islams," and Zaman (2002) has demonstrated that the religious and political practices of the ulama cannot be reduced to their caricature as atemporal, lethargic, and conservative interpreters of faith. Meanwhile, the works of Talal Asad (1993, 2003) problematize the multilayered history of faiths such as Christianity and Islam. Second, one should not assume that the Islamic world is just as saturated with old and new media as the rest of the world. According to data from the World Bank and UNESCO, there is a sizable gap between the Muslim world and other regions in new media reach. The data show that while the Arab world fares better than the Islamic world in terms of overall media benchmarks, the gap between it and other parts of the world, particularly when it comes to new media, is still enormous.

Media: Shaper or Enforcer?

We should not exaggerate the influence of media as a catalyst for change or overstress its impact on the targeted audience. The fact remains that media transmit messages to an audience whose minds are not empty vessels. Theories on the effect of media are varied, and the field of media studies is saturated with studies debating whether consumption of media creates activation (new belief), reinforcement (confirmation of existing belief), or conversion (change to a different belief).

Some studies maintain that media has an absolute effect on an audience, while other studies argue that individuals tend to take from the news only what confirms their preexisting beliefs. *Cultivation* theory predicts that heavy media use will result in a public expressing beliefs and opinions similar to those featured predominantly in public media. *Agenda-setting* theory postulates that media consumers will assign greater importance to issues predominant in media messages without necessarily mimicking the views of the media.[5] The *memory-based* model suggests that an individual's opinion can be influenced by memory, which can subsequently make certain ideas more salient and accessible, thus affecting the individual's expressed opinions.[6] The theory of *cognitive misers* states that people employ information shortcuts to form attitudes and reach decisions, relying on "preexisting views and the information most readily available to them in the news media as the mutable material from which to mold their opinions."[7] Finally, the theory of *selective exposure* postulates "filters of selectivity" (selective exposure, selective attention, selective perception, and selective retention) that prompt individuals to pay attention to topics and opinions in which they are already interested.[8] Kelly and Etling (2008, p. 12) explain that the complex processes of selective exposure helps to illuminate the manner in "which people choose what media to experience, interpret what is experienced, and remember or forget the experience according to their prior interests and beliefs."

Media and the International Relations of the Muslim World

The technology of contemporary communications gives the media unprecedented power to describe and narrate events, often beyond the organized capabilities of governments. As Edward Said (1993, 1997) demonstrated, the Western-dominated international media form a remarkably independent and capable "world system... which articulates and produces culture, economics, and political power along with their military and demographic coefficients."[9] At the same time, not an island, the media have been used as an instrument by a wide variety of religious and political groups seeking change, whether peacefully or violently, through the mass dissemination of their grievances. Media have enabled these actors to utilize new spaces for ideological polemics, civic action, and, alas, sectarianism and warfare. As José Casanova has argued, today "all world religions can be reconstituted for the first time truly as de-territorialized, global imagined communities, detached from the civilizational settings in which they have been traditionally embedded."[10] Communication technology allows for not only deterritorialization of imagined religious communities but also decontextualization of concepts, keywords, and discourses by cutting their umbilical cord to the milieu in which they first germinated, making them vagabonds. Media also allow religious communities to channel their iconoclastic energy into mainstream culture, to be appropriated by consumer industries.

While the impetus for satellite-based telecommunications services in the Arab states can be traced back to the formation of the Arab Satellite Communication Organization (ARABSAT) in 1976, it can be argued that the powerful longing for regional satellite television stations in the Arab world came as a reaction to the coverage of regional wars and conflicts in the 1980s and 1990s. With the emergence of the Cable News Network (CNN) as the first global news network in 1980, CNN's around-the-clock news coverage led to its emergence as a global actor in international relations. Real-time coverage of conflict creates an imperative for prompt action and decision making. The so-called CNN effect became important not in directly changing policy but in affecting the environment in which policy is made. The pervasiveness of global news coverage certainly played an important role in the formation of new media in the Muslim world.

The dominance of CNN's coverage of international news and, in particular, its coverage of the first Palestinian Intifada and the 1990–91 Gulf War opened eyes in the Arab world to the ways in which important crises and conflicts were covered by Western media, while concurrently creating aggravation at the predominance of Western perspectives in the coverage of regional events. This annoyance would eventually lead to the creation of regional satellite television stations like Al Jazeera and Al Arabiya. Al Jazeera—started in 1996 by the Emir of Qatar—is considered to have set the standard, and the tone, for Arab television news. Al Jazeera's format of open discussion, rarely attempted by other broadcasters in the region, and its focus on issues of broad Arab concern have helped to make it the pinnacle of Arab-language broadcasting.[11]

Al Jazeera's propulsion to international prominence came with its coverage of the war in Afghanistan in 2001. Henceforth, the Al Jazeera effect encouraged new "public diplomacy" initiatives by the U.S. government, including the launching of its own Arab-language Radio Sawa in 2002 and television station Al Hurra in 2004. Not to be left out, the Islamic Republic of Iran joined the war of the airwaves by launching its own Arabic-language international television news channel, Al-Alam, in 2003 and an English language mouthpiece, Press TV, in 2007. Also, one should not omit the soft power impact of the in-house media outlets of nonstate actors like Al Qaeda (As-Sahab) and Hizbollah (Al Manar).[12] Analyzing the summer 2006 war between Hizbollah and Israel, Arab media expert Marwan Kraidy (2006) maintains that "during the period of July 1–15, the station was ranked 81st among satellite stations in the Middle East, while during the period of July 15–28 it shot up to number 8." He goes on to argue that the programming of Al Manar (founded in 1991) "was just one branch of Hezbollah's overarching propaganda campaign, which orchestrated the speeches of [its leader] Hassan Nasrallah with military actions and the media campaign to effectively portray the party's message that they were fighting a war for all of Lebanon, not simply a sectarian battle." In other words, Hizbollah adopted the media strategy of a government in wartime, namely, to intimidate the enemy, legitimize its activities, and propagate support.[13] Hizbollah embraced the nature of modern war, which now requires choreographed media campaigns and infomercials to prepare friend and foe.

Media and Intra-Muslim Relations

New media are increasingly enabling the Arab world and the Muslim world to have not only an argument with the West but also an internal argument in its own ranks. These new media make it much easier to expose the incestuous relationships between wealth and political power, to criticize the self-serving speeches of governing elites, and to challenge the government-controlled media. Lynch (2005) has argued that satellite TV and the Internet are helping to create a "new Arab public" that is embracing a more liberal and pluralistic politics. Consider the Internet phenomena of YouTube and Facebook. On YouTube, one can find hundreds of video clips showing demonstrations for human rights in the Muslim world, speeches by liberal activists, and sermons by reformist Muslim clerics, all captured on handheld cameras, even cell phones. Young activists create groups on Facebook to respond to human rights violations or to call for religious tolerance. The so-called Twitter Revolution after the 2009 contested Iranian presidential elections drove home the point that people are trying to create a new type of public space by moving around the censorship mechanisms.[14]

Meanwhile, secular politicians and religious groups use virtual fora such as Facebook, MySpace, and Twitter to communicate with and mobilize their power base. Today on Facebook, one can find profiles and fan clubs for Lebanese and Malaysian politicians, Bangladeshi and Pakistani political parties, Saudi princes and muftis, Iraqi ayatollahs, Iranian religious thinkers, South Asian Isma'ili Muslims, the Egyptian Muslim Brotherhood, and the Turkish Gülen movement.

The Blogosphere

Pierre Nora (1996, p. 10) has argued that now "a secondary or prosthetic memory complements our actual experience (witness the effect of live news broadcasts on the event being covered)." This historicized memory "comes to us from without…[and] we internalize it as an individual constraint. The transition from memory to history requires every social group to redefine its identity by dredging up its past. The resulting obligation to remember makes every man his own historian."

Muslim bloggers are some of our newest historians. Some invoke memory to wax nostalgic about a radiant and pristine past, and others to relive past experiences of victimization. Young people in the Muslim world have turned to blogging as a leisure activity and a way to bypass the restrictions on free expression imposed by their predominantly authoritarian governments. According to a 2008 study, Iran—a country ranked nearly last (166 out of 169 countries) in the 2007 World Press Freedom Index—has a blogosphere of "approximately 60,000 routinely updated blogs featuring a rich and varied mix of bloggers."[15] The study concludes that "given the repressive media environment in Iran today, blogs may represent the most open public communications platform for political discourse. The peer-to-peer architecture of the blogosphere is more resistant to capture or control by the state than the older, hub and spoke architecture of the mass media model."[16] However, this does not mean that the Iranian regime is comfortable with the free use of the Internet by some 18 million of its citizens. Quite to the contrary, many in the ruling elite have a rather hostile view of the Internet and new communication technologies such as SMS, Bluetooth, and social networking sites. They consider them to be potential tools for a "color" revolution such as the 2004–05 Orange Revolution in Ukraine.[17] In November 2008, a high-level official in the Iranian judiciary reported that the government filters some 5 million "unethical and anti-social" Internet sites that threaten the country's "religious identity."

Nor is the struggle over online expression always between bloggers and governments. In Egypt, a "Quranist blogger" was first interrogated by the legal affairs department of the powerful Al-Azhar (the world's leading center of Sunni Islamic learning) and, apparently at the behest of the chief of Al-Azhar, was subsequently arrested by the Ministry of Interior's State Security Intelligence on account of his religious statements questioning the validity of the *Sunnah*.

While blogs in the Middle East still number in the thousands,[18] they are becoming increasingly influential and important sources of unfiltered news, political information, counterintuitive opinions, and religious-political activism.[19] The anonymity and decentralization of communications online are empowering women and marginalized Muslims (homosexuals, dissenters and apostates, and small sects) to overcome the *chador* of foreignness, the solitariness of living a hidden life, and the stigma of marginality. The Internet has put a limitless marketplace of ideas at the fingertips of many Muslims. Today online one can seek fatwas from a cyber mufti, join an Islamic nongovernmental organization (NGO) or an e-Jihad, partake in charitable, humanitarian, and philanthropic causes, pay one's religious taxes, do a word search in an online Qur'an, consult the electronic Hadith, perform a cyber-prayer, send an Islamic e-card, sign an online petition, use the Ramadan calculator, locate a mosque, join the fandom of a popular Egyptian sheikh on Al Jazeera TV, treat oneself to a cyber-pilgrimage, check out matrimonial opportunities, or even learn Islamic pickup lines![20]

Yet the Internet, with its anonymity, has also provided a fertile ground for "hacktivism, hacking and cracking in the name of Islam." *Hacktivism* has been defined as "the convergence of hacking with activism…[it] includes electronic civil disobedience, which brings methods of civil disobedience to cyberspace."[21] In 2008, thanks partly to the sectarian tensions in places such as Iraq and Lebanon, the Muslim world witnessed a major cyberwar between Sunni and Shiite hackers. Armies of hackers from both sides brought down hundreds of portals belonging to seminaries, satellite TV channels (Al Arabiya), and leading clerics and preachers. In 2009, the fighting between Israel and Hamas in Gaza acquired a cyber dimension as "more than 10,000 sites were compromised by hackers."[22]

Furthermore, by disseminating and often magnifying stories about individual incidents of scripture and religious desecration, the new media help to fuel political protest and religious tension. Recent examples include stories characterizing the Taliban's destruction of statues of Buddha (2001), a Qur'an being flushed down a toilet in the Guantánamo Bay detention center (2005), and another Qur'an being riddled by the bullets of an American soldier in Afghanistan (2008). Similarly, cases involving the desacralization of religious icons (Salman Rushdie's *Satanic Verses*, the Danish cartoons of Prophet Muhammad, the Dutch films *Submission* and *Fitna*) have demonstrated the power of media in fanning the flames of international crisis. In short, globalization and the Internet have now allowed groups to attack each other in new ways.

Conclusion

As religious life progressively migrates from physical places of worship toward the virtual world, faith becomes inextricably tied to globalized images, sound bites, and personal tastes. Meanwhile, media shape the perceptions of religion and things "religious" among the public and the foreign policy elite, by artic-ulating, transmitting, promoting, and legitimizing knowledge and information. In recent times, the body of work on Muslims and media seems to have moved beyond past scholarship that dissected the Western voyeuristic gaze cast on Muslims (i.e., Said 1997, Shaheen 2001) to begin to look at how Muslim actors and groups are using media to achieve their own interests in a globalized econ-omy transformed by communications technology.

The vista is decidedly mixed. While savvy Muslim cybernauts have initiated an exciting voyage of discovery and expression, the more numerous members of the religious chattering class live confidently in their own information ghetto. One finds ample evidence to support Appadurai's claim that mass media provoke individual reaction in the forms of "resistance, irony, selectivity and in general *agency*."[23] Whether reactions are manifested in resisting the CNN effect by establishing rival stations, taking collective offense at President George W. Bush's use of such words and phrases as *crusade* and *axis of evil*, participating in resistance movements after seeing gruesome images of war (Abu Gharib, Najaf, Beirut, or Gaza), or acting out of benevolence to help earthquake and tsunami victims in Pakistan and Indonesia, there is no doubt that students of international relations need to pay more attention to how the media frame events in the Muslim world.

Michel Foucault argued that language antedates and constructs subjectivity. In the same vein, one can maintain that global media shape our imagination and historical memory. Yet we should keep in mind that regardless of whether we consider globalization a policy or a process, the fact remains that the Muslim world is not a tabula rasa completely shaped by globalization's impact. The culture contains formidable repertoires of traditions and narrative templates, complex and empowering universes of discourse, and nonephemeral notions of valor and virtue.

Furthermore, as the proponents of the communication theory of selective exposure have argued, we should not succumb to the naïve premises that became the hallmarks of modernization theory. The introduction of personal computers to Muslim societies was not tantamount to somehow Westernizing them. Instead, local actors used the technologies of the PC and the Internet to accomplish what they were doing or wanted to do already—only better, faster, and cheaper.[24]

Acknowledgment

We are thankful to Jonathan Lyons, Todd Fine, Sarah Marusek, and Ebrahim Soltani for their comments on this chapter. Epigraph: Elaine Sciolino and Souad Mekhennet, "Warrior for Al Qaeda Rallies Jihad Recruits with Her Online Fury," *New York Times*, May 28, 2008, A10.

Notes

1. "Whereas for the first ten years of use, from 1969 to 1979, the Internet consisted of no more than 188 hosts, and a relative handful of users, by January 2003, 171,638,297 host computers and more than 600,000,000 users were linked to the network, demonstrating the Internet's phenomenal growth." Deborah L. Wheeler, *The Internet in the Middle East: Global Expectations and Local Imaginations in Kuwait* (Albany: State University of New York Press, 2005), 2.

2. Appadurai uses the new word *mediascapes* to refer to the "distribution of the electronic capabilities to produce and disseminate information which are available to a growing number of private and public interests." Arjun Appadurai, *Modernity at Large: Cultural Dimensions of Globalization* (Minneapolis: University of Minnesota Press, 1997), 35.

3. "Old media" refers to technologies such as broadcast and cable television, the printing press, books, newspapers, magazines, and videos and movies. "New media" refers to digital and computerized technologies (such as the Internet) that allow for networked information and communication.

4. Betigül Ercan Argun masterfully demonstrates how the Turkish community living in Germany can remain "indexed to homeland politics" and live a "self-segregated" life courtesy of the media and their virtual neighborhoods. (See Argun, *Turkey in Germany: The Transnational Sphere of Deutschkei* [New York: Routledge, 2003].) The equally impressive work of Hamid Naficy shows the semiotic impact of exilic media—with its nostalgic narratives of homeland, authenticity, and return—on the identity formation of the Iranian American community. (See Naficy, *The Making of Exile Cultures: Iranian Television in Los Angeles* [Minneapolis: University of Minnesota Press, 1993].)

5. See Beth Olson, "Media Effects Research for Public Relations Practitioners," in the *Handbook of Public Relations*, ed. Robert L. Heath (Minneapolis, MN: Sage, 2004), 271–278.

6. Eric C. Nisbet, Matthew C. Nisbet, Dietram A. Scheufele, and James E. Shanahan, "Public Diplomacy, Television News, and Muslim Public Opinion," *International Journal of Press/Politics* 9 (2004), 21.

7. Ibid., 20

8. See Stuart P. Oskamp and P. Wesley Schultz, *Attitudes and Opinions*, 3rd ed. (Mahwah, NJ: Lawrence Erlbaum, 2004), chapter 9.

9. Edward Said, *Culture and Imperialism* (New York: Alfred Knopf, 1993), 309.

10. José Casanova, "Public Religions Revisited," paper presented at the Politics of Religion-Making conference, Hofstra University, October 4–6, 2007.

11. See Samantha M. Shapiro, "The War inside the Arab Newsroom," *New York Times Magazine*, January 2, 2005, 28; and Mohamed Zayani, ed., *The Al Jazeera Phenomenon: Critical Perspectives on New Arab Media* (New York: Paradigm, 2005), 4.

12. As Joseph Nye has pointed out in *Power in the Global Information Age*, the simultaneous broadcast of so many varied stations vying to influence a targeted audience generates a case of the "paradox of plenty," where "attention rather than information becomes the scarce resource." Cited in Mohammed el-Nawawy, "U.S. Public Diplomacy and the News Credibility of Radio Sawa and Television Al Hurra in the Arab World," in *New Media and the New Middle East*, ed. Philip Seib (New York: Palgrave Macmillan, 2007), 124.

13. Hanna Rogan, "Abu Reuter and the E-Jihad: Virtual Battlefields from Iraq to the Horn of Africa," *Georgetown Journal of International Affairs* 8:2 (Summer–Fall 2007), 90.

14. Real-time reactions to the June 2009 Iranian elections were observed via Iranian citizens posting updates to Facebook profiles and Twitter lists. In addition, graphic images of violence against protestors were disseminated via Flickr pages and YouTube accounts. Protesters utilized new media to coordinate meetings and communicate with the outside world, despite an Iranian government crackdown on media and the Internet.

15. John Kelly and Bruce Etling, *Mapping Iran's Online Public: Politics and Culture in the Persian Blogosphere* (Cambridge, MA: Berkman Center for Internet & Society, Harvard Law School, 2008), 2, 41, http://cyber.law.harvard.edu/publications/2008/Mapping_Irans_Online_Public.

16. Ibid.

17. It helps to remember that the conservative Iranian clergy—who were historically opposed to such "sinful" media of mass communication (cinema, prerecorded music and video, tapes, radio, and television) on religious grounds—were willing to undergo a change of heart once they came to appreciate the effectiveness of these vehicles in disseminating their

message on the eve of the 1979 revolution. Similarly, in postrevolutionary Iran, they have warmed up to the Internet for the purposes of propagating their religious-political message. Today every single grand ayatollah in Iran has his own Web site (see www.salehin.com/fa/sites/sites_2.htm). The portal of the supreme leader (www.wilayah.net/) is available in ten different languages, while that of another grand ayatollah is available in twenty-five languages (see www.lankarani.net/).

18. A recent study found a network of approximately 35,000 active Arabic language blogs (see http://cyber.law.harvard.edu/publications/2009/Mapping_the_Arabic_Blogosphere).

19. Marc Lynch has drawn attention to the efforts of young bloggers affiliated with Egypt's Muslim Brotherhood who are questioning the policies of the older generation of leaders heading the organization. (See Lynch, "Young Brothers in Cyberspace," *Middle East Report* 245 [Winter 2007], www.merip.org/mer/mer245/lynch.html.)

20. For more discussion of Islam online, see Miriam Cooke and Bruce B. Lawrence, eds., *Muslim Networks: From Hajj to Hiphop* (Chapel Hill: University of North Carolina Press, 2005); and Mohammed Ibahrine, *New Media and Neo-Islamism: New Media's Impact on the Political Culture in the Islamic World* (Saarbrücken: VDM Verlag, 2007).

21. Gary R. Bunt, *Islam in the Digital Age: E-Jihad, Online Fatwas and Cyber Islamic Environments* (London: Pluto, 2003), 37.

22. San Kaplan, "Web defacements escalate as Israel moves farther into Gaza," *SC Magazine*, January 5, 2009, www.scmagazineus.com/web-defacements-escalate-as-israel-moves-farther-into-gaza/article/123542/.

23. Appadurai, *Modernity at Large*, 7.

24. For example, seminaries in Iran were not interested in adopting Western notions but wanted to create a searchable database of every one of Ayatollah Khomeini's speeches/sermons, to digitalize Shiite theological and jurisprudential texts, and so forth.

Annotated Bibliography

Al-Azmeh, Aziz, 1993. *Islam and Modernities*. London: Verso.

Anderson, Benedict, 1992. *Long-Distance Nationalism: World Capitalism and the Rise of Identity Politics*. Amsterdam: Centre for Asian Studies.

Appadurai, Arjun, 1997. *Modernity at Large: Cultural Dimensions of Globalization*. Minneapolis: University of Minnesota Press.

Argun, Betigül Ercan, 2003. *Turkey in Germany: The Transnational Sphere of Deutschkei*. New York: Routledge.

Asad, Talal, 1993. *Genealogies of Religion: Discipline and Reasons of Power in Christianity and Islam*. Baltimore: Johns Hopkins University Press.

Asad, Talal, 2003. *Formations of the Secular: Christianity, Islam, Modernity*. Stanford, CA: Stanford University Press.

Bunt, Gary R., 2003. *Islam in the Digital Age: E-Jihad, Online Fatwas and Cyber Islamic Environments*. London: Pluto.

Casanova, José, 2007. "Public Religions Revisited." Paper presented at the conference on the Politics of Religious Making, Hofstra University, October 4–6.

Cooke, Miriam, and Bruce B. Lawrence, eds., 2005. *Muslim Networks: From Hajj to Hiphop*. Chapel Hill: University of North Carolina Press.

el-Nawawy, Mohammed, 2007. "U.S. Public Diplomacy and the News Credibility of Radio Sawa and Television Al Hurra in the Arab World." In *New Media and the New Middle East*, ed. Philip Seib, 119–135. New York: Palgrave Macmillan.

Giddens, Anthony, 1987. *The Nation-State and Violence*. Berkeley: University of California Press.

Giddens, Anthony, 1990. *The Consequences of Modernity*. Stanford, CA: Stanford University Press.

Ibahrine, Mohammed, 2007. *New Media and Neo-Islamism: New Media's Impact on the Political Culture in the Islamic World*. Saarbrücken: VDM Verlag.

Kaplan, San, 2009. "Web Defacements Escalate as Israel Moves Farther into Gaza." *SC Magazine*, www.scmagazineus.com/Web-defacements-escalate-as-Israel-moves-farther-into-Gaza/article/123542/.

Kelly, John, and Bruce Etling, 2008. *Mapping Iran's Online Public: Politics and Culture in the Persian Blogosphere*. Cambridge, MA: Berkman Center for Internet & Society, Harvard Law School, http://cyber.law.harvard.edu/publications/2008/Mapping_Irans_Online_Public.

Kraidy, Marwan, 2006. "Hizbollywood: Hizbollah's Information War Viewed from Lebanon." Washington, DC: Woodrow Wilson International Center for Scholars, www.wilsoncenter. org/index.cfm?topic_id=1426&fuseaction=topics.event_summary&event_id=201758.

Lull, James, 2007. *Culture-On-Demand: Communication in a Crisis World*. New York: Wiley-Blackwell.

Lynch, Marc, 2005. *Voices of the New Arab Public: Iraq, al-Jazeera, and Middle East Politics Today*. New York: Columbia University Press.

Lynch, Marc, 2007. "Young Brothers in Cyberspace," *Middle East Report* 245 (Winter), www. merip.org/mer/mer245/lynch.html.

Naficy, Hamid, 1993. *The Making of Exile Cultures: Iranian Television in Los Angeles*. Minneapolis: University of Minnesota Press.

Nisbet, Erik C., Matthew C. Nisbet, Dietram A. Scheufele, and James E. Shanahan, 2004. "Public Diplomacy, Television News, and Muslim Opinion," *Harvard International Journal of Press/Politics* 9, 11–37.

Nora, Pierre, 1996. "General Introduction: Between Memory and History." In *Realms of Memory: Rethinking the French Past*, vol. 1, ed. Pierre Nora, trans. Arthur Goldhammer, 1–20. New York: Columbia University Press.

Olson, Beth. 2004. "Media Effects Research for Public Relations Practitioners." In *Handbook of Public Relations*, ed. Robert L. Heath, 271–278. Minneapolis, MN: SAGE.

Oskamp, Stuart, and P. Wesley Schultz, 2004. *Attitudes and Opinions*, 3rd ed. Mahwah, NJ: Lawrence Erlbaum.

Rogan, Hanna. 2007. "Abu Reuter and the E-Jihad: Virtual Battlefields from Iraq to the Horn of Africa," *Georgetown Journal of International Affairs* (Summer–Fall), 89–96.

Said, Edward W., 1993. *Culture and Imperialism*. New York: Alfred Knopf.

Said, Edward W., 1997. *Covering Islam: How the Media and the Experts Determine How We See the Rest of the World*, rev. ed. New York: Vintage.

Sciolino, Elaine, and Souad Mekhennet, 2008. "Warrior for Al Qaeda Rallies Jihad Recruits with Her Online Fury," *New York Times*, May 28, A10.

Shaheen, Jack G., 2001. *Reel Bad Arabs: How Hollywood Vilifies a People*. New York: Olive Branch.

Shapiro, Samantha M., 2005. "The War inside the Arab Newsroom," *New York Times Magazine*, January 2, 26–54.

Wheeler, Deborah L., 2005. *The Internet in the Middle East: Global Expectations and Local Imaginations in Kuwait*. Albany: State University of New York Press.

Zaman, Muhammad Qasem, 2002. *The Ulama in Contemporary Islam: Custodians of Change*. Princeton, NJ: Princeton University Press.

Zayani, Mohamed, ed., 2005. *The Al Jazeera Phenomenon: Critical Perspectives on New Arab Media*. New York: Paradigm.

15 }

Old Monks, New Media, and the Limits of Soulcraft

Diane Winston

In August 2007, the Burmese military junta[1] raised the price of fuel by 500 percent, sparking panic in an already poverty-stricken nation.[2] Subsequent reports of civilian protests were buried deep in international newspapers, but several weeks later, when the nation's Buddhist monks joined in, the world took notice. A small trickle of wire service stories gave way to a tsunami of print, broadcast, and online coverage, including blogs, YouTube videos, and multimedia background pieces. Increased awareness of Burma's economic woes spurred world leaders, including U.S. President George W. Bush, to initiate sanctions against the junta. On the grassroots level, thousands worldwide joined social networking sites where they could learn about the monks' campaign and support Burma's prodemocracy efforts.

Why, how, and when did the American press take note of events in Burma, and what role did religion play in capturing public attention? What was the impact of new media on the coverage and its reception? What role did Buddhism play in galvanizing public opinion? How did the story affect U.S. foreign policy, and what are the limits of "soulcraft," the religious dimension of statecraft? This essay examines events in Burma between mid-August and late September 2007, as well as why Buddhism is central to understanding them.

Ever since *Newsweek* proclaimed 1976 "the year of the evangelical," American news outlets have sought to cover religion's role in public life.[3] But according to critics in the academy, the nonprofit world, and the religious sector, their efforts consistently fall short. Much of the criticism centers on the mainstream media's inability to capture nuance, communicate substance, and convey the elusive yet essential role that belief and concomitant opinions and behavior have on individuals' orientation to culture and society. According to this perspective, most newspapers, newscasts, and newsmagazines bungle, sensationalize, or just don't get evangelicals, Muslims, Catholics, and Jews—much less Mormons, "Moonies," and Scientologists.

On a deeper level, the critique reflects frustration with the media's gatekeeping function: reporters and editors decide who is interviewed, how the story is organized,

229

and which issues and ideas are paramount. Notwithstanding its claims of objectivity, balance, and neutrality, the news media's control over source selection and narrative structure gives it significant sway over public opinion and, by extension, the formation of public policy. Consider coverage of the Israeli-Palestinian conflict. Advocates on both sides exegete sourcing, language, and reporting because these components are the building blocks for articles that turn news consumers into activists, seeking to influence policy decisions.

In recent years, the Internet has diminished the mainstream news media's monopoly on public storytelling and dramatically altered how information is produced, disseminated, and received. The Saffron Revolution,[4] the name given to the Burmese monks' campaign, is a case in point. A story at the intersection of religion and politics, unfolding in a far-off corner of the globe with exotic religious actors, the monks' actions easily could have been overlooked or misunderstood by the mainstream American media. Instead, the demonstrations became a national and global cause célèbre, captured online in videos, photography, and blogs posted by citizen journalists. These new forms of communication, as much as the mainstream media, created the context for soulcraft in the Internet age.

Crisis, Response, Reaction

On August 15, 2007, Burma's military junta eliminated governmental subsidies that kept the price of fuel and natural gas artificially low.[5] The junta, the State Peace and Development Council (SPDC), acted without warning, but the financial problems behind the policy change were no secret. Just two years earlier, the SPDC completed work on a new capital, built from the ground up, in the middle of the jungle. Outside observers estimated the cost of the new complex to be upward of 2 percent of the nation's gross domestic product, a significant burden for a very poor population.[6] Burma is rich in natural resources, including oil, jade, and timber, but the junta's military spending and fiscal mismanagement had impoverished citizens. When the subsidies ended, the subsequent 500 percent spike in natural gas prices and the doubling of fuel and diesel costs reverberated through the economy, raising the prices of basic goods and services beyond the reach of many citizens.

Within days, members of the '88 Generation student movement, which had led antigovernment protests nineteen years earlier, organized a demonstration against the regime. Some 500 activists marched in Rangoon, the country's largest city and former capital.[7] Over the next ten days, rallies continued spreading nationwide.[8] In response, the government arrested the protest's leaders, and militia members attacked those who continued to march. Then, in early September, an unexpected development nudged what had been minimally reported events onto the global stage. Scores of Buddhist monks paraded in Pakokku, a religious enclave near Mandalay. Hailed by bystanders, the monks held signs protesting the price hike. The army, interceding for the first time, fired warning shots and then attacked the marchers.

Since Buddhist monks occupy an esteemed place in Burmese society, news of the beatings prompted outraged civilian journalists to post on blogs and to send photos and videos to expatriate activists and international news outlets.

Pakokku's civil authorities apologized to the monks, but the state-run media was less conciliatory. It condemned the monks' behavior and threatened reprisals if demonstrations continued. Within days, a new group, the Alliance of All Burma Monks (ABMA), called for a religious boycott if the SPDC did not meet its requests: an apology for the army's attacks, reinstated subsidies on key consumer goods, the release of all political prisoners, and the initiation of a democratic dialogue. In response, the SPDC ratcheted up antiprotester rhetoric and shut down communications links that served journalists as well as protest organizers.

On September 14, the ABMA declared that Burma's monks would no longer accept alms from the government. This act, symbolized by an overturned beggar's bowl, effectively excommunicated SPDC leaders. The significance of the monks' refusal of government money illustrates the interpenetration of religion and politics in Burmese culture. In normal circumstances, the monks refrain from worldly activities, but they do engage in "religious antipolitics" if they perceive a threat to Buddhist teachings. The ultimate expression of that "public moralizing without direct engagement in politics," according to Ingrid Jordt, a professor at the University of Wisconsin–Milwaukee, is refusing to accept donations.[9] The act is known in the Pali language as *pattam nikkyjjana kamma*—turning over the bowl.[10]

In essence, the monks' boycott prevented the junta's leaders, their families, and their allies from gaining merit, "a moral condition that produces real world power and felicitous circumstances on one's future life." Thus, the simple act of marching with overturned bowls, as the monks did on September 17, signaled a challenge to the regime's legitimacy. The message became explicit when monks around the country read aloud an excommunication decree: "The clergy boycotts the evil, sadistic, pitiless and immensely thieving military rulers! Excommunication together with rejection of their donations of four material things and abstaining of preaching to them has come into effect!"[11]

On September 19, monks led marches in many Burmese cities.[12] Demonstrations typically started with several hundred holy men, but local citizens soon swelled their ranks. A few marches ended in police violence, but more often, they proceeded peacefully: monks and laypeople, arm-in-arm, reciting prayers in the heavy autumn rains. Then, on September 22, an unexpected encounter added a political charge to the monks' prayerful protest. According to eyewitnesses, the monks persuaded police guarding the Rangoon home of opposition leader Aung San Suu Kyi to let them approach. Under house arrest for more than a decade, Suu Kyi had not been seen in public for four years. Now she was allowed to walk outside and greet the monks, albeit from behind a police line.

Emboldened by the meeting between the monks and the opposition leader, some 20,000 protesters took to the streets of Rangoon the next day, followed by more than 60,000 the day after.[13] Instead of marching silently, many called for releasing

Suu Kyi, freeing political prisoners, and ending the SPDC regime. Equally large numbers of demonstrators followed suit in some two dozen other Burmese cities. That the demonstrations kept growing amid increasingly bold calls for democratic reform convinced a majority of the junta that it was time to crack down.[14] That night, the military leader in charge of religious affairs called the protesters "destructionists." The government's handpicked committee of Buddhist leaders announced that the monks had overstepped their bounds and should return to prayer and meditation.

Nevertheless, thousands of protesters returned to the streets. The ABMA and the '88 Generation leaders called for reform and promised to persevere, even in the face of government suppression. For the first time in twenty years, many Burmese citizens believed change was possible. But the regime proved resistant: the SPDC arrested key opposition leaders and assigned militia and riot police to patrol Rangoon's streets. On September 26, when the monks tried to leave the Shwedagon Pagoda—a historic Buddhist site and a staging area for the demonstrations, troops used live warning shots, teargas, rubber batons, and smoke bombs to stop them. Some monks were herded into trucks for detention and arrest. Others—including many who were sitting and praying—were beaten. Bystanders were shocked by the violent assaults on revered religious leaders, yet groups of monks and civilians continued to rally around the city. In some instances, soldiers fired into the crowds; other times, marchers were able to proceed unharmed. By day's end, hundreds of monks and civilians had been rounded up, and estimates of fatalities ranged from one to four (including two monks).

That night, the police raided monasteries throughout Rangoon. After beating and dispersing residents, they confiscated any items of value. The following day, when citizens protested the monks' treatment, many were beaten, and some were shot. With the monks detained or trapped inside the monasteries, laypeople convened the demonstrations. But they were set upon by security forces that, failing to dissuade them, fired live ammunition into crowds. One soldier, spotting a journalist videotaping the melee, shot him point-blank.[15] Throughout the day, whenever protesters tried to regroup, soldiers forcefully stopped them. By nightfall, hundreds had been detained and an unknown number killed. In the days that followed, soldiers and riot police took control of Rangoon's streets, blocked traffic, and prevented pedestrians from congregating. In the meantime, monks were driven from the monasteries—many were beaten, some fled, and others were taken away. By early October, the demonstrations had all but ended. The number of those arrested is unknown, as the state media and independent sources varied wildly—ranging from 2,000 to 6,000. Likewise, the number killed is estimated to be as low as thirteen and as high as several thousand.

Burmese Buddhism

State-supported violence against Burma's religious leaders magnified the news value of the Saffron Revolution. Even more dramatic than photos of red-robed, marching monks were the images of police and militia beating, dragging, and firing on red-robed, marching monks. The power of the images lay in conjuring, then skewing, the trope of bald, bare-armed, otherworldly ascetics. But the dialectic between religion and politics is complex, especially in Burma—one of the most Buddhist countries in the world. Nearly 90 percent of the population is Buddhist, and the percentage of monks to laypeople is among the world's highest. On a structural level, Buddhism provides the rhythm and texture for daily life— pagodas (houses of worship) dot Burma's cities and countryside, and religious holidays set the cultural calendar, providing a sense of meaning and belonging for a destitute population. Most Burmese children receive a Buddhist education, and many boys spend time in monasteries as novice monks.

Burmese Buddhists follow the Theravada school, which had spread throughout Southeast Asia by the tenth century.[16] Like other Buddhist traditions, Theravada, the oldest, focuses on spiritual development. It stresses individual enlightenment, but it also assumes that the *sangha* (the religious community) will ensure that the social order conforms to the *dhamma* (the right path) and that the *sasana*, the Buddha's teachings, will suffuse society. At the heart of those teachings, especially for ordinary folk, is giving, and Burma provides more financial support to Buddhism than any other nation. Giving to the *sangha*, when done with the proper intention, spiritually elevates the giver, providing benefits both in the present moment and in the future. In its purest sense, giving enables the donor to intuit the joy of selflessness. But as widely practiced, the act is key because it bestows merit (well-being) on the giver. Accordingly, every morning monks visit local households, silently holding out their bowls for small donations of food. By accepting several scoops of rice, the monks confer blessings on the householder.

This reciprocity also occurs on a societal level. Until the late nineteenth century, when Britain conquered Burma, the *sangha* provided a religious underpinning for the indigenous monarchy. In turn, Buddhist kings supported the interests of the religious community, giving generously and helping to spread the *sasana*. During colonial rule, the *sangha* functioned as an alternate communal authority, sustaining national identity. Following independence in 1948, Buddhism became the official state religion. Subsequent governments supported the *sangha*, which in turn legitimated their patrons' worldview, even when it ran counter to the interests of the people.[17] Accordingly, the SPDC has supported monasteries, published Buddhist texts, funded public ceremonies, refurbished holy sites, and also persecuted members of other religions, including Muslims and Christians. Still, the government cannot support all of Burma's monks, and since it is wary of those who are not beneficiaries, the SPDC appointed a supreme religious council to monitor and discipline the rest of the *sangha*.

Feeding the junta's suspicion of potentially dissident monks is the specter of socially engaged Buddhism.[18] Denoting an activist approach to embodying compassion, the term "socially engaged Buddhism" was popularized by Thich Nhat Hanh, a Zen Buddhist monk and teacher, during the Vietnam War. In the early

1960s, Nhat Hanh began providing direct relief to his Vietnamese countrymen who had been impoverished and displaced by years of warfare. Later in the decade, he toured the United States, encouraging the antiwar movement's quest for peace. In the intervening years, socially engaged Buddhism has been studied by scholars and adopted by practitioners worldwide.

In covering the protests, American reporters needed to grasp the interrelationship between Burma's sacred and secular domains, as well as the notion of religious antipolitics. They also had to abandon their native assumptions: church-state separation is meaningless in a nation where Buddhism is the official religion, and the American mash-up of religion and politics, whereby religious leaders are often active political partisans, is unknown. Writing for *Religion in the News*, Jordt, the Wisconsin professor, expressed concern about uninformed coverage.

> At the height of the protests, I was contacted by Seth Mydans, the Southeast Asia correspondent for the *New York Times*. For 20 years, I have studied the relationship between religion and politics in Burma. Mydans said he was preparing a Week in Review article about "militant monks" and he wanted some quotes from me on the subject.
>
> "Well," I said. "You've got it all wrong."
>
> I told Mydans that if he did write up the protest as a story of militant monks, he would be endangering the movement and putting the monks at risk. That was because "militancy" contradicts Burmese society's dominant view of the role monks can take vis-à-vis worldly society. It would also have been inaccurate reporting. The protests were almost uniformly peaceable.[19]

According to Jordt, focusing on the monks' "militancy" would not only misrepresent the *sangha*'s intention but also strengthen the junta's contention that demonstrators violated the *sasana* by engaging into political activities. If that were true, the SPDC would be justified in sending the monks back to their spiritual activities. Yet the very nature of the monks' authority, as well as their relationship to the sociopolitical order, made the protests difficult to categorize as simply sacred or secular. For example, the reciprocal notion of giving, which bound the monks to donors, made monks sensitive to the elimination of subsidies. Cognizance of the people's suffering provided a spiritual base for the monk's protests, but they also saw their own donations shrinking. Writing in the *Fletcher Forum of World Affairs*, Kyaw Lin Hlaing, a Burmese native and assistant professor of Asian and International Studies at the City University of Hong Kong, presented the monks' perspective:

> We basically live on the support of our lay disciples. In our country, monks had to get involved in politics when the government was not fixing the problems of the people. Whenever there were problems our people expect us to do something about it. The current military government has been doing a terrible job of fixing

the country's problems. The problem lies in the fact that these generals are more interested in enriching themselves.... We therefore wanted to do something to make them realize they could not remain in power without doing anything for the people and the country. We just waited for the right time, and when that time came, we all came together and staged peaceful demonstrations.[20]

Hlaing argues that the monks, adhering to *sasana*, modeled the spiritual discipline of a peaceful protest, even though many also sought democratic reform.[21] "In fact the peaceful form of protest proved to be quite effective. When blocked in one place in downtown Rangoon, some Buddhist monks kneeled down and paid homage to soldiers in the way their lay disciples paid homage to them. In Burmese society, people believe it is sinful to be paid homage by people who are older or superior to them. Thus, these tributes frightened the soldiers, who then let the monks pass."[22]

The SPDC blamed outside agitators and foreign governments for galvanizing the monks, but Hlaing discounts the charges.[23] In most cities, the monks did not allow lay protesters to join them, and when they did, the monks directed the laypeople to pray, too. As the demonstrations continued without government interference, the marchers became emboldened. But when monks joined the activists in calling for democratic reforms, the government cracked down—forcibly ending the demonstrations despite the swell of negative reports.

Press Reports and Diplomatic Responses

When the junta eliminated subsidies and demonstrations began, international wire services reported events in short, stark stories. Among American news providers, *AP Worldwide* led the coverage. Its briefs appeared in news outlets nationwide, including the *New York Times*,[24] which ran an AP wire before dispatching Seth Mydans, its Southeast Asia correspondent, to the scene. Mydans picked up the story on August 23, reporting on a "small demonstration" in Rangoon.[25] During the initial weeks of the demonstrations, before the monks were heavily involved, the *Times*, similar to other mainstream news outlets, provided episodic news briefs. The paper ran fewer than ten stories between August 18 and August 31, and only two were under Mydans's byline (the rest were wire). Still, given Burma's lack of consequence for most Americans and the modest size of the demonstrations, the coverage was not insignificant. As Mydans wrote on August 31, photos and videos transmitted by citizen journalists had "given the small demonstrations a disproportionate impact, both abroad and at home."[26]

That impact grew after the melee in Pakokku. In addition to coverage in the mainstream media, exiled prodemocracy activists posted dramatic images and on-site commentaries documenting the military's attacks. But surprise overtook outrage when the monks "fought" back: excommunicating Burma's leaders and marching with overturned bowls. These peaceful demonstrations, dubbed the Saffron Revolution, lifted the story from back burner to banner headline in the *Times* and other American news outlets.[27] Striking images of the red-robed processions captivated millions who saw them on Web sites and YouTube, newspapers and television. Even the SPDC was mindful of the world's gaze. According to Mydans,[28] the publicity, along with their own scruples, made the leaders reluctant to use force against the monks. Some of the junta's supporters and family members were especially wary of disrespecting the monks' prayerful marching.

Bloggers posted from inside and outside Burma; some were longtime democratic activists, and others were citizens deeply disturbed by what they saw in the streets.[29] *Asia Times* cited a "poignant blog, by a young, 'sensitive' Myanma woman who identifies herself as Dawn," as well as a "popular blogger [who] created a 'prosaic collection of vivid text and photos.'"[30] Less than 1 percent of the population had Internet access, but those who did were savvy about using new technology.[31] Collecting information via instant messaging, chat rooms, mobile phones, Flickr, and Facebook, citizen journalists uploaded images and commentary to mainstream news organizations, as well as to news sites run by Burmese exiles, such as Irrawaddy[32] in Thailand, Mizzima[33] in India, and Democratic Voice of Burma[34] in Norway. The tide of publicity and subsequent international support buoyed protesters, but in September's waning days, the junta tried to cut off[35] the flow of information by disabling the Internet and shutting down cell towers.[36] Still, dissidents found ways to communicate with the mainstream media and outside supporters.[37]

Online media also provided a focus for citizens worldwide to show support the protesters. Within a week of appearing on Facebook, a group supporting the monks grew to 100,000;[38] a year later, more than 400,000 people had signed up to donate money, join campaigns, attend local events, sign petitions, and share updates on Burma. Likewise, when exiled activists launched the Panties for Peace campaign,[39] sending women's underwear to SPDC leaders allegedly fearful of such garments, news of the drive spread online much faster than through the mainstream media. At the same time as grassroots activists sought to support the protesters, American leaders also responded to the monks' plight. Even before August, President Bush was "personally engaged in the cause of Burmese freedom," pushing for democratic reform in the United Nations, as well as in high-level diplomatic meetings.[40]

After August, the president called for sanctions. Many were already in place, including President Bill Clinton's 1997 executive order prohibiting U.S. companies from making new investments in Burma and a subsequent congressional act banning Burmese imports to the United States.[41] (Despite these bans, Chevron has continued oil and gas trade with Burma.)[42] The United States also had suspended aid to Burma and opposed loans to the junta from international financial organizations. After the Saffron Revolution, President Bush announced restrictions on visas to the United States for junta leaders and their families;[43] pushed for critical statements from the UN Security Council and the Association of Southeast Asian Nations (ASEAN), and unsuccessfully pressed China, Burma's primary trade partner, to condemn the regime.[44] But the impact of these initiatives was limited because of a lack of support from Burma's economic allies: China, India, and Thailand.

In sum, the monks' activities raised popular awareness of the problems in Burma, which in turn increased pressure for action on the American government. Thus the *sangha*'s soulcraft elicited a multitude of grassroots activities and several diplomatic initiatives. However, U.S. policy to Burma did not change since it already supported democratic reform, and sanctions, albeit ineffectual, were already in place. Some new moves were taken, but notwithstanding the media success of the Saffron Revolution, neither American diplomacy nor populist campaigns affected the junta's subsequent actions.

Lessons Learned

The dramatic images of Burma's monks prayerfully protesting against the government had resonance with another even more spectacular image of a Buddhist demonstration. On the morning of June 11, 1963, several hundred Buddhist monks and nuns paraded to a busy Saigon intersection, where they stood and blocked traffic in the thoroughfare. As this solemn procession lined the streets, Thich Quang Duc, an elderly monk, emerged from a parked car and assumed a lotus position on the ground. As a second monk doused him with gasoline, Duc lit a match and burst into flames. The fire burned for ten minutes, filling the square with a terrible stench, but the monk never said a word. His supporters spoke for him, waving banners that read, in English and Vietnamese, "A Buddhist Priest Burns for Buddhist Demands" and "A Buddhist Priest Burns for Five Requests."[45]

Malcolm Browne, the only reporter on the scene, shot roll after roll of photographs, mechanically snapping, he later explained, to distance himself from the horror.[46] The shot that subsequently appeared in newspapers worldwide won a World Press Photo Award, and Brown, who was working for the *Associated Press*, received a Pulitzer Prize for his Vietnam War coverage. Yet from the first, the photograph of "burning monk" was nonpareil, searing viewers with a heat that leapt from the page. Seeing it in the morning papers, President John F. Kennedy was said to have cried, "Jesus Christ!"[47] Later that day, meeting with Henry Cabot Lodge, the newly appointed ambassador to South Vietnam, the president noted, "These were the worst press relations in the world today." This was no small observation since competing events included civil rights struggles—Old Miss was desegregated the week before and Medger Evers would be assassinated that very night—the recent death of Pope John XXIII, and Kennedy's controversial call for a nuclear test-ban treaty.

By lighting a spark that fueled Americans' doubts about the conflict in Vietnam, the photo of the burning monk galvanized American sentiment against the South Vietnamese government of Ngo Dinh Diem and helped to mobilize a nascent antiwar movement. Thich Quang Duc's attempt at soulcraft did not immediately change American foreign policy, but it did prepare the way for the administration's split with the Diem regime that autumn. Like the photos and videos of the Saffron Revolution, it used the emotional power of religious images to raise awareness of a local struggle in a faraway place. But eliciting an emotional response is only a first step. Shaping the meaning of the image through an interpretative frame is key for mobilizing popular support and shaping foreign policy, which is why journalists have enjoyed an outsize influence in places like Washington, D.C. "In the domain of foreign policy," write Lisa Skow and George Dionisopoulos on the media struggle to frame the "burning monk," "the struggle over images 'is more than a distraction—it is central.'"[48]

The SPDC knew that, too, which is why it waited several weeks before attacking the monks. According to some accounts, the junta was wary of going against Buddhist spiritual authority.[49] But it is also true that leaders understood that the monks had strong international support. In the United States, that support was a product, in part, of the new media that facilitated the flow of images and the mobilization of cause-oriented social networks. But it also arose from Americans' growing familiarity with and interest in Buddhism. In the forty-four years between Duc's self-immolation and Saffron Revolution, the number of Buddhists in the United States had grown from about 200,000 to close to 2 million, and the number of "white" Americans practicing Buddhism had dramatically increased.[50]

During this period, too, sympathy for the Dalai Lama's struggle for Tibetan autonomy had normalized the notion of Buddhist soulcraft. In fact, the Dalai Lama, along with almost all things oriental, held a privileged place in American popular culture.[51] According to Jane Iwamura, the oriental monk in film and television became a popular foil for American ambivalence about Western values. "American consciousness plagued by the demands of modernity—imperialist strength and will, Christian progress, disembodied instrumental reason, capitalist accumulation and greed—find peace and resolution through the Oriental monk.... This bridge figure represents salvation, not only for America, but also for Asia."[52] Thus, when the Dalai Lama released a statement on September 23 supporting "the recent peaceful movement for democracy in Burma," his words were reported worldwide.[53]

It is not surprising, then, that the Saffron Revolution caught America's eye. The sea of scarlet robes tapped into deep reservoirs of respect, reverence, and sympathy. The monks' decision to demonstrate ratcheted up the visual imagery (and concomitant coverage), even as it spurred American orientalism, which fed on the online information flow. New media made the revolution immediate and accessible. Internet users could read, see, and hear much more on blogs, YouTube, and international news sites than what American print and broadcast media offered even on their own Web sites.[54] Moreover, much of the Internet information was unfiltered; without gatekeepers to frame the story, users could interpret it for themselves. These interpretations called into being networks of activists wielding soft power:

boycotts, letter-writing campaigns, rallies, and even panties. They did not, however, affect the policy decisions that occurred on a wholly different level. As much as the media helped drive President Bush's desire to influence events, the complex reality of relationships on the ground, especially the unwillingness of Burma's Asian trading partners to criticize the junta, diminished the impact of his diplomatic interventions.[55]

Despite the autumn crackdown, Burma's monks returned to the front lines of socially engaged Buddhism less than six months later. In May 2008, after a catastrophic cyclone killed more than 134,000 Burmese and left many more hungry and homeless, monks took the lead in providing social services. Whether distributing supplies gathered within the country or soliciting help overseas, the monks—not the junta—directed relief efforts. Yet their very success at helping to meet critical needs further antagonized military leaders. According to one press report, "A young monk in the Chaukhtatgyi Paya monastery district in Yangon predicted trouble ahead. 'You will see it again because everyone is angry and everyone is restless,' said the monk, who said he joined the September 'saffron revolution' and had a large gash over his right eye from a soldier's beating to show for it."[56]

What, then, is to be taken from this interplay of religion, media, and soulcraft? The monks succeeded at their task of focusing the global gaze on their religious antipolitics. Their efforts did not lead to immediate wholesale change, but there have been improvements. In 2010, Aung San Suu Kyi was allowed to move freely, and a new semi-civilian government, installed in August 2011, has taken steps to improve the country's human rights record.[57] These developments are a product of many factors, but the power of religious images to incite and unite, along with the Internet's capacity for circulation and dissemination, offers religious and secular actors the possibility of mobilizing a new form of track-three diplomatic initiatives. These images not only live on through YouTube; now *Burma VJ*, a documentary film making the rounds of film festivals, reprises "materials shot by underground reporters."[58] Nevertheless, it's too early to determine the efficacy of media and online campaigns. For every successful effort (consider Barack Obama's Web-based organizing), there are dozens that evoke only armchair interest. How and why some catch fire and what they can accomplish is worthy of further study.[59]

For journalists, the impact of new media on reporting at the intersection of religion and politics is equally instructive. The circulation of unfiltered images and reports, and their resonance with the public, may indicate a need to rethink journalistic norms such as "objectivity." The prospects for intercultural understanding, as well as exemplary reporting, are not bound to finding balance or modeling impartiality. Rather, they require recognition of one's own bias, specifically the imprint of cultural presuppositions, and a concomitant openness to something different, especially when that something involves the slippery prospect of putting belief into action.

Notes

The author wishes to thank Rebecca Sheehan, Nick Street, and participants in the Religion and Public Life Seminar at the University of Southern California for their contributions to this paper.

1. The Burmese military junta changed the country's name to Myanmar. However, since Burmese democratic activists, as well as the American government and many media outlets, use the name Burma, it is used here.

2. Burma "ranks 132 out of 177 countries in the United Nations Development Program's Human Development Index. Most experts, who doubt the government's statistics, think the reality is worse." Daniel Pepper, "Aftermath of a Revolt: Myanmar's Lost Year," *New York Times*, October 5, 2008. www.nytimes.com/2008/10/05/weekinreview/05pepper. html?_r=1&scp=2&sq=daniel pepper&st=cse.

3. See www.newsweek.com/id/44543.

4. The Saffron Revolution was named for the color of the monks' robes. The actual colors were closer to red and maroon but "saffron" is more redolent of exotic orientalism.

5. The summary of events is drawn from several sources including the AP Worldwide, Agence-France Presse, *New York Times*, *Washington Post*, *BBC*, and Human Rights Watch (www.hrw.org/en/reports/2007/12/06/crackdown).

6. See www.hrw.org/en/node/10572/section/6.

7. "Hundreds Protest in Myanmar over Fuel Price Hikes," Agence France Presse, August 19, 2007.

8. "Buddhist Monks Join Pro-Democracy Protesters in Myanmar," Agence France Presse, *New York Times*, August 28, 2007, A11.

9. See Ingird Jordt, *Burma's Mass Lay Meditation Movement: Buddhism and the Cultural Construction of Power* (Athens: Ohio University Press, 2007).

10. See http://www.trincoll.edu/depts/csrpl/RINVol10No3/turning%20over%20the%20 bowl.htm.

11. See www.hrw.org/en/node/10572/section/8. According to a footnote in the Human Rights Watch summary, the four material things that monks can accept are robes, medicine, shelter, and rice.

12. Onlookers understood the religio-political context for the protests. In an article in *The Irrawaddy*, an online news site started by Burmese exiles, a student expressed dismay about government attacks on the monks: " 'It is not appropriate as Burma is ruled by Buddhist believers,' he said, adding that the government should seek a peaceful compromise with the monks, 'They [the junta] should apologize as the monks asked and ask the monks what they want'" (www. irrawaddy.org/article.php?art_id=8663).

13. Some news outlets reported there were as many as 100,000 demonstrators.

14. Larry A. Niksch, "Burma-U.S. relations (report)," *Congressional Research Service (CRS) Reports and Issue Briefs*, 2007.

15. The shooting of Japanese journalist Kenji Nagai was subsequently aired on Japanese television. See www.timesonline.co.uk/tol/news/world/asia/article2550369.ece.

16. The summary of Burmese Buddhism is based on several sources, including Juliane Schober, "Communities of Interpretation in the Study of Religion in Burma," *Journal of Southeast Asian Studies* 39:2 (June 2008), 255 (13); Kyaw Lin Hlaing, "Protests in Burma,"

Fletcher Forum of World Affairs 32:1 (Winter 2008), 125–144; www.timesonline.co.uk/tol/comment/faith/article3052917.ece; and www.fpif.org/fpiftxt/4582.

17. Hlaing, "Protests in Burma, 125–144.

18. For example, Christopher Queen, Charles Prebish, and Damiam Keown, eds., *Action Dharma: Bew Studies in Engaged Buddhism* (London: RoutledgeCurzon, 2004).

19. See www.trincoll.edu/depts/csrpl/RINVol10No3/turning over the bowl.htm.

20. Hlaing, "Protests in Burma," 134.

21. George Packer writes, "In general, the monks I interviewed were far more unsentimental in their political calculations than students and artists were; they thought like dedicated organizers who understood just how long and hard the battle would be." George Packer, "Drowning: Can the Burmese People Rescue Themselves?" *New Yorker*, August 25, 2008, www.newyorker.com/reporting/2008/08/25/080825fa_fact_packer.

22. Hlaing, "Protests in Burma," 137.

23. On the other hand, some studies found foreign funds were used to help the protests, including contributions from George Soros's Open Society, which has a Burma initiative: www.soros.org/initiatives/bpsai.

24. I focused on the *New York Times* because it is viewed as an exemplar of American journalism, and it was one of the few American newspapers to have a reporter in Burma.

25. Seth Mydans, "Steep Rise in Fuel Costs Prompts Rare Public Protest in Myanmar," *New York Times*, August 23, 2007, A5.

26. See www.nytimes.com/2007/08/31/world/asia/31myanmar.html.

27. The spike in stories can be seen across media platforms. According to Proquest, the *New York Times* and *Los Angeles Times* ran six stories on Burma between August 16 and August 28, 2007; they had thirty-five stories between September 17 and September 26. During this same period, the *Wall Street Journal* had eight articles. National Public Radio broadcast no coverage until September 21. Then between September 23 and 30, it ran forty-seven pieces (a count from all their programs). *Time* had no coverage in August and two pieces in early September. Between September 19 and 30, the magazine ran nine articles. (The *Time* and NPR numbers come from their respective Web sites.)

28. See www.nytimes.com/2007/09/21/world/asia/21myanmar.html.

29. A blog by Burmese Buddhist monk Ashin Mattacara was in the running for the Best Asian Blog of 2008. Begun in 2004 to explore religion, the blog focused on politics after the 2007 protests. For more, see www.mizzima.com/news/regional/1526-burmese-blogger-in-running-to-win-qbest-asian-blogq.html. Another well-respected blogger on the crisis was Jotman, a non-Burmese interested in "global citizenship" (http://page1.jotman.com-a.googlepages.com/home). Besides compiling reports from news sites to create a daily timeline of the crisis, Jotman featured interviews with escaped monks and other members of the Burmese resistance.

30. See www.atimes.com/atimes/Southeast_Asia/1129Ac0s.html.
http://www.atimes.com/atimes/Southeast_Asia/II29Ae02.html; accessed 10/9/11

31. Stephen Kauffman, USINFO, State Department Documents and Publications, November 1, 2007.

32. See www.irrawaddy.org/.

33. See www.mizzima.com/.

34. See www.dvb.no/english/index.php.

35. See www.washingtonpost.com/wp-dyn/content/article/2007/08/22/AR2007082202488_pf.html.

36. Kauffman, USINFO, State Department Documents and Publications, November 1, 2007; Seth Mydans, "Monks Are Silenced and for Now, the Web Is Too," *New York Times*, October 4, 2007, A1; and www.irrawaddy.org/article.php?art_id=8803.

37. See blogswork.wordpress.com/2007/09/26/burma-the-web-is-watching/; http://online.wsj.com/article/SB119090803430841433.html?mod=hpp_us_editors_picks. See also www.thirdworldtraveler.com/Burma/Burma_watch.html. For a case study of Burma's citizen journalists, see www.columbia.edu/itc/sipa/nelson/newmediadev/Citizen journalism.html.

38. See www.guardian.co.uk/world/2007/sep/29/burma.topstories32.

39. See www.ctv.ca/servlet/ArticleNews/story/CTVNews/20080527/burma_embassy_080527/20080527.

40. See www.washingtonpost.com/wp dyn/content/article/2007/08/22/AR2007082202488_pf.html.

41. In July 2008, a new U.S. law banned the import of Burmese gems, including from third-party suppliers. (See www.hrw.org/en/news/2008/07/28/us-burma-gem-ban-strengthened.)

42. See www.sofmag.com/wp/2008/07/24/us-lawmakers-vote-to-extend-sanctions-against-burma/.

43. See http://uk.reuters.com/article/latestCrisis/idUKWAT00815420070925?sp=true. See, too, www.america.gov/st/texttrans-english/2007/October/20071019171340xjsnommis0.1622736.html and www.whitehouse.gov/news/releases/2007/10/20071019-15.html.

44. David E. Sanger and Steven Lee Myers, "U.S. Steps Up Confrontation with Myanmar's Rulers," *New York Times*, September 26, 2009, A6.

45. Ann Blair, "The Buddhist Crisis in South Vietnam and the American Press," *Melbourne Historical Review* 20 (1990), 27.

46. Malcolm Browne, *Muddy Boots and Red Socks: A Reporter's Life* (New York: Random House, 1993), 11–12.

47. Lisa M. Skow and George N. Dionisopoulos, "A Struggle to Contextualize Photographic Images: American Print Media and the 'Burning Monk,'" *Communications Quarterly* 45:4 (Fall 1997), 396.

48. Ibid., 406; Blair, "The Buddhist Crisis," 34.

49. For example, http://english.aljazeera.net/news/asia-pacific/2007/10/2008525185945871910.html.

50. See http://www.bffct.net/id65.html accessed 10/9/11
http://religions.pewforum.org/reports accessed 10/98/11

51. Rudy Busto, "'*Chiariidaa o Sukue, Sekai o Sukue!*': Nuclear Dread and the Pokémonization of American Religion in Season One of Heroes," in *Small Screen, Big Picture: Television and Lived Religion*, ed. Diane Winston (Waco, TX: Baylor University Press, 2009), 293.

52. Jane Iwamura, "The Oriental Monk in American Popular Culture," in *Religion and Popular Culture in America*, ed. Bruce David Forbes and Jeffrey H. Mahan (Berkeley: University of California Press, 2004), 37.

53. For example, "Dalai Lama Offers Support to Myanmar Monks," Agence France-Presse, September 24, 2007.

54. The U.S. coverage paled in breadth and depth to what was available online, especially after the protests led the junta to cut off visas for foreign journalists. The blogger Jotman criticized the American media for being "asleep at the wheel": http://jotman.blogspot.com/2007/10/us-media-asleep-at-wheel-on-burma.html.

55. See Niksch, "Burma-U.S. relations (report)," for a detailed report on why sanctions failed.

56. See www.nytimes.com/2008/05/31/world/asia/31myanmar.html?_r=1&scp=1&sq= monks succeed in cyclone relief&st=cse.

57. For example, see www.newsweek.com/id/72026 and www.newsweek.com/id/71984?tid= relatedcl.

58. See http://burmavjcom.title.dk/.

59. For sources in the popular media, see, for example, www.nytimes.com/2009/01/25/magazine/25bloggers-t.html?scp=1&sq=revolution facebook-style&st=cse.

Annotated Bibliography

Books

Religion and the news media is a vastly understudied subject, and many of the key works are more than a decade old, written before the advent of new media. However, several of these works still remain timely and informative.

Badaraco, Claire, *Quoting God: How Media Shape Ideas about Religion and Culture*. Waco, TX: Baylor University Press, 2004.

Explores the reflexive relationship between religion and media in essays by scholars and journalists that go behind the headlines of stories on cults, Muslims, and religion and foreign policy, including Paul Boyer's excellent piece on biblical prophecy and international relations.

Lobdell, William, *Losing My Religion: How I Lost My Faith Reporting on Religion in America and Found Unexpected Peace*. New York: HarperCollins, 2009.

An inside-out view of the relationship between religion and the media can be found in this memoir. A former *Los Angeles Times* religion reporter, Lobdell describes how his experience on the beat chipped away at his evangelical faith.

McCloud, Sean, *Making the American Religious Fringe: Exotics, Subversives and Journalists, 1955–1993*. Chapel Hill: University of North Carolina Press, 2004.

An engaging case study of how magazines shaped cultural perspectives of nonmainstream religious groups. McCloud helps explain how and why stereotypes about Muslims, Buddhists, and Christian fundamentalists took hold in the popular imagination and the societal consequence of these depictions.

Sloan, William David, ed., *Media and Religion in American History*. San Ramon, CA: Vision Press, 2000.

Includes essays on religion and colonial newspapers, the mass media and revivalism, and journalists and the Scopes trial. It's an uneven collection, but it features several excellent essays by historians whose work is a distillation of subsequent books and projects.

Articles

Flory, Richard, "Promoting a Secular Standard: Secularization and Modern Journalism, 1870–1930," in *The Secular Revolution*, ed. Christian Smith. Berkeley: University of California Press, 2003.
Providing historical context for Rosen's argument, Flory explores the impact of secularization on the journalistic profession.
Rosen, Jay, "Journalism Is Itself a Religion." www.therevealer.org/archives/timeless_000149. php. http://blogcritics.org/culture/article/journalism-is-itself-a-religion/ accessed 10/9/11
Among the best descriptions of the underlying tensions between religion and the media. Rosen reveals the clash of authoritative domains that helps explain why religion is frequently marginalized or trivialized by the mainstream media.
Winston, Diane, "Back to the Future: Religion, Politics and the News Media," *American Quarterly* 59:3 (2007).
Provides a case study on how stories becomes headlines

Web Sites

www.getreligion.org/ provides a daily update about how the mainstream media gets or misses the role of religion in the news.
To the left of Getreligion, http://therevealer.org/ provides a quirkier take on religion in media.
http://uscmediareligion.org/ offers updates on trends in coverage from the Knight Chair on Media and Religion at the University of Southern California.
http://www.realclearreligion.org/ good aggregate for religion news online
http://pewforum.org/ religion news, surveys and analyses

PART VI

Religion and American Foreign Policy

16 }

God's Country?
Walter Russell Mead

Evangelicals and Foreign Policy

Religion has always been a major force in U.S. politics, policy, identity, and culture. Religion shapes the nation's character, helps form Americans' ideas about the world, and influences the ways Americans respond to events beyond their borders. Religion explains both Americans' sense of themselves as a chosen people and their belief that they have a duty to spread their values throughout the world. Of course, not all Americans believe such things—and those who do often bitterly disagree over exactly what they mean. But enough believe them that the ideas exercise profound influence over the country's behavior abroad and at home.

In one sense, religion is so important to life in the United States that it disappears into the mix. Partisans on all sides of important questions regularly appeal to religious principles to support their views, and the country is so religiously diverse that support for almost any conceivable foreign policy can be found somewhere.

Yet the balance of power among the different religious strands shifts over time; in the last generation, this balance has shifted significantly, with dramatic consequences. The more conservative strains within American Protestantism have gained adherents, and the liberal Protestantism that dominated the country during the middle years of the twentieth century has weakened. This shift has already changed U.S. foreign policy in profound ways.

These changes have yet to be widely understood, however, in part because most students of foreign policy in the United States and abroad are relatively unfamiliar with conservative U.S. Protestantism. That the views of the evangelical Reverend Billy Graham lead to quite different approaches to foreign relations than, say, those popular at the fundamentalist Bob Jones University is not generally appreciated. But subtle theological and cultural differences can and do have important political consequences. Interpreting the impact of religious changes in the United States on U.S. foreign policy therefore requires a closer look into the big revival tent of American Protestantism.

Why focus exclusively on Protestantism? The answer is, in part, that Protestantism has shaped much of the country's identity and remains today the majority faith in the United States (although only just). Moreover, the changes in Catholicism (the second-largest faith and the largest single religious denomination in the country) present a more mixed picture with fewer foreign policy implications. And finally, the remaining religious groups in the United States are significantly less influential when it comes to the country's politics.

A Question of Fundamentals

To make sense of how contemporary changes in Protestantism are starting to affect U.S. foreign policy, it helps to understand the role that religion has historically played in the country's public life. The U.S. religious tradition, which grew out of the sixteenth-century Reformations of England and Scotland, has included many divergent ideologies and worldviews over time. Three strains, however, have been most influential: a strict tradition that can be called fundamentalist, a progressive and ethical tradition known as liberal Christianity, and a broader evangelical tradition. (Pentecostals have theological differences with non-Pentecostal evangelicals and fundamentalists, but Pentecostalism is an offshoot of evangelical theology, and thus the majority of American Pentecostals can be counted with evangelicals here.)

It would be wrong to read too much precision into these labels. Most American Christians mix and match theological and social ideas from these and other strands of Protestant and Christian thought with little concern for consistency. Yet describing the chief features of each strand and their implications for the United States' role in the world will nevertheless make it easier to appreciate the way changes in the religious balance are shaping the country's behavior.

Fundamentalists, liberal Christians, and evangelicals are all part of the historical mainstream of American Protestantism, and as such, all were profoundly affected by the fundamentalist-modernist controversy of the early twentieth century. For much of the 1800s, most Protestants believed that science confirmed biblical teaching. When Darwinian biology and scholarly "higher criticism" began to cast increasing doubt on traditional views of the Bible's authorship and veracity, however, the American Protestant movement broke apart. Modernists argued that the best way to defend Christianity in an enlightened age was to incorporate the new scholarship into theology, and mainline Protestant denominations followed this logic. The fundamentalists believed that churches should remain loyal to the "fundamentals" of Protestant faith, such as the literal truth of the Bible.

The fundamentalists themselves were divided into two strands, originally distinguished as much by culture and temperament as by theology. The "separatists" argued that true believers should abandon churches that compromised with or tolerated modernism in any form. As U.S. society and culture became more secular and pluralistic, the separatists increasingly withdrew from both politics and culture. The other strand of the original fundamentalist movement sought continual engagement with the rest of the world. This strand was originally called neo-evangelical. Today, the separatists proudly retain the label of fundamentalist, while the neo-evangelicals have dropped the prefix and are now simply known as evangelicals.

The three contemporary streams of American Protestantism (fundamentalist, liberal, and evangelical) lead to very different ideas about what the country's role in the world should be. In this context, the most important differences have to do with the degree to which each promotes optimism about the possibilities for a stable, peaceful, and enlightened international order and the importance each places on the difference between believers and nonbelievers. In a nutshell, fundamentalists are deeply pessimistic about the prospects for world order and see an unbridgeable divide between believers and nonbelievers. Liberals are optimistic about the prospects for world order and see little difference between Christians and nonbelievers. And evangelicals stand somewhere in between these extremes.

Self-described fundamentalists are a diverse group, partly because there are many competing definitions of the term *fundamentalist* and, in keeping with the decentralized and sectarian character of American Protestantism, there is no generally accepted authoritative body to define what fundamentalists are or believe. As used here, the term *fundamentalist* involves three characteristics: a high view of biblical authority and inspiration; a strong determination to defend the historical Protestant faith against Roman Catholic and modernist, secular, and non-Christian influence; and the conviction that believers should separate themselves from the non-Christian world. Fundamentalists can be found throughout conservative Protestant Christianity, and some denominations more properly considered evangelical (such as the Southern Baptists and the Missouri Synod Lutherans) have vocal minorities that could legitimately be called fundamentalist.

Fundamentalist denominations, such as the ultra-Calvinist Orthodox Presbyterian Church, tend to be smaller than liberal and evangelical ones. This is partly because fundamentalists prefer small, pure, and doctrinally rigorous organizations to larger, more diverse ones. It is also because many fundamentalist congregations prefer to remain independent of any denominational structure.

Many outsiders think of fundamentalism as an anti-intellectual and emotional movement. And it is true that most conservative American Protestants attach great importance to emotional and personal spiritual experience. But the difference between fundamentalists and evangelicals is not that fundamentalists are more emotional in their beliefs; it is that fundamentalists insist more fully on following their ideas to their logical conclusion. Fundamentalists are more interested than evangelicals in developing a consistent and all-embracing "Christian worldview" and then in systematically applying it to the world. It is one thing to reject (as many evangelicals do) Darwinian evolution because personal experience leads one to consider the Bible an infallible guide. It is something else entirely to develop (as some fundamentalists do) an alternative paradigm of "scientific creationism," write textbooks about it, and seek to force schools to teach it or withdraw one's children from those schools that will not. Fundamentalist-dominated institutions, such as the Independent Baptist movement and Bob Jones University, are not hotbeds of snake-handling revivalist Holy Rollers but host intense, if often unconventional, scholarship.

Devastated by a string of intellectual and political defeats in the 1920s and 1930s, fundamentalists retreated into an isolation and a pessimism that were foreign to the optimistic orientation of nineteenth-century American Protestantism. The effect of this retreat was to give fundamentalists a defensive and alienated outlook that bore a marked resemblance to the Puritan Calvinism of early New England. Like the Puritans, many fundamentalists hold the bleak view that there is an absolute gap between those few souls God has chosen to redeem and the many he has predestined to end up in hell. Calvinists once labored to establish theocratic commonwealths—in Scotland by the Covenanters and the Kirk Party, in England during Oliver Cromwell's ascendancy, and in New England, all during the seventeenth century. But in the last three centuries, theocratic state building has become both less attractive to and less feasible for hard-line fundamentalists. It is not only that demographic changes have made it difficult to imagine circumstances in which fundamentalists would constitute a majority. The experience of past commonwealths also shows that successor generations usually lack the founders' fervor. Sadder and wiser from these experiences, contemporary American fundamentalists generally believe that human efforts to build a better world can have only very limited success. They agree with the nineteenth-century American preacher Dwight Moody, who, when urged to focus on political action, replied, "I look upon this world as a wrecked vessel. God has given me a lifeboat and said, 'Moody, save all you can.'"

If fundamentalists tend to be pessimistic about the prospects for social reform inside the United States, they are downright hostile to the idea of a world order based on secular morality and on global institutions such as the United Nations. More familiar than many Americans with the stories of persecuted Christians abroad, fundamentalists see nothing moral about cooperating with governments that oppress churches, forbid Christian proselytizing, or punish conversions to Christianity under Islamic law. To institutions such as the UN that treat these governments as legitimate, they apply the words of the prophet Isaiah: "We have made a covenant with death, and with hell we are at agreement." It is no coincidence that the popular Left Behind novels, which depict the end of the world from a fundamentalist perspective, show the Antichrist rising to power as the secretary-general of the UN.

Fundamentalists, finally, are committed to an apocalyptic vision of the end of the world and the Last Judgment. As biblical literalists, they believe that the dark prophecies in both the Hebrew and the Greek Scriptures, notably those of the book of Revelation, foretell the great and terrible events that will ring down the curtain on human history. Satan and his human allies will stage a final revolt against God and the elect; believers will undergo terrible persecution, but Christ will put down his enemies and reign over a new heaven and a new earth. This vision is not particularly hospitable to the idea of gradual progress toward a secular utopia driven by technological advances and the cooperation of intelligent people of all religious traditions.

Liberal Thinking

Liberal Christianity finds the core of Christianity in its ethical teachings rather than in its classic doctrines. As far back as the seventeenth century, this current of Christian thinking has worked to demythologize the religion: to separate the kernel of moral inspiration from the shell of legend that has, presumably, accreted around it. Liberal Christians are skeptical about the complex doctrines concerning the nature of Jesus and the Trinity that were developed in the early centuries of the church's history. They are reluctant to accept various biblical episodes— such as the creation of the world in seven days, the Garden of Eden, and Noah's flood—as literal narrative. And their skepticism often also extends to the physical resurrection of Jesus and the various miracles attributed to him. Rather than believing that Jesus was a supernatural being, liberal Christians see him as a sublime moral teacher whose example they seek to follow through a lifetime of service—often directed primarily at the poor. The Unitarian Church, introduced to the United States in 1794 by the English scientist and theologian Joseph Priestly, is a denomination organized around these core ideas. Priestly was a friend of Benjamin Franklin and a significant theological influence on Thomas Jefferson, although both Franklin and Jefferson attended Episcopalian services when they went to church. As Darwinism and biblical criticism led others to question the literal accuracy of many biblical stories, liberalism spread widely through the mainline Protestant denominations—including the Methodist, Presbyterian, American Baptist, Congregational, Episcopal, and Lutheran churches—to which the United States' social, intellectual, and economic elites have generally belonged.

Although more doctrinally conservative Christians often consider progressives to be outside the Christian mainstream, liberal Christians claim to represent the essence of Protestantism. The Reformation, in their view, was the first stage of reclaiming the valuable core of Christianity. The original reformers purged the church of the sale of indulgences and ideas such as purgatory, papal infallibility, and transubstantiation. In attacking such established Christian doctrines as the Trinity, original sin, and the existence of hell, liberal Christians today believe they are simply following the "Protestant principle."

Liberal Christianity has a much lower estimate of the difference between Christians and non-Christians than do the other major forms of American Protestantism. Liberal Christians believe that ethics are the same all over the world. Buddhists, Christians, Hindus, Jews, Muslims, and even nonreligious people can agree on what is right and what is wrong; every religion has a kernel of ethical truth. The idea of the church as a supernatural society whose members enjoy special grace plays very little role in liberal Christianity.

Because most liberal Christians (with the important exception of "Christian realists" such as the theologian Reinhold Niebuhr) discard the doctrine of original sin, liberal Christianity leads to optimism both about the prospects for a peaceful world order and about international organizations such as the UN. Indeed, liberal Christians have often seen the fight to establish the kingdom of God as a call to support progressive political causes at home and abroad. They argue that the dark prophecies of Revelation point to the difficulty of establishing a just social order on earth—but that this order will nonetheless come to pass if everyone works together to build it.

Liberal Protestantism dominated the worldview of the U.S. political class during World War II and the Cold War. Leaders such as Franklin Roosevelt, Harry Truman, Dean Acheson, Dwight Eisenhower, and John Foster Dulles were, like most American elites at the time, steeped in this tradition. The liberal Christian approach also opened the door to cooperation with Roman Catholics and Jews, who were then becoming much more influential in the United States. Some of the optimism with which many liberal Christians today approach the problems of world order and cooperation across ethnic and religious lines reflects their earlier success at forming a domestic consensus.

In recent years, however, liberal Christianity has been confronted with several challenges. First, liberal Protestantism tends to evanesce into secularism: members follow the "Protestant principle" right out the door of the church. As a result, liberal, mainline denominations are now shrinking—quickly. Second, liberal Christians are often only tepidly engaged with "religious" issues and causes. Liberal Christians may be environmentalists involved with the Sierra Club or human rights activists involved with Amnesty International, but those activities take place in the secular world. Third, alienated from the Catholic hierarchy by their position on issues such as abortion and gay rights, and from Jews by their decreasing support for Israel, liberal Christians are losing their traditional role as the conveners of an interfaith community. Finally, the mainline denominations themselves are increasingly polarized over issues such as gay rights.

Consumed by internal battles, they are less able to influence U.S. society as a whole.

Evangelicals and the Middle Path

Evangelicals, the third of the leading strands in American Protestantism, straddle the divide between fundamentalists and liberals. Their core beliefs share common roots with fundamentalism, but their ideas about the world have been heavily influenced by the optimism endemic to U.S. society. Although there is considerable theological diversity within this group, in general it is informed by the "soft Calvinism" of the sixteenth-century Dutch theologian Jacobus Arminius, the thinking of English evangelists such as John Wesley (who carried on the tradition of German Pietism), and, in the United States, the experience of the eighteenth-century Great Awakening and subsequent religious revivals.

The leading evangelical denomination in the United States is the Southern Baptist Convention, which, with more than 16.3 million members, is the largest Protestant denomination in the country. The next-largest evangelical denominations are the African American churches, including the National Baptist Convention, U.S.A., and the National Baptist Convention of America (each of which reports having about 5 million members).The predominantly African American Church of God in Christ, with 5.5 million members, is the largest Pentecostal denomination in the country, and the rapidly growing Assemblies of God, which has 2.7 million members, is the largest Pentecostal denomination that is not predominantly black. The Lutheran Church–Missouri Synod, which has 2.5 million members, is the second-largest predominantly white evangelical denomination. Like fundamentalists, white evangelicals are often found in independent congregations and small denominations. So-called parachurch organizations, such as the Campus Crusade for Christ, the Promise Keepers, and the Wycliffe Bible Translators, often replace or supplement traditional denominational structures among evangelicals.

Evangelicals resemble fundamentalists in several respects. Like fundamentalists, evangelicals attach a great deal of importance to the doctrinal tenets of Christianity, not just to its ethical teachings. For evangelicals and fundamentalists, liberals' emphasis on ethics translates into a belief that good works and the fulfillment of moral law are the road to God—a betrayal of Christ's message, in their view. Because of original sin, they argue, humanity is utterly incapable of fulfilling any moral law whatever. The fundamental message of Christianity is that human efforts to please God by observing high ethical standards must fail; only Christ's crucifixion and resurrection can redeem man. Admitting one's sinful nature and accepting Christ's sacrifice are what both evangelicals and fundamentalists mean by being "born again." When liberal Christians put ethics at the heart of their theology, fundamentalists and evangelicals question whether these liberals know what Christianity really means.

Evangelicals also attach great importance to the difference between those who are "saved" and those who are not. Like fundamentalists, they believe that human beings who die without accepting Christ are doomed to everlasting separation from God. They also agree with fundamentalists that "natural" people—those who have not been "saved"—are unable to do any good works on their own.

Finally, most (although not all) evangelicals share the fundamentalist approach to the end of the world. Virtually all evangelicals believe that the biblical prophecies will be fulfilled, and a majority agree with fundamentalists on the position known as premillennialism: the belief that Christ's return will precede the establishment of the prophesied thousand-year reign of peace. Ultimately, all human efforts to build a peaceful world will fail.

Given these similarities, it is not surprising that many observers tend to confuse evangelicals and fundamentalists, thinking that the former are simply a watered down version of the latter. Yet there are important differences between the fundamentalist and the evangelical worldviews. Although the theological positions on these issues can be very technical and nuanced, evangelicals tend to act under the influence of a cheerier form of Calvinism. The strict position is that Christ's sacrifice on the cross was only intended for the small number of souls God intended to save; the others have no chance for salvation. Psychologically and doctrinally, American evangelicals generally have a less bleak outlook. They believe that the benefits of salvation are potentially available to everyone, and that God gives everyone just enough grace to be able to choose salvation if he wishes. Strict Calvinist doctrine divides humanity into two camps with little in common. In the predominant evangelical view, God loves each soul, is unutterably grieved when any are lost, and urgently seeks to save them all.

All Christians, whether fundamentalist, liberal, or evangelical, acknowledge at least formally the responsibility to show love and compassion to everyone, Christian or not. For evangelicals, this demand has extra urgency. Billions of perishing souls can still be saved for Christ, they believe. The example Christians set in their daily lives, the help they give the needy, and the effectiveness of their proclamation of the gospel—these can bring lost souls to Christ and help fulfill the divine plan. Evangelicals constantly reinforce the message of Christian responsibility to the world. Partly as a result, evangelicals are often open to, and even eager for, social action and cooperation with nonbelievers in projects to improve human welfare, even though they continue to believe that those who reject Christ cannot be united with God after death.

Evangelicals can be hard to predict. Shocked by recent polls showing that a substantial majority of Americans reject the theory of evolution, intellectuals and journalists in the United States and abroad have braced themselves for an all-out assault on Darwinian science. But no such onslaught has been forthcoming; U.S. public opinion has long rejected Darwinism, yet even in states such as Alabama, Mississippi, and South Carolina, which have large actively Christian populations, state universities go on teaching astronomy, genetics, geology, and paleontology with no concern for religious cosmology, and the United States continues to support the world's most successful scientific community. Most evangelicals find nothing odd about this seeming contradiction. Nor do they wish to change it—unlike the fundamentalists. The pragmatism of U.S. culture combines with the somewhat anti-intellectual cast of evangelical religion to create a very broad public tolerance for what, to some, might seem an intolerable level of cognitive dissonance. In the seventeenth century, Puritan Harvard opposed Copernican cosmology, but today evangelical America is largely content to let discrepancies between biblical chronology and the fossil record stand unresolved. What evangelicals do not like is what some call "scientism": the attempt to teach evolution or any other subject in such a way as to rule out the possibility of the existence and activity of God.

Evangelicals are more optimistic than fundamentalists about the prospects for moral progress. The postmillennial minority among them (which holds that Christ will return after a thousand years of world peace, not before) believes that this process can continue until human society reaches a state of holiness: that the religious progress of individuals and societies can culminate in the establishment of a peaceable kingdom through a process of gradual improvement. This is a view of history very compatible with the optimism of liberal Christians, and evangelicals and liberal Christians have in fact joined in many common efforts at both domestic and international moral improvement throughout U.S. history. Although the premillennial majority is less optimistic about the ultimate success of such efforts, American evangelicals are often optimistic about the short-term prospects for human betterment.

In his 2005 book *Imagine! A God-Blessed America: How It Could Happen and What It Would Look Like*, the conservative evangelical Richard Land describes and justifies this evangelical optimism: "I believe that there could be yet another Great Awakening in our country, a nationwide revival.... Scripture tells us that none of us can know with certainty the day or hour of the Lord's return. Thus, we have no right to abandon the world to its own misery. Nowhere in Scripture are we called to huddle pessimistically in Christian ghettoes, snatching converts out of the world."

The Balance of Power

Recent decades have witnessed momentous changes in the balance of religious power in the United States. The membership of the liberal, historically dominant mainline Protestant churches mostly peaked in the 1960s. Since then, while the number of American Christians has grown, membership in the mainline denominations has sharply dropped. According to *Christianity Today*, between 1960 and 2003, membership in mainline denominations fell by more than 24 percent, from 29 million to 22 million. The drop in market share was even more dramatic. In 1960, more than 25 percent of all members of religious groups in the United States belonged to the seven leading mainline Protestant denominations; by 2003, this figure had dropped to 15 percent. The Pew Research Center reports that 59 percent of American Protestants identified themselves as mainline Protestants in 1988; by 2002–03, that percentage had fallen to 46 percent. In the same period, the percentage of Protestants who identified themselves as evangelical rose from 41 percent to 54 percent.

In 1965, there were 3.6 million Episcopalians in the United States—1.9 percent of the total population. By 2005, there were only 2.3 million Episcopalians—0.8 percent of the population. Membership in the United Methodist Church fell from 11 million in 1965 to 8.2 million in 2005. In the same period, that in the Presbyterian Church (U.S.A.) fell from 3.2 million to 2.4 million, and the United Church of Christ saw its membership decline by almost 50 percent.

Meanwhile, despite some signs of slowing growth after 2001, the Southern Baptist Convention gained more than 7 million members to become the nation's largest Protestant denomination. Between 1960 and 2003, the Southern Baptists gained more members than the Methodists, Presbyterians, Episcopalians, and the United Church of Christ together lost. In 1960, there were almost 2 million more Methodists than Southern Baptists in the United States; by 2003, there were more Southern Baptists than Methodists, Presbyterians, Episcopalians, and members of the United Church of Christ combined.

The impact of these trends on national politics has not been hard to find. Self-identified evangelicals provided roughly 40 percent of George W. Bush's total vote in 2004. Among white evangelicals, Bush received 68 percent of the national vote in 2000 and 78 percent in 2004. (The majority of African American evangelicals continue to vote Democratic. Among Hispanics, Bush ran much stronger among the growing Protestant minority than among Catholics; however, both Hispanic Protestants and Hispanic Catholics were more likely to support Bush if they were religiously observant.) Evangelicals have been playing a major role in congressional and Senate elections as well, and the number of self-identified evangelicals in Congress has increased from around 10 percent of the membership in both houses in 1970 to more than 25 percent in 2004.

Fundamentalists, despite some increase in their numbers and political visibility, remain less influential. This is partly because the pervasive optimism of the United States continues to limit the appeal of ultra-Calvinist theology. Moreover, religious politics in the United States remains a coalition sport—one that a fundamentalist theology, which continues to view Catholicism as an evil cult, is ill equipped to play. To make matters more complicated, fundamentalists themselves are torn between two incompatible political positions: a sullen withdrawal from a damned world and an ambitious attempt to build a new Puritan commonwealth.

Finally, many evangelicals remain resistant to fundamentalist attitudes. "I believe the Word of God, I'm just not mad about it," explained the Reverend Frank Page, the new president of the Southern Baptist Convention, after his election in June 2006.

Out in the World

The growing influence of evangelicals has affected U.S. foreign policy in several ways; two issues in particular illustrate the resultant changes. On the question of humanitarian and human rights policies, evangelical leadership is altering priorities and methods while increasing overall support for both foreign aid and the defense of human rights. And on the question of Israel, rising evangelical power has deepened U.S. support for the Jewish state, even as the liberal Christian establishment has distanced itself from Jerusalem.

In these cases as in others, evangelical political power today is not leading the United States in a completely new direction. We have seen at least parts of this film before: evangelicals were the dominant force in U.S. culture during much of the nineteenth century and the early years of the twentieth. But the country's change in orientation in recent years has nonetheless been pronounced.

Evangelicals in the Anglo-American world have long supported humanitarian and human rights policies on a global basis. The British antislavery movement, for example, was led by an evangelical, William Wilberforce. Evangelicals were consistent supporters of nineteenth-century national liberation movements—often Christian minorities seeking to break from Ottoman rule. And evangelicals led a number of reform campaigns, often with feminist overtones: against suttee (the immolation of widows) in India, against foot binding in China, in support of female education throughout the developing world, and against human sexual trafficking (the "white slave trade") everywhere. Evangelicals have also long been concerned with issues relating to Africa.

As evangelicals have recently returned to a position of power in U.S. politics, they have supported similar causes and given new energy and support to U.S. humanitarian efforts. Under President Bush, with the strong support of Michael Gerson (an evangelical who was Bush's senior policy adviser and speechwriter), U.S. aid to Africa has risen by 67 percent, including $15 billion in new spending for programs to combat HIV and AIDS. African politicians, such as Nigeria's Olusegun Obasanjo and Uganda's Yoweri Museveni, have stressed their own evangelical credentials to build support in Washington, much as China's Sun Yat-sen and Madame Chiang Kai-shek once did. Thanks to evangelical pressure, efforts to suppress human trafficking and the sexual enslavement of women and children have become a much higher priority in U.S. policy, and the country has led the fight to end Sudan's wars. Rick Warren, pastor of an evangelical megachurch in Southern California and the author of *The Purpose-Driven Life* (the single best-selling volume in the history of U.S. publishing), has mobilized his 22,000 congregants to help combat AIDS worldwide (by hosting a conference on the subject and training volunteers) and to form relationships with churches in Rwanda.

Evangelicals have not, however, simply followed the human rights and humanitarian agendas crafted by liberal and secular leaders. They have made religious freedom—including the freedom to proselytize and to convert—a central focus of their efforts. Thanks largely to evangelical support (although some Catholics and Jews also played a role), Congress passed the International Religious Freedom Act in 1998, establishing an Office of International Religious Freedom in a somewhat skeptical State Department.

Despite these government initiatives, evangelicals, for cultural as well as theological reasons, are often suspicious of state-to-state aid and multilateral institutions. They prefer grass-roots and faith-based organizations. Generally speaking, evangelicals are quick to support efforts to address specific problems, but they are skeptical about grand designs and large-scale development efforts. Evangelicals will often react strongly to particular instances of human suffering or injustice, but they are more interested in problem solving than in institution building.

(Liberal Christians often bewail this trait as evidence of the anti-intellectualism of evangelical culture.)

United States policy toward Israel is another area where the increased influence of evangelicals has been evident. This relationship has also had a long history. In fact, American Protestant Zionism is significantly older than the modern Jewish version; in the nineteenth century, evangelicals repeatedly petitioned U.S. officials to establish a refuge in the Holy Land for persecuted Jews from Europe and the Ottoman Empire.

United States evangelical theology takes a unique view of the role of the Jewish people in the modern world. On the one hand, evangelicals share the widespread Christian view that Christians represent the new and true children of Israel, inheritors of God's promises to the ancient Hebrews. Yet unlike many other Christians, evangelicals also believe that the Jewish people have a continuing role in God's plan. In the seventeenth and eighteenth centuries, close study of biblical prophecies convinced evangelical scholars and believers that the Jews would return to the Holy Land before the triumphant return of Christ. Moreover, while the tumultuous years before Jesus' return are expected to bring many Jews to Christ, many evangelicals believe that until that time, most Jews will continue to reject him. This belief significantly reduces potential tensions between evangelicals and Jews, since evangelicals do not, as Martin Luther did, expect that once exposed to the true faith, Jews will convert in large numbers. Luther's fury when his expectation was not met led to a more anti-Semitic approach on his part; that is unlikely to happen with contemporary evangelicals.

Evangelicals also find the continued existence of the Jewish people to be a strong argument both for the existence of God and for his power in history. The book of Genesis relates that God told Abraham, "And I will make of thee a great nation, and I will bless thee.... And I will bless them that bless thee, and curse him that curseth thee: and in thee all families of the earth be blessed." For evangelicals, the fact that the Jewish people have survived through the millennia and that they have returned to their ancient home is proof that God is real, that the Bible is inspired, and that the Christian religion is true. Many believe that the promise of Genesis still stands and that the God of Abraham will literally bless the United States if the United States blesses Israel. They see in the weakness, defeats, and poverty of the Arab world ample evidence that God curses those who curse Israel.

Criticism of Israel and of the United States for supporting it leaves evangelicals unmoved. If anything, it only strengthens their conviction that the world hates Israel because "fallen man" naturally hates God and his "chosen people." In standing by Israel, evangelicals feel that they are standing by God—something they are ready to do against the whole world. Thus John Hagee—senior pastor of an 18,000-member evangelical megachurch in San Antonio, Texas, and author of several *New York Times* bestsellers—writes that if Iran moves to attack Israel, Americans must be prepared "to stop this evil enemy in its tracks." "God's policy toward the Jewish people," Hagee writes, "is found in Genesis 12:3," and he goes on to quote the passage about blessings and curses. "America is at the crossroads!" Hagee warns. "Will we believe and obey the Word of God concerning Israel, or will we continue to equivocate and sympathize with Israel's enemies?"

The return of the Jews to the Holy Land, their extraordinary victories over larger Arab armies, and even the rising tide of hatred that threatens Jews in Israel and abroad strengthen not only the evangelical commitment to Israel but also the position of evangelical religion in American life. The story of modern Jewry reads like a book in the Bible. The Holocaust is reminiscent of the genocidal efforts of Pharaoh in the book of Exodus and of Haman in the book of Esther; the subsequent establishment of a Jewish state reminds one of many similar victories and deliverances of the Jews in the Hebrew Scriptures. The extraordinary events of modern Jewish history are held up by evangelicals as proof that God exists and acts in history. Add to this the psychological consequences of nuclear weapons, and many evangelicals begin to feel that they are living in a world like the world of the Bible. That U.S. foreign policy now centers on defending the country against the threat of mass terrorism involving, potentially, weapons of apocalyptic horror wielded by anti-Christian fanatics waging a religious war motivated by hatred of Israel only reinforces the claims of evangelical religion.

Liberal Christians in the United States (like liberal secularists) have also traditionally supported Zionism, but from a different perspective. For liberal Christians, the Jews are a people like any other, and so liberal Christians have supported Zionism in the same way that they have supported the national movements of other oppressed groups. In recent decades, however, liberal Christians have increasingly come to sympathize with the Palestinian national movement on the same basis. In 2004, the Presbyterian Church passed a resolution calling for limited divestment from companies doing business with Israel (the resolution was essentially rescinded in 2006 after a bitter battle). One study found that 37 percent of the statements made by mainline Protestant churches on human rights abuses between 2000 and 2004 focused on Israel. No other country came in for such frequent criticism.

Conspiracy theorists and secular scholars and journalists in the United States and abroad have looked to a Jewish conspiracy or, more euphemistically, to a "Jewish lobby" to explain how U.S. support for Israel can grow while sympathy for Israel wanes among what was once the religious and intellectual establishment. A better answer lies in the dynamics of U.S. religion. Evangelicals have been gaining social and political power, while liberal Christians and secular intellectuals have been losing it. This should not be blamed on the Jews.

The New Great Awakening

The current evangelical moment in the United States has not yet run its course. For secularists and liberals in the United States and abroad, this is a disquieting prospect. Measured optimism, however, would be a better response than horror and panic. Religion in the United States is too pluralistic for any single current to dominate. The growing presence and influence of non-Christian communities in the country—of Jews, Muslims, Buddhists, Hindus, and, above all, secularists—will continue to limit the ability of any religious group to impose its values across the board.

Liberals, whether religious or not, may want to oppose the evangelical agenda in domestic politics. For the most part, however, these quarrels can cease at the water's edge. As the rising evangelical establishment gains experience in foreign policy, it is likely to prove a valuable—if not always easy—partner for the mostly secular or liberal Christian establishment. Some fears about the evangelical influence in foreign policy are simply overblown. After the attacks of September 11, for example, fears that evangelical Christians would demand a holy war against Islam were widespread. A few prominent religious leaders (generally fundamentalists, not evangelicals) made intemperate remarks; Jerry Falwell, for one, referred to the Prophet Muhammad as "a terrorist." But he was widely rebuked by his colleagues.

United States evangelicals generally seek to hold on to their strong personal faith and Protestant Christian identity while engaging with people across confessional lines. Evangelicals have worked with Catholics against abortion and with both religious and secular Jews to support Israel; they could now reach out to Muslims as well. After all, missionary hospitals and schools were the primary contact that most Middle Easterners had with the United States up until the end of World War II; evangelicals managed more than a century of close and generally cooperative relations with Muslims throughout the Arab world. Muslims and evangelicals are both concerned about global poverty and Africa. Both groups oppose the domination of public and international discourse by secular ideas. Both believe that religious figures and values should be treated with respect in the media; neither like the glorification of casual sex in popular entertainment. Both Islam and evangelicalism are democratic religions without a priesthood or hierarchy. Muslims and evangelicals will never agree about everything, and secular people may not like some of the agreements they reach. But fostering Muslim-evangelical dialogue may be one of the best ways to forestall the threat of civilizational warfare.

Nervous observers, moreover, should remember that evangelical theology does not automatically produce Jacksonian or populist foreign policy. A process of discussion and mutual accommodation can in many cases narrow the gap between evangelicals and others on a wide range of issues. Worrying that evangelical politics will help lock the United States into inflexible and extreme positions is a waste of time; working with thoughtful evangelical leaders to develop a theologically grounded approach to Palestinian rights, for example, will broaden the base for thoughtful—though never anti-Israel—U.S. policies.

Similarly, engaging evangelicals in broader foreign policy discussions can lead to surprising and (for some) heartening developments. A group of leading conservative evangelicals recently signed a statement on climate change that stated that the problem is real, that human activity is an important contributing cause, that the costs of inaction will be high and disproportionately affect the poor, and that Christians have a moral duty to help deal with it. Meanwhile, evangelicals who began by opposing Sudanese violence and slave raids against Christians in southern Sudan have gone on to broaden the coalition working to protect Muslims in Darfur.

Evangelicals are likely to focus more on U.S. exceptionalism than liberals would like, and they are likely to care more about the morality of U.S. foreign policy than most realists prefer. But evangelical power is here to stay for the foreseeable future, and those concerned about U.S. foreign policy would do well to reach out. As more evangelical leaders acquire firsthand experience in foreign policy, they are likely to provide something now sadly lacking in the world of U.S. foreign policy: a trusted group of experts, well versed in the nuances and dilemmas of the international situation, who are able to persuade large numbers of Americans to support the complex and counterintuitive policies that are sometimes necessary in this wicked and frustrating—or, dare one say it, fallen—world.

Note

This essay is reprinted here by permission of *Foreign Affairs* (85:5, September–October 2006). Copyright (2006) by the Council on Foreign Relations, Inc. www.ForeignAffairs.com.

17 }

America's International Religious Freedom Policy

Thomas F. Farr

In early 2006, a serious dilemma for U.S. international religious freedom (IRF) policy came briefly but sharply into focus. A man named Abdul Rahman was being tried in Kabul, Afghanistan, for the crime of changing his religion. If convicted, Mr. Rahman would be executed. The circumstances surrounding the trial revealed a great deal about Afghan democracy, and the role of religious freedom in American foreign policy.

Just five years earlier, U.S.-led forces had ousted from Afghanistan the brutal and theocratic Taliban regime. The Taliban had harbored Osama bin Laden and Al Qaeda as they planned their attack on the United States. It had stoned women and summarily executed men for the slightest deviation from its version of Islamic purity. By 2004, however, Afghans had drafted and ratified a democratic constitution and elected a new government. In its own words, the constitution sought to create "a civil society free of oppression, atrocity, discrimination, and violence and based on the rule of law, social justice, protection of human rights, and dignity, and ensuring the fundamental rights and freedoms of the people."[1]

According to the U.S. State Department, Afghanistan had achieved a democracy grounded in religious freedom.[2] This achievement was deemed by the Bush administration critical to its new national security strategy, which argued that only a democratic Afghanistan could eliminate the pathologies feeding Islamist extremism.[3] And yet here in a democratic courtroom, Abdul Rahman was being tried for apostasy, a crime meriting death under the prosecution's interpretation of the constitution.

The initial response of the State Department was to insist that the trial be "transparent," as if the issue were mere openness.[4] Soon, however, public outrage led the administration to pressure the Afghan government for Rahman's release. Ultimately the charges were dropped on "technical grounds," not because of any principle enunciated in the Afghan constitution. Rahman fled the country in fear of his life.

In one sense, the freeing of Abdul Rahman was a success for the U.S. policy mandated by the 1998 International Religious Freedom Act (IRFA). In the years since the passage of that law, a new religious freedom office at the State Department had managed cases of religious persecution, incidents that prior to IRFA had not always been pursued with alacrity. Now, in the wake of Rahman's escape, the head of that office told a congressional hearing that he had "never been more proud of our government's work than I was with regard to this case." Both the president and the secretary of state, he said, had made it clear to the world how important this issue was to the United States.[5]

But what *was* the issue? Saving Mr. Rahman was certainly a worthy humanitarian act. There was, however, a far deeper problem. With the Rahman trial, Afghan democracy had officially declared that there was no contradiction between constitutional governance grounded in human rights and the judicially required execution of a man for his peaceful religious practices. Nor was the issue merely one of apostasy from Islam; the Afghan government routinely brought blasphemy charges against mainstream Muslim citizens seeking to debate the provisions of Islam through speech and publications.[6] But American diplomacy continued to insist that Afghanistan had achieved religious freedom. Whatever the State Department meant by that term, it did not appear to exclude illiberal religious practices that were destructive of religious freedom and incompatible with the consolidation of democracy.

What accounts for these anomalies in U.S. foreign policy and, in particular, its approach to advancing international religious freedom? What have been the goals of IRF diplomacy, and what has been its relationship to broader policy purposes, including the soft power aspects of democracy promotion? This essay explores these and other questions in assessing the policy mandated by IRFA. We begin with a brief discussion of the legislative campaign that produced the IRFA and follow with an exploration of the law's operation during the period 1998–2008. We then turn to the critics of the new initiative, who emerged from all sides of the American ideological spectrum. The essay concludes with an assessment of U.S. IRF policy after its first decade.

The Origins of America's International Religious Freedom Policy

The idea for a national political campaign on religious freedom was first widely broached among faith-based activists during a January 1996 conference in Washington, D.C., sponsored by the National Association of Evangelicals. An impressive group of scholars, religious leaders, and politicos, drawn mainly (but not exclusively) from evangelical Protestant ranks, produced a "Statement of Conscience."[7] This document served as the rallying cry, if not always the blueprint, for the legislative campaign. After the conference, a lobbying coalition came together, spearheaded by Michael Horowitz, a Jewish scholar and activist at Washington's Hudson Institute, and Nina Shea, a Roman Catholic and founder of Freedom House's Center for Religious Freedom.[8] The fruits of their work emerged in May 1997 as the "Freedom from Religious Persecution Act." Drafted by

Horowitz and sponsored by Representative Frank Wolf (R, Virginia) and Senator Arlen Specter (R, Pennsylvania), the bill became known as Wolf-Specter.

The bill's centerpiece was the imposition of automatic sanctions on governments guilty of severe persecution. Wolf-Specter went through significant changes before passing overwhelmingly (375–41) in the House. But it was controversial from the outset and staunchly opposed by the Clinton administration. Even revised versions were known to have little chance in the Senate. Driven by a broader vision of how U.S. foreign policy should address religious persecution, a group of Hill staffers led by John Hanford produced an alternative bill that afforded policy makers more flexibility.[9]

In March 1998, this new bill was introduced in the Senate as the International Religious Freedom Act, cosponsored by Senators Don Nickles (R, Oklahoma) and Joseph Lieberman (D, Connecticut). After months of disputation within the coalition, negotiations in Congress, and persistent efforts by the State Department to gain amendments, and despite widespread predictions that it could not pass, the IRF Act became law in October.[10] Ultimately, a confluence of political circumstances led most of the coalition, Congress, the State Department, and the White House to accept the legislation. Those circumstances included upcoming congressional elections (no one wanted to be labeled "soft on religious persecution"), late concessions that made the statutory language more palatable to the administration, the president's looming impeachment trial, the single-mindedness of the act's authors, and the willingness of Republican leaders to ensure a floor vote. The most important long-term explanation for the act's passage, however, was the new faith-based human rights coalition that had conducted the legislative campaign.[11] Despite significant differences between the two versions of the bill, most members of the coalition were in the end able to support the new law.

The outlines of IRFA as passed were reasonably clear. Its twin goals were "to condemn violations of religious freedom and to promote . . . freedom of religion."[12] To achieve these goals, it created an overlapping triad of actors, the center of which was an office of international religious freedom at the State Department, headed by a very senior diplomatic official—an ambassador at large. This official was styled "principal advisor to the President and Secretary of State" and authorized to represent the United States abroad in bilateral and multilateral venues. One of the ambassador's key policy tools was the annual IRF Report that would characterize the status of religious freedom in every country and describe U.S. actions to oppose violations and advance freedom.

In a peculiarly American (one might say Madisonian) twist, IRFA established a watchdog agency, the U.S. IRF Commission, to review the facts presented in State Department reports and provide independent recommendations on IRF policy. The commission was initially a temporary experiment, set to expire four years after its appointment. However, in due course, its work was deemed valuable enough that Congress extended its life to 2011. Given its direct, annual appropriation of some $3 million and the high quality of its personnel, the commission has made a significant impact on the public debate over U.S. IRF policy.

Finally, the IRF Act urged, but did not require, the establishment of a special IRF adviser to the president, to be located in the staff of the National Security Council. This position was not formally filled by either President Clinton or President Bush. However, in both administrations, other White House officials sometimes performed the role envisioned by the law, such as liaison with the ambassador, the commission, and religious nongovernmental organizations.

Most of the actions *required* of the United States by the statute were negative in nature. Each fall, the State Department described violations of religious freedom in the annual reports and took some action against violators. In the vast majority of cases, this requirement was satisfied by an official, private demarche in which an American official raised the issue of the violation with the government concerned. Although the report and the demarches were typically the responsibility of junior officers at U.S. embassies abroad, the very requirement for the report has had an impact on American diplomacy, especially among younger officers. The reports themselves—each one extending to hundreds of pages—have become valuable benchmarks and data sources.

The most significant mandate of IRFA, however, was a very public focus on the most serious problems of persecution. Soon after the IRF Report was issued each year, the department was required to publish a list of "countries of particular concern" (CPCs)—governments guilty of perpetrating or acquiescing in "particularly severe violations" of religious freedom, such as torture, rape, abduction or clandestine detention, and "other flagrant violations of the right to life, liberty or the security of persons."[13]

In deciding what nations should be designated as CPCs, the secretary of state was obliged to take into account evidence from the department's own reports, the recommendations of the IRF commission, and data from outside sources. After the CPCs were chosen, IRFA mandated that the secretary take some "action" against each designated country, ranging from very serious economic sanctions to a waiver of any action at all. A waiver could be exercised in any of three circumstances: the secretary determined that the violations had ceased, the waiver was required by "important national interests," or a waiver "would further the purposes" of IRFA itself.[14]

The law also encouraged, but did not require, a broad array of direct and indirect initiatives by U.S. foreign policy agencies, led by the State Department's ambassador at large, designed to advance the institutions of religious freedom. These included the use of foreign aid and grants to nongovernmental organizations (NGOs). Most of its language on this subject was nonbinding: for example, "in the allocation of foreign assistance, the United States should make a priority of promoting and developing legal protections and cultural respect for religious freedom." Title V of the law amended existing laws on foreign aid, international broadcasting, international exchanges, and Foreign Service awards to incorporate the advancement of religious freedom as a goal but not a mandate.[15]

One further aspect of the law merits emphasis: the bureaucratic and functional status of the IRF ambassador at large and his office within the Department of

State. As noted, IRFA named this official as "principal advisor to the President and the Secretary of State." The authors of the act believed that statutory provision, combined with the title of ambassador at large, would ensure the office's placement directly under the secretary of state or somewhere else high in the department's bureaucracy. An ambassador at large was a very senior official, situated below undersecretaries and above assistant secretaries. However, Clinton Secretary of State Madeleine Albright decided to house the ambassador and his office in the bureau of Democracy, Human Rights and Labor, thereby rendering him a subordinate of that bureau's assistant secretary. This arrangement was continued under President Bush and both his secretaries of state, Colin Powell and Condoleezza Rice.

Implementation, 1998–2008

During the first decade of the law's implementation, certain patterns of diplomatic action emerged, usually centered on the annual designations. The CPC lists typically contained six to ten countries, including five perennials—China, Sudan, Burma, Iran, and North Korea.[16] Others appearing on the list during the first decade were Iraq, Serbia, Afghanistan, Vietnam, Saudi Arabia, Uzbekistan, and Eritrea. Four were, in due course, "undesignated": Saddam Hussein's Iraq, Slobodan Milosevic's Serbia, the Taliban's Afghanistan, and Vietnam.[17] In the first three cases, the cause of their removal from the CPC list was not U.S. IRF policy but the military overthrow of the respective tyrannical governments. As we shall see, Vietnam was the sole example of a country eliminated from the list because of its response to IRF diplomacy.

Sanctions were actually applied to only one CPC country, Eritrea, and they had no positive effect.[18] Most of the countries appearing on the list had already been subject to U.S. sanctions for human rights violations. Here the IRF Act permitted the administration to "double hat" the existing sanction, that is, to cite it as satisfying the legal requirement. No further action need be taken. This provision and the rather liberal provisions of the waiver were two key concessions in statutory language won by the Clinton administration.

Regional bureaus at Foggy Bottom typically resisted the designation of countries recommended by the IRF ambassador. China, for example, appeared on the first CPC list despite vigorous opposition from the East Asian bureau and the staff of the National Security Council. The IRF Ambassador Robert Seiple won the battle over China because he persuaded Secretary Albright on the merits and because of lobbying by the IRF Commission chair, Rabbi David Saperstein, at the White House.[19] Seiple's victory was so unexpected that the IRF Commission had actually predrafted a press release condemning the department for omitting China.[20] During the ensuing years, however, neither the Clinton nor the Bush administrations developed a program that would have a significant impact on religious persecution or religious freedom in China. Despite attempts by Seiple's successor, John Hanford, to build institutions that might influence the Chinese, U.S. IRF policy has not had much traction there.[21]

The U.S. policy in Vietnam has provided an interesting contrast to China. For several years, the East Asian bureau and U.S. embassy in Hanoi were able to prevent the designation of Vietnam as a CPC, even though the facts were reasonably clear. Modeled to an extent on the Chinese approach to controlling religion, Vietnam's system was more flexible but still repressive. Indigenous Buddhists and Hoa Hao were at constant risk of arrest or worse, and Protestant Christians in the highlands were subject to forced renunciations, displacement, and church destruction. Catholics had lesser, but still serious, disabilities. John Hanford, who took office in 2002, used his first two years to build his case, and in 2004 he convinced Secretary Colin Powell to list Vietnam as a CPC. Hanford then negotiated a binding agreement with Hanoi (one of the options from the menu of actions in the IRF Act). Ultimately, the agreement led Hanoi to reduce persecution, and in 2006 Vietnam was removed from the list.[22] It remains to be seen whether these actions will result in permanent improvements, but the case is to date the most singular success of U.S. IRF policy.

A more tentative example of progress may be seen in Saudi Arabia, where the utter absence of religious freedom has had a direct impact on U.S. security. It was here that Osama bin Laden and other Al Qaeda terrorists imbibed the Wahhabism that provided much of the theological oxygen for their movement. Preeminent among its theological premises is the belief that non-Wahhabis, Muslim and non-Muslim, are infidels deserving of harsh repression and even death. As U.S. attitudes about the kingdom shifted after 9/11, Ambassador Hanford and other senior Bush officials secured the designation of Saudi Arabia in 2004. By 2006, they had negotiated an informal (nonbinding) Saudi agreement to a series of principles, including a cessation of official funding for Wahhabi imams and literature overseas and a revision of bigoted Wahhabi language in Saudi textbooks.[23] By 2008, neither agreement had been fully implemented; indeed, there was evidence of Saudi resistance.[24] But the agreement was an important, if isolated, example of positive steps in U.S. IRF policy precisely where they were most needed for U.S. national security.

For the most part, however, the IRF initiative was quite limited in its scope. This was in part due to the bureaucratic and functional isolation of the ambassador and his office within the bureau of Democracy, Human Rights and Labor (DRL). Under the Clinton administration, IRF Ambassador Robert Seiple was not satisfied with this arrangement but decided not to fight it. Seiple's subordination to the DRL assistant secretary was somewhat alleviated by his participation in regular senior staff meetings. This helped identify him as a senior official and created some leverage for him in the department.[25] As noted, both of President Bush's secretaries of state continued to house the IRF ambassador in DRL. But they also barred him from the regular senior staff meetings chaired by the secretary. Other ambassadors at large and all assistant secretaries were part of that meeting. This treatment of the IRF ambassador and the IRF function, especially by the Bush administration, communicated to officials inside the department, in Washington, and in foreign capitals that the issue was unconnected to the broader imperatives of U.S. foreign policy.[26]

In sum, IRF policy during its first decade tended to emphasize the punitive measures required by IRFA, especially the CPC designations. Both ambassadors employed this method with modest success, but neither succeeded in integrating the new policy into the mainstream of foreign affairs. With the possible exceptions of Vietnam and Saudi Arabia, neither was able to develop programs and policies that would actually promote religious freedom in a political and cultural sense. And both lacked the authority to employ with any consistency the positive steps authorized but not required by the law, such as the use of foreign aid or democracy funding for NGOs who sought to advance religious liberty. Both had overseen a growing staff of excellent officers, but most came from outside the diplomatic service. For the most part, foreign service officers feared, with considerable justification, that working in the IRF office would harm their careers.[27]

IRFA's Discontents

During and after the debate over IRFA, three key objections emerged that highlighted weaknesses of the legislation and its later implementation. The first objection reflected a profound distrust of the State Department among many leaders of the legislative campaign—especially, but not entirely, the conservatives. They believed that American diplomacy was biased against religion in general and Christianity in particular. Accordingly, they initially sought to create a structure that would circumvent Foggy Bottom altogether. The first Wolf-Specter bill simply cut out the secretary of state; the statute's key official was a director of persecution monitoring who worked directly for the president and who had almost sole authority to impose punitive sanctions against offending governments. There was to be little substantive input from the State Department, nor any direction from the president's chief foreign policy official.[28]

This structure was stiffly opposed by the Clinton administration, and later drafts of the bill moved the director of persecution monitoring into the State Department. As noted, the IRF Act ultimately established an ambassador at large to head an office of international religious freedom at State. But suspicion of American diplomacy remained strong, even as supporters shifted their allegiance from Wolf-Specter to the IRF Act. While skepticism about the training and capacity of diplomats to engage religious ideas and actors is certainly warranted, the idea that a fundamental shift in U.S. foreign policy could occur in the face of the State Department's direct opposition— especially a shift on the subject of religion—was and is unrealistic. But disdain for U.S. diplomacy in general and for the State Department in particular remains to this day influential among some who supported the legislative campaign.

The lingering effects of this problem are indicated in the roles played by the IRF Commission. Distrust of the State Department has led some in Congress and elsewhere to view the commission, not the ambassador at large and his office, as the core agency of U.S. religious freedom policy.[29] Unfortunately, this preference for the commission has had the unintended effect of reducing scrutiny of the State Department. The commission's work itself has often been quite creative. It has induced debate over U.S. policies that were shortsighted, occasionally followed by corrective action from policy makers. A key example was the commission's role, along with that of the ambassador at large, in ensuring at least a rhetorical commitment to religious freedom in the Iraqi constitution. American diplomats were not initially prepared to fight for this provision, and commission pressure on the department was important.

But the commissioners' activity also diverted congressional and public attention from the compartmentalization of the IRF ambassador at large and his office inside the State Department. As early as 2003, the Department's inspector general (IG) concluded that this arrangement was hindering America's IRF policy: "The current structure that places the congressionally mandated office of the Ambassador at Large for International Religious Freedom within DRL [the human rights bureau] is at odds with the Department's organizational guidelines and has proved to be unworkable. As a consequence, *the purposes for which the religious freedom function was created are not being adequately served*" (emphasis added).[30] No action was taken on the IG report by Congress, the White House, or the State Department.

A second element of the legislative battle that foreshadowed persistent criticism, both domestic and foreign, was Wolf-Specter's emphasis on Christians to the apparent detriment of other persecuted religious groups, most notably Muslims.[31] This impulse was in part understandable—Christians are routinely abused in trouble spots around the world, including several Muslim countries. Growing awareness of this tragedy motivated many members of the coalition to get involved in the legislative campaign. Ironically, the statement of conscience that had emerged from the January 1996 conference in Washington, D.C., provided a Christian rationale for *universal* religious freedom, not an exclusive focus on Christians. In retrospect, it seems unlikely that Wolf-Specter highlighted Christian victims from a desire to exclude non-Christians. Rather, the focus on Christians reflected a tactical calculus of what would energize supporters and pass in Congress.

In the end, however, the seemingly Christian-centered approach permitted domestic and international critics to charge that the Christian right was behind the law and that their objectives were narrowly sectarian, such as clearing the way for American missionaries and undermining Islam. In fact, the IRF Act as passed was universal in scope and backed by a wide variety of groups from across the political spectrum.[32] However, some Clinton administration officials, domestic observers, and foreign governments continued this criticism during the Bush presidency.[33] It both fed and reflected the perception at home and abroad that U.S. IRF policy was an act of American religious imperialism.

A third criticism emerged inside Foggy Bottom itself. It was a principled objection that would linger during the ensuing years and contribute to the continued isolation of the IRF office and its function. Put simply, there was a profound skepticism among department officials about the legitimacy of public religious expression. Led by Secretary Albright, the department charged that IRF legislation would construct an "artificial hierarchy of human rights" in foreign policy, privileging religious freedom over other equally important or more important rights.[34] This charge was rooted in larger reservations about religious ideas and communities—especially, but not exclusively, evangelical Christian ideas and communities. These reservations were intensified by the department's natural tendency to resist any new policy imposed by Congress.

Critics of the hierarchy objection pointed out that it was difficult to sustain on practical grounds.[35] Several offices in the State Department already focused on other vulnerable groups, including the senior coordinator for international women's issues and the ambassador at large for war crimes issues. Moreover, the Clinton administration was emphasizing what it called the "nontraditional rights," such as a broadened concept of the rights of women and children and reducing the world's population growth by guaranteeing abortion rights. Given these facts, objecting to a focus on religious freedom seemed an inconsistent position to take. To some members of the legislative coalition, it merely confirmed the rationale for their efforts—a State Department bias against religion in general and Christians in particular.

Some at the State Department indeed feared that a separate office devoted to religious issues would expose U.S. diplomacy to what they saw as the divisiveness of the Christian right, especially its goals of conversion and employing religion-based arguments in the public square.[36] These goals ran counter to the minimalist understanding of religious liberty prevalent at Foggy Bottom—the idea of "religious tolerance." Promoting tolerance usually means countering those habits, natural to many religious groups, that are associated with intolerance, including proselytizing and asserting absolute truth claims. In this sense, religious tolerance is very different from religious freedom.

A typical example was the views of Assistant Secretary John Shattuck, the department's point man in resisting IRF legislation. In a speech at Harvard Law School after leaving government, he laid out his position:

> The idea of "freedom of religion" is predicated on the existence of more than one religion. But a multiplicity of religions has always meant conflict, and religious conflict often led to war and human devastation. This ... is hardly a ringing endorsement of religious freedom. Then, in the mid-twentieth century, a new concept emerged in the Universal Declaration of Human Rights. ... This was the idea of *tolerance of religious difference*—an idea that was offered in response to the long and bloody history of religious conflict that had included, in Europe alone, the Crusades, the Islamic conquests, the Inquisition, the Thirty Years War, and most recently the Holocaust. ... The modern concept of religious tolerance grew not out of the west, but out of a universal revulsion after World War II to genocide and crimes against

humanity—many of which had been committed against or in the name of religion.

Shattuck then outlined contemporary threats to religious tolerance. First was the fanaticism represented by the likes of Osama bin Laden, Serb President Slobodan Milosevic, and others "who rise to power by fomenting religious intolerance and conflict." The second threat to religious tolerance was closer to home. It consisted of "efforts ... by the American religious right to advance a political agenda within the United States government that seeks to promote special religious interests overseas." He was referring to the International Religious Freedom Act and its supporters.[37]

Here was a major element of the hierarchy objection to a U.S. IRF law. As the Clinton-Albright team saw it, religious persecution should be vigorously opposed, but religion itself is not a human good to be nourished. Rather, it is a potential source of conflict to be managed. Shattuck's argument was that religious tolerance, largely an achievement of the United Nations and the international community, overcame the conflict inherent in religion, represented in modern America by the religious right. This helps to account for why the IRF ambassador and his function were isolated within the State Department, where such views were typical, if not dominant.[38]

Conclusion: IRF Policy after Ten Years

What can be said about the overall performance of U.S. IRF policy during its first decade? In the broadest sense, it has been a wise policy experiment for the times. The late twentieth and early twenty-first centuries have been characterized by a resurgence of public forms of religious expression in most parts of the world. For better or worse, religious ideas, actors, and movements have had an increasing influence on societies, politics, economics, and global trends. In such a context, religious freedom provides a potentially fruitful framework within which these ideas and actors can operate in peaceful competition and, within societies, toward the common good.

At its base, religious freedom means the right of every person to believe or not and to enter or exit religious communities. As such, it lies at the heart of human dignity. But it also entails the right of religious *communities* to defend themselves against violent or rapacious proselytizing, to present their religious truth claims, and to engage in public policy debates. A successful democracy nourishes public religious expression, while it also establishes broad limits that apply to all who enter the political realm, whether they are believers or secularists. This is akin to what political theorist Alfred Stepan has dubbed "the twin tolerations."[39] Muslims, Orthodox Christians, Hindus, and others are more likely to accept such limits if they do not banish expressions of faith or religious motivations to the purely private domain. If American diplomats can learn to advance the twin tolerations, U.S. democracy promotion (and counterterrorism) efforts will become far more effective.

But despite its title, the International Religious Freedom Act has been less concerned with constructing regimes of religious freedom than with condemning religious persecution, the distinctly negative side of religion's resurgence. This concern is understandable, and the focus on persecution has yielded positive results. There are hundreds of people who owe their freedom, and some their lives, to the American antipersecution project. But in a world where millions suffer because of their religious beliefs or those of others, this record is surely a modest one.

Not only has religious persecution failed to decline during the past decade[40] but also it has been supplemented by a particularly poisonous variation: religion-based extremism and transnational terrorism. For centuries, men have killed others because of what they perceive as religious obligation. In recent years, we have seen these and similar motives at work among Buddhists of Sri Lanka, Hindus of India, Christians of the Balkans, and Muslims in several countries. Islamist terrorism of the Al Qaeda variety has had a major impact on American national security.

It is a supreme irony that the choices made by a religious president to counter Islamist terrorism—the implantation of democracies in the greater Middle East—was attempted with very little attention to religious actors or the political idea of religious freedom. Such factors have played little part in the American democracy projects for Iraq or Afghanistan, let alone elsewhere. Surely that has handicapped the U.S. contribution to the consolidation of democracy in those countries.[41]

A significant reason for the narrow application of IRF policy has been the dominance of the CPC method, which has taken most of the energy dedicated to the project. With the exception of Vietnam, IRF actions have been primarily punitive in nature and reactive rather than anticipatory. These methods focused the meager resources allocated by the department on a handful of authoritarian countries. It addressed the problem of persecution almost entirely through (empty) threats of sanctions, and it made little effort to analyze or alter the structures and causes of persecution. More often than not, this approach reduced IRF diplomacy to raising the issue with governments and handing over lists of prisoners. Sometimes, as with the case of Abdul Rahman, those prisoners were set free. But persecuting governments too often saw these cases as a matter of "America management." And as in Afghanistan, U.S. policy makers saw them primarily as humanitarian problems rather than serious obstacles to the consolidation of democracy.

Moreover, the department's emphasis on the worst persecutors left even fewer resources to engage the much larger group of countries that did not meet the high legal standard for severe persecution but were sometimes close to the line. Many of these nations were vital to American interests, such as Russia, Pakistan, India, Indonesia, and Egypt. Most were highly influenced by religious ideas, actors, and communities. They might well have profited from programs designed to advance religious liberty in a broader sense, that is, working out a democratic accommodation between religion and state that protected religious liberty while also benefiting majority religious communities.

Underlying all these considerations, however, is a deeper pathology in the American diplomatic establishment: a secularist conviction about how the world ought to work. In a 2006 book, former Secretary of State Madeleine Albright wrote that diplomats and policy makers in the 1990s ignored the role of religion in shaping the world. To them, she wrote, the subject of religion "was above and beyond reason; it evoked the deepest passions; and historically, it was the cause of much bloodshed. Diplomats in my era were taught not to invite trouble, and no subject seemed more inherently treacherous than religion."[42] Notwithstanding the events of recent years, this world view remains thoroughly entrenched at the State Department.

It is therefore somewhat ironic that most majority religious communities continue to believe that the primary goal of U.S. IRF policy is to clear the way for American missionaries. Many also believe that the United States seeks to weaken majority religious communities by banishing them from the political realm. The latter perception is far closer to the truth. American diplomacy must develop the vocabulary and the will to convince religious actors that religious freedom and the twin tolerations will over the long term *benefit* them and need not banish their truth claims to the purely private realm. Diplomats can derive sound historical arguments (including those derived from the histories of the religious traditions in question) to show that the control of civil power by religious groups will destroy democracy and harm religion. They can also draw on contemporary research in the social sciences indicating that religious freedom is necessary if democracy is to be stable and lasting.[43]

The trial of Abdul Rahman, with which this essay began, was a harbinger of more than a single humanitarian tragedy. It was a stark demonstration of an illiberal constitutional order that would lead to many human rights violations. But it also reflected a continuing dearth of the kind of religious freedom that could help root democracy and make it stable. The establishment of a robust regime of religious freedom would be good for Afghanistan, for all its citizens and its religious communities, and for the security of the United States. Thus is the advancement of international religious freedom critical to the achievement of American purposes in the world.

Notes

This chapter is adapted from Thomas F. Farr, *World of Faith and Freedom: Why International Religious Liberty Is Vital to American National Security* (New York: Oxford University Press, 2008).

1. The Constitution of Afghanistan, Preamble, §8.

2. See the op-ed by the U.S. Ambassador to Afghanistan Zalmay Khalilzad, "Afghanistan's Milestone," *Washington Post*, January 6, 2004, A17. Also see the Afghan chapter of the State Department's 2005 Annual Report on International Religious Freedom, which asserted that "the constitution provides for religious freedom."

3. See the National Security Strategy of the United States, 2006, §II. Available at http://georgewbush-whitehouse.archives.gov/nsc/nss/2006/. Also see the National Strategy for

Combating Terrorism, September 2006, 1: "Through the freedom agenda, we ... have promoted the best long term answer to Al Qaeda's agenda: the freedom and dignity that comes when human liberty is protected by effective democratic institutions."

4. At a March 6, 2006, State Department press conference, Under Secretary Nicholas Burns related his private remarks to visiting Afghan Foreign Minister Abdullah: "I said on behalf of our government that we hope very much the judicial case ... would be held in a transparent way. And of course, as our government is a great supporter of freedom of religion and as the Afghan constitution affords freedom of religion to all Afghan citizens, we hope very much that ... the right of freedom of religion will be upheld in Afghan court." Again, on March 20, Department spokesman Sean McCormack: "it's important, we believe, that the Afghan authorities conduct this trial and any proceedings that lead up to it in as transparent a manner as possible. Our view ... is that tolerance, freedom of worship is an important element of any democracy and these are issues as Afghan democracy matures that they are going to have to deal with increasingly." Statements accessed at www.state.gov/r/pa/prs/2006/html.

5. Statement of ambassador at large for International Religious Freedom to the Congressional Human Rights Caucus, April 7, 2006.

6. In 2002, Afghanistan's Chief Justice Fazul Hadi Shinwari publicly denounced the new women's affairs minister, Sima Samar, for telling a magazine that she did not believe in shari'a. She was formally charged with the crime of blasphemy and ultimately resigned for fear of her life. See Commission on International Religious Freedom Press Release, "Afghanistan: Freedom and Electoral Democracy," September 13, 2004, www.uscirf.gov. In a more recent case, Afghan citizen Sayed Perwiz Kambakhsh was sentenced to death for blasphemy in 2007 after downloading material from the Internet relating to the role of women in Islamic societies. The court also threatened to arrest any reporters who protested against Kambakhsh's sentence. See http://news.bbc.co.uk/2/hi/south_asia/7204341.stm.

7. NAE Statement accessed at www.pcahistory.org/pca/3-476.doc.

8. For an insightful survey of the movement, Michael Horowitz, and Nina Shea, see Jeffrey Goldberg, "Washington Discovers Christian Persecution," *New York Times*, December 21, 1997.

9. Hanford was a congressional fellow in the office of Senator Richard Lugar (R-Indiana).

10. Hanford and his coauthors decided that the tactics employed by Horowitz were corrosive enough to warrant secrecy in drafting their bill. See Thomas F. Farr, *World of Faith and Freedom: Why International Religious Liberty Is Vital to American National Security* (New York: Oxford University Press, 2008), 119.

11. Allen Hertzke, *Freeing God's Children: The Unlikely Alliance for Global Human Rights* (Lanham, MD: Rowman and Littlefield, 2004).

12. IRF Act, Section 1 (a) 2 (b): Policy.

13. IRF Act, Section 1 (b), 3 (11): Definitions.

14. IRF Act, Section 407, (a) (1)-(3).

15. IRF Act, Title V.

16. North Korea was first designated in 2001.

17. Technically, the first three regimes were "identified" by the State Department but not "designated" under the statute, because none constituted governments recognized by the United States.

18. Sanctions were applied after designation in 2005. Two years later, conditions had "further deteriorated." Department of State, Annual Report on International Religious Freedom for 2007, Eritrea chapter.

19. Farr, *World of Faith and Freedom*, 150–154.

20. Statement from Steve McFarland, Executive Director of the IRF Commission. See "Religion Today by the Associated Press," September 30, 1999.

21. Farr, *World of Faith and Freedom*, 362–373.

22. Ibid., 373–377.

23. Ibid., 377–379.

24. See, for example, a 2008 report by the Hudson Institute, "Saudi Arabia's Curriculum of Intolerance," www.hudson.org/files/documents/saudi_textbooks_final.pdf.

25. Farr, *World of Faith and Freedom*, 141–142.

26. Ibid., 193–195.

27. See Thomas Farr. "Diplomacy in an Age of Faith: Religious Freedom and National Security," *Foreign Affairs* 87:2 (March–April 2008), 118.

28. The statute required the director to "consult" the secretary of state in making policy recommendations to the president and to "coordinate" with the secretary "to ensure that the provisions of the Act are fully and effectively implemented." See H.R. 1685, May 20, 1997, Section 5 (e). But this language did not provide any direct authority to the secretary and, in any case, did not affect the sanctions decision, which rested with the director alone.

29. Farr, *World of Faith and Freedom*, 118–121.

30. Office of Inspector General, U.S. Department of State and the Broadcasting Board of Governor, Monthly Report of Activities, September 2003, 13.

31. Farr, *World of Faith and Freedom*, 121–124.

32. Hertzke, *Freeing God's Children*, 197–199, 225–227, 234–236. Among the religious groups that supported the IRF Act were the Christian Coalition, the National Jewish Coalition, the National Association of Evangelicals, the Washington Office of the Episcopal Church, the Conference of Catholic Bishops, and the Religious Action Center of Reformed Judaism.

33. See, for example, John Shattuck, "Religion, Rights and Terrorism," *Harvard Human Rights Journal* (Spring 2003), 183–188. Also see the remarks in Jean-Paul Marthoz and Joseph Saunders, "Religion and the Human Rights Movement," http://hrw.org/wr2k5/religion/1.htm.

34. Madeleine K. Albright, October 23, 1997, speech on religious freedom at the Catholic University of America, http://publicaffairs.cua.edu/speeches/albright97.htm.

35. See, for example, Jeremy Gunn's comments in *Religious Persecution as a U.S. Policy Issue*, ed. Rosalind I. J. Hackett, Mark Silk, and Dennis Hoover (Hartford, CT: Center for the Study of Religion in Public Life, 2000), 49. Also Stephen Rickard, "Religion and Global Affairs: Repression and Response," *SAIS Review* (Summer–Fall 1998), 56.

36. Cf. Noah Feldman, "Imposed Constitutionalism," *Connecticut Law Review* (Summer 2005), 876–877.

37. Shattuck, "Religion, Rights and Terrorism,"183–188.

38. Farr, *World of Faith and Freedom*, 124–132.

39. Alfred Stepan, "Religion, Democracy and the 'Twin Tolerations,'" in *World Religions and Democracy*, ed. Larry Diamond, Mark F. Plattner, and Philip J. Costopoulos (Baltimore: Johns Hopkins University Press, 2005).

40. In 2007, one of the world's leading authorities on religious persecution, Paul Marshall, noted that "violations of religious freedom worldwide are massive, widespread, and, in many parts of the world, intensifying." See Marshall, "The Range of Religious Freedom," in *Religious Freedom in the World*, ed. Paul Marshall (Lanham, MD: Rowman and Littlefield, 2007), 11. This phenomenon is not limited to what used to be called the Third World. Marshall notes, "Despite these countries' continuing openness, much of Europe seems to be becoming less religiously free," 8.

41. See Thomas F. Farr, "Islam's Way to Freedom," *First Things* (November 2008), www.firstthings.com/article.php3?id_article=6381.

42. Madeleine Albright, *The Mighty and the Almighty: Reflections on America, God, and World Affairs* (New York: HarperCollins, 2006), 8.

43. Brian J. Grim, "The Social and Political Impact of Religious Freedom Worldwide," paper presented to a Georgetown University symposium on U.S. IRF policy, February 25, 2008. A version of Grim's paper appears as "Religious Freedom: Good for What Ails Us?" in *Review of Faith and International Affairs* 6:2 (June 2008), 3–7. Also see Grim and Roger Finke, "Religious Persecution in Cross-National Context: Clashing Civilizations or Regulated Religious Economies," *American Sociological Review* 72:4 (2007). For a discussion of the religious competition model of religious freedom and how it can lead to social capital, see Rodney Stark and Roger Finke, *Acts of Faith: Explaining the Human Side of Religion* (Berkeley: University of California Press, 2000). For the relationships between religious belief and economic growth, see Robert J. Barro and Rachel M. McCleary, "Religion and Economic Growth across Countries," *American Sociological Review* (October 2003).

Annotated Bibliography

Danan, Liora, and Alice Hunt, *Mixed Blessings: U.S. Government Engagement with Religion in Conflict Prone Settings*. Washington, DC: Center for Strategic and International Studies, 2007.
One of the first systematic studies of how U.S. foreign policy agencies do and do not engage religious ideas and actors. It concludes that, while there are some bright spots, there are also significant deficiencies in the U.S. approach, deficiencies that harm America's position in the world.
El Fadl, Khaled Abou, *The Great Theft: Wrestling Islam from the Extremists*. San Francisco: HarperSanFrancisco, 2005.
El Fadl, Khaled Abou, *Islam and the Challenge of Democracy*. Princeton, NJ: Princeton University Press, 2004.
These two works by the reformer Abou El Fadl point the way to a broad-based Islamic defense of democracy and human rights in general and religious freedom in particular.
Farr, Thomas F., *World of Faith and Freedom: Why International Religious Liberty Is Vital to American National Security*. Oxford: Oxford University Press, 2008.
An argument for advancing religious freedom internationally for two reasons: first, as a matter of justice and human dignity and, second, as a diplomatic, nonmilitary means of pursuing fundamental American interests abroad.
Farr, Thomas F., and Dennis R. Hoover, *The Future of U.S. International Religious Freedom Policy: A Policy Report with Recommendations for the Obama Administration*. Washington,

DC: Berkley Center for Religion, Peace and World Affairs and the Center on Faith and International Affairs, 2009, http://berkleycenter.georgetown.edu/publications/940.

A comprehensive set of recommendations on improving U.S. international religious freedom policy, based on the experiences, strengths, and weaknesses of that policy under the Clinton and Bush administrations. These recommendations stem from three symposia held at Georgetown University during 2008, the tenth anniversary of the passage of the 1998 International Religious Freedom Act.

Grim, Brian J. and Roger Finke. *The Price of Freedom Denied: Religious Persecution and Conflict in the Twenty-First Century.* New York: Cambridge University Press, 2011.

A summary of Grim and Finke's pioneering work, arguing that the evidence demonstrates a causal connection between the absence of religious freedom and the presence of religion-related violence, conflict, and terrorism.

Hamburger, Philip, *The Separation of Church and State.* Cambridge, MA: Harvard University Press, 2002.

The best treatment of historic and current confusions among American elites, including religious elites, on the meaning of *separation* in U.S. constitutional and political discourse. This confusion has had a significant impact on U.S. foreign policy in general and international religious freedom policy in particular.

Hertzke, Allen D. *Freeing God's Children: The Unlikely Alliance for Global Human Rights.* Lanham, MD: Rowman and Littlefield, 2004.

The best treatment of the genesis and development of the legislative campaign for the International Religious Freedom Act of 1998. Hertzke's work emphasizes the tension, in the legislative campaign, between those who sought vigorous condemnation of persecutors and those who sought to employ quiet diplomacy.

Marshall, Paul and Nina Shea. *Silenced: How Apostasy and Blasphemy Codes are Choking Freedom Worldwide.* New York: Oxford University Press, 2011.

A near encyclopedic survey of anti-blasphemy and apostasy laws and practices in Muslim-majority countries, and the effort to criminalize blasphemy in international forums by Muslim countries. The book contains an excellent analysis of the effects of these laws and practices, as well as essays by three leading Muslim scholars Islam and religious freedom.

Marthoz, Jean-Paul, and Joseph Saunders, "Religion and the Human Rights Movement." http://hrw.org/wr2k5/religion/1.htm.

An extraordinarily candid discussion of the deep divisions between the modern liberal human rights movement—the point of view of the authors—and the movement for international religious freedom.

Murray, John Courtney, *We Hold These Truths: Catholic Reflections on the American Proposition.* Lanham, MD: Rowman and Littlefied, 1960.

The classic American Catholic defense of religious liberty and the First Amendment. Murray influenced the Roman Catholic Declaration on Religious Freedom at the Second Vatican Council.

Philpott, Daniel, "The Catholic Wave," *Journal of Democracy* (April 2004), 32–46.

Philpott, Daniel, "The Challenge of September 11 to Secularism in International Relations," *World Politics* (October 2002).

Philpott, Daniel, "Explaining the Political Ambivalence of Religion," *American Political Science Review* 101 (August 2007), 505–525.

Philpott, Daniel, *Revolutions in Sovereignty: How Ideas Shaped Modern International Relations*. Princeton, NJ: Princeton University Press, 2001.

Philpott's conceptualization of the role of religion in the international order is creative and extraordinarily helpful to anyone interested in the subject.

Toft, Monica Duffy, Daniel Philpott and Timothy Samuel Shah. *God's Century: Resurgent Religion and Global Politics*. New York: W.W. Norton and Co., 2011.

The best study of the resurgence of public religion during the last half century and its implications for democracy, stability, terrorism, and world peace.

18 }

Navigating in the Fog

IMPROVING U.S. GOVERNMENT ENGAGEMENT
WITH RELIGION

Frederick D. Barton, Shannon Hayden, and
Karin von Hippel

Background

In the 2007 report *Mixed Blessings: U.S. Government Engagement with Religion in Conflict-Prone Settings*,[1] the Post-Conflict Reconstruction (PCR) Project at the Center for Strategic and International Studies (CSIS) concluded the following:

- United States government officials are often reluctant to address the issue of religion, whether in response to a secular U.S. legal and political tradition, in the context of America's Judeo-Christian image overseas, or simply because religion is perceived as too complicated or sensitive.
- Current U.S. government frameworks for approaching religion are narrow, often approaching religions as problematic or monolithic forces, overemphasizing a terrorism-focused analysis of Islam, and sometimes marginalizing religion as a peripheral humanitarian or cultural issue.
- Institutional capacity to understand and approach religion is limited because of legal restrictions, lack of religious expertise or training, minimal influence for religion-related initiatives, and a government primarily structured to engage with other official state actors.

One year later, as part of the follow-on work to address these shortcomings, CSIS President John Hamre referred to the "intellectual blinders" in place at the public policy level, given the extreme sensitivity around religion.[2] As a result, policy makers are not always aware of the full range of options, partners, and strategies that might be available and will require further guidance to make religion a more "comfortable" issue for practitioners and policy makers, not only in conflict zones but also in foreign affairs more generally.

Introduction

Religion features prominently in many of the major foreign policy challenges facing the new Obama administration, notably in Afghanistan, Iran, Iraq, Nigeria, Pakistan, Somalia, and, of course, the Middle East as a whole. Yet beyond the experts, most government officials and implementing partners still do not have the requisite tools or necessary understanding of the issues to factor religion into policy and practice in an appropriate manner. Even among the experts, how many foreign policy officials—military and civilian—could comfortably answer the following questions?

- Are there differences in the way Islam is interpreted by the Afghan Taliban, the Pakistan Taliban, the Haqqani Network (HQN), the Hezb-e Islami Gulbuddun (HiG), Al Qaeda, or other militia groups operating in the tribal regions that straddle the Afghan-Pakistan border? How would potential differences factor into military planning, development strategies, or potential negotiation strategies?
- Can the radical madrassas in Pakistan be reformed, and, if so, what is the best approach?
- If the extremist and militant al-Shabaab religious youth group in Somalia should *not* be viewed as a monolithic terrorist group, how do the constituent parts interpret Islam? Which members or factions within al-Shabaab should be confronted with force, which could be marginalized, and is it possible to integrate any of them?
- How important a factor is religion when considering the appeal of Hamas and Hizbollah among their constituencies?
- And how can these issues cohere with the increasingly confused U.S. notion of separation of church and state?

These types of questions have only recently been addressed in policy circles and by no means as consistently or thoroughly as they should. Despite some improvements in understanding Islam in particular in the years since 9/11, the average U.S. diplomat, soldier, or aid worker does not get the necessary training or appropriate guidance from political and legal offices as to how to interact with religious actors, organizations, and movements in many parts of the world.

This article discusses U.S. engagement with religion in two parts.[3] The first outlines the difficulties and challenges in conflict zones and discusses the legal issues that arise. The second proposes concrete recommendations intended to clarify guidance and harmonize practice. Because conflict zones are complex and fluid environments, and religion can be interpreted very differently in each situation, it is not possible to develop a generic framework that can be applied in all contexts. Aid workers, soldiers, diplomats, and other practitioners need new tools, but they must also be prepared to work with ambiguity and rely on their own judgment.

Challenges and Legal Issues

THREE CASE STUDIES

Three examples from recent fieldwork in conflict zones help illustrate the challenges that still need to be overcome. In the first, an American director of a small development project funded by the U.S. Agency for International Development (USAID) in Afghanistan holds weekly staff meetings, which include Afghan and U.S. government employees. One day, an Afghan employee tells the American project manager that the Afghan staff would like to start the meetings with a prayer.

The manager considers her dilemma. If she agrees, she is respecting the culture of the host country and its people, probably creating goodwill, and improving overall office relations and potentially the success of the project. If she declines, she is doing so because she is concerned that allowing prayer would violate the principle of separation of church and state in the U.S. Constitution—even though she probably does not understand how those principles relate to the law. While she is worried about imposing her own Western values in a country that is "faith-saturated," her overriding concern is that an American supervisor at headquarters or at the embassy in Kabul might hear about the prayers and shut down her project entirely. After weighing the risks, she decides *not* to approve the prayer.

In the second example, a U.S. Army colonel in Iraq is worried that a particular imam might start working with the insurgency and therefore wants to help rebuild his mosque to prevent this from happening. He submits an application to the U.S. embassy to use CERP[4] funds, and his request is rejected. He subsequently changes the word *mosque* to *cultural site* on the application and resubmits it, and funding is approved. He helps rebuild the mosque and forges a trusting relationship with the imam.

In the third example, U.S. soldiers in several southern provinces of Afghanistan are building madrassas, with U.S. government approval and funding. These new schools are to have a mixed religious and secular curriculum and are officially sanctioned by the Afghan government. The American and Afghan officials hope that parents will send their children to these schools rather than to the more radical madrassas.[5] It is not clear what official overall legal guidance enabled these schools to be built—guidance that would also be applicable to other parts of the world—or if the "national security concern" justification was invoked. Moreover, these schools were built with relatively little fanfare in the press, positive or negative. Nor did they engender any public discussion as to whether this violated the First Amendment. The soldiers just built the schools.

In the first two cases, the field workers had enough religious literacy to understand the importance of respecting local traditions and working with religion, but they chose different outcomes. Even if they understood the importance of religion, they did not know what was legal according to U.S. law. This is because there is little case law to draw on as to how the Establishment Clause should be interpreted extraterritorially. It is also because the U.S. government has not consistently applied practice from one situation to another. Witness the distinction between the second and third cases, when direct permission given to soldiers in Afghanistan versus the hurdles that had to be overcome in Iraq.

The ambiguity and general reluctance to confront issues of religion in many programs, agencies, and embassies interfere with successful foreign policy outcomes. One major stumbling block arises from legal concerns. What are the current legal limitations and guidance concerning working with religion overseas?

LEGAL ISSUES

A lack of clear court rulings, the evolution of Constitutional interpretation, and the strict antiterrorist legislation imposed after September 11 (such as the Patriot Act) have all contributed to the aforementioned uncertainty and often fear in dealing with religion.[6] The long-standing tradition of "separation of Church and State" is also an underlying factor. Americans understand that there are significant restrictions on mixing government and religion domestically, and they naturally assume the same would apply to activity conducted abroad. Yet, this is not necessarily the case.

The First Amendment to the Constitution states, "Congress shall make no law respecting the establishment of religion, or prohibiting the free exercise thereof." In evaluating the application of the Establishment Clause domestically, courts are guided by the Lemon Test, which stipulates that a statute must have a secular purpose, the primary effect must neither advance nor inhibit religion, and it must not foster "an excessive government entanglement with religion."[7] Yet an evolution in jurisprudence involving both the Establishment and Free Exercise Clauses has occurred over the last four decades since the Lemon case was decided.[8] The result is that, in some ways, legal restrictions have become more relaxed, allowing for activities by faith-based groups that would have been prohibited before.[9]

At the same time, little case law exists regarding the extraterritorial application of the Establishment Clause. The most relevant case, at least regarding funding issues, is the *Lamont v. Woods* (2d. Cir. 1991) decision,[10] in which taxpayers sued USAID for violating the Establishment Clause by funding Jewish and Catholic schools abroad. The court found that "the operation of the Establishment Clause strongly indicates that its restrictions should apply extraterritorially" but implied that the analysis may be different than it is domestically.[11] In particular, the court indicated that the government could be permitted exceptions, for example, for reasons of national security.[12]

The dozens of legal experts consulted for this work agreed, however, that this case would now have only limited applicability. In other words, the ruling does not provide enough direction for the range of issues confronted around the world today. Nonetheless, *Lamont* remains the only relevant ruling to date. Two major obstacles obstructing further clarity are the legal principle of standing, which requires a plaintiff to show he is actually harmed by the law, and context (the difficulty in getting a case that meets the criteria to settle an issue definitively). Given today's complex conflicts, it is hard to imagine one case settling these larger questions, and thus direction may have to come from different parts of the government.

The lack of clear guidelines to U.S. government interaction with religious issues and organizations overseas also leaves undefined the extent to which the United States can appropriately promote Islamic principles that support democracy. Projects that support moderate strains of Islam could run into trouble because of the endorsement and encouragement of one form of religion over another—in this case one version of Islam over another. This would be strictly prohibited by the Establishment Clause as applied domestically, though some experts argue that the case could be interpreted differently abroad, particularly if the country's government has endorsed similarly moderate interpretations of the same religion.[13] This question has also not been decided.

A former lawyer at the Department of Commerce remarked that one goal during her time in office was to eschew the issue of the Establishment Clause and its application abroad entirely. She commented that everyone does the same thing— religion is seen as so sensitive, both domestically and internationally, that it is best to avoid the subject.[14] The Department of Justice's Office of Legal Counsel, the highest authority on these issues for executive branch officials, has yet to offer guidance on the extraterritorial applications of the First Amendment. Many government officials and implementing partners therefore do not know the limits of engagement and thus would probably provide contradictory advice in a number of situations.[15]

With little guidance on offer, the choices available are perceived as seriously risky, with potentially negative repercussions for both the U.S. official personally and for the outcome of a given project.[16] There are a few practitioners who prefer the space that ambiguity provides and will take the necessary risks, but far too many will adopt a risk-avoidance strategy, even if these diplomats, soldiers, and aid workers may be working in a faith-saturated society. Thus, while official permission in extreme cases may be granted, overall guidance needs clarification for greater consistency, particularly in day-to-day, nonextreme situations.

Conclusions and Recommendations

Given that religion plays a fundamental role in many foreign policy crises today, it is critical that officials and implementing partners improve their understanding of religions and religious actors. This is especially important in conflict zones, which are by definition extremely challenging, dynamic, and fluid environments. Improved direction will make an enormous contribution to U.S. officials, who need far greater comfort to work in these fast-paced environments. This is not to say that all potential outcomes can be anticipated, that religion is the most important factor in all conflicts, or that detailed guidelines should be provided. Field personnel require as much flexibility as possible, but they also need to be armed with better knowledge and tools to work with religion in more constructive ways when it is an important factor.

Improved policy and practice can be achieved through top-down efforts, such as clear guidance from the Department of Justice, but also from the bottom up, using social networking and other Web 2.0 tools to enhance information-sharing and practice. The PCR Project has developed a "Five Critical Steps Model" to improve overall response to states at risk. These five can also provide the framework for the recommendations section of this chapter.

FIVE CRITICAL STEPS FOR IMPROVING ENGAGEMENT WITH RELIGION

1. Improved Anticipation, Analysis, and Planning. Generally, U.S. officials and partners need more relevant and accessible methods for anticipating, analyzing, and planning for states at risk. This includes an improved understanding of the local political, cultural, social, religious, and economic dynamics on the ground, even though it is extremely difficult to obtain accurate, real-time information in conflict zones.

Recommendation: Training and Exercises

Enhance training for U.S. government personnel for different potential scenarios, and ensure that all training programs have a mix of civilian and military personnel from all parts of the expanded interagency. This should include a range of learning methodologies, from normal coursework, war-gaming, role-playing, and other simulations to e-learning and further education in-country.

While civilian and military training currently does include some focus on religion, it is not as comprehensive as should be the case. For example, before deployment to Iraq, two military officials remarked that they were provided with only enough guidance during training to "stay out of trouble." At the Foreign Service Institute (FSI), the 2011–2012 course catalogue offers only three courses explicitly focusing on religion, and all are on Islam, including one introductory course in the Area Studies Division. While religion is included as a topic in several Area Studies courses, along with history, politics, economics, society, and culture, there are no introductory courses that deal with the world's religions broadly.

One of the better examples of preparation for dealing with religion was found in the Army Field Manual 3–06.11, *Combined Arms Operations in Urban Terrain.*[17] As part of Appendix G—Intelligence Requirements Checklists for Urban Operations, the following checklist is provided:

What is the religious structure? (1) Beliefs; (2) Percent of population; (3) Importance in society; (4) Leaders; (5) Practices; (6) Bias of one religion toward another; (7) Is one religious group dominant? If so, why? (8) Physical boundaries of influence; (9) Boundary overlaps; (10) Role in conflict; (11) Key personnel and location.

Using these eleven points as a checklist, an individual can research and determine the critical information about the role of religion before deploying. This appendix, which includes similar checklists for ethnic groups, tribal structure, refugee populations, organized gangs, economic classes, and more, demonstrates that the concept of religion is taken seriously by the military in some instances.

If the U.S. government does not have the capacity to inform its staff to the level desired, what are the alternatives? One possible way to augment training is through the use of nongovernmental institutions, such as universities and think tanks.[18] These nongovernment institutions, with targeted programming, could help fill the gap, and government institutions could encourage employees to attend relevant events and provide easy access to podcasts from iTunes U and other sites.

Despite some improvements over the past few years, overall training needs to expand significantly, with integration of training efforts between and among civilian and military actors to mirror the real-life blend in conflict zones. By increasing the knowledge base and comfort level of officials before, during, and after deployment, they will be better able to address ongoing challenges at headquarters and in the field.

> *2. Integrated Strategies.* In most conflict environments, international actors still have not managed to integrate their strategies and priorities in an effective manner, not only within and between bilateral and multilateral partners but also, critically, with the host government and local people.

Recommendations: Interagency Legal Task Force

Given that the lack of legal clarity in the United States is one main obstacle to improved performance, as a first step, the Department of Justice should spell out basic guidelines for compliance that encourage better understanding of the Establishment and Free Exercise clauses of the Constitution and other relevant statutes. These guidelines should be made in consultation with other U.S. agencies, expert academics, and practitioners and aim to provide clarity, flexibility, and maneuverability, rather than impose greater restrictions.

The Department of Justice will also need to ensure buy-in from all relevant legal counsels within the interagency, including State, USAID, the Pentagon, the National Security Council, Agriculture, Treasury, the White House Office of Faith-Based and Neighborhood Partnerships, and the intelligence community. Thus, a related recommendation would be to convene quarterly interagency legal working groups to discuss areas of concern and share guidance and advice.

The proceedings from these meetings should be available to all diplomats, soldiers, and aid workers, with the ability to feed back into the legal working group on a regular basis. This would help issues that arise in changing conflict environments, provide a debating forum for different views, and share ongoing challenges. Web sites as well as new tools, such as Webinars, can help those in the field interact more regularly with various advisers and counsels at headquarters and in embassies.

286 { Religion and American Foreign Policy

These meetings would be used to develop the political argument for engaging and taking risks and help to focus the administration and Congress so that they can assume appropriate leadership roles. They would also move the debate beyond the threat-based, Islam-focused analysis of religion, with the overall aim of providing clarity and reducing the fear of dealing with religious issues and actors abroad.

      3. *Innovative Operations.* The U.S. government and its major partners need new tools to ensure more agility and innovation in planning, implementing, and managing stabilization and reconstruction activities. They could include the systematic application by donors and practitioners of new research approaches and techniques from management sciences, industry, Silicon Valley, and other fields to help solve many development challenges and accelerate change in fundamental ways.

RECOMMENDATIONS: IMPROVE CONNECTIVITY

Clarity is critical for civilian and military personnel working in conflict zones and at headquarters—not only in terms of understanding the guidelines and approaches but also for improving knowledge of general religious dynamics abroad. New platforms should be developed to collect and share relevant information on religious groups, movements, and actors, using online networking and other open-sourced, information-sharing tools. This would help expand the communities of policy makers and practitioners, as well as develop a common language, new policy tools, and baseline assumptions about different ways to approach and conceptualize religion in conflict settings.

      Experts from the private sector, as well as the growing community of practitioners working on knowledge management, should be engaged so that new links could be forged between the numerous practitioners and scholars working in conflict zones, far beyond the current concept of human terrain teams. These meetings and tools would help break down cultural barriers that often interfere with collaboration between different groups, such as between academics and the military.

      These virtual platforms can also host new government initiatives, if they can be publicly shared. One example could be the new toolkit for engaging with religion in conflict settings developed by the USAID's Office of Conflict Management and Mitigation (CMM). This document, which was released in September 2009, presents lessons learned from case studies in different countries.[19] While not describing itself as taking a cookie-cutter approach, the toolkit endeavors to share wisdom gained from past difficult situations. Other ideas can be generated through the use of open competitions, with cash prizes, for expanding the pool of problem solvers beyond the so-called experts.

      4. *Measures of Progress (MOP).* The PCR Project has developed a distinct methodology for measuring progress in reconstruction operations from the perspective of local actors, which is critical to the success of any mission. In reconstruction operations, claims of success or failure are meaningless

in the absence of baseline information, knowledge of where reconstruction efforts are heading, and an understanding of the ultimate goal. The PCR Project methodology tries to circumvent the problem of imperfect information typical to conflict zones by combining and balancing a variety of sources, and it presents the final results in a simple grid that policy makers can easily digest.

Recommendations: Regular Surveys and MOPs

In-country surveys will help U.S. officials gain a deeper insight into their conduct and a better understanding of the religious dynamics. Many polling organizations, such as the Pew Global Attitudes Project and other media companies, already examine many issues related to religion, and these can be collated and complemented by additional interviews and focus groups with national and international actors conducted by independent organizations.

> 5. *Communication, Connectivity, and Community.* A more integrated response—by definition—requires a robust communication strategy to ensure that it is understood and disseminated properly, among both international and national actors. A successful communication strategy requires flexibility, new partners, risk taking, and a mix of tools to implement and disseminate it. Well-placed television and radio ads that establish U.S. respect for religious freedom and values would also have value—greetings during the Eid holidays, for example.

Recommendations: New Tools and Partners

The strategy needs to utilize revolutionary communications concepts, as well as low-tech and no-tech options, to improve information sharing and best practices—on the ground and in the virtual world. This means Web 2.0 open-source technologies, social networking tools, cell phones, radios, and even the tea house.

New partners should include local civil society organizations and religious institutions, as well as other nongovernment organizations working on improving understanding of religion in U.S. foreign policy. In particular, the network of Luce Foundation–funded universities and institutions should be tapped.[20]

An improved understanding of religion in conflict settings is necessary for successful U.S. foreign policy. It should be possible to provide greater clarity and guidance without adding undue bureaucratic and other restrictions on policy and programs.

Notes

This essay was written while the authors were codirectors and project coordinator, respectively, of the Post-Conflict Reconstruction (PCR) Project at the Center for Strategic and International Studies and was subsequently updated by the PCR Project.

1. For previous work on this subject, see *Mixed Blessings: U.S. Government Engagement with Religion in Conflict-Prone Settings* (Washington, DC: CSIS, 2007), http://csis.org/files/media/csis/pubs/070820_religion.pdf.

2 See http://csis.org/event/role-faith-based-groups-foreign-assistance

3. Since the publication of *Mixed Blessings*, the PCR Project has worked to implement the recommendations by hosting three legal working group meetings, convening 15 to 20 public meetings, conducting individual interviews with experts, and continuing institutional partnerships in and outside of Washington.

4. CERP—Commander's Emergency Response Program, http://www.dtic.mil/doctrine/jel/jfq_pubs/0937.pdf.

5. See February 1, 2008, *Stars and Stripes* article, *Report: U.S. Military Funds Building of Islamic Schools*, www.stripes.com/article.asp?section=104&article=52094.

6. See more on this discussion in July 25, 2008, CSIS event, Religion in Foreign Policy, http://csis.org/event/religion-foreign-policy-john-mansfield-recent-supreme-court-rulings.

7. *Lemon v. Kurtzman*, 403 U.S. 602 (1971).

8. The Obama administration seems set to "mend, not end" President Bush's programs working with faith-based organizations. See www.washingtonpost.com/wp-dyn/content/article/2008/07/03/AR2008070302453.html.

9. President Barack Obama has announced that NGO hiring rules will be reviewed on a case-by-case basis, in the event of conflict with faith-based groups' hiring practices. See www.washingtonpost.com/wp-dyn/content/article/2009/02/05/AR2009020500834.html?referrer=emailarticle.

10. See *Lamont v. Woods*, 948 F.2d 825, 835 (2d Cir. 1991).

11. *Lamont v. Woods*, 948 F.2d 825, 835 (2d Cir. 1991).

12. Jessica Powley Hayden, "Mullahs on a Bus: The Establishment Clause and U.S. Foreign Aid," *Georgetown Law Journal* 95 (2006).

13. See CSIS event on July 25, 2008, with Harvard University Professor John Mansfield, http://csis.org/event/religion-foreign-policy-john-mansfield-recent-supreme-court-rulings; Mansfield is one of the earliest scholars working on these issues, publishing "The Religion Clauses of the First Amendment and Foreign Relations" in the *DePaul Law Review* in 1986.

14. Interview, Washington, DC, December 18, 2007.

15. During 2008, the PCR Project at CSIS convened three off-the-record sessions to discuss in detail the legal obstacles concerning religion and its impact on official work in conflict countries. The goal has been to help, through discussions and research, translate the legal language into practical guidance. The organizations included The American Jewish Committee, American Enterprise Institute, The Brookings Institution, Council on Foreign Relations, Creative Associates International, Embassy of Afghanistan, Embassy of Canada, Gallup, George Washington University, Georgetown University, The Henry L. Stimson Center, International Center for Religion and Diplomacy, IREX, Lutheran Immigration and Refugee Services, NationsCourt, Inc., Pew Forum on Religion & Public Life, Religious Action Center of Reform Judaism, The Asia Foundation, Secular Coalition for America, Syracuse University, Tharwa Foundation, USAID, U.S. Army, U.S. Commission on International Religious Freedom, U.S. Department of State, and U.S. Institute for Peace.

16. There are some attempts to help. For example, the Web site www.religionandsocialpolicy.org contains a wealth of information, articles, and essays on issues related to how the government and religion interact.

17. See www.globalsecurity.org/military/library/policy/army/fm/3-06-11/index.html.

18 As part of the recommendation to increase knowledge of religious dynamics, the PCR Project initiated a speaker series focusing on key faith figures throughout the world who are understudied. PCR hosted three public events on Moqtada al-Sadr with Patrick Cockburn, author, *Muqtada*, interviewed by Nadia Bilbassy-Charters, Senior Correspondent, Middle East Broadcasting Centre, http://csis.org/event/muqtada-muqtada-al-sadr-shia-revival-and-struggle-iraq; on Ayatollah Khamenei with Karim Sadjadpour, author, *The Writings of Khamenei*, interviewed by Sally Quinn, *The Washington Post*, http://csis.org/event/under-standing-khamenei-writings-irans-supreme-leader; and on Maulana Sami ul-Haq (the so-called Father of the Taliban) with Imtiaz Ali, Special Correspondent, *The Washington Post*, interviewed by Arnaud de Borchgrave, Director, Transnational Threats Project, CSIS, http://csis.org/event/maulana-sami-ul-haq-father-taliban.

19. "Religion, Conflict and Peacebuilding: An Introductory Programming Guide," U.S. Agency for International Development, September 2009, www.usaid.gov/our_work/cross-cutting_programs/conflict/publications/docs/Religion_Conflict_and_Peacebuilding_Toolkit.pdf.

20. The Chicago Council Religion Task Force recently released a comprehensive set of recommendations for improved U.S. government engagement with religion, with strong sections on training and religious literacy. See *Engaging Religious Communities Abroad: A New Imperative for U.S. Foreign Policy* (Chicago: Chicago Council on Global Affairs, 2010), www.thechicagocouncil.org/Files/Studies_Publications/TaskForcesandStudies/Religion_2010.aspx.

Annotated Bibliography

Alterman, Jon, and Karin von Hippel, eds., *Understanding Islamic Charities*. Washington, DC: CSIS, 2007.
This book explores the variety of roles that Muslim philanthropies play in different countries, their interactions with national and international institutions, and the boundaries and connections between their philanthropic roles and their political impacts. See http://csis.org/publication/understanding-islamic-charities.
Blair, Tony. Speech at the National Prayer Breakfast, February 10, 2009.
Argues strongly for the importance of understanding and appreciating the role of faith. See http://tonyblairfaithfoundation.org/2009/02/tony-blair-speech-to-the-natio.html.
Hayden, Jessica, "The Establishment Clause and U.S. Foreign Aid," *Georgetown Law Journal* 95:171 (2006).
An excellent examination of foreign aid issues and how they fit into the national security environment. See www.georgetownlawjournal.com/issues/pdf/95-1/hayden.pdf%5B1%5D.pdf.
Holenstein, Anne-Marie, "Role and Significance of Religion and Spirituality in Development Cooperation: A Reflection and Working Paper." Swiss Agency for Development and Cooperation, March 2005.
A practical review of the cultural and religious issues practitioners may confront when implementing development projects. See www.deza.admin.ch/ressources/resource_en_24892.pdf.

Johnston, Douglas L., "Religion and Foreign Policy" In *Forgiveness and Reconciliation: Religion, Public Policy, and Conflict Transformation*, ed. Raymond Helmick. Philadelphia: Templeton Foundation Press, 2001.

Discusses nuanced ways to use religion for positive effect in conflict resolution. See www. icrd.org/index.php?option=com_content&task=view&id=209&Itemid=133.

Lupu, Ira, and Bob Tuttle, "Constitutional Change and Responsibility of Governance Pertaining to the Faith-Based and Community Initiative," working paper for the Conference on Innovations in Effective Compassion, September 2008.

Offers an in-depth discussion of legality and faith-based organizations. See www.religionandsocialpolicy.org/docs/Lupu_Page263.pdf.

Lupu, Ira, and Bob Tuttle, "The State of Law—2008: A Cumulative Report on Legal Developments Affecting Government Partnerships with Faith-Based Organizations." *Roundtable on Social Welfare Policy* (2008).

A comprehensive analysis of legal issues and faith-based groups in the United States. See www.religionandsocialpolicy.org/docs/legal/state_ofthe_law_2008.pdf.

Mansfield, John H., "The Religion Clauses of the First Amendment and Foreign Relations," *DePaul Law Review* 36:1 (1986).

One of the earliest pieces to discuss the legal issues surrounding religion and foreign policy. Mansfield's article explores the issues raised in the debate over the extraterritorial application of the religion clauses.

UNFPA, "Culture Matters: Working with Communities and Faith-Based Organizations: Case Studies from Country Programmes." 2004.

Provides recommendations for appropriate ways to work in-country, dealing with sensitive issues and faith-based groups. See www.deza.admin.ch/ressources/resource_en_94204.pdf.

U.S. Department of the Army, *Combined Arms Operations in Urban Terrain*. FM 3.06–11, 2002.

Useful for understanding the military's operational approach to religion within a cultural context. See www.globalsecurity.org/military/library/policy/army/fm/3-06-11/index.html.

APPENDIX

Internet Resource Guide

Compiled by M. Christian Green
with Nicole Greenfield

As religion and international affairs continues to emerge as an active subfield of political science and international relations, as well as an undeniably important nexus of concerns in the composition and analysis of public policy, so, too, has the number of valuable resources accessible on the Internet increased. During the various meetings of the Religion and World Affairs Working Group at the Social Science Research Council (SSRC), contributors to this book found themselves referring to certain Web sites over and over again in discussion and in the notes to their individual chapters. A consensus emerged that a collection of these Web sites with descriptive and evaluative commentary would be helpful to readers of this book.

Methodology

At an initial meeting of the working group, contributors were interviewed individually about the Web sites they consult most frequently in their work. These Web sites were compiled into a master list. At a subsequent meeting, contributors were asked to indicate which of these Web sites they use in their work or know by reputation and to rank these in descending order, with a five-star ranking indicating excellence in the field. A second list collated these rankings, cross-referencing them with the number of contributors ranking them at each level.

With this list in hand, researchers at the SSRC reviewed each Web site individually. The key evaluative questions were as follows: (1) Does the Web site, whether oriented primarily toward religion or international affairs, address issues at the *nexus* of both fields? (2) If the Web site and its sponsoring organization are situated in one field more than the other, does it convey information that would be *essential* for scholars in both religion and international affairs to understand new and emerging issues in the field? (3) Does the Web site provide *content* (articles, data, analysis, etc.) that would be useful for external researchers and the general public, rather than being limited to description or promotion of the sponsoring organization, its productions, events, and the like? (4) Does the Web site include, in particular, Web-based *new media* (audiocasts, videocasts, blogs, etc.) in addition to more traditional print content?

In a third and final phase, groups of the compiled Web sites and their descriptions were sent to individual contributors for their evaluation. In most cases, the evaluators were the individuals who initially recommended these Web sites or who gave them the highest ranking. In some cases, contributors have been asked to evaluate Web sites that emerged as significant and meriting inclusion after the ranking phase and during the review process. Thus, the evaluators are generally individuals who are familiar with the Web sites themselves or with the work of their sponsoring organizations. However, to assure neutrality, evaluators have not been allowed to review any organization with which they have a significant ongoing or past affiliation.

Descriptions

The following descriptions were written by the compilers and other members of the research team at the SSRC. Each entry begins with a *basic description* of the Web site, its sponsoring organization, and the organization's purpose or mission. In general, these were clipped or paraphrased from the front page or mission statement of the sponsoring organization, under the principle that, with regard to its basic mission, the organization can reasonably be expected to represent itself accurately.

The basic descriptions are followed by specific information about the *location of material* on religion and international affairs on the Web site. The interaction of religion and international affairs is so timely that many of these organizations have major research projects and Web site areas dedicated to these issues. In some cases, however, finding the material on religion and international affairs required a deeper search of the Web site. In those cases, we have provided instructions for readers about where to look or how to search.

We have also endeavored to give the reader a sense of the *type of issues* that each Web site covers. Where major research projects or topic areas are featured on the Web site, we have listed these. Where the content search required deeper investigation, we have culled the issues from searches of where religion and international affairs are featured in the organization's publications, events, and other proceedings.

Wherever it is present, *new media* content is specifically referenced. Given the timeliness and global range of the issues and the impact of globalization through new technology and methods of communication, it seems essential to highlight the availability of these resources. The new media have global reach and general accessibility and are increasingly a feature of both research and teaching in the academic world. As they are the cutting edge, they deserve special mention.

Analysis

The list collects the twenty-five top-ranked Web sites, based on this two-stage analysis. A longer and more inclusive list will be posted and regularly updated on Georgetown University's Berkley Center for Religion, Peace, and World Affairs Web site: http://berkleycenter.georgetown.edu/resources/topics/religion-and-international-affairs.

(1) Adherents.com
www.adherents.com
Adherents.com is a growing collection of more than 43,870 adherent statistics and religious geography citations: references to published membership/adherent statistics and congregation statistics for more than 4,200 religions, churches, denominations, religious bodies, faith groups, tribes, cultures, and movements around the world. It presents data from both primary research sources such as government census reports, statistical sampling surveys, and organizational reporting and citations from secondary literature that mention adherent statistics. The site's main feature is an alphabetized list of religious groups, ranging from the Aaronic Order to Zurvanism. Clicking on individual religions reveals statistics on number and population percentages of adherents in the countries where they are located, as well as numbers of congregations and units within the denomination. Adherents.com is an Internet initiative and not affiliated with any religious, political, or educational organization; it claims to be the Web's second most frequently visited general religion site.

(2) Association of Religion Data Archives (ARDA)
www.thearda.com
ARDA's purpose is to democratize access to the best data on religion. Online since 1998, the initial archive was targeted at researchers interested in American religion. The target audience and the data collection have both greatly expanded since 1998, now including both American and international collections and developing features for educators, journalists, religious congregations, and researchers. ARDA's international surveys and data include cross-national, multiple-nation, and single-nation surveys. Its national profiles page lists alphabetical links to information on religion in nations around the world. There are also regional profiles, a handy calculator to compare nations, and regions on religious adherents and historical information. The list of data sources (with links) is itself a very helpful resource, as is the general search feature that permits searching by subject by topics ("abortion," "religious freedom") and other specific indices. The ARDA site is a singularly useful resource for scholars in a variety of disciplines, as well as more general audiences, who want information about religion in the United States and around the world.

(3) Berkley Center for Religion, Peace, and World Affairs
berkleycenter.georgetown.edu
Through research, teaching, and service, the Berkley Center at Georgetown University supports the interdisciplinary study of religion and its role in world

affairs. Its faculty-led programs focus on religion as it relates to global challenges, including war and peace, global development, U.S. foreign policy, and interreligious dialogue. Two premises guide the center's work: that scholarship on religion and its role in world affairs can help to address these challenges effectively and that the open engagement of religious traditions with one another and with the wider society can promote peace.

(4) Brookings Institution
www.brookings.edu
The Brookings Institution supports independent scholarship and research that contributes to the public policy debate in the United States. The Institution supports a number of in-house programs and centers dedicated to studying particular issues and world regions, as well as external operational centers in China and Qatar. Its "World" section focuses on a variety of issues related to global governance, global economics, development, security, and foreign policy issues; current research projects include initiatives on democracy in the Middle East and security policy for the twenty-first century. Brookings provides educational courses for corporate and government leaders and is a leading publisher in the area of public policy through its Brookings Institution Press. The institution's Web site provides a number of e-mail services and news roundups and feeds, along with articles written by Brookings scholars, with many addressing religion in U.S. domestic politics and in public affairs around the world.

(5) Carnegie Council for Ethics in International Affairs
www.cceia.org
The Carnegie Council is a leading voice promoting ethical leadership on issues of war, peace, religion in politics, and global social justice. It convenes agenda-setting fora and creates educational opportunities and information resources for a worldwide audience of teachers and students, journalists, international affairs professionals, and concerned citizens. Its work focuses on three broad themes: ethics, war, and peace; global social justice, and religion in politics. In addition to public affairs lectures, the Council offers a broad array of reference material and other resources, many of which are now online articles and audio and video webcasts and podcasts. Its flagship publication is the quarterly journal *Ethics & International Affairs*. It also offers a free electronic newsletter and a regular print *Bulletin*. The organization provides a wealth of material on the ethical dimensions of international affairs to government, corporate, media, academic, and other audiences.

(6) Center for Strategic and International Studies (CSIS)
www.csis.org
The Center for Strategic and International Studies is a bipartisan, nonprofit organization that seeks to advance global security and prosperity by providing strategic insights and practical policy solutions to decision makers in government,

international institutions, the private sector, and civil society. CSIS has twenty-five programs grouped under three themes: defense and security policy, global challenges, and regional transformation. The center's Web site offers further information on events, publications, programs, press releases, and CSIS experts. Though no programs are specifically dedicated to religion, the site contains many articles on religion and its impact on world affairs and international security. With its focus on justice and reconciliation, the CSIS Program on Crisis, Conflict, and Cooperation (formerly the Post-Conflict Reconstruction (PCR) Project), in particular, has a significant religious dimension. The Henry Luce Foundation has provided the center with funding for various projects, including those focused on U.S. government engagement with religion in conflict-prone settings.

(7) Center for the Study of Islam and Democracy (CSID)
https://www.csidonline.org
Founded in March 1999, the Center for the Study of Islam and Democracy is a Washington, D.C.–based organization dedicated to studying Islamic and democratic political thought and merging them into a modern Islamic democratic discourse in the United States and around the world. The center also hopes to improve Americans' understanding of Islam's approach toward a variety of public issues. In addition, CSID sponsors an annual conference, international workshops, public lectures and seminars, publications, and education and training programs on Islam, democracy, citizenship, law, and human rights. The Web site has an automatic translation feature from English into Arabic and Persian. Complete issues of multiple years' worth of its quarterly bulletin, *Muslim Democrat*, and its monthly bulletin, *Democracy Watch*, are posted online (the latter in Arabic as well as English), along with other articles, bulletins, and book descriptions.

(8) Central Intelligence Agency (CIA): The World Factbook
https://www.cia.gov/library/publications/the-world-factbook/index.html
The annual publication of the Central Intelligence Agency's *The World Factbook* disseminates information on countries around the world to an even wider audience, particularly now that it is available exclusively and entirely online and no longer available in print form. The online version is updated every two weeks. Population information includes data on religious affiliation. The CIA is the principal agency in the United States collecting intelligence agency related to national security. It provides intelligence data and analysis to the president, Congress, policy makers, and military personnel.

(9) Council on Foreign Relations (CFR)
www.cfr.org
www.cfr.org/about/outreach/religioninitiative
The New York City–based Council on Foreign Relations is a foreign policy membership organization that publishes the bimonthly journal *Foreign Affairs* and promotes understanding of American foreign policy through meetings, debate,

and dialogue among its members, government officials, and interested citizens. Its main page allows for searches on a variety of issues. Although religion is listed as a subissue under the main issue heading of "Society and Culture," entering "religion" on the main search vehicle produces an even wider range of results. The Council aims to nurture future foreign policy leaders and to create a comprehensive knowledge base for policy recommendations. Notable members include Zbigniew Brzezinski, George H. W. Bush, Henry Kissinger, George Soros, Alan Greenspan, and Dick Cheney. In 2006, the Council received a generous two-year grant from the Henry Luce Foundation for a program on religion and foreign policy.

(10) Forum 18
www.forum18.org
Forum 18 is a Christian news and archive service that monitors religious freedom primarily in Russia, Eastern Europe, and Central Asia. Its geographic reach also includes China/Tibet, North Korea, and Burma, as well as other Communist, post-Communist, and authoritarian nations and places where religious freedom is routinely violated. One of its best-known services is a daily news e-mail providing succinct but highly detailed reports on violations of religious freedom on a country-by-country basis. The search and archive feature also permits searches by country and by religion, including a wide range of religious traditions besides Christianity. The Forum is committed to hosting at least one international convention each year and also engages in policy debates over issues pertaining to international religious freedom. Named after the religious freedom principles in Article 18 of the Universal Declaration of Human Rights, Forum 18 is based in Oslo, Norway.

(11) Freedom House
www.freedomhouse.org
Freedom House promotes democracy and freedom and opposes dictatorships around the world with ideologies from across the political spectrum (including religiously based totalitarian regimes). Its work combines analysis of trends of freedom and democracy and their abuse, advocacy on behalf of human rights and democracy, and action to strengthen civil society, promote open government, defend human rights, and facilitate the free flow of information and ideas. It actively supports democratic change, freedom, and human rights by urging U.S. policy makers, international organizations, and governments to adopt policies supporting the tenets of democracy. It also assists "young democracies" in escaping legacies of tyranny, dictatorship, and political repression. Its efforts are focused in regions where freedom is threatened—Central Asia, Central and Eastern Europe, the Middle East, Africa, Latin America, and the former Soviet Union. Its Web site contains articles, press releases, and other resources in English, Spanish, Russian, Chinese, Korean, Arabic, and Farsi versions.

(12) Grim and Finke International Religion Indexes
www.thearda.com/Archive/Files/Descriptions/IRFAGG.asp
This data set, produced by Brian Grim and Roger Finke, converts the narrative information found in the U.S. State Department's International Religious Freedom (IRF) reports into more than 100 different variables describing religious freedom in 195 countries. Grim and Finke develop three standardized indexes to facilitate cross-national comparison. These indexes measure government regulation of religion (GRI), government favoritism of religion (GFI), and social regulation of religion (SRI). Files for individual years and an aggregate file of coded data from the 2001, 2003, and 2005 IRF reports are available on the ARDA Web site. Because the data set derives from the IRF reports, it depends on the varying detail and quality of the reports. However, by translating the massive amount of information in the IRF reports into a format that greatly facilitates cross-national comparison, it offers a pathbreaking means to analyze the value of religious liberty to economic, social, and political development.

(13) Institute on Culture, Religion, and World Affairs (CURA)
www.bu.edu/cura
Founded by internationally renowned sociologist of religion Peter L. Berger, the Institute on Culture, Religion, and World Affairs (CURA) at Boston University has served as a research and publication center for issues on culture and global development for more than twenty years. As both an academic and policy center, CURA works closely with government, business, and media partners in exploring these topics. Recent conferences and publications have focused on issues ranging from secularism in Europe to moderation in Islam. In 2005, CURA received a three-year grant from the Henry Luce Foundation in support of a program to improve the U.S. policy community's awareness of the role of religion in world affairs, and in 2010, the institute received an additional three-year Luce grant to focus on religious pluralism and civic peace in multicultural societies.

(14) International Crisis Group (ICG)
www.crisisgroup.org
The International Crisis Group is a leading independent, nonpartisan source of analysis and advice to governments and intergovernmental bodies like the United Nations, European Union, and World Bank on the prevention and resolution of deadly conflict. Its work combines field-based analysis, policy prescription, and high-level advocacy to warn of emerging crises and offer pragmatic solutions to ongoing conflicts. ICG publishes *CrisisWatch*, a monthly bulletin that provides updates on significant situations of conflict or potential conflict; past issues are archived in a searchable database. With resources in more than eight languages, the Web site contains a variety of other reports and databases, as well as press releases, articles, op-eds, interviews, speeches, multimedia webcasts, and resources for journalists. As an example of its coverage, ICG's Uganda information section includes a detailed history of the conflict involving the Lord's

Resistance Army, updates on the Juba Peace talks, and policy briefs and updates on the situation on the ground.

(15) The Joan B. Kroc Institute for International Peace Studies
kroc.nd.edu/
Located at the University of Notre Dame, the Kroc Institute sponsors academic research on peacemaking and helps practitioners become more effective. Kroc offers classes at the undergraduate and graduate level; programming emphasizes a productive dialogue between Notre Dame's Catholic heritage and other religious and secular traditions. Current research initiatives focus on nonmilitary enforcement of international norms and the peacebuilding. role of international institutions, religious elements in contemporary conflict, and nonviolent social change. In addition, the Kroc Institute developed the Peace Accords Matrix, a comparative, interactive online database of peace accords. Other online resources include free and downloadable peace studies courses, a reflective peacebuilding toolkit handbook, and links to faculty experts. The institute also publishes the online journal *Peace Policy* and coordinates the Catholic Peacebuilding Network.

(16) The Pew Forum on Religion and Public Life
www.pewforum.org/
Launched in 2001, the Pew Forum on Religion and Public life at the Pew Research Center uses rigorous social science research methods to promote a deeper understanding of issues at the intersection of religion and public affairs and deliver timely, impartial information to national opinion leaders, including government officials and journalists. In 2008, it released the landmark "US Religious Landscapes Survey," which discusses the religious affiliation, beliefs and practices, and social and political attitudes of the American public. The Pew-Templeton Global Religious Futures Project, sponsored by the Pew Charitable Trusts and John Templeton Foundation, encourages expanded global knowledge of religion and released its first survey on Islam and Christianity in sub-Saharan Africa in April 2010. The forum's Web site offers extensive access to its research, events, and multimedia resources; for instance, its "Religion & Politics 2010" page offered news, analysis, and data on religion-related aspects of the midterm elections.

(17) Pew Global Attitudes Project
www.pewglobal.org/
Started in 2001, the Pew Global Attitudes Project is a series of surveys on worldwide public opinion on a range of topics. With more than 175,000 interviews in fifty-five countries conducted for the project, the site offers a wealth of information to scholars, journalists, and researchers on public opinion. Reports dating back to 2001 are available online. Some examples include "Unfavorable Views of Jews and Muslims on the Increase in Europe," "Muslims in Europe: Economic Worries Top Concerns about Religious and Culture Identity," and "The Great

Divide: How Westerners and Muslims View Each Other." All of the data sets related to the reports are available for download. The Web site also features commentaries on poll findings and news items from 2002 to the present. At the bottom left navigation, a useful links button provides links to other sites that offer surveys, most of which are centered on global opinions.

(18) Religion and the State Project (RAS)

www.religionandstate.org/

Sponsored by Bar-Ilan University, the Religion and the State Project gauges the intersection of government and religion by examining policies on religion. The resulting data set measures this intersection for 175 states yearly between 1990 and 2002 and categorized the various types of relationships between government and religion. The data set and codebook are available for download on the site, as are the data sets from the Minorities at Risk project (link to MAR entry). The site provides a bibliography of related books, articles, and dissertations that use the RAS data set. The links page offers information on other useful resources about religion and the state. RAS is an official Association of Religion Data Archives affiliate.

(19) Religion Monitor

www.religionsmonitor.com

Sponsored by the Bertelsmann Foundation, the Religion Monitor is a data collection instrument that surveys traditional and new forms of religiosity and examines the changing face of religion in the context of pluralism. It was started in 2007 on the basis of a poll of 21,000 people in twenty-one countries. Future rounds will expand the survey to more than 100 countries. The survey encompasses six core dimensions of religiousness: interest in religious affairs, belief in God or something divine, public and private religious practices, religious experiences, and the general relevance of religion to everyday life. It analyzes theistic as well as pantheistic semantics and other specific subjects, such as spirituality. The question modules are identical for all nationalities and all religions, and the random sample takes into account sociodemographic factors such as gender division or various age groups as a percentage of the overall population.

(20) United Nations: Office of the Special Rapporteur on Freedom of Religion or Belief

www2.ohchr.org/english/issues/religion/index.htm

Under the purview of the United Nations Human Rights Council, the Special Rapporteur on Freedom of Religion or Belief has a twofold mandate: to identify barriers to the right to freedom of religion or belief and to work to provide workable solutions to overcoming these barriers. The Web site includes links to the Rapporteur's annual reports on religious freedom, which contain accounts of the situation of religious freedom in the places where the Rapporteur's office conducts visits in a particular year. These reports are often highly detailed, containing information on specific individuals, religious organizations, and religious traditions and the particular kinds of restrictions on religious freedom that they are encountering. In August 2010, Heiner Bielefeldt of Germany assumed the office of Special Rapporteur; Asma Jahangir of Pakistan was Special Rapporteur from 2004 to 2010.

(21) United States Commission on International Religious Freedom (USCIRF)
www.uscirf.gov
The United States Commission on International Religious Freedom is a federally funded independent commission created by the International Religious Freedom Act of 1998. It monitors the status of freedom of thought, conscience, and religion or belief throughout the world and makes nonbinding policy recommendations to the U.S. government. While the Office of International Religious Freedom at State is responsible for the Annual Report on International Religious Freedom, USCIRF prepares its own annual report and makes recommendations to the State Department on which countries to designate as Countries of Particular Concern (CPCs) for ongoing, egregious violations of religious freedom; the Secretary of State makes the final determination on CPC status. USCIRF also publishes a Watch List of countries that require further close monitoring. USCIRF commissioners travel widely to conduct country visits, hold public hearings in the United States, and testify before Congress on religious freedom issues; trip reports and transcripts of hearings and testimony are available online.

(22) United States Department of State: International Religious Freedom Reports
www.state.gov/g/drl/rls/irf/
The Department of State's Office of International Religious Freedom issues annual international religious freedom reports to Congress. Each of these provides a global summary of religious demographics, as well as social and political conditions related to U.S. religious freedom policy. The individual country reports include sections describing religious demography, the country's legal/policy framework toward religion, restrictions and abuses, forced conversions, improvements, social attitudes toward religious communities, and details of U.S. religious freedom policy initiatives in the country in question. The Office of International Religious Freedom prepares the reports using data collected by U.S. embassy officials and from a variety of government and nongovernmental sources in each country, as well as other country and religion experts. The reports are a helpful source for up-to-date summaries of political, social, and sometimes historical context regarding religion in a particular country.

(23) United States Institute of Peace (USIP): Religion and Peacemaking Program
www.usip.org/issue-areas/religion
The Religion and Peacemaking program at the United States Institute of Peace (USIP) conducts research, identifies best practices, and develops new peacebuilding. tools for religious leaders and organizations; helps define and shape the field of religious peace building; and in cooperation with USIP's other centers, develops and implements integrated strategies for the institute's conflict-specific work,

including projects with religious communities in zones of conflict. For example, it is working with Islamic scholars to develop curricula for madrasa education. Program-related reports, event transcripts, and lesson plans are on the USIP Web site, along with an online certificate course in interfaith conflict resolution. Special reports address the role of religion in conflict and peace, religious perspectives on war and peacemaking, teaching about the "religious other," and Islamic teachings on peacemaking and democracy. The program is currently working in Pakistan, Afghanistan, Iraq, Iran, Colombia, Sri Lanka, and Northern Uganda.

(24) World Christian Database

worldchristiandatabase.org

The World Christian Database is an online resource with data on religious adherents worldwide, classified by major denominations. This information is available at various levels of geographic aggregation and can also be viewed alongside other current demographic statistics. Based at the Center for the Study of Global Christianity at Gordon-Conwell Theological Seminary, the database grew from the *World Christian Encyclopedia* and is updated regularly. Access to the database is by paid subscription. The database is one of the few sources for cross-national, time-series religious statistics and is quoted widely in the mainstream media. One of the most valuable features is the customizable data tables, which can be exported in PDF or Excel format. Because of the project's historical emphasis on evangelization, the data is weighted heavily toward Christianity. It often relies on estimates self-reported by religious groups or based on affiliation with umbrella organizations.

(25) The World Values Survey

www.worldvaluessurvey.org/

The World Values Survey, directed by Ronald Inglehart at the University of Michigan, is an ongoing academic project by social scientists to assess cultural, moral, political, and religious values and changes around the world. The geographic breadth and historical depth of the survey data make it a particularly valuable social science resource. The project's Web site makes much of its research available. Visitors to the site can view findings of the World Values Survey, an overview of its four waves, a list of links to publications based on its data, and links to its past conferences and workshops. In the left-hand column, there is a list of shortcuts that allow visitors to download data files and analysis. Some publications that have been based on survey findings include *The Worldviews of Islamic Publics in Global Perspective* (2005) and *Islam, Gender, Culture, and Democracy* (2003).

INDEX

Abrahamic faiths, 151, 152
Abu-Nimer, Mohammed, 151
Acheson, Dean, 252
Ackerman, Bruce, 30, 61
Adelkhah, Fariba, 93
Adherents.com, 293
Afghanistan
  blasphemy laws in, 104, 113, 114, 263, 274n6
  on CPC list, 266
  democracy and religious freedom, 262–263, 273, 274n4
  external jihad and Soviet-occupied, 135
  Islamic political movements in, 73
  mujahideen in, 128, 135
  proselytism allegations, 112
  religious militancy in, 2
  support for truth-telling, 158
  terrorists campaigns, 129
  women's rights in, 63
African American Church of God in Christ, 253
African American churches, 253
Afro-American religions, 33
agenda-setting theory, 219
Ahmadinejad, Mahmoud, 116
Ahmed, Leila, 89, 90
Ahmedis, 76
aid agencies, 165–166, 168
AIDS, 191, 193–194, 257
Ajami, Fouad, 130
Al-Alam (TV station), 221
Al Arabiya (TV station), 220, 223
Al-Azhar (Sunni learning center), 222
Al-Azmeh, Aziz, 218
Al Hurra (TV station), 220
Al Jazeera (TV station), 220
Al Manar (TV station), 221
Al Qaeda, 3, 127, 141, 221, 262, 267
Albania
  Islamic majority in, 64
  Muslims in, 63
Albright, Madeleine, 18, 266, 270, 273
Algeria, 85
  Islamic fundamentalists in, 63
  Islamic political movements in, 73
  religious violence, 131–132
Ali, Kecia, 90

Alkire, Ssabina, 193, 195
Allem, Nichole J., 9, 217–224
Alliance of All Burma Monks (ABMA), 231, 232
Alliance of Civilizations and the World
  Economic Forum (UN), 210
American Joint Jewish Distribution Committee, 168
American Political Science Review (APSR), 4
American Protestant Zionism, 258
American Revolution, 68
American secularism, 75, 81
America's international religious freedom
  policy, 262–263
  implementation, 1998–2008, 266–268
  IRF policy after ten years, 271–273
  IRFA's discontents, 268–271
  origins of, 263–266
Amnesty International, 252
An-Na'im, Abdullahi Ahmed, 90, 91
Anderson, Benedict, 217
Anglican Church/Anglicanism, 32, 76, 151, 156
anti-Muslim prejudice, 206–207
antiapartheid movement, 19
anticlericalism, 68, 75
antidemocratic doctrines, 59–60, 65
AP Worldwide, 235
apostasy, 91, 105, 112–113, 262
Appadurai, Arjun, 33, 217, 224
Appleby, Scott R., 40
Arab Human Development Report (UNDP), 186–187
Arab Muslim countries, 87
Arab nationalism, 135
Arab Satellite Communication Organization
  (ARABSAT), 220
Argentina, and religious influence on
  transitional justice, 156
Arminius, Jacobus, 253
Army Field Manual, 284
As-Sahab (TV station), 221
Asad, Talal, 218
Asia Times, 236
Assemblies of God, 253
Associated Press, 237
Association of Religion Data
  Archives (ARDA), 293